324.24106 DOU

D0519040

Th
sta

11. J

4

16.

10. M

27. MAY 2

LIBERALS

General election poster, 1929

UWE BRISTOL
WITHDRAWN
LIBRARY SERVICES

Liberals

A History of the Liberal
and Liberal Democrat Parties

Roy Douglas

UWE, BRISTOL

- 5 SEP 2005
His
Library Services

Hambledon and London

London and New York

Hambledon and London

102 Gloucester Avenue, London NW1 8HX

175 Fifth Avenue
New York, NY 10010
USA

First Published 2005

ISBN 1 85285 353 0

Copyright @ Roy Douglas 2005

The moral rights of the author have been asserted.

All rights reserved.

Without limiting the rights under copyrights
reserved above, no part of this publication may be
reproduced, stored or introduced into a retrieval system,
or transmitted, in any form or by any means (electronic, mechanical,
photocopying, recording or otherwise), without the prior
written permission of both the copyright owner and
the above publisher of the book.

A description of this book is available from the
British Library and from the Library of Congress.

Typeset by Carnegie Publishing, Lancaster,
and printed in Great Britain by Cambridge University Press.

Distributed in the United States and Canada
exclusively by Palgrave Macmillan,
A division of St Martin's Press.

UWE, BRISTOL LIBRARY SERVICES

Contents

Illustrations

Text Illustrations

Illustration Acknowledgements

The author and publishers are most grateful to *Lib Dem News* for permission to reproduce plates 5–19.

Introduction

Just when the Liberal Party came into existence is a matter for debate, but it was well established by the late 1860s. It remained one of the two great parties of the state, either as the government or as the acknowledged opposition, down to the 1914 war. Thereafter it underwent a rapid decline, and ten years later it was reduced to just over forty MPs, of whom the majority owed their seats to the absence of opposition from either the Conservatives or Labour. The Labour Party established itself as the principal challenger to the Conservatives during the same period, raising the question of whether the primary reason for the change was the inherent attraction of Labour or the shortcomings of the Liberals. With a few short-term rallies, the decline continued, so that by the middle 1950s there were only six Liberal MPs, and briefly only five. An objective observer might easily have concluded that the parliamentary extinction of the Liberal Party was just round the corner.

Much has been written about the causes of the Liberal decline, but what happened to the Liberals and their successors in the succeeding half century has been every bit as remarkable as their earlier decline, perhaps more so. By the late 1950s, it was clear that the funeral had been indefinitely postponed, even if Liberal fortunes fluctuated wildly over the next two decades. There were good moments – as when the Liberals won more than six million votes in February 1974 – but also ones when the party seemed to be getting nowhere.

Most of the 1980s was occupied by the stormy and astonishing love affair between Liberals and the new Social Democratic Party, which had started life as a breakaway from Labour. At one moment the 'Alliance', which the two parties formed, seemed to be carrying everything before it, and for months opinion poll ratings set it ahead of Conservative and Labour alike. At others, the whole venture seemed likely to collapse in farce. After a long period of uncertainty the two parties united in 1988 to form what would become the Liberal Democrats.

In the 1990s the Lib Dems began to establish themselves as a real force in politics, and by 2001 they had captured fifty-two seats. No less remarkably, Lib Dems performed spectacularly well in parliamentary by-elections. In the 1987 Parliament they captured three seats from the Conservatives, in

the 1992 Parliament four, and in the 1997 Parliament one. Up to the end of
2004, there had only been four by-elections in the 2001 Parliament. All took
place in what looked like impregnable Labour seats. Two were won by Lib
Dems, who came close to victory in both the others. Nobody, not even the
most optimistic Liberal, would have considered that sort of result remotely
possible a quarter of a century earlier.

In the hundred and fifty years since the party's foundation, Liberal attitudes
to public questions, not surprisingly, have evolved, and in each generation
commentators, and Liberals themselves, have asked whether the 'new' Liberals of their own time would have been recognised as true successors by
those who had preceded them. In the 1870s people wondered whether
Palmerston would have acknowledged Gladstone as his true successor, and
similar questions have been asked ever since. Despite all the changes, a continuous skein of Liberal thought, going back at least as far as Gladstone, can
be identified. Although the Liberal Party was by no means the historic Whig
Party under another name, the Liberal Party did inherit two important legacies from the Whigs. The first of was the idea of liberty. The Liberal starts
from a presumption of liberty. People should be allowed to do as they wish,
unless some good reason can be shown to the contrary. The burden of proof
lies on the objector to liberty, not on the person who seeks to uphold it.

The second recurring idea which the Liberals inherited from the Whigs
was the idea that a government should act within a fixed framework of rules,
not according to the arbitrary decision of particular individuals. The sovereign, or ministers acting with the sovereign's authority, may have special
legal powers – the prerogative – but these powers should be kept to a minimum. Judges are appointed to apply an ascertainable corpus of law, not to
enforce the wishes of any particular person, however exalted.

Just as law should be universal, so governments must follow universal
principles. The eighteenth- and early nineteenth-century House of Commons, with its enormous variations in constituency size and entitlement to
vote, did not represent the nation in a logical or equitable manner. The
Whigs began to rectify that state of affairs through the 1832 Reform Act. The
Liberals went much further. They saw that it was individuals who ought to
be represented, not property, and embarked on a course of action which
eventually led to universal franchise and the ballot. This demand for fair
voting procedures was continued in the twentieth century by the Liberal
campaign for proportional representation.

Liberals have a rooted dislike for all kinds of privilege attached to particular groups of people, and this attitude goes a long way towards explaining
their attitude to religious questions, particularly in the nineteenth century.

Members of the nonconformist sects in England and Wales, and opponents of the religious establishments in Scotland and Ireland, were attracted to the Liberal Party because it opposed the privileges attached to the Church of England,. The same dislike of privilege, joined to the recognition that 'knowledge is power', led Liberals to press for wider educational opportunities. It is no accident that the Education Act of 1870, which laid the foundations of universal elementary education, was carried by a Liberal government and that Liberals remained particularly interested in educational reform thereafter.

From the moment the Liberal Party came into existence, its supporters saw the cause of Free Trade as a major element in its policy. There were many good reasons for Liberals to take that view, but not least which was their belief in liberty. To Liberals, Free Trade meant that governments should allow people to trade as they wished, without either impediment or favour, unless there was some overwhelming reason – such as the safety of the purchaser or others – which dictated to the contrary.

In a narrow sense, the term 'Free Trade' was used to mean the abolition of customs duties and embargoes, designed to restrict the quantity of imports, for the benefit of home producers. Many Liberal Free Traders, however, regarded the repeal of protectionist duties as only the first instalment of a wider policy. Indirect taxes on goods produced within Britain were also impediments to trade. Gladstone in particular greatly reduced the incidence of indirect taxes. On innumerable occasions in the nineteenth and twentieth centuries, Liberals defended Free Trade against encroachments by Protectionists. For much of the twentieth century, the one policy which the ordinary voter recognised as a clear badge of Liberal identity was Free Trade.

In the mid nineteenth century, many Liberals appear to have believed that Free Trade would suffice to remedy all economic anomalies, insofar as they were capable of being remedied at all. As the century advanced, however, it became increasingly clear that poverty and social injustice remained largely untackled. Without some radically new approach, there was no good reason for thinking that they would solve themselves. In the 1870s and 1880s, many Liberals came to the conclusion that more positive action was required. Governments began to legislate in the direction of what came to be called 'social reform'. Many Liberals also became committed to land reform, particularly the 'Land Value Taxation' ideas associated with the American economist and philosopher Henry George. A strong interest in welfare issues has remained an abiding Liberal concern.

At the very moment when Liberals were preparing to confront social problems on a scale which nobody had attempted before, a great new issue cut

across politics, deflecting attention in a different direction. By the end of
1885 Gladstone as Prime Minister had reached the conclusion that the overwhelming majority of the people of Ireland demanded, and would
eventually attain, legislative independence. The sooner that demand was
granted the better it would be for Britain and Ireland alike. In the following
year he made his first attempt to enact Home Rule. It failed and split the
Liberal Party split asunder. As Gladstone had foreseen, the Home Rule question did not go away. The tragic long-term consequences of the failure to
grant Home Rule are well known, and the ghost of the controversy continues to walk in Northern Ireland to this day.

The Liberal government formed in December 1905, and which remained
in office until the First World War, was in many ways the epitome of developed Liberal thought. It had a clear electoral mandate to maintain Free
Trade against the challenge of what was called Tariff Reform. A large proportion of its active members were enthusiastic supporters of Land Value
Taxation, but, as land reform would take time, the initial focus was on radical social reform. The government introduced old age pensions, national
insurance and unemployment insurance. In the teeth of opposition from the
Lords, it carried the radical budget of 1909, and then proceeded to curtail
the power of the Lords for the future.

The 1914 war changed everything. Despite victory in 1918 and the vigorous leadership of Lloyd George, by 1922 the Liberal Party was reduced to the
third party of the state, and there were echoes of the internecine Liberal disputes which had arisen in wartime and its immediate aftermath for several
decades to come. Labour was the principal beneficiary of the Liberals' misfortune. By the end of the 1920s most people had abandoned the idea that
a Liberal government was possible in the foreseeable future. The choice now
seemed to lie between Conservatives and Labour. A number of leading Liberals, including some of the most important names in the party, defected.
The Liberal Party nevertheless continued to proclaim a comprehensive
range of policies, as if a Liberal government was on the cards. It was kept
alive because there were still many people who believed that those policies
were appropriate and necessary, and that there was no prospect of attaining
their aims through either of the other parties.

What lies ahead is anybody's guess; the one forecast which one can make
with confidence is that it will be a fascinating story. Every political party
experiences fluctuations in its fortunes, but those of the Liberals and their
successors the Liberal Democrats have been a good deal more spectacular
than most.

Acknowledgements

More than thirty years ago, I wrote a *History of the Liberal Party, 1895–1970*, for which the Rt. Hon. Jeremy Thorpe kindly wrote a preface. The present book is a completely different one, covering a period from the nineteenth-century beginnings of the Liberal Party, through the fusion with the Social Democratic Party in 1988, down to the activities of the Liberal Democrats in the early twenty-first century.

Necessarily the present book draws on some of the written material and conversations which I used when writing the earlier work. I must therefore renew the acknowledgments I made there to the very helpful people who assisted at the time, many of whom are now, alas, dead. These people include R. Humphrey Davies, who started to work at Liberal headquarters in 1895, and was able, in his late nineties, to give lucid accounts of experiences and personalities more than a century ago. W. R. Davies and T. D. (Tommy) Nudds both occupied leading positions among professional workers before the 1939 war, and remained in place for many years afterwards. Others who helped with recollections included Lady Asquith of Yarnbury (Lady Violet Bonham-Carter), George Awdry, Desmond Banks, Ronald Banks, Barbara Bliss, Geoffrey Block, Lord Boothby, William Glanville Brown, Pat Cavanaugh, Chris Cook, Mrs K. Cossar, Lord Drumalbyn, C. R. Dudgeon, H. J. Glanville, David Goldblatt, Edgar Hardy, Derek Hudson, Lady Megan Lloyd-George, Barry McGill, Andrew McLaren, Mrs Lucy Masterman, Richard Moore, Mrs Doris Norris, Frank Owen, Lord Rea, Sir Steven Runciman, Sir Geoffrey Shakespeare, Lady Simon of Wythenshawe, Reginald Smith, Lancelot Spicer, A. J. Sylvester, A. J. P. Taylor, Viscount Tenby (Gwilym Lloyd George), F. C. Thornborough and Sir Ronald Walker.

I also express gratitude for help which has been received from three people who have read and criticised the whole, or part, of the manuscript: my wife Jean, Lord Rennard, Chief Executive of the Liberal Democrats, and Jeremy Thorpe. Deirdre Razzall, of *Lib Dem News*, has been extremely helpful in providing illustrations for the plate section. I need hardly say that the responsibility for any errors of fact or dubious opinions is exclusively mine.

1

Origins

But the liberal deviseth liberal things; and by liberal things shall he
stand.

Isaiah 32:8

There has been much debate as to when the Liberal Party as such came into
existence.[1] Almost any date between 1830 and 1868 might be chosen.

The once widespread view that the Liberal Party was essentially the historic Whig Party under another name is untenable. William Gladstone,
whose influence on the Liberal Party was greater than that of any other man,
had entered politics as a Tory and at no stage in his career could he be
labelled a Whig. On the other side of the political fence, the 14th Earl of
Derby served for a time in a Whig Cabinet, yet he was later to preside over
three governments in the 1850s and 1860s which are usually called 'Conservative'. Many Liberal Party activists in the middle and late nineteenth century
would have repudiated the labels 'Whig' and 'Tory' with equal indignation.

Like both 'Whig' and 'Tory', the word 'Liberal' in its political sense was
first used in a highly pejorative manner, with overtones suggesting that the
people to whom it was applied were not only deplorable characters, but 'un-
English' as well.[2] As with both earlier names, 'Liberal' was soon proudly
adopted by the people for whom it was meant as an insult. When Richard
Cobden in 1842 declared that Sir Robert Peel, the Conservative Prime Minister of the day, was 'as Liberal as' the Whig leader Lord John Russell, he
meant this as a compliment, not an insult. Perhaps the safest way to think
about party origins is to consider that, around 1830, the Whig and Tory
Parties both began to disintegrate; and it was not until the late 1860s that
the Liberal and Conservative Parties had come into existence in a fully
recognisable form.

To appreciate the atmosphere when the Liberal Party was coming into
existence, it is vital to remember that politics in the eighteenth and early
nineteenth centuries was very different from later times. The labels 'Whig'
and 'Tory' often said more about a politician's family, friends and clubs than
about his ideas on public questions, and it is sometimes difficult to decide
which label is more appropriate for a particular individual. Writing about a

later period, one influential author has declared that 'only 28 [MPs] could honestly be described as Whigs by birth and connection'[3] The figure was probably considerably greater around 1830, but genuine Whigs cannot have been more than a small minority of the MPs, although they formed a much greater proportion of the House of Lords. The term Whig, though very loose, is nevertheless convenient to describe parliamentarians who found themselves in general agreement with the consensus of opinion among members of the Whig aristocracy.

In any event, the return of a candidate to Parliament seldom depended on his party affiliation. In the great majority of cases, a constituency returned two MPs, and unopposed returns were very common. A candidate would normally be expected to provide much, or all, of the expenses from his own resources or those of his patron, and would be unlikely to do that unless he thought he had a fair chance of success. Thus, at the General Election of 1761, there were only 53 contests in all. There was nevertheless a tendency for contests to become more common as time went on. At the General Election of 1818 the number of British contests had risen to 105.

Voting qualifications varied considerably from place to place, but nowhere was the electorate more than a small minority of the male population. Until 1872, voting was public, and many, though by no means all, constituencies were dominated by a single individual, or a small group of individuals, who could control the representation by bribery, intimidation, or a mixture of the two.[4] But to suggest that such 'influences' were the only factors producing a compliant electorate would be wrong. Respect for the candidates or their patrons was often genuine. Yet the voters in Gatton or Old Sarum, each constituency with fewer than ten electors, and each returning two members to the House of Commons down to 1832, were hardly able to make a free choice. These were extreme cases; but there were a great many other 'rotten boroughs'. In some of the larger constituencies, pressures of a different kind discouraged contests. Like Old Sarum, Yorkshire was a single constituency, but it had over 20,000 voters, and no interest could dominate such a vast area. Yet it was seldom contested. In 1807, when three candidates contended for the two seats, two of those candidates spent not much less than £100,000 each, while the third (who, incidentally, finished top of the poll) spent a mere £28,000.[5] These figures must be multiplied by perhaps forty or fifty to provide modern equivalents. Yet the two constituencies ranking next after Yorkshire in the size of their electorates – London, and Westminster, with around 10,000 or 12,000 voters each – were regularly the scenes of contests.

For most of the early nineteenth century, a succession of Tory governments held office. Then, quite suddenly, a chain of unpredictable events took place which changed everything dramatically. In 1829, the formidable Duke of Wellington was Prime Minister, and the government's chief representative in the House of Commons was Sir Robert Peel. The government decided, for reasons which are outside the present story, that it was necessary to grant 'Catholic Emancipation' – that is, to remove most of the existing public disabilities attending Roman Catholics. This infuriated many of the Government's Tory followers, but was carried with support of the Whig Opposition, which tended to take a more laid-back attitude to such matters. The Whigs hoped, and probably expected, to secure a share of office in some kind of coalition under Wellington, which would restore stability to a shaken government. But there was no sign that this concession would be granted. Thus the government was confronted simultaneously by disaffected Tories and disappointed Whigs. Then, in June 1830, George IV, never the most loved of British sovereigns, died, and was succeeded by his brother William IV. As the law stood, demise of the sovereign required a General Election. Parliament was dissolved four weeks later. At that election, the number of reliable government supporters was reduced by about fifty; but there seemed no immediate reason for the government to resign.

If there was one political idea which more or less united the Whigs, it was 'reform': a term which was understood to include some reduction in the number of 'rotten boroughs', enfranchisement of the growing industrial cities, and perhaps an increase in the electorate as well. In the aftermath of the 1830 General Election, the Whig opposition raised the question of reform in a very moderate way. Wellington could almost certainly have brushed the criticism aside with little damage to the government; but instead he chose to defend the existing system in uncompromising terms. The Whigs were provoked, while those Tories who had deplored Catholic Emancipation were prepared to do anything necessary to bring down a government which they hated. A fortnight later, the government was defeated in the House of Commons on a completely different issue, and resigned. The King called on the Whig leader, Earl Grey, to form a government. The Whigs decided to make reform a Cabinet measure. The man set in charge of the government's proposals was Lord John Russell, third son of the 6th Duke of Bedford, who had been a staunch supporter of reform for a long time.

The Bill which Russell submitted in March 1831 went much further than many had anticipated. He sought to disenfranchise sixty boroughs, and to reduce another forty-seven from two MPs to one. The seats would be allocated to more populous places, notably county constituencies and industrial towns. After many difficulties with the Bill in the House of Commons, the government offered to resign. The King refused to accept the resignation, but agreed to call another General Election. In most of the constituencies where there was a contest, the main issue was reform. There was widespread excitement. Where the voters had any real choice, the upshot was usually an impressive victory for the reformers, though there were a few rather surprising triumphs for the other side.

When the new Parliament met, Russell brought forward another Reform Bill, essentially similar to the one he had proposed earlier. This time the majority in the Commons was overwhelming, but the House of Lords threw it out. The government obtained the King's assent to create enough peers to swamp that majority, should need arise. Whether the King liked this or not, supporters of reform pretended that he genuinely approved, and he acquired the awful punning nickname of 'Reform Bill'. The threat of mass creation of peers was enough; and in April 1832 the Lords passed the government's measure with a small majority. The worst of the 'rotten boroughs' were abolished. Qualifications for the vote were made more uniform. The electorate was also increased substantially, though it still fell far short of 'democracy'. No women received the vote, and only about one in eight adult men did so. The Reform Act referred only to England and Wales; but similar measures for Scotland and Ireland were passed almost immediately. The Scottish measure had a much greater effect than the English one, for only around 4500 people in the whole country had previously possessed the vote. For many years to come, the country's political representation would be overwhelmingly Whig or Liberal.

At the end of 1832, a General Election was held under the new system. There were 401 constituencies in the United Kingdom – many returning two MPs, and a few returning three. Only 124 were uncontested. The result was a massive victory for the government. Three political groups, none of them clearly defined, could be recognised. The Whigs broadly supported the Ministry. Other MPs, often called 'Radicals', were avid for further reforms. On the other side of the House, the Tories, whose differences over Catholic Emancipation had been largely thrust aside by events, were now beginning to be known as Conservatives: a term which Peel had used in the General Election of 1831. This was much more than a mere change of name. Peel envisaged a great change in the nature of political parties, in which a party which was conservative in ideology as well as name would confront a party aiming at political change.

The direct consequences of reform were perhaps less dramatic than enthusiasts on either side had anticipated; but they were nevertheless considerable. The power of the great 'borough-mongers' had been curtailed, thiough there were still many constituencies where the influence of a particular individual, or small group of individuals, was overwhelming. The idea that electoral contests would be fought everywhere on some great public issue had become firmly established. The events of 1830–32 ushered in 'the golden age of the private MP': a period in which neither great patrons nor party machines, with their tempting offers of favours, were able to exercise as much influence as in the past. Politicians were disposed to exercise their personal judgement on public issues, conscious that local electorates would eventually decide whether that judgement was acceptable or not. As late as 1893, a wholly credible authority 'remarked on thirty members at least who came down to the House to listen to debate, and voted as reason and conscience inclined'.[6] A seat in Parliament was an honour to be coveted, not the key to a remunerative career. Although Ministers received salaries, MPs were unpaid, and would remain so until 1911. The expense of nursing and contesting a constituency was likely far to exceed any financial return. Necessarily, most MPs were men of considerable fortune.

Whatever else the reform agitation had done, it certainly brought forward issues which had been discussed for many years, usually without much sense of urgency. Parliamentarians inside and outside the government were anxious to press for these matters to be resolved. In 1833, slavery was abolished throughout the British Empire, and substantial contributions were made from public funds to compensate slave-owners. The same year saw an important Factory Act regulating conditions of employment, while major changes in the Poor Law followed in 1834. The Municipal Corporations Act of 1835 laid the foundations of responsible local government.

Reform had other political implications, as well as the obvious ones. In 1834, Grey retired from the Premiership, and was succeeded by Viscount Melbourne, who was less than enthusiastic for the job. Later in the year, the new Prime Minister had an interview with the King which resulted in Melbourne's dismissal. Some historians have suggested that the dismissal was 'collusive', with Melbourne as pleased to go as the King was to be rid of him. Just how far that was the case is a matter of dispute. The Conservatives took office – at first under Wellington, but almost immediately under Peel – and called for a new General Election. They failed to secure a majority, but remained in office for several months. In April 1835 they were compelled to resign, and Melbourne returned. This chain of events had long-term consequences. The royal power to dismiss a Minister, which had once been a reality, had not produced the intended result and was never used again. Peel's own campaign for election as MP for Tamworth was accompanied by issue of a 'manifesto', ostensibly addressed to the voters of that particular constituency but in practice widely used as a statement of his party's policy. Very gradually, and over many years, voters came more and more to assess the suitability of a parliamentary candidate in the light of his attitude to questions which had been promulgated by party leaders.

The authority of the Whigs was slowly eroded. In 1834, an important question arose concerning the Church of Ireland. This was a Protestant establishment, similar to the Church of England in doctrine and organisation, and – like the Church of England – entitled by law to various privileges. Yet the large majority of the people of the country adhered to the Roman Catholic Church, and a considerable proportion of the Protestants adhered to 'dissenting' or 'nonconformist' denominations. Russell, whose influence among the Whigs was immense, declared that the revenues of the Church of Ireland were unnecessarily great. This precipitated the resignation of four members of the Cabinet, who had been visibly unhappy with developments in the government for some time. The fact that they eventually departed on an ecclesiastical question casts significant light on the importance of church matters in nineteenth century politics. All four were soon received into the Conservative Party, and one of them – Lord Stanley, the future 14th Earl of Derby – would eventually become Prime Minister. Peel's own strategy certainly assisted such moves; for he made it clear that the Reform Act, whether wise or not, was irreversible.

The death of William IV and the accession of Victoria in 1837 occasioned another General Election, and the Whig position was again eroded. A further election in 1841 gave the Conservatives a substantial majority. The practice of the time did not require the government to resign immediately, as would be the case today, but soon the Whigs were defeated in the new House and Peel became Prime Minister for a second time. The ministry which he formed was a very impressive one, including no fewer than six men who had been or would later become Prime Minister.

Peel doubled up as Chancellor of the Exchequer. His 1842 Budget swept away literally hundreds of indirect taxes, and reintroduced Income Tax as an alternative source of revenue. Income Tax in the nineteenth century and well into the twentieth, was paid exclusively by people in comparatively comfortable circumstances. The Budget fitted well with Peel's vision of Conservatism. Not only was he unwilling to resist change when it was palpably inevitable, he was willing to bring change about when there were evident merits in so doing. By the early 1840s, it looked very much as if Peel's general vision of the political future had been achieved. Yet events would soon prove otherwise.

In the wake of reform, many ordinary people decided that what happened in Parliament was likely to exert a real effect on their lives. At the same time a great many non-parliamentarians, whether enfranchised or not, decided to act collectively to influence the behaviour of MPs. In this period, agitation for political change took place largely outside the recognised political parties. Two great movements could be discerned. Their objectives were very different, but not incompatible, yet they often perceived each other as a rival, for each was appealing to the people as a whole to exert pressure on the parliamentarians. 'Chartism' may be regarded as a response to the failure of reform to enfranchise the majority of working-class people. The 'People's Charter', from which it took its name, sought various constitutional changes, which included manhood suffrage and the secret ballot. The movement attracted great public attention, winning eager support in some quarters and bitter opposition in others. After a massive meeting in 1848, where a perceived risk of violence was countered by the enrolment of a quarter of a million special constables, Chartism gradually declined as a political force; but the underlying ideas remained, and an important precedent was established for action in the future.

The second great popular movement, the Anti-Corn Law League, sought immediate economic changes. The Corn Laws had been introduced in 1815, at the end of the French wars. They set an embargo on wheat importation when the price was below £4 a quarter. The Corn Laws were varied from time to time; but a body called the Anti-Corn Law League was set up to achieve their complete abolition. At a time when bread was a major item in most working-class budgets, high corn prices could result in something near starvation, and the idea that the laws which tended to keep up prices should be immediately repealed became increasingly popular both among workers themselves and among industrial employers, who perceived that high food prices would produce an effective demand for high wages.

The Anti-Corn Law League was largely inspired by the genius of its principal speaker, publicist and organiser, Richard Cobden. Without any obvious social advantages, Cobden became a successful calico printer; but the Anti-Corn Law cause drew him into public life, and at one point he nearly bankrupted himself through his zeal. At the same time, sums of money which seemed vast by the standards of the time were raised for the League. Innumerable leaflets were produced, innumerable public meetings held. The force of the League was largely moral: an appeal at least as much to men's consciences as to their pecuniary interests. Like many of his supporters, Cobden made no secret that repeal of the Corn Laws was but part of his agenda, which aimed at a general system of Free Trade.

In the mid-1840s, famine developed in Ireland on a most appalling scale, killing something like one in eight of the population and driving enormous numbers of people to leave the country, many of them in conditions of extreme destitution. The Irish famine exerted relatively little direct effect on politics; but many people feared similar developments on the British

mainland. The result was victory for the League. First most of the Whig
Opposition were converted, then Conservative Prime Minister Peel. Most
ministers favoured repeal; most back-bench Conservatives opposed it
because they feared adverse effects on agriculture; but in 1846 it was carried
by the 'Peelite' Ministers and the Whigs together. Almost immediately, the
government was defeated on a different issue and resigned. The Whigs, now
led by Russell, took office.

Peel, who – more than any other man – had created the original Conservative Party, had effectively destroyed it. The anger felt by his 'Protectionist'
opponents within the party was even more protracted and bitter than the
anger which had been felt over Catholic Emancipation. Although Peel
himself died four years later, most people who had followed him over the
Corn Law question were never again able to work with a Conservative ministry. Thus a relatively small, but exceedingly able and influential, group of
'Peelites' came into existence, who would eventually play a very important
part in the genesis of the Liberal Party.

The government gradually lost support, and in 1851 Russell resigned.
Attempts to form an alternative government collapsed, and he soon
returned to office. The Whig discomfiture continued nevertheless, and in
February of the following year a new Conservative ministry was formed,
headed by Stanley (who had recently become the 14th Earl of Derby), with
Benjamin Disraeli, a man with no aristocratic connections and very much a
political maverick, as his Chancellor of the Exchequer. The Derby-Disraeli
ministry had a weak base, for it represented only a section of the original
Conservative Party. It may perhaps have wished to restore Protection, but
lacked either the power or the determination, or both, to do so. Indeed, it
soon became clear not only that no serious politician would attempt to
restore the Corn Laws, but also that a rapid extension of Free Trade in all
directions was taking place.

A General Election in the summer of 1852 resulted in the Conservatives
falling some way behind the Whigs, and a substantial contingent of 'Peelites' holding the balance between them. By this time, there were signs that
a new grouping was beginning to form. 'Peelites', Whigs and Radicals were
drifting together, for all of them agreed that Free Trade must be defended
and extended. This grouping would eventually constitute the basis of the
Liberal Party, though at the time there was little reason for considering it
much more than a temporary expedient. In December 1852, the first government of the new grouping took office, headed by a 'Peelite', the 4th Earl
of Aberdeen, who had served as Foreign Secretary in Peel's second administration, and was regarded as the leader of the Peelites. The choice of
Aberdeen appears at first sight remarkable,[7] for several men seemed to have

more impressive qualifications, and there were anxious meetings before Aberdeen 'emerged' as Prime Minister, with general support of Whigs and Peelites, and some of the Radicals. Perhaps the vital factor in the selection was that his background was Peelite rather than Whig. Whigs and Radicals could be expected to support a Peelite Free Trader against Conservatives who in their hearts hankered for a return to Protection; while if a Whig were made Prime Minister, there was always a chance that Peelites might eventually drift back to rejoin the remainder of their former party.

The composition of the new government was no less remarkable. In a cabinet of thirteen, no fewer than five were 'Peelites', including the Chancellor of the Exchequer, W. E. Gladstone, who was approaching the zenith of his powers. Whigs formed the largest single grouping, and Russell became Foreign Secretary. The Home Secretary was Viscount Palmerston – one of the great 'characters' of the period, whose ideas did not fit comfortably with any political party, though at this time he was generally accounted as a Whig. Only one 'Radical' was included, Sir William Molesworth, whose very promising career was to be cut short by death a few years later. Neither Cobden nor his second-in-command John Bright joined the ministry, and Cobden was disposed to think that Molesworth had almost apostatised by accepting office; but in other respects it really did look like a new 'Ministry of All the Talents'. Gladstone's first Budget, in 1853, carried on the tradition of Peel's measure eleven years earlier, and is widely regarded as one of the most impressive in Britain's fiscal history. More than a hundred items were freed from tax. These included soap, and this relief proved particularly beneficial to working-class people. Another important change was the extension of legacy duty to real estate as well a personal property: a measure which would gradually reduce the economic and social grip of the landowning class.

Very soon, however, this apparently strong and stable ministry was blown off course by Britain's involvement in the war with Russia which began in March 1854. Cobden, who had strong pacifist proclivities, incurred much unpopularity through his dislike for the whole episode; but the element of sheer blundering incompetence in the conduct of the war was significantly greater than in most conflicts. The most impressive performance in the government was that of the Chancellor of the Exchequer. Gladstone contrived to raise the money required for the war, not by the common expedient of borrowing (which transfers the burden to future generations of taxpayers), but by a temporary increase in income tax. Aberdeen received much of the blame for wartime blunders, perhaps unjustly. In February 1855, the Prime Minister was dropped and a new ministry formed by Palmerston, whose prestige rose rapidly. A General Election in 1857, which has been described as 'unique in our history, the only election conducted as a simple plebiscite in favour of an individual',[8] confirmed the government in office. Early in 1858, Palmerston's enthusiasm for Emperor Napoleon III of France led to a government defeat, and a second Derby-Disraeli Ministry was formed; though, lacking a majority in the House of Commons, it could not be expected to last for long. Palmerston's authority suffered only a temporary setback, and was soon as high as ever. His 'insouciance, easy approachability and common touch' were immensely popular.[9] Many of Palmerston's ideas could hardly be called liberal and certainly not radical, yet he retained to the end of his life an enormous prestige among people whose aspirations were very different from his own.

By this time, the idea of further parliamentary and electoral reform was beginning to gain favour in many quarters, although neither Derby nor Palmerston evinced much enthusiasm for it. But how much reform, and when? At what point should the line be drawn between the 1832 franchise, which was widely seen as inadequate, and a modern democracy which few politicians wanted – at least for the time being? Neither party was agreed as to what particular changes might be appropriate.

In March 1859, the Conservative government proposed some significant extensions to the franchise. Two ministers resigned in protest, and the Bill was attacked from many different angles. In the end it was defeated, and a new General Election was called. This resulted in the miscellaneous Opposition politicians who were by now becoming generally known as 'Liberals' losing a certain amount of ground but retaining their majority in the House of Commons. By common consent, the anomaly of a Conservative Government with a predominantly Liberal House of Commons could not be maintained for much longer, and when the new Parliament met at the end of May it was plain that a new government would soon take office.

On 6 June 1859, a meeting of Liberal MPs was held at Willis's Rooms in London. This meeting is sometimes considered to represent the formal establishment of the Liberal Party, although there is little evidence to suggest that contemporaries saw it in so dramatic a light. Rather should it be seen as a move to ensure that the disparate 'Liberals', whose majority in the new House was not very great, could achieve a measure of cooperation and form a viable Ministry. The attendance was impressive. Of around 356 MPs who ranked as 'Liberals', 274 turned up, although absentees included both Gladstone and Cobden. A major part in the discussions was taken by the Marquis of Hartington, heir to the Duke of Devonshire, who would play an important role in politics for many years to come. His 'courtesy' marquisate did not give him a seat in the House of Lords, nor disable him from being elected to the House of Commons. The 'Liberals' had no acknowledged overall leader, but Palmerston and Russell, who had been on bad terms for some time, indicated that each would be willing to serve under the other. The remaining 'Peelites' were also willing to cooperate. As for the 'Radicals', John Bright expressed his readiness to support a Liberal government, though he made no secret of his doubts about Palmertson's attitude on foreign policy, which he considered far too bellicose. But, whatever reservations may have existed in a few places, the overall result of the meeting was that nearly all present resolved to bring down the Derby government, and there seemed a fair chance that they would give support to any Liberal administration which was likely to be established in its place.

The Conservative Ministers were soon defeated on a vote of confidence and resigned; but this left open the question who should be the new Prime Minister. There would be difficulties with either Palmerston or Russell, and the Queen – who did not like either of them – contemplated calling another Liberal, Earl Granville, to resolve competing claims. In the end, however, it appeared that Palmerston had widespread public support, and he emerged as Prime Minister. Russell became Foreign Secretary, and Gladstone Chancellor of the Exchequer. Palmerston and Russell both tried to persuade Cobden to join the Cabinet as President of the Board of Trade, but he eventually refused. Later another of the early anti-Corn Law campaigners, C. P. Villiers, did join the Cabinet, though in a different capacity. Many years later, Villiers would attain some distinction as the oldest man ever to sit in the House of Commons – still an MP when he died at the age of 96.

Soon the government made further important advances in the direction of Free Trade. Cobden, though not a Minister, engaged in negotiations with France on the matter of a commercial treaty, with more or less support from the government. The treaty which emerged in 1860 required mutual tariff reductions by the two countries. In the same year Gladstone produced another of his great Budgets. In part, this was just an implementation of Cobden's treaty, but it went a good deal further than that. Hundreds more items were freed from liability for customs duties, and income tax was increased to compensate. Only forty-eight items were still subject to customs duties, and (as the Chancellor put it) 'nothing whatever [remained] in the nature of protective or differential duties, unless you apply that name to the small charges which will be levied upon timber and corn which amount in general, perhaps, to about 3 per cent.'

One defeat which Gladstone sustained over the 1860 Budget is almost as famous as these victories. The overwhelmingly Conservative House of Lords, at the instigation of Derby, decided to throw out Gladstone's proposal to repeal the duties on paper, which affected the price of books and other publications, and were seen as a 'tax on knowledge'. The repeal proposal was contained in a Bill separate from other fiscal proposals, and constitutional practice of the time still permitted the Lords to reject, though not to amend, financial Bills from the Commons. In the following year Gladstone annexed similar proposals to his other financial recommendations in a single Bill. The Lords, who dared not reject all the financial provisions for the year, had to accept defeat. By the early 1860s, one might say that Free Trade, at least in the narrow sense of the term, had been achieved. Not many people wished to see that state of affairs reversed, and fewer still thought that it was possible to do so.

If the Liberals' financial policy was a great success, in other respects they ran into serious difficulties. The American Civil War began in 1862, and one of the first consequences in Britain was a dramatic decline in cotton supplies, resulting in much hardship for the Lancashire cotton industry. But although the 'cotton famine' ended within a year or two, and English prosperity was restored, the chronic distress of Ireland remained, and seeds were being sown for many serious troubles in the future. Neither the cotton famine nor the troubles of Ireland generated much effective pressure, inside or outside Parliament, for drastic economic measures. Most people seem to have believed that Free Trade, accompanied by some financial assistance from local authorities, would do more or less all that could be done to mitigate distress. An early suggestion that much more economic reform was possible came from Cobden. In his last public speech, at Rochdale in November 1864, he declared that, if he were younger, 'I would take Adam Smith in hand, and I would have a League for free trade in land just as we had a League for free trade in corn.' Just what Cobden meant by 'free trade in land' is not clear; but he certainly regarded radical land reform as essential for future development. At a later date, many Liberals would take up Cobden's words, and would come to the view that land reform was vital to deal with many remaining social problems.

Except for fiscal matters, and some significant law reforms, Palmerston's second government did not leave behind many great achievements. Then, in 1865, important events took places, which between them changed the political scene in several directions. Cobden died in April: a man still at the height of his powers, who surely had much yet to give to the life of his country and party. In July, a new General Election was called, which resulted in a small improvement in the Liberals' position. Perhaps the most sensational feature of that election was Gladstone's defeat, by a mere twenty votes, in the representation of Oxford University. He promptly decamped for South Lancashire, where he was returned triumphantly. In October, the octogenarian Prime Minister died. Palmerston, in the judgement of the formidable Duke of Argyll, 'had no ideals for the future of the world, and had a profound distrust of those who professed to be guided by such ideals'. A recent assessment is similar: 'For Palmerston, politics was about holding things together.'[10] 'Holding things together' certainly does not summarise the aims of any of the very disparate men who would lead the Liberals after Palmerston.

Palmerston was succeeded by the seventy-three year old Russell, who by this time had become an earl. 'Reform' had been Russell's great political interest for many years, and he evidently hoped to crown his career with another constitutional measure comparable with that which he had carried a third of a century earlier. In the end, a Reform Bill – necessarily a compromise – was brought before Parliament. As Russell was a peer, Chancellor of the Exchequer Gladstone was put in change of the measure in the House of Commons. Immediately, the Bill ran into trouble, not least with government supporters. The leading personality among the Liberal rebels was Robert Lowe, an albino who had acquired a deep dislike for anything resembling democracy from his earlier experiences in Australia. His associates soon acquired the nickname 'Adullamites', from the cave to which David and 'every one that was discontented' repaired in the time of King Saul.[11] The Second Reading of the Reform Bill passed the Commons with a desperately small majority; but it ran into further trouble in its later stages, and the government resigned. The poisoned chalice passed, and Derby was called to form another Conservative government.

The new ministry could not escape the problems which had confronted its predecessor. In July 1866, serious riots in Hyde Park, London, appear to have convinced some waverers that resistance to Reform was even more dangerous than acceptance, and in March 1867 a new Reform Bill was brought forward, not very different from its predecessor. Like the Liberals before them, the Conservative government had great difficulty with some of its putative supporters. An intense period of political manoeuvring followed, with Disraeli and Gladstone playing the leading roles on the two sides. By this time, there was little doubt that some kind of Reform Act would soon be passed. The two sides in Parliament appeared more eager to ensure that people likely to vote for their own party came on to the register than to exclude others who seemed likely to vote for the other side. Thus the Bill became increasingly radical as it passed through Parliament. When it was eventually passed, as the so-called 'Second Reform Act' of 1867, it provided for a substantial measure of redistribution of seats in favour of the more populous places; but the most sensational feature was application of the 'Household Franchise' in the boroughs, though not in the county constituencies. Under this arrangement, most urban householders, whether owners or tenants, received the vote. This meant that in many constituencies working men came to constitute a large majority of the electorate. The total number of voters was multiplied more than three-fold. Here was one of the great ironies of nineteenth century politics; for Derby, whose dislike of anything resembling democracy was particularly intense, presided over a measure much more radical in some ways than the Act of 1832 – or, indeed, the 'Third Reform Act' of 1885. The 'Second Reform Act' of 1867 affected only England and Wales, but legislation for Scotland and Ireland followed in the first half of 1868.

The wrath of the Adullamites was nothing compared with the anger of many Conservatives, who considered themselves utterly betrayed. Viscount Cranborne, who, as Marquis of Salisbury, would eventually become a Conservative Prime Minister, spoke of 'perfidy'. The best-remembered lines of the poet Coventry Patmore described 1867 as

> ... the year of the great crime
> When the false English nobles and their Jew
> By God demented, slew
> The Trust they stood twice pledged to keep from wrong.

The effect of the smouldering resentment of disaffected Conservatives has some parallels with what had happened twenty, and forty, years earlier.

Derby had long suffered from gout, but a serious new attack caused him to resign the premiership in February 1868. Disraeli was the inevitable successor. It is perhaps a telling contrast between the two men that the classicist Derby was author of a good translation of Homer's *Iliad*, while the romantic Disraeli had achieved early fame as a novelist whose works had strong social overtones.

Throughout the brief period of Disraeli's first Ministry, a Conservative government coexisted with a Liberal majority in the House of Commons, while it was certain that a new General Election must take place, with an enormously extended electorate, once the new registrations were complete. Parliament was eventually dissolved in November 1868, and a General Election followed swiftly. The result was a large majority for the Liberals, who received well over a hundred more seats than their rivals. They were overwhelmingly strong in Scotland, and predominated considerably in Ireland and Wales. In England, the Liberal majority was smaller, but sufficient. It was noted that the Liberals did particularly well in the towns, evidently benefiting from the new enfranchisement. A remarkable exception to this rule was the fate of the philosopher and economist John Stuart Mill, who was defeated at Westminster. Mill's liberalism was evidently too much for his supporters. He had advocated extensive land reform in Ireland; and had even supported votes for women. In a number of English County seats, too, the Liberals fell back. Gladstone and Hartington were both casualties in Lancashire, though they were able to secure election elsewhere. The county had witnessed massive Irish immigration, and this had strong religious overtones. The Chief Whip concluded that 'Lancashire has gone mad, and the contest there has been one of race, Saxon against Celt.'[12]

General Elections in those days were spread over several weeks, but as soon as the overall picture was clear Disraeli resigned, without waiting to be defeated in the new Parliament: a precedent which has been followed ever since when defeat of an existing government was not in doubt. Russell may have had some claim on the premiership, but he manifestly wished to retire, and there was not the slightest doubt that the Queen's commission would go to Gladstone, who accepted office on 3 December 1868.

The political scene in 1868 was profoundly different from what it had been a third of a century earlier. The difference was not just that new parties with new ideas had replaced old ones, but that the whole structure and organisation of parties had changed radically, in response to the need to appeal to a very different kind of electorate in very different constituencies. Important changes in one party usually sparked off similar changes in the other. Although Britain was still far short of being a democracy in the modern sense of the word, it was already apparent that any party which sought to govern the country must win the support of large numbers of people of very modest means in order to do so; and that the 'influence' of important men alone would not suffice to rally that support.

Before 1832, candidates would normally appoint an election agent – usually a local solicitor – whose job was to ensure that potential supporters went to the poll (with suitable inducements where appropriate).[13] Once the contest was over, the electoral machinery usually disintegrated quickly. The 1832 Act introduced the principle of an electoral register which was compiled annually. Only those whose names appeared on the register were entitled to vote. At first a registration fee of one shilling was demanded, but this requirement was later abolished. The need for registration made it important for political activists to ensure that their own supporters were put on the register, and opponents with dubious qualifications were excluded. This led to the establishment of 'registration societies', most particularly in constituencies whose political allegiance was in doubt. As a General Election might be called at short notice, and no party could afford to be caught unprepared, the work of registration societies was continuous, and they provide early examples of local political organisations of a more or less permanent character. For many years to come, however, arrangements varied widely from constituency to constituency. A wealthy candidate would often prefer to defray registration and other expenses himself, rather than set up a more broadly-based organisation which might have ideas of its own. During the most intense period of the Corn Law agitation, the Anti-Corn Law League also established registration societies, designed to ensure that all Free Traders were included on the register. As time went on, such local organisations developed complex canvassing arrangements, designed not only to persuade waverers but also to ensure that supporters were identified and, where necessary, taken to the poll.

While this process was taking place at the 'grass roots' level, other developments were taking place at the centre. The old pattern of more or less self-contained constituencies whose elected Members would then decide to support or break a government was changing. It was becoming a matter of importance to many ordinary people which party dominated Parliament and controlled the government. Active politicians, whether on the government side or in opposition, became increasingly interested not just in what was happening in their own constituency but in what was happening throughout the country. 'Reformers', Chartists and Anti-Corn Law campaigners sought to take their message everywhere. But these organisations of the 1830s and 1840s were designed essentially to produce some specific changes in the fairly near future. Once those changes had taken place, or public interest had receded, the organisation behind them must either disintegrate or change its character.

By the 1850s and 1860s, however, continuing parties rather than ad hoc campaigns were becoming the centre of political activity. This applied both in parliament and in the country. A politician as experienced as Viscount Althorp, Chancellor of the Exchequer under Grey and Melbourne, had a strong dislike for the organisation of MPs through a whipping system.[14] Two or three decades later, not only the whipping of MPs but also close organisation of ordinary voters were taken for granted in all parties. People were not just concerned with current issues; they were coming to support the incipient Liberal or Conservative Parties because they thought that those parties expressed a general point of view which was likely to be relevant to problems which would arise in the future.

Establishment of permanent central organisations for political parties followed as a natural consequence of these developments. In 1831, opponents of reform set up the Carlton Club in London, partly as a social centre, but also as a means of building up political organisation in the constituencies and – a little later – assisting the work of registration. Five years later, the Whigs and their associates established a similar but rival body, the Reform Club. Provincial supporters of the two parties would repair to the appropriate London club, and discuss problems like registration techniques and choice of candidates with the Party Whips, or with a salaried Chief Agent.

As time went on, the Reform Club became less important as a centre for what was to become the Liberal Party, but the importance of central party machinery did not diminish.

An important factor in encouraging the growth of central machinery of political parties was the special problem of 'outvoters' – that is, of people who had votes in places where they did not reside. They constituted something like 15 per cent of the whole electorate, and in close contests it was very important for the party they were likely to support to ensure that they voted. Before 1832 it had been considered necessary in some exceptional cases to bring in outvoters from foreign countries; but the outvoter problem later became much more general. At one time, very generous 'travelling expenses' were sometimes offered to induce outvoters to do their public duty; but in 1858 the law was changed, and the candidate or agent was only permitted to provide means of conveyance – which usually meant a railway ticket – to enable them to vote. As no constituency organisation had a strong interest in polling other people's outvoters, the central machinery of the party was the obvious body for handling the problem.

In February 1860 a body initially known as the Liberal Registration Association, later called the Liberal Central Association, was set up under the aegis of the Chief Liberal Whip, Sir Henry Brand (who was later to play an important role as Speaker of the House of Commons).[15] The LCA soon came to deal with a variety of problems, including registration, polling of outvoters, provision of candidates, and financial assistance for candidates unable or unwilling to defray expenses from their own resources. It also began to establish constituency Liberal Associations in places where none existed. This central machinery necessarily required substantial financing from wealthy members of the party.

Other changes were exerting a great influence on developing parties during the middle years of the nineteenth century. By the late 1860s, transportation had been revolutionised, and something like 12,000 miles of railway track were in use. Politicians and political organisers could reach any substantial town in the country with much greater ease and speed than they could have travelled a few dozen miles in the early years of the century. Ordinary people could, and did, travel considerable distances to hear famous orators. There was also a great 'information revolution'. Although the first Act making elementary education compulsory and universal was not passed until 1870, a great many adults could read long before that. Even in the 1830s, journalism was adapting rapidly to a widening market. The stamp duty on newspapers was reduced from 4d. (rather less than 2p) to 1d. in 1836; in 1855 it was repealed altogether. This made newspapers much more affordable to people of limited means. Many of the newspapers appearing in

the mid-century were promoted by individuals or syndicates with strong
political interests. Satirical periodicals like *Figaro in London* became important in the 1830s, and often carried political cartoons not wildly different in
character from those of the present. *Punch* first appeared in 1841; by the later
1860s there were several competing publications, including the Conservative
Judy. All this was stimulating political interest at many social levels.

The importance of religion in nineteenth century politics would be difficult to overstate. Churches were not just places where people met on
Sundays and holy days to worship; they were also places where all kinds of
gatherings would be held on week days, and so they formed a major
medium of social contact. The national Churches of England, Ireland and
Scotland enjoyed various legal and economic privileges which were
inevitably resented by members of other denominations,

In Ireland, religious differences corresponded to a large extent with class
differences. Through most of the country, the peasantry was overwhelmingly Catholic, the higher social classes overwhelmingly Protestant, although
in some places, particularly in Ulster, Protestants preponderated in all social
classes. Protestants, however, were not all of one kind. In the south, and in
some parts of Ulster, they were overwhelmingly members of the Church of
Ireland, which closely resembled the Church of England. In the extreme
north east, they were mainly Presbyterians. As the nineteenth century
advanced, ideas of national independence became particularly strong among
Catholics, while members of the Church of Ireland were deeply conscious
of affinities with co-religionists in England. Attitudes among Presbyterians
changed over time.

In England, Catholics were relatively few in number except in areas of
heavy Irish immigration, and the great division lay between members of the
Church of England and 'nonconformists' of various denominations. Anglicans and nonconformists were present in comparable numbers, and there
was sometimes intense rivalry between them. There were theological disputes involved; but social aspects of the division were of particular
importance in politics. Nonconformistry tended to be particularly strong in
the industrial towns, and among the working classes. Some denominations
had elaborate systems of lay preachers, which meant that working men
acquired experience in organisation: experience which many of them later
applied to activities like Trade Unionism, temperance agitation – and
politics. Enfranchisement of urban working-class householders in 1867
meant that issues which interested nonconformists came increasingly to the
fore. The Church of England, by contrast, was widely seen as the church of
the squire and the parson, and was particularly strong in some (though not
all) rural areas, and in the wealthier districts of towns. As the nineteenth

century advanced, the link between Anglicanism and Conservatism, and the link between nonconformistry and Liberalism, became increasingly strong. There were many exceptions both ways – the staunch Anglican Gladstone was the most famous – but the general correlation could not be denied. In the 1850s and 1860s, there had been deep discussions about matters like payment of church rates, and religious tests for the older English universities, in which attitudes followed closely the Anglican-nonconformist line of division. More disputes would soon follow.

In Wales the Church of England also enjoyed establishment, but the proportion of nonconformists was much higher than in England. The various nonconformist denominations had spread like wildfire from the 1830s onwards, most particularly in the Welsh-speaking areas where the Anglican liturgy must have been as incomprehensible as the Latin Mass. The little Bethels and Zions of the villages had mostly been built through local effort within living memory, and there was an immense feeling of pride in their popularity and efficacy.

In Scotland, Presbyterians of one kind or another predominated heavily over other denominations, although there were some parts of the country where Catholics were numerous, and others where there were many Episcopalians, whose practices resembled those of the Church of England. The Church of Scotland was Presbyterian and was also established. In 1843 it underwent the 'disruption', which resulted in the formation of the Free Church of Scotland, whose members showed attitudes which in many ways paralleled the English and Welsh nonconformists. The close correspondence between religious and political affiliations are very clearly brought out in the voting figures for the Scottish universities in the 1868 General Election. Among ministers of the established church, Conservatives led Liberals by 1221 to 67, and among Episcopalians by 78 to four; while among Free Church and United Presbyterian Ministers the Liberals led by 1081 to 34.[16]

The Liberal Party derived much of its later character from the rising personality of Gladstone, just as the character of the Conservative Party was being influenced by Disraeli. The great period of the Gladstone-Disraeli duel lasted barely a dozen years; but in that time the two men exerted an influence on their respective parties vastly greater than that of any other nineteenth century statesmen: an influence which is not extinct to this day. Morally, intellectually, and by sheer force of character, Gladstone towered above his contemporaries. As a young man, he had inclined towards a career in the church, but was over-persuaded by his father. His sense of an all-seeing God imposing heavy responsibilities on the statesman never left him. Politics, for Gladstone, had no meaning except as the vindication of underlying moral and religious principles; though the way in which he applied those principles developed greatly during his long life. His first book had argued the interdependence of church and state, and had stirred Macaulay to the famous description of its author as 'the rising hope of [the] stern unbending Tories'. Yet there is a real consistency. As a Tory, Gladstone believed fervently in reciprocal rights and duties of people belonging to different classes. What shook his Toryism was the growing conviction that the privileged classes were failing to adhere to their side of the social bargain. The young ultra-Tory was still essentially the same man as the Prime Minister who would later defend the right of the atheist Bradlaugh to sit in the House of Commons; and the man who would emerge from retirement at the age of nearly eighty-seven to campaign on behalf of the persecuted Armenians.

Gladstone was a classicist of considerable standing, who – like Derby, and like both of the Pitts – was particularly devoted to Homer. He is, perhaps, the only politician of whom one might say that, if he had not become Prime Minister, he could easily have become a great archbishop, or a distinguished professor of Greek. His knowledge of more recent literature in several tongues was considerable. Far into old age, his physical and intellectual energy was enormous. He was still famous for taking long walks, and for his propensity to cut down large trees.

As for the political body over which Gladstone was to preside for so long, and with such overwhelming authority, there was no doubt that the Liberal Party was very much a political reality by the late 1860s, and was set to endure for a long time to come. It had an immensely able leader, and a strong and growing organisation. Enormous numbers of people in all social classes had no hesitation in describing themselves as Liberals. We may still debate which – if any – of the governments of the 1830s, 1840s, 1850s and earlier 1860s should properly be called 'Liberal'. There is no doubt at all that the government over which Gladstone presided at the end of 1868 fully merited that name.

2

Exhausting the Volcanoes

Gladstone ... spent his declining years trying to guess the answer to the
Irish Question; unfortunately, whenever he was getting warm, the Irish
secretly changed the Question.

W. C. Sellar and R. J. Yeatman: *1066 and All That*

In the late 1860s, a revolutionary Irish body known as the Fenians commenced a campaign of violence, first in Ireland and then in Britain. No
doubt Fenian terrorism could be contained, though at high cost; but the real
need was to remove its causes. When Gladstone's realised that he would
soon be Prime Minister, his first noteworthy comment had been, 'My mission is to pacify Ireland'. In one form or another, the 'Irish Question' would
recur for the remainder of Gladstone's long life, and would prove of major
importance to his party for decades after his death.

Gladstone took personal charge of Irish parliamentary business. The first
major action of the new government was to deal with an Irish complaint which
was not primarily concerned with the economic condition of the country,
but was real and widespread nevertheless, and had some economic overtones. During the period of Disraeli's brief first Ministry, and particularly at
the General Election of 1868, the future of the Protestant establishment in
Ireland had been widely debated. The Liberals, and Gladstone in particular,
urged the need to disestablish the Church of Ireland – that is, to remove its
special legal privileges. In general, the British electorate appeared to support
the Liberal view on the subject. In some areas, particularly where there had
recently been a good deal of recent Irish immigration, there was a Protestant
backlash, and matters went the other way. It is likely that the surprising
defeats of Gladstone and Hartington in Lancashire constituencies may be
explained at least partially by that factor. In Ireland itself there was no doubt
about popular support for disestablishment, and nearly two-thirds of the
MPs returned were Liberals. Irish Catholics would necessarily support it.
Presbyterians, who formed the third strongest denomination in the country,
were split, but seemed mainly to favour disestablishment. This may explain
several Liberal successes in Ulster.[1]

In 1869, Gladstone introduced a Bill to disestablish the Irish Church. The contest was sharp, but even the House of Lords thought it best to submit to the popular will on the most vital aspects of the dispute, and the measure passed into law. The Church of Ireland became a voluntary body without special privileges, although people who might have suffered personally from disestablishment received compensation. Many Church of Ireland land-holdings passed into the hands of tenants, though they were required to repay the value through what were in effect long-term mortgages.[2] This set an important precedent for Irish land purchase, which became a great issue later in the century.

In 1870, Gladstone turned to his next piece of Irish legislation, which eventually became his first Irish Land Act. One of the great paradoxes of the Anglo-Irish Union, which had been brought out with fearful poignancy in the Famine, was the great disparity between land relationships in the two kingdoms. Substantive land law was almost identical in England and Ire-land. This misled many English people into thinking that social realities ought to be the same in the two countries, and – if they were not – this was due to some national eccentricity of the Irish. In fact, social relations were wildly different. In most cases, English landlords lived on their estates, spoke the same language and worshipped at the same church as their tenants. In Ireland, landlords and tenants were usually of different religions and often spoke different languages, for the Gaeltacht was much more extensive than it is today. To a growing extent Irish landlords were absentees, living in Dublin, London or elsewhere. The Irish landlord was likely to leave man-agement of his estate to an agent whose main remit was to draw as much rent as possible, on an essentially short-term view. The resident English landlord was far more likely to be an active 'improver', willing to provide capital and anxious to cooperate with his tenants to develop the estate according to the best practice of the time, and to play an active part in many local activities. In law, any improvements made on the land reverted to the landlord on expiry of a tenancy. In England, where the landlord had usually created those improvements, this may seem reasonable enough; but in Ire-land, where they had often been made by the tenant, matters were very different. Not surprisingly, tenants were therefore disinclined to introduce improvements, and this was a significant factor in the general poverty of Irish farms which had been so important at the time of the Famine. In some parts of Ireland, holdings were so tiny that the potato was the only crop which was likely to yield enough harvest – in a good year – to feed the farmer and his family. The overriding reason why Ireland suffered an appalling famine in the 1840s and England did not was the Irish dependency on that single crop. When the potato failed, everything failed.

Agricultural conditions varied widely in different parts of Ireland. At the time of the Famine, Ulster suffered noticeably less than the other three provinces of Ireland. This was widely regarded as the result of a practice known as 'Ulster Custom', under which a tenant vacating his tenancy was entitled to the value of improvements he had introduced. Gladstone's particular concern in the Irish Land Bill of 1870 was to secure the application of 'Ulster Custom' throughout Ireland. Another important feature of the Irish Land Act was the so-called 'Bright Clauses', which owed their existence to the President of the Board of Trade. They provided for a measure of land purchase – the principle which Bright had also inspired in the Irish Church Act of the previous year. When a landlord and his tenant agreed in principle on the sale of a holding, the Board of Works was authorised to advance up to two-thirds of the price, which would be repaid, with interest, over 35 years. In one sense this proved something of a damp squib, for fewer than 500 loans were ever made under these terms; but in another sense it was significant, for a very important principle which had appeared in the Irish Church Act of the previous year was reaffirmed, and would be copied in later legislation which had much greater effect.

Yet the Land Act profoundly disappointed many people by what it failed to do. While Irish tenants were doubtless pleased to obtain compensation for improvements, they had been even more anxious to obtain security of tenure. They considered that a tenancy should normally be renewed when it came for annual review, provided that the agreed rent had been paid and other covenants had been followed. The government refused to accede to that demand; and from this refusal much trouble would later arise.

The year 1870 witnessed another famous measure, the Education Act which is linked with the name of W. E. Forster. Unlike most leading politicians on both sides of the House, Forster started life in modest circumstances, though he later became a successful millowner. Before the Education Act, children of the wealthy, and of the moderately prosperous, received private education; but provision for the bulk of the population was erratic. Two great systems of charitable schools existed, the National Society schools which were presided over by Anglican authorities, and schools operated by the British and Foreign School Society, which were controlled by nonconformists. Both societies had received small grants from public funds since the 1830s, and their schools were subject to public inspection. Outside those societies were elementary schools which were not inspected, where the standard of teaching was in many cases very low. Even when all these disparate schools were added together, the number of places available was far less than the number of children. There was widespread and general concern to improve and rationalise the educational system, but for many years the problem had been unresolved.

The Bill which Forster introduced in February 1870 applied only to England and Wales. It sought to establish a general system of elementary education for children aged between five and twelve, making use of the existing charitable schools. The country would be divided into educational districts. Where there were not enough school places for the children in a particular district, an elected School Board would be charged to remedy the situation. Women as well as men were authorised both to vote and to stand for election. In some places, though not in all, the elections were conducted by secret ballot. Parents who could afford to do so would be required to provide part of the cost of their children's education, but the poorest children would be taught free. School Boards would raise funds for the scheme through education rates. It was intended that the School Boards should be authorised to make by-laws imposing penalties on parents failing to send their children to school, once adequate places had been provided.

At first Forster's Bill was greeted with general enthusiasm, but soon serious difficulties arose. Some of these difficulties were financial; but the most serious ones related to religious teaching. Many nonconformists bitterly resented the idea of giving financial support to church schools where Anglican doctrine, and the Anglican catechism, would be taught. After much argument, a compromise emerged. The schools operated through the societies would continue to teach religion according to their own principles, while the 'Board Schools' would teach a sort of non-denominational 'Bible Christianity'. The measure introduced a 'Conscience Clause', under which parents objecting to the religious teaching given would be authorised to withdraw their children from that aspect of their studies. In the end the Bill passed into law more or less as originally intended. Many nonconformists continued to feel deeply aggrieved at the compromise, and Forster – though himself of nonconformist origin – encountered considerable difficulties thereafter with other Liberals in his own Bradford constituency.

The following year, 1871, saw new army legislation, sponsored by Edward Cardwell. Cardwell's Bill introduced many important reforms, designed essentially to increase the army's efficiency, and he is sometimes regarded as the most effective Secretary for War of his century. But its most controversial feature was the proposal to abolish purchase of army commissions. There were many instances of rich young men almost completely lacking in experience or capacity securing high rank in that manner. The proposal encountered considerable resistance in the Commons, and was halted at the Second Reading in the Lords. The government's response was remarkable, and provides a striking example of the Prime Minister's well-known propensity to be 'terrible on the rebound'. Gladstone, who was still on good terms with the Queen at this date, advised her to issue a royal warrant to abolish purchase. This annoyed some Liberals, while the House of Lords was enraged. The real irony of the aftermath, however, was that their Lordships now became willing to pass the Bill, because it provided for compensation for officers who would suffer pecuniary loss through abolition of purchase.

Forster, fresh from his Education Act of the previous year, was set in charge of a new Ballot Bill in 1871. At the 1868 General Election there had been some notorious cases of tenants evicted by aggrieved landlords for supporting Liberal candidates, and the whole question of secret voting had acquired considerable importance. In spite of some filibustering by the Conservative opposition, the measure passed the Commons, but it was rejected by the Lords. This meant that it was lost for the 1870–71 session, and had to be reintroduced in 1872. Again the Ballot Bill passed the Commons, more or less in its original form, and again it went up to the Lords. This time the peers decided that discretion was the better part of valour, and allowed the measure to pass.

The same year 1872 also saw the concluding stages of a long controversy with the United States. During the American Civil War, the rebel Confederate States obtained a number of naval vessels, including the cruiser *Alabama*, from British sources. After the war, the American government sought compensation from Britain for damage done and expenses incurred as a result. The matter was referred to arbitration, and $15 million – a very large sum by the standards of the time – was awarded against Britain. This the government duly paid. The decision to go to arbitration set a very important precedent in international dealings which would be generally approved today, but which at the time was widely criticised by the government's opponents.

Another important measure of 1872 which would eventually have widespread repercussions was the new licensing legislation which the Home Secretary H. A. Bruce first proposed in 1871, and which – with modifications – took legislative shape as the Licensing Act of the following year. The context is important. 'Temperance' was a deeply controversial issue, and remained so far into the twentieth century. The idea that the sale and consumption of alcoholic drink should be severely controlled had roots in the eighteenth century, but it was not until the quality of public water supplies improved in the mid-nineteenth century that the temperance movement grew substantially. It was particularly strong among nonconformists, but had supporters among people of all religions and none. Not only did advocates of temperance deplore drunkenness, but, at a time when working class wages were close to the margin of subsistence, they could readily show that a man who drank substantial quantities of alcohol almost necessarily pushed his family below the poverty line.

The Act controlled the issue of new licences for public houses, which had to be confirmed by the Home Office. Fines for drunkenness were increased, and hours within which drink could be sold were restricted. In Parliament, it was not a matter of deep controversy, and licensed victuallers on the whole accepted it. One may guess that many publicans were relieved both by the restrictions on new entrants to their business and by the greater leisure they now received. The measure fell very far short of the aims of the temperance extremists, and one of its most powerful critics in the House of Commons was the Liberal Sir Wilfrid Lawson, who considered it too moderate. Once the Act took effect, however, there was agitation on the opposite side. Deputations of protest were launched, and several riots took place. It is likely that this measure was a major factor in the government's growing unpopularity.

Even before the Licensing Act took effect, the Conservative Opposition began to redouble its efforts to undermine the government. In perhaps the most famous speech of his life, at Manchester on 3 April 1872,[3] Disraeli compared the Ministers with 'exhausted volcanoes'. This was less than fair. The Liberals were by no means 'exhausted'; even the Ballot Act had not yet become law. But there was much to be said for the view that Gladstone's government had nearly worked itself out of a job. In 1872, there were twenty by-elections in Britain, five of which recorded Conservative gains from Liberals. In Ireland the position was even worse. There were six by-elections, all of them in Liberal seats. Five resulted in government defeats: just one to a Conservative and four to advocates of what was becoming known as Home Rule.[4]

The Home Rule movement represented a new factor in politics – or rather an old factor in a new form. In 1870, Isaac Butt (who had once sat briefly as a Conservative MP for an English constituency) set up the Irish Home Government Association, which aimed at restoration of a separate Irish parliament. This harked back to O'Connell's campaign for 'Repeal' a quarter of a century earlier. Butt (like Parnell in later times) was a Protestant, and the link between renascent Irish nationalism and Catholicism was not as close at first as later became the case.

Two factors had been particularly important in the appearance of a strong Home Rule movement.[5] Agricultural tenants were disappointed with the limited effects of the 1870 Land Act; while the fate of Fenians who had participated in violent disturbances in the 1860s caused much concern. The initial violence received scant support in Ireland; but the severe punishment meted out to the perpetrators led to a wave of sympathy. Butt acquired a great reputation as the lawyer who defended Fenians at their trials, and who later campaigned actively but unsuccessfully for an amnesty for them. In the early 1870s, Home Rulers made inroads into both Liberal and Conservative support in Ireland, though the Liberals suffered the more. Butt himself was returned in a by-election of 1871, capturing the Liberal seat of Limerick city without a contest.

For reasons both of ideology and of interest, the Liberal Government remained anxious to 'pacify Ireland', and in 1873 this concern led to further serious difficulties. The structure of the Irish universities might seem a somewhat arcane issue, of little concern outside Ireland and a matter of less than universal interest even there, for only a tiny minority of the Irish people could aspire to tertiary education at all. The question, however, was long-standing, and involved the extremely sensitive issues of nationalism and religion. Legislation introduced by the Liberal government in 1871 had permitted non-Anglicans to be appointed to lay posts in the Oxford and Cambridge colleges, and in the following year Henry Fawcett, a blind and very independent-minded Liberal MP, proposed a similar measure for Trinity College, Dublin. This would have cut across the wider ideas which the government had for a general reform of Irish academic institutions, but it received widespread support among Liberal MPs, and was only defeated through extraordinary pressure by the government whips. Early in 1873 the government's own Bill was published, and Gladstone himself took charge of the measure, overriding his Chief Secretary for Ireland Lord Hartington, who had quite different ideas from his chief on the matter. All Irish institutions of the appropriate academic standard were to be brought together in a single university. Trinity would lose its special status, and the religious tests would be abolished; but in most respects the autonomy of the component units would be unimpaired. At first there was widespread support for the Bill, not least among Catholics; but it soon fell between two stools.[6] Most of the Irish hierarchy decided to oppose it as 'being framed on the principle of mixed and purely secular education'. Many Protestants, including some Liberal critics, saw it as an unwarranted concession to Catholicism. The Conservative opposition was eager to bring about a government defeat, and no doubt this issue was as good as any. On 11 March, the government failed on the second reading of the Bill by 287 votes to 284 – a number of Liberals, British and Irish, voting with the Opposition.

A curious political crisis followed. Gladstone may have contemplated dissolution of Parliament and an appeal to the electorate; but, if so, he was dissuaded, and instead tendered the government's resignation. Disraeli refused to take office. He produced subtle and diffuse arguments for the refusal; but the main reason was almost certainly party-political. The longer the government remained in office, the worse its fate was likely to be when the eventual reckoning came. Gladstone perforce resumed office.

From now on, almost everything went wrong for the government. In the early summer of 1873, a Liberal MP, G. O. Trevelyan, proposed extension of the franchise to rural residents on similar terms to those which the 1867 Act afforded to residents in the towns. This was not a government Bill, but Gladstone indicated his personal support. That precipitated the resignation of a member of the Cabinet, Lord Ripon.[7] Next, serious charges of overspending were levelled at the Post Office and the Department of Works. Lowe, the Chancellor of the Exchequer was implicated in a technical sense through his ministerial responsibility, and with considerable difficulty was persuaded to move from the Exchequer to the Home Office. Gladstone eventually decided to double up the Chancellorship with the office of Prime Minister.

That presented an awkward technical problem. As the law then stood (and would stand for many years to come), an MP accepting a ministerial post was required to vacate his seat and submit to a by-election. What was by no means clear law was whether a man who was already a Minister, but accepted a further ministerial post, was required to do the same. The two Law Officers assured Gladstone that there was no such requirement; Brand, the former Liberal Chief Whip who had by this time become Speaker, was less certain. The nub of the problem was that Gladstone's seat, Greenwich, was by no means a safe one, and defeat of the Prime Minister would be a calamity for his government. Perhaps fortunately the ministerial move took place in August, and several months passed before Parliament met again. When it did, the legality of the business was not seriously impugned, but there was always the risk that a full challenge might be made, probably at a highly inopportune moment. All this, of course, destabilised a tottering government even further.

On 18 January 1874, Gladstone began to discuss the possibility of an early dissolution with some colleagues.[8] A couple of days later, he listed reasons for dissolution with considerable bluntness, commencing with 'We gain time and avoid for the moment a ministerial crisis'. The Greenwich difficulty was not among the points listed. On 23 January, the Cabinet agreed to a dissolution. There has been much discussion as to why Gladstone chose that particular moment for an election. If the Greenwich problem may be discounted, as it probably can, one likely explanation may be the threat of a 'ministerial crisis' at which he hinted. Both George Goschen at the Admiralty and Cardwell at the War Office were pressing for high spending estimates, which Gladstone could be expected to resist, both as a stern upholder of public economy and as a man to whom war was particularly abhorrent. If the Liberals won the election, his own prestige would be overwhelming, and would enable him to beat down opposition from the Service departments. If the Liberals lost, they would be able to regroup themselves in opposition.

The 1874 General Election campaign was brief. The most important new issue raised on the Liberals side was Gladstone's proposal to abolish Income Tax. This was quite realistic, and Disraeli's observations during the election did not suggest otherwise. Income Tax stood at 3d. in the pound, or 1.25 per cent on taxable income. The anticipated yield in the current year was between £5 and £6 millions. A budget surplus of £4 millions was expected; thus revenues would go most of the way towards meeting the sum. Additions to indirect taxes would be anathema to a free trader like Gladstone, but various other measures, such as increases in death duties, were open for consideration, and economies might be made in expenditure, particularly on the Service departments. It may well be that Gladstone raised his proposal to abolish income tax in order to thwart pressure for higher spending rather than as an inducement to the electorate.

Most of the election results were in by the end of the first week in February 1874, the remainder by the middle of the month. The government suffered a heavy defeat. The new House contained approximately 350 Conservatives to 242 Liberals and 60 Home Rulers. Apparently reliable authorities give substantially different figures of numbers of MPs returned in various interests. It is clear, however, that the result was of exceptional importance. For the first time in a quarter of a century, the Conservatives had won a clear majority. Gladstone was disposed to blame the result on reactions to the Licensing Act. 'We have been swept away', he wrote, 'by a torrent of beer and gin'.[9] Defending his own seat in the closely-fought two-member constituency of Greenwich, the Prime Minister at least retained his place, but sustained the minor indignity of running second of the four candidates, trailing behind a Conservative distiller. A careful analysis of the Liberal MPs returned in 1874 suggests that the social composition of the party which Gladstone led had not changed greatly over recent years. The largest single group, though not an overall majority, were landowners, with men engaged in industry and commerce running them fairly close, while considerable numbers of lawyers were also present.[10]

Two of the British Liberal successes of 1874 were specially significant for the future, for they carried into Parliament candidates with working-class origins, promoted by a body known as the Labour Representation League. Stafford was a two-member borough, both seats being held by Conservatives at the time of the dissolution. Much against the national trend, one of those seats was captured by a Liberal backed by the LRL. The victor was Alexander Macdonald, President of the Miners' National Association, who began his working life in the pits, although he later became a successful businessman. The other LRL success was no less remarkable. Thomas Burt of

Morpeth commenced work in the coal mines at the age of ten. As his biographer noted, Burt 'was returned almost solely by workmen as a workmen's member, at a time when he had not long left the pit, and was the ill-paid and hard-worked secretary of a miners' organisation'.[11] Burt was to remain Liberal MP for Morpeth until his retirement in 1918, at the age of 81. Later in the nineteenth century, a number of other working-class men were returned to the House of Commons. They were often described by contemporaries as 'Labour', 'Liberal Labour' or 'Lib–Lab', but in the large majority of cases they sat as Liberals.

From a long-term point of view, the results in Ireland would prove particularly important for British, as well as Irish, politics. With the usual reservations about exact numbers, one may say that, in addition to the sixty seats which went to Home Rulers, thirty-three went to Conservatives and only ten to Liberals. Chichester Fortescue, the only Irish MP who sat in Gladstone's Cabinet, was one of the Liberal casualties. The Conservatives, who had greatly increased their representation in Britain, actually lost some ground in Ireland. Five of their seats in Ulster were captured by the Liberals.[12] Most of the remaining Irish Conservative seats were in Ulster, with a few in Leinster.

In the immediate aftermath of the election, it was not easy to say to what extent the Home Rulers should be regarded as a new and separate force in politics and to what extent they should be regarded as a section of the Liberals. As recently as the previous November, they had held a conference at which they sought to reorganise themselves as something like a distinct political party, but the reorganisation was far from complete when the General Election overtook them. An Irish historian has commented that

> In all, eighteen of the sixty Home Rulers had sat as Liberals in the previous
> Parliament and a further twelve or so were of typical Liberal stamp. It can
> safely be said that a clear majority of the Home Rule MPs would have stood as
> Gladstonians if that was what the political need of the time had dictated.[13]

This suggests that the great impetus which the 1874 General Election afforded to the Home Rule cause may have owed at least as much to the government's temporary unpopularity as to any burning enthusiasm for Home Rule. Thus the state of the parties in Ireland was by no means clear in the immediate aftermath of the 1874 election. In the light of subsequent events, however, it appears that Liberalism had suffered a blow in Ireland from which it would never recover. In 1868, the great majority of Irish voters had supported a party which sought to satisfy Irish grievances within the existing union with Britain; by 1874 most Catholic, and some Protestant, Irish voters had come to the conclusion that further rectification of Irish grievances would require at least a substantial measure of self-government. The country had already adopted a pattern which would persist for many years to come, with Conservatives dominant in most Protestant areas and Home Rulers dominant in most Catholic areas.

Like Disraeli in 1868, Gladstone accepted the voters' verdict as final, and did not await defeat in the new House. On 17 February 1874, he tendered the ministry's resignation to the Queen. Later in the day, she summoned Disraeli to form his second administration.

THE IN-"JUDICIOUS BOTTLE-HOLDER."

GHOST OF PAM. "AHA, DEAR BOY! WE MANAGED THINGS RATHER DIFFERENTLY WHEN I WAS BOTTLE-HOLDER!"

A *Punch* cartoon of February 1871 showing the ghost of Palmerston
addressing Gladstone and observing the marked difference between
their ways of 'managing things'.

3

In the Wilderness

No Chancellor of the Exchequer is worth his salt who is not ready to save what are meant by candle-ends and cheese-parings in the cause of his country.

W. E. Gladstone at Edinburgh, 29 November 1879

Although in retrospect the 1874 General Election may be recognised as one of considerable importance, matters must have looked very different indeed to people actually living through the contest, for there seemed to be no great issue of controversy between the two parties as to the policies which should be followed in the aftermath. It looked much like a battle of 'outs' and 'ins'.

Once the election was over, there was speculation about Gladstone's intentions. He soon wrote to Lord Granville, Foreign Secretary in the old administration and Liberal leader in the House of Lords. He was willing, if the party so desired, to withdraw at once; but, if he continued for the time being, he proposed to consider his position again before the beginning of the 1875 session. Predictably, the Liberals were glad enough to keep him on such terms. For the remainder of the year he devoted a large part of his impressive energies to a close study of the question of Ritualism in the Church of England, which interested him a good deal more than did many political controversies. The *Annual Register* describes his attendance in Parliament during the remainder of the session as 'fitful and uncertain'.

Little happened at this stage to suggest that Disraeli's government was following policies with which Gladstone disagreed passionately. Even Gladstone's own proposal to abolish Income Tax seemed to find an echo. The new Chancellor, Sir Stafford Northcote (later Lord Iddesleigh), had been Gladstone's secretary many years earlier, and appeared still to be influenced by Gladstonian ideas. His 1874 Budget reduced Income Tax to a mere 2d. in the pound – under 1 per cent, and the lowest level at which it had stood from Peel's reintroduction of the tax in 1842 down to the present. In the same Budget, a significant further step was taken in the Free Trade direction, by abolition of the sugar duties. In other respects it seemed to be performing a job of which the Liberals could heartily approve. There was some important social legislation. The legal status of Trade Unions was improved, and public health promoted. A Factories Act considerably reduced the exploitation of women and children, while the Artisans' Dwellings Act gave local authorities enhanced powers of slum clearance, and an Agricultural Holdings Act pleased many tenant farmers. A new Judicature Act extended the principles of earlier Liberal legislation.

Ten months after his earlier missive, Gladstone wrote again to Granville. This time he definitely decided to withdraw, indicating that 'this retirement is dictated to me by my personal views as to the best method of spending the closing years of my life'. There has been scholarly debate about Gladstone's real intentions,[1] but it is likely that he meant what he said. By the time of the next General Election he would probably be over seventy. He had many interests outside politics, and had little liking for the practice of scoring silly points off opponents which seems to fascinate many politicians. On top of that, he considered that the Liberal Party was so deeply split on so many issues that coordinated action was impossible. If the new Conservative government was prepared to pursue policies of which, on the whole, he approved, he had no intention of leading factious opposition to those policies. If he remained in politics at all, it would be in order to do some important job.

Gladstone had completely overshadowed all other members of his government, and there was no obvious successor. Three names were considered seriously: the Marquis of Hartington, W. E. Forster and George Goschen. The last of these was soon dropped. On the face of it, Forster seemed much the better qualified of the two remaining men. He had been responsible for two of the most important pieces of legislation under the old government, and his record of achievement during that period was second only to that of Gladstone himself. Hartington, however, had two obvious advantages. He was about fifteen years younger than Forster and his rank as heir to a dukedom carried not only a snob appeal but also an assurance to nervous Liberals that he was not likely to support dangerously radical policies.

There were indications that the contest, if it came, would be a close one. Some evidence exists to suggest that, contrary to expectations, Hartington's main support would be from Radicals, and that of Forster from Whigs. What was perhaps critical in the contest was that 'those who disliked Forster did so very strongly, whereas most of those who preferred him could be induced to accept Hartington, however unenthusiastically'.[2] Eventually Forster was persuaded to withdraw. And so, on 3 February 1875, when the Liberal MPs met at the Reform Club in London to choose a new leader, the only candidate was Hartington, who was appointed with more or less universal approval. Nobody could call Hartington charismatic, but he had a reputation for good sense, and his ideas – as would soon be proved – were by no means hidebound.

Hartington did not succeed to the full inheritance of his predecessor. Gladstone had been acknowledged leader of the party as a whole. Only the MPs had been engaged in the recent contest, and so Hartington could only be considered leader of the MPs. At a time when a Prime Minister was as likely to be a peer as an MP, it could not be taken for granted that he would be the natural choice for Prime Minister if the Liberals were again able to form a government. It has been suggested that the most likely candidate in such circumstances would have been Granville.[3]

After 1875 the flood of reforming legislation began to abate, and the Conservatives started to encounter difficulties for other reasons. Disraeli's famous acquisition of the bankrupt Khedive's shares in the Suez Canal on behalf of the British government towards the end of 1875 added to the Premier's popularity, but it also encountered serious criticism on grounds more elevated than mere party jealousy. Then, in the course of 1876, a matter arose which today seems of little more than ceremonial significance, but which exercised contemporaries considerably. Disraeli, perhaps hoping to end the widowed Queen's withdrawal from public life, sought to award her the new title Empress of India. This proposal was disliked by Liberals of all kinds: by Whigs, who were disposed to cut monarchs down to size, by Radicals who in those days were often more or less republican in their sympathies, by off-beat men like Lowe who did not fit into either category, and by Gladstone himself, who was beginning to recover his interest in contemporary politics. The Prime Minister's proposals were, of course, carried; but the Queen was much distressed by the Liberals' attitude, and this may have played a significant part in her general alienation from the party during her later years.

In the middle 1870s, the pattern of British politics was changed dramatically as a result of events in south-eastern Europe. Apart from Greece, most of the southern Balkans were still part of the Ottoman, or Turkish, Empire; but the subject peoples, who were predominantly Orthodox Christians, had a deep sense of grievance against their rulers. The empire was corrupt and incompetent, and its authority was often enforced in a savage and brutal manner. Turkey's traditional antagonist was Russia, who had natural sympathy for her co-religionists in the Balkans. Unfortunately Russia also had ambitions of her own, which included acquisition of the Ottoman capital Constantinople. This was a matter of great concern to the controllers of British foreign policy, who feared that a Russian presence on the Mediterranean might interrupt their own interests in the area, particularly communications with India and the Far East. Thus, on the whole, British foreign policy tended to support Turkey, as in the Crimean War of the 1850s.

In 1875, there were disorders in Herzegovina, Bosnia and Serbia; but in May 1876 irregular Turkish troops suddenly massacred some 15,000 people, many of them completely innocent, in a new Balkan 'trouble spot', Bulgaria. To people of our own time, who recall the vastly greater wickedness of Hitler, Stalin and Mao, the scale of these atrocities seems small; but the Victorians were less familiar with such horrors, and there was a huge and largely spontaneous public revulsion. The Liberal leaders were becoming increasingly critical of the government for its pro-Turkish leanings. In September 1876, while this agitation was in full spate, Gladstone published a pamphlet *The Bulgarian Horrors and the Question of the East.* Its most famous passage was a call for the Turks to be driven 'bag and baggage' from their European provinces. The pamphlet was an immediate sensation, and 200,000 copies were sold within a month. Disraeli, who had recently become Earl of Beaconsfield, did what he could to defend an increasingly unpopular policy. There is reason for thinking that he had been put in a false position through erroneous information supplied by the British Ambassador at Constantinople, but the Prime Minister's occasional flippancy helped to rouse public fury against him.

The Bulgarian agitation ran its course; but even when it was over there remained a great feeling of hostility towards the Sultan's government among a large section of the British public. In April 1877, war broke out between Turkey and Russia. There was not, and never could be, any question of Britain actively intervening in favour of Russia; but a strong argument exists for the view that Gladstone's action was an important factor in averting intervention in favour of Turkey. Soon a marked difference opened up between Beaconsfield and his Foreign Secretary, the 15th Earl of Derby, who had succeeded his father a few years earlier. Eventually Derby left the government, and was to reappear as a Liberal a little later. The international crisis ended in mid-1878 with the Congress of Berlin, at which all the acknowledged Great Powers, including both Russia and Turkey, assembled to work out a settlement. Turkish oppression of the Bulgarians ended, while Russia did not acquire a base on the Mediterranean. Britain received a protectorate over the Turkish island of Cyprus. Beaconsfield's government stood at the peak of its popularity.

While these events were taking place at the top level of politics, some great changes were occurring at the grass-roots, which would have very important long-term consequences. The Reform Act of 1867 provided that certain large towns would return three MPs, but that an individual voter in those towns would only receive two votes. The object of this odd arrangement was to ensure that a party which was in a minority, but nevertheless polled sub-stantially, would normally be expected to win one of the seats in the town concerned.[4] In most towns, the arrangement worked more or less as intended.

In one place, however, the intended result was not achieved. Birmingham was an overwhelmingly Liberal town, and the local Liberal activists decided that it was not necessary to share representation with Conservatives at all. In 1868, the Liberal organisation advanced three candidates for the three seats. Liberal supporters in some wards of the town were advised to vote for candidates A and B, in other wards for A and C, in others for B and C. As a result of this strategy, three Liberals were returned for the town. In the General Election of 1874, despite the national swing to their party, the Birm-ingham Conservatives were so demoralised that the three Liberals were returned unopposed.

The Birmingham Liberals introduced other innovations too. They advanced candidates on a party 'ticket' for local government. This device was also successful, and resulted in the election of a Liberal council. In 1873 Joseph Chamberlain, who would play a major part in the Liberal Party's future, was chosen mayor. Chamberlain, who had amassed a considerable fortune in industry at an early age, retired on the proceeds and devoted the remainder of his life to politics. Under his lead, an extensive programme of public works was adopted, including slum clearance and improvements to sanitation and street paving, which attracted national attention. Soon the Birmingham Liberals extended their activities even further, infiltrating gov-erning bodies of schools and charitable organisations.

Chamberlain worked closely with an extremely able political organiser, the Birmingham Liberal Association's secretary Francis Schnadhorst. The Liberal Association which they dominated was open to all inhabitants of the town, voters or non-voters. A subscription of one shilling a year was suggested, but this was not obligatory and those unwilling or unable to pay were admitted as members after signifying adherence to the organisation's objectives. Anybody who wished to exert an influence on the town's future who was not an intransigent Conservative was likely to join the Liberal Association. Final authority lay in a representative body with 594 members, usually known as the 'Liberal 600'. The exceptionally pervasive Liberal organisation in Birmingham was often styled the 'caucus' – though this was really a gross misuse of a term which had acquired a pejorative meaning in America.

Interest in the 'Birmingham Plan' soon began to spread among Liberals. Schnadhorst and Chamberlain visited other towns, and about twenty paid emissaries were appointed to continue the work. Sometimes established

Liberals fell foul of these local 'caucuses'. The most famous case of this arose
in Bradford shortly before the 1874 election, when the local 'caucus' made
an unsuccessful attempt to coerce their MP, W. E. Forster, to toe the 'caucus' line. After 1874, a number of Liberal associations in towns like
Manchester, Leeds and Sheffield, where results had been particularly disappointing, introduced reconstruction plans of their own. These plans were
not, for the most part, designed primarily in order to create a representative
body, but for essentially practical reasons.[5] In various towns 'Hundred' bodies were set up – '300s', '400s' and so on – which roughly paralleled the
Birmingham '600'.[6]

While the Bulgarian agitation lasted, the various Liberal bodies which had
been inspired by the Birmingham 'caucus' played a large part in sparking off
indignation meetings. Soon a link was made between this agitation and the
activities of several non-party bodies.[7] The National Education League was
a formidable organisation which strongly opposed grants from local education rates to support denominational schools. There were several other
'one-issue pressure groups', which were also organised on a more or less
national scale. Chamberlain urged them to join forces with overtly Liberal
organisations which had representative structures comparable with that of
Birmingham, and to set up a national body. On 31 May 1877, a conference
was called in Birmingham, at which delegates from 93 places met under the
chairmanship of Chamberlain, to establish what became known as the
National Liberal Federation. Non-representative Liberal Associations were
not invited; in practice, the meeting was almost confined to delegates from
the English boroughs.

Hartington was invited to support the new movement, but he preferred
to remain aloof. Chamberlain then approached Gladstone, who – no doubt
eager to win support for his mounting campaign against 'Beaconsfieldism'
– was glad to comply. After the business part of the meeting was over,
Gladstone addressed a crowd of more than thirty thousand people. A man
who had been present reflected, many years later, that 'it would be impossible to express in words the feelings by which the whole multitude appeared
to be inspired'.[8] In our own age, which is profoundly cynical about politicians of all brands, it is difficult to appreciate the enthusiasm which
Gladstone, and to a measure Disraeli as well, were able to generate among
their followers.

Gladstone's presence gave the National Liberal Federation a sort of semi-
official status in the party. At first there was some risk of general conflict
with older Liberal bodies, about a hundred in number, which had been set
up under the aegis of the Liberal Central Association. Those bodies were
usually more or less self-appointed groups of individuals who were able and

willing to subscribe substantially to the local organisation. Reactions in the constituencies varied. In some places, the NLF was seen as the best way to restore the party's fortunes; in others the 'hundreds' were viewed with marked suspicion.[9] Occasionally there was a compromise. Thus, Chester was a two-member constituency, close to Gladstone's residence at Hawarden. In 1868, and again in 1874, it had returned one Liberal and one Conservative. The local Liberals were both fearful for their own holding and covetous for the Conservative seat. An arrangement was worked out under which there would be a governing '300', of whom 200 were chosen by democratic ward associations, and 100 by the traditional élite. This compromise proved successful, for at the next General Election both Chester seats were won by Liberals. As a general rule, however, the town Liberal associations soon came to copy the Birmingham model.[10]

As time went on, and a substantial Liberal victory began to appear increasingly likely, the NLF began to take an aggressive attitude towards the old, narrow groups of substantial subscribers. At the Darlington meeting of the NLF Council in February 1880, Chamberlain declared that

> If there be anywhere any Liberal Association which is not at the present time truly representative of every class and section of the Liberal Party ... it is the duty of all who are interested in its success to endeavour by all means to invite, to entreat, nay almost to compel outsiders to come in.[11]

Members of the various bodies linked to the NLF were concerned to use it as a vehicle for propaganda as well as political organisation. It began almost immediately to issue pronouncements on public issues, which did not necessarily correspond with the views, or at least the priorities, of the existing party leadership. The NLF never claimed any right to make *ex cathedra* pronouncements on policy which could be expected to commit a future Liberal Government, but what it had to say was certainly likely to influence the highest circles in the party. In general, it used that influence in a very responsible manner, and avoided behaviour of a factional kind. A modern writer has noted that 'when the party was divided the NLF acted as a force for party unity, for it embodied the belief of the rank and file that there was an identifiable Liberalism upon which most Liberals were agreed'.[12]

The leaders of the NLF, most of the 'Hundreds', and the various pressure groups which were giving more or less support to the Liberal Party, had one important feature in common: they were mainly nonconformists. Most nonconformist denominations had a much more democratic organisation than the Church of England, and many had elaborate systems of lay preaching as well. A coal miner or a farm labourer who could conduct a service, or run a Sunday School or a chapel choir, was already a leader, and in many areas that meant that there was an alternative source of leadership to the traditional village authorities.

The Balkan troubles of the mid-1870s were apparently resolved at the Congress of Berlin in 1878, and Britain acquired a protectorate over the Turkish island of Cyprus in the bargain. All this looked like a great diplomatic triumph for Beaconsfield. Soon, however, the Conservative Government began to run into serious difficulties, both at home and abroad. Early in 1879, British troops advanced into Zululand, but were massacred at Isandhlwana. Many doubted both the justice and the wisdom of the initial attack, while even those who approved of it were hard-put to excuse the military incompetence which marked the operation. In the end, Isandhlwana was avenged; but at the cost of an unnecessary war.

Even more serious difficulties were encountered in Afghanistan. In the summer of 1878 there were apprehensions that Russia as in process of acquiring control of Afghanistan, perhaps with the long-term aim of conquering India, and the British Government countered by invading the country. Soon the Afghans were compelled to accept British control over foreign policy; but in September 1879 the British residency which had recently been established at Kabul was stormed and the occupants massacred. The immediate political effect in Britain was similar to that of Isandhlwana. The government came under double attack, from those who regarded the initial advance as unwise or immoral, and from those who had approved of the aggression but censured the government for its failure.

A couple of months after news of the Kabul massacre reached Britain, Gladstone commenced his sensational 'Midlothian Campaign', which would prove a personal *tour de force* without parallel before or since. Earlier in 1879, Gladstone had resolved to offer himself as candidate at the forthcoming General Election for Midlothian, which bordered Edinburgh. The constituency had usually been Conservative, though a Liberal had won it in 1868, only to lose it in 1874. Gladstone's campaign lasted for a fortnight at the end of November and beginning of December. It involved a considerable number of speeches, some of them 'whistle-stop' affairs at towns *en route* from Liverpool to Scotland. There were many demonstrations of popular enthusiasm, including decorations of various kinds, bonfires and torchlight processions. The principal financial burden fell on Gladstone's Scottish host, the young Earl of Rosebery, who would later play a major part in Liberal affairs.

Gladstone delivered a series of attacks against Beaconsfield's government. He criticised it for reckless expenditure, but above all for its aggressive foreign and imperial policy. His words about the Afghan campaign are well remembered, expressing at the same time his deep religious conviction, his hatred of war and his detestation of the narrow racist outlook which was all too common at the time:

> Remember that the sanctity of life in the hill-villages of Afghanistan, among the winter snows, is as inviolable in the eye of Almighty God as can be your own. Remember that He who has united you as human beings in the same flesh and blood, has bound you by the law of mutual love; that that mutual love is not limited by the shores of this island, is not limited by the boundaries of Christian civilisation; that it passes over the whole surface of the earth, and embraces the meanest along with the greatest in its unmeasured scope.[13]

The whole campaign represented something of a watershed in British politics. The idea of a major statesman making what was in effect a direct appeal to the electorate, not only in his own constituency but generally, was not wholly without precedent; but there was a marked difference of degree from anything which had happened before.

The Conservative Government was running into other difficulties. Public expenditure and taxation were both rising. Income Tax, which for two years stood at only 2d. in the pound, was rising, and reached 5d. in 1879. Much more serious was the general decline in prosperity. The *Annual Register* paints a fearful picture of conditions at the beginning of the year:

> The distress produced by the want of employment has been aggravated by a winter of great severity. From all the large towns came the same sorrowful tale. Thousands of families, which in times of ordinary prosperity lived in decent comfort, were said to be on the brink of starvation ... The pressure was peculiarly severe on those who struggled against pauperism to the last. Many were found by benevolent visitors in a state of absolute famine, having pawned all their scanty possessions and even their clothes to obtain food.[14]

The industrial depression abated a little in the course of 1879, but at the same time one of the wettest years on record inaugurated what would prove to be a very long-term slump in agriculture. In England, rain wrecked the grain harvest. In 1878, the wheat yield was around 30.5 bushels per acre; in 1879 it was 15.7.[15] Free importation of grain from abroad saved workers in the towns from starvation; bu many farmers were ruined. In Ireland, the staple potato crop again suffered the blight which had brought on the famine of the 1840s. In 1878 the yield had been 2527 tons to the acre; in 1879 it was only 1114.[16] This time it was not quite famine; but it was very near it.

Early in 1880, Beaconsfield's government saw two shafts of light in the political gloom. By-elections had mostly been going badly for them for a considerable time. Then the Conservatives contrived to hold a vulnerable seat in Liverpool. Soon they actually captured a Liberal seat in the London constituency of Southwark. The government decided that this was as good an opportunity as any to confront the electorate, and – to general surprise – dissolution of Parliament was announced early in March. Formal party manifestos were still not the rule in those days, but Beaconsfield issued what was generally regarded as equivalent of a manifesto in the form of a public letter to the Duke of Marlborough, Lord Lieutenant of Ireland. This document laid its main emphasis on the supposed benefits which had derived from the Union with Great Britain, thus opposing the cause of Home Rule. Superficially, this seems a remarkable issue for a Prime Minister to choose as the main plank of his election platform, for at that date nobody except the Irish Home Rulers themselves and a very small number of advanced Liberals opposed the continuance of the Union. But the choice of an Irish issue had much to do with events of the previous six years.

The Home Rulers elected in 1874 had represented a wide range of political views. At one extreme were men whose avowed objective was a sovereign Irish republic, completely separated from Britain. At the other extreme, many, and perhaps most, of the Home Rulers were still receiving the Liberal whip a year after the election.[17] In 1875, however, Hartington effectively removed any remaining uncertainty about the separateness of the two parties. Butt, who had been presenting highly rational arguments for Home Rule, and followed all the accepted rules of gentlemanly political conduct, soon came under heavy fire from his own supporters. In April 1875, a young Protestant landowner, Charles Stewart Parnell, was returned to Parliament at a by-election in County Meath. In the course of the following year he made himself leader of a small group of aggressive Home Rulers who were determined to exploit, or to break, all existing rules of parliamentary procedure in order to force attention on Irish problems. These 'obstructionists', as they were commonly called, managed largely to disrupt ordinary parliamentary business. Most MPs, including many Home Rulers, were deeply shocked by these tactics, and in 1877 there was public disagreement between Parnell and Butt.

In May 1879 Butt died – worn out, perhaps, by the strains of leading his highly fissile party. His successor, William Shaw, is a somewhat shadowy figure who had originally sat as a Liberal: the current *Dictionary of Irish Biography* does not even give him an entry. At the time of Butt's death, an important new issue was about to enter Irish political affairs. Relations between Irish landlords and tenants slumped rapidly from bad to worse with the onset of the agricultural depression in 1879, and soon a savage 'land war' was in operation. The contest was conducted at two distinct levels. At the political level, tenants sought changes in land law; at the grass-roots the 'war' involved not only rent strikes but also numerous acts of peasant violence against unpopular landlords, their agents, and even their livestock. In October 1879, Parnell was chosen President of the new National Land League of Ireland which soon came to direct the peasant campaign. The Land League not only pressed its own agrarian policy but also supported the cause of Home Rule.

By the time of the 1880 General Election, the 'land war' was being waged with great bitterness. The attitude of the government and of a large section of British opinion was predictable: fury at the 'agrarian crimes' committed by the peasant rebels, conjoined with resentment at the earlier 'obstructionism' of certain Home Rulers. In some minds this blurred into a racist hostility to everybody and everything Irish. English cartoonists often portrayed 'Paddy' as a destructive ape. The fact that many British people were of that frame of mind goes some way towards explaining Beaconsfield's preoccupation with the putative iniquities of Irish Home Rule, at a time when he might have been expected to lay stress on British, Imperial or international issues.

With the usual reservations about exact numbers of MPs elected in various interests, the upshot of the 1880 General Election was a nearly exact reversal of the 1874 results. The Liberals, who had received 242 seats at the earlier election, eventually secured 352; the Conservatives who had had 350, won only 237; while the Home Rulers eventually secured 63 seats, against 60 in 1874. Thus the Liberals had a clear overall majority. The widespread view that this result was more or less a foregone conclusion at the start of the campaign is wrong.[18] There is abundant evidence, from both Liberal and Conservative sources, to show that well-informed people were astonished. During the election, men like the Home Secretary Richard Cross had warned electors, not of the risk of a runaway majority for an opposing party whose leadership and future policy were both uncertain, but of the danger of a hung Parliament in which the Irish would call the tune. Beaconsfield's warnings about the perils of Home Rule fit into the same context.

To whom, or what, should the credit (or blame) for this remarkable turnabout be attributed? No doubt factors quite outside the control of politicians played a part, not least the appalling weather of 1879 and its economic consequences. Gladstone's personal effect on the results was widely believed by friends and foes alike to have been crucial, though he had no official standing in the party. From the mid-1860s onwards, he acquired a prestige and authority among Liberals which has few parallels in Britain or in any other free society. No doubt Gladstonian finance played a large part in strengthening the British economy; but his main appeal was not based on calculations of interest, but on sheer moral force. He was seen to be fighting for great causes because they seemed to him right, and people of all classes were proud to enrol themselves under his banner.

It would be wrong, however, to view Hartington as a mere *roi fainéant*. His leadership, if not inspired, had achieved a high level of competence and even vigour. Against fifteen major speeches attributed to Gladstone during the election campaign itself (in course of which he triumphantly captured Midlothian), Hartington made twenty-four.[19] Nor may the third element in the victory of 1880 be ignored. Chamberlain advanced a strong argument for the view that 'caucus' politics had had a major influence on the result.[20] Gladstone's moral appeal, the solid if unglamorous work of men like Hartington, and the careful organisation of the 'caucus' had all played vital parts in the victory. It is not accidental that those three men derived from the three distinct headstreams which fed into the current of mid-Victorian Liberalism. By 1880, most party supporters would not have considered themselves Whigs, or Radicals, or Peelites; they were just Liberals.

In ordinary circumstances, Beaconsfield would probably have tendered his resignation immediately the result was clear, but there were two snags. The Queen was out of the country, and did not see cause to return promptly in order to transfer ministerial offices; and there was great doubt as to who should head a new Liberal administration.[21] As has been seen, Hartington had proved a considerable success, both as parliamentary leader and as a platform orator. For a long time, right until the General Election results were no longer in doubt, the press appeared to agree that Granville was the likeliest Prime Minister. There was no doubt that Gladstone had been the star performer on the Liberal side; but it was not until a very late stage that the *Daily News*, the principal Liberal newspaper, began to campaign for Gladstone to become Prime Minister again. When Victoria eventually deigned to return, Beaconsfield recommended her to invite Hartington to form a ministry, and she followed constitutional precedent by acting on the outgoing Prime Minister's advice. Hartington soon discovered that Gladstone would only be prepared to join the government at all if he held the first office. A Liberal ministry without him was unthinkable, and so Hartington and Granville went together to explain to the Queen that she would have to accept Gladstone. On 23 April it was announced that Gladstone would form an administration. Neither Hartington nor Granville wanted the job; it is reported that both showed unfeigned delight when they learnt the news of Gladstone's appointment from the Queen's secretary. By this time, the Queen had conceived her famous distaste for Gladstone, and accepted him only with great reluctances. Perhaps if she had returned promptly when the result of the election was clear, instead of tarrying so long in a German spa, she might have had Hartington or Granville instead.

To a considerable extent, the new Cabinet resembled the one which had left office in 1874. Gladstone again doubled up the offices of Prime Minister and Chancellor of the Exchequer. Three incomers to the Cabinet would be of great importance in the future. Gladstone clearly needed to include representatives of the younger Radicals in the government. A close relationship existed between Joseph Chamberlain and Sir Charles Dilke – who at that moment seemed the more important of the two. Gladstone first offered Dilke a post which did not carry a seat in the Cabinet. Dilke indicated that he would not serve unless either he or Chamberlain was taken into the Cabinet. The Queen had strong objections to Dilke, and so the Presidency of the Board of Trade, with a seat in the Cabinet, was given to Chamberlain. Dilke was made Under-Secretary of State for Foreign Affairs. As his principal Granville was in the Lords, Dilke became chief government spokesman for the Foreign Office in the Commons. At the end of 1882, he did at last receive a post in the Cabinet.

The other two newcomers to the Cabinet were Earl Spencer and Sir William Harcourt. Spencer was one of the few Whigs who would follow Gladstone after the Home Rule split of 1886, and at the time of Gladstone's final withdrawal from politics in 1894 the old Prime Minister was prepared to recommend him as his successor. Harcourt, who became Home Secretary, would later become an important Chancellor of the Exchequer. The most remarkable omission was Goschen. In 1877, Hartington had declared in favour of extending the Household Franchise to rural as well as urban constituencies. Goschen disagreed, and as the new government plainly intended to enact the reform he disliked, he refused to join. His Liberalism became increasingly tenuous as time went on.

At the moment when Gladstone's second government was formed, the Liberal Party had undergone such profound changes that Palmerston would have had great difficulty in recognising it as the institution which he had headed only fifteen years before. It was a fair guess that a Liberal Government, whoever led it, would seek to extend the franchise further: a policy which Palmerston had deplored. Attitudes to foreign policy had departed even further from Palmerstonian views. It is unthinkable that he would have taken a similar line to Gladstone on such matters as the compensation agreement with the United States over the actions of the *Alabama*, or the Russo-Turkish dispute, or Afghanistan. The Liberal Party was also showing interest in 'social' legislation on matters like improving the legal status of Trade Unions, reducing hours of employment and encouraging slum clearance. It certainly wasn't Palmerston's party at all.

THE NEW SUIT.

Lord D——:—"I HAVE HITHERTO DEALT WITH DIZZY & CO."

*Gladstone (Liberal Tailor):—*SO I SHOULD HAVE THOUGHT, MY LORD   A VERY OLD-FASHIONED CUT, AND
.THER A TIGHT FIT FOR A GENTLEMAN OF YOUR PROPORTIONS.   I FLATTER MYSELF THAT IF YOU
.VOUR US WITH YOUR CUSTOM *WE* SHALL BE ABLE TO GIVE YOU EVERY SATISFACTION."

Gladstone, the tailor, is about to cut a new outfit for the 15th Earl of Derby,
son of the former Conservative Prime Minister, who was moving strongly
in the Liberal direction. The tailor's clerk is Hartington.
A cartoon from the satirical journal *Fun*, 1879.

4

Events Take Charge

When you are up to your neck in alligators, it's difficult to remember
that you went there to drain the swamp.

Anon.

The Liberal Government of 1868 had usually held the initiative. The Liberal
Government of 1880 certainly had positive ideas of its own, and was eventually able to claim quite an impressive body of legislation; but to a large
extent it was forced to respond to events, some of them the legacy of the
previous administration.

Almost as soon as the new Parliament met, an issue arose which today
seems absurdly trivial, but which generated a great deal of excitement for
several years to come. One of the Liberals returned for the two-member
constituency of Northampton was Charles Bradlaugh. He held opinions
on various subjects which were guaranteed to upset polite opinion of the
day; but what attracted immediate attention was his oft-publicised atheism.
When MPs were invited to swear an oath of allegiance, Bradlaugh
demanded the right to affirm instead. There was some doubt whether pre-
vailing rules allowed him to do this, and so the Speaker referred the matter
to a Select Committee, which eventually decided, by the narrowest of
majorities, that it was not permitted. There followed a long, convoluted,
chain of events (including three by-elections in Northampton), which are
fascinating to study, but are rather outside the remit of the present work.
To complete the story, Bradlaugh was returned at the following General
Election, and a new, more sensible, Speaker permitted him to take the oath.
Two years later, legislation was at last passed which authorised affirmation.
It is noteworthy that some of Bradlaugh's most vigorous opponents were
men like Lord Randolph Churchill who were not noted for their piety, but
who loved to embarrass the government; while some devoutly religious men
like Gladstone and Bright did what they could to help him.

Long before the Bradlaugh saga had reached its end – indeed, when it had
barely commenced – the new government was confronted with much more
serious difficulties in connection with Ireland. In May 1880, the Home Rule
MPs met in Dublin to select a chairman for the ensuing parliamentary

session. William Shaw sought re-election, but was narrowly defeated by Parnell.[1] Not only did the Home Rulers choose an inveterate rebel rather than a moderate, but the leader they selected was already President of the Land League. Thereafter for many purposes the peasant movement and the Home Rule parliamentarians could be regarded as one.

The Land League's principal demands became known as the 'Three Fs'. 'Fixity of Tenure' meant that a tenant who paid his rent and observed the other covenants of the tenancy could not be evicted. 'Free Sale' meant that when a tenancy ended, the tenant should be entitled to the value of any improvements he had introduced. 'Fair Rent' had a much less certain meaning, because when a landlord and his tenant disagreed about the rent, each side was almost certain to declare that his own view of what it should be represented a 'fair' sum.

The agricultural distress in Ireland which followed the ghastly harvest of 1879 was made worse by a spate of evictions, largely of tenants who defaulted on rent. The average for the five years ending in 1877 was 503; in 1878 it was 743; in 1879 it was 1098; and by the middle of 1880 it was clear that this figure would be exceeded considerably in the current year. Evictions had to be supported by force, and there was growing difficulty in maintaining order. The government first proposed the Compensation for Disturbance Bill, to authorise compensation to tenants evicted for non-payment of rent. The Bill encountered difficulties in the House of Commons. On the Second Reading, twenty Liberals voted against it and fifty abstained. Eventually it passed the Commons, but it was thrown out by the Lords with a five to one majority. Unsuccessful though it was, the Bill sufficed to dislodge from the government one Whiggish junior Minister who would eventually play an important part on the other side of politics: the Marquis of Lansdowne.

Not surprisingly, agitation in Ireland increased. Pending some statutory arrangement about rents, the Land League proposed that tenants on an estate should reach their own decision as to what rent was fair. This should be offered to the landlord, and, if he refused, they should pay nothing. With Parnell's support, the Land League recommended that people who acted in violation of Land League precepts should be 'boycotted' – the word deriving from the name of a County Mayo land agent. As an Irish historian has commented, 'The "moral" force of the boycott gave way quite easily in the circumstances to physical violence [which] could range from the burning of ricks of hay, to the maiming of animals, to bodily assault and even murder.'[2] Soon W. E. Forster, Chief Secretary for Ireland, was confessing that 'No man dares take a farm from which another person has been ejected, nor work for a man who pays his rent, or who refuses to join the Land League'.

Civil order in Ireland was rapidly breaking down. In 1880, there were more than 1200 'outrages' – as agrarian crimes were commonly called – and two-thirds of these took place in the last three months of the year. If a miscreant was brought to trial, nobody would dare testify against him. In the early phase of the agitation, northern Protestants usually stood aloof from Land League activities; as time went on, signs began to appear that they might soon cooperate with their southern Catholic counterparts. The Land League itself was under growing pressure from the Fenians, alias the Irish Republican Brotherhood, which condemned its moderation.

For many years, governments of various kinds had reacted to the occasional spates of unlawful activity by passing 'Coercion Acts', which gave the Irish Executive special powers, including authority to detain people without trial. Coercion Acts were all designed to expire automatically after a limited period, unless they were formally renewed. When the Liberals took office in 1880, a Coercion Act was in force, but it soon expired and the government did not seek to renew it. By early 1881, however, Forster was driven to propose a return to coercion. The Chief Secretary's personal distress was unconcealed. He declared that he would never have accepted the office if he had thought that the duty to reintroduce coercion would have devolved upon him.[3] The Irish MPs did what they could to obstruct the legislation, and one famous sitting of the House of Commons lasted for a record 41½ hours.

The Conservatives, like any opposition, were willing to embarrass the government, but they could not feel much *Schadenfreude* about the Liberals' Irish difficulties. There was always a serious risk that the government would collapse, and they would find themselves in office, perhaps with Ireland on, or over, the brink of civil war. Beaconsfield died in April 1881, and thereafter the Conservative leadership was as uncertain as that of the Liberals had been in the later 1870s. Sir Stafford Northcote led in the Commons, the Marquis of Salisbury in the Lords. Neither was acknowledged as overall leader of the party.

There was only one man in the whole range of politics with the ability and prestige necessary to attempt a resolution of the current Irish difficulties, and that was Gladstone himself. Shortly after Parliament adopted coercion, the Prime Minister introduced a new Irish Land Bill. The Bill proposed to grant all of the 'Three Fs'. When there was dispute over the rent payable on a property, a judicial body would decide on the sum. These 'judicial rents' would then hold for fifteen years. In addition, further facilities were made for land purchase by occupying tenants. A Land Commission would be authorised to advance up to three-quarters of the purchase price of a holding to the landlord, and would be repaid by the tenant over a long period.

John Morley later reflected about the measure which Gladstone was proposing: 'The Whigs were disaffected by it, the Radicals doubted it, the Tories
thought that property as a principle was ruined by it, the Irishmen, as the
humour seized them, bade him send the Bill to line trunks'.[4] In the end, the
Irish Land Bill passed the Commons. When the Third Reading division was
taken in July, only fourteen voted against it, though there were many
abstentions. After long and complex debates, it was accepted by the Lords
in the following month. Lord Derby reported that the commonest judgement was, 'We were bound to try something, and, on the whole, there
seemed nothing else to try'.[5] Derby was already well on his way to joining
the Liberals, and would soon become the only man to serve in Cabinet
under both Disraeli and Gladstone. Against the support of Derby, however,
Liberals had to set the loss of the very influential Duke of Argyll, who found
the Free Sale clauses intolerable, taunting his erstwhile Liberal colleagues as
'jellyfish'. He was not the only great Whig landowner who was beginning to
find the Liberal Party increasingly uncomfortable. The third Earl Grey, son
of the 'Reform' Prime Minister, and the Earl of Zetland, a major landowner
in north Yorkshire, both departed for the Conservative camp about the
same time.

Passage of the Irish Land Act did not result in an immediate drop in
agrarian crime. In October 1881, the government used its 'Coercion' powers
to arrest Parnell and other Land League leaders. They replied with a 'no-rent
manifesto', urging the peasants to refuse all payment to their landlords. The
Land League was promptly declared an illegal organisation; furthermore,
'no-rent', repudiated by most of the clergy, proved ineffectual. Nor were
the efforts of a 'Ladies' Land League', headed by one of Parnell's sisters,
particularly successful.

Parnell had correctly prophesied that 'Captain Moonlight' would take
over while he was under detention. By early 1882 it was visibly in the interest both of the British authorities and of the leaders of the erstwhile Land
League to come to terms. With Gladstone's approval, Chamberlain played a
considerable part as a go-between. In April, Gladstone and Parnell reached
an understanding, known from the location of Parnell's gaol as the 'Treaty
of Kilmainham'. Most of the Land League leaders were to be released from
prison. The government would introduce legislation to relieve tenants who
were in arrears of rent, and the Irish politicians would do what they could
to restrain violence and give the Land Act a fair test.

There was a political explosion. Forster deplored the 'Treaty', and
resigned. His tenure of office had been a spectacular example of the maxim
that the Irish Chief Secretaryship was 'the graveyard of political reputations'.
His successor was Lord Frederick Cavendish, brother of Hartington and

nephew by marriage of Gladstone's wife. On his arrival in Ireland a few days later, Cavendish and his Permanent Under-Secretary were murdered in Phoenix Park by terrorists belonging to a small splinter-group calling itself the 'Invincibles'. This tragic event produced the inevitable shock reaction, but both the government and the Irish leaders soon addressed themselves to the practical task of applying the Kilmainham agreement. The Arrears Bill which Gladstone had promised under the Kilmainham arrangements provoked furious parliamentary discussion later in the year, but it eventually passed in a form more or less acceptable to the government and to the Irish.

The long 'Land War' produced a great effect on the character of the Irish movement, and indirectly on British politics as well. Parnell had acquired a prestige and authority in his own country unmatched since O'Connell. In the autumn of 1882 the Home Rulers were reconstituted as the Irish National League, under Parnell's leadership. They began to look like a disciplined army rather than a ragged collection of people whose sole unifying feature was a vague aspiration for some kind of Irish Parliament. For the time being there was some relaxation in political tensions over Ireland, though these would return long before the end of Gladstone's second administration.

In the first period of the 1880 government, progress was made towards changes in the foreign policy which Gladstone had called 'Beaconsfieldism', and against which he had inveighed during the Midlothian campaign. By the spring of 1881, British troops had been withdrawn from most of Afghanistan. In southern Africa, problems were more complex. The Zulu troubles of 1879 had been closely linked with questions affecting a much wider area. The Cape and Natal were British colonies; the Orange Free State was a Boer-controlled republic. The Transvaal, where also Boers were the most numerous white settlers, had been annexed by Britain as recently as 1877. The nature of the Liberal campaign in 1880 encouraged many Boers in the Transvaal to seek a restoration of independence. Just before the end of the year a republic was proclaimed, and early in 1881 Boer forces entered Natal. In February the Boers won a significant victory over the British at Majuba Hill. There was considerable pressure in Britain for avenging the defeat and restoring control, but the government refused to be deflected from its long-term intentions, and soon concluded peace with the Boers on terms which gave them full internal self-government, while Britain obtained control over external relations of the Transvaal.

At the other end of Africa, the immediate legacy of 'Beaconsfieldism' would pose even more acute problems. Disraeli's purchase of the Suez Canal shares had been popular, but Liberals warned at the time that it might produce great difficulties in the future. They could hardly have foreseen just how dire those consequences would prove. The profligacy of Khedive Ismail, which had given Disraeli his opportunity in 1875, continued thereafter, occasioning great sufferings for the Egyptian people and considerable problems for Europeans. In theory, however, Egypt was still part of the Ottoman Empire, and in 1879, the Sultan, nominal suzerain of Egypt, was prevailed upon to proclaim the deposition of Ismail, in favour of his son Tewfik.

Thus matters had stood when the Liberals took office in 1880. There followed a lull. In September 1881, a military revolt occurred in Egypt, under the leadership of a certain Arabi Bey, later Arabi Pasha. To what extent the insurrection could be regarded as a truly nationalist movement is open to doubt. If Gladstone could be convinced that this was indeed the case, he would be certain to view it with sympathy.[6] Soon Arabi was brought into the Khedive's government, and in the ensuing months his authority in Egypt increased steadily. But as 1882 advanced, evidence accumulated which suggested that Arabi was in truth a mere military adventurer. By June, Gladstone considered that Arabi intended to depose the Khedive 'to the placing of whom on the Throne we are parties'.[7]

The major international port of Alexandria at the western end of the Delta soon became the focus of attention, and in May 1882 British and French naval vessels were positioned nearby. In the following month there was a serious riot in Alexandria, in course of which some fifty people, a few of them British, were killed, and the British Consul injured. British officials on the spot reported that the rioting had been started by the military.[8] Whether or not this information was correct, the damage had been done. Most of the British Cabinet came to favour some kind of intervention, though for a time it was hoped that this might be performed by Turkey, or through a general action by the powers.

At the beginning of July, Arabi seemed to be fortifying Alexandria with hostile intent. The French then withdrew their fleet. They were willing enough to defend the Suez Canal, but that was a good hundred miles distant. The British vessels remained in place, and on 11 July bombarded the fortifications. Authorisation of this move appears, at first sight, the most out-of-character action of Gladstone's whole career. It can perhaps best be explained by the view that the Prime Minister had decided that Britain had a moral obligation to uphold the Khedive; furthermore that Arabi's removal was essential for the restoration of peace in Egypt.[9]

Some Liberals challenged the wisdom and the morality of the bombardment immediately. The Radical MP Sir Wilfrid Lawson described it as 'a cowardly, a cruel and a criminal act'.[10] He went on to draw a vivid picture of the fury with which Gladstone, Hartington, Chamberlain and the Home Secretary Sir William Harcourt might have greeted similar action by a

Conservative government. A day or two later, Bright resigned from the Cabinet. For some time he had observed regretfully 'how much of the "jingo" or war spirit can be shown by certain members of a Liberal Cabinet'.[11] In his resignation speech he expressed his 'profound regard' for Gladstone – which was warmly reciprocated. Yet Bright felt constrained to describe the bombardment as 'a manifest violation both of international law and of the moral law'.[12] The bombardment of Alexandria was followed by military intervention in Egypt. A small body of marines was landed two days later, and these were soon followed by a larger force which took control of the city. Tewfik placed himself under British protection. In September a British force under Sir Garnet Wolseley destroyed Arabi's force at Tel-el-Kebir.

Wars seldom end where they began. Late in 1882, news arrived that a military prophet who called himself the Mahdi, or deliverer, had appeared in the Sudan. 'The waste Sudan' had been conquered by Egypt some decades earlier, and Egyptian rule there was peculiarly iniquitous.[13] The Mahdi's rising had aspects of a Muslim jihad, but it could also be seen as a national liberation movement undertaken by what Gladstone later described as 'a people struggling rightly to be free'.

In February 1883, the Cabinet decided, against Gladstone's advice, to send troops to the Sudan. The operation proved not only bloody, but futile. In November news came that an Egyptian army in the Sudan, under British officers, had been annihilated by the Mahdi's forces. From almost any point of view, the wisest course would be for British and Egyptian troops to withdraw. In January 1884 the government took the fateful decision to appoint the brave, resourceful and charismatic, but highly unstable, General Charles Gordon to take charge of evacuation operations. Even before the appointment was made, Gladstone was much concerned that instructions given to Gordon should not permit him to 'shift the centre of gravity as to political and military responsibility for that country'.[14] On Gordon's arrival in Egypt, the Khedive appointed him Governor-General of the Sudan for such time as was necessary to achieve the evacuation. A leading British official in Cairo asked Gordon pointedly whether he concurred in 'the policy of abandoning the Sudan'. He emphatically agreed.

In the course of 1884 and the very beginning of 1885, the situation became increasingly confused. Gordon rapidly convinced himself that his real duty was not to evacuate the Sudan but to occupy it. He was soon besieged in the capital Khartoum, where he remained for ten months – though by no means incommunicado. There was intense debate, not least in the Cabinet, whether a British expedition should be sent to relieve him. Hartington favoured sending a large military contingent. Chamberlain argued for a small striking force to extricate Gordon. Gladstone and Granville were at first highly dubious about the wisdom of any operation in the Sudan. The government ran into serious trouble in Parliament. A motion of censure which was moved in the House of Commons in May was defeated by a margin of only 28 votes. For the first time in the parliament, the Irish Nationalists voted with the Opposition on a critical issue: fair warning of trouble to come.

Eventually a force was mounted under Wolseley, the victor of Tel-el-Kebir. The operation, however, required much preparation, and when it began its progress southwards the campaign encountered many difficulties. On 18 January 1885 the relief force at last reached Khartoum, only to discover that the place had been captured, and Gordon killed, just two days earlier. There was a furious public reaction, and the Queen made known her personal distress by a telegram *en clair* to the Prime Minister. Inevitably, there was a bitter parliamentary inquest. A vote of censure was moved from the Conservative benches. The figures were close: 302 for the government, 288 against it. Forty Home Rulers and twelve Liberals, including Goschen and Forster, voted with the Opposition, and another fourteen abstained.

There is something to be said for the view that the government would have handled Sudanese matters better if it had not been simultaneously involved in a domestic problem of a very different kind. There had never been much logic in the 1867 franchise, which gave the vote to most householders in urban areas but still retained a much narrower electorate in the county constituencies. Gladstone later pointed out that a man who had the vote because he lived in a burgh constituency on one side of the Clyde could lose that vote if he moved house to a county constituency on the other side of the river.

The astonishing thing is that the arrangement lasted as long as it did; but the Liberal government set out to rectify matters. Any large increase in the number of voters would highlight another problem. There was already a massive disparity in the size of the electorate in different constituencies, and this disparity would be increased further by franchise reform; so a major redistribution of seats would be expected to accompany a change in the electorate. The Opposition appears to have feared that redistribution might be used in a very partisan way, and new constituency boundaries might be drawn in order to help the party designing the legislation. If a single Bill was submitted in which the two issues of franchise reform and redistribution were raised, much cross-voting was likely to occur, and it would prove difficult to pilot the measure through Parliament. If, however, the issue of franchise reform could be settled first, this might reduce the government's difficulties with redistribution.

So, when the government's proposals were submitted to the House of

Commons in February 1884, these referred to the franchise alone, reserving the question of constituency redistribution for later attention. Qualifications for the franchise in county constituencies would be similar to those obtaining in the boroughs. The government's Bill was to apply not only to Great Britain but to Ireland as well. It passed the Commons comfortably, but ran into trouble in the Lords, where an amendment seeking to link franchise reform with redistribution was carried by a substantial majority. In the end, tacit agreement was reached. There would be a special autumn session of Parliament to resolve the franchise issue, which the Lords would not obstruct further. The government agreed to consult with the Opposition on redistribution, and a separate Bill on the subject was introduced early in 1885. There was much argument over the details of the 'Seats Bill', but the broad principle of inter-party agreement was followed: a precedent which has been observed ever since: and the measure completed its passage in June 1885. By that time, the government had fallen; but that is another story.

In that way massive changes were brought about, more or less by consensus. The electorate was more than doubled. Redistribution involved the extinction of many small boroughs, whose electorates were assimilated in their counties. Other boroughs which formerly had two MPs were reduced to one. The strange expedient of large boroughs having three MPs while electors there had only two votes was abolished, and those boroughs were divided into single-member constituencies. A number of boroughs of intermediate size continued to return two MPs, and the electors there continued to have two votes. In the course of the discussions, there was considerable support for further reforms. The proposal that women should receive the parliamentary vote was taken far more seriously than had been the case in 1867. An amendment to that effect was strongly supported. It might well have been carried but for an announcement that the government could not accept responsibility for the Bill if so. There was also substantial support for 'manhood suffrage': the proposal that virtually all men should receive the vote at the age of 21.

The composition of the new electorate was open to several serious objections. The omission of women was the most obvious of these, although it is probably fair to say that in the 1880s most women would have followed male guidance in political matters. Omission of men who were not householders meant that an adult son living under his father's roof normally did not receive a vote. However, astute political agents were often able to circumvent that rule by a sort of legal fiction under which the son became ostensibly a rent-paying lodger and was thus entitled to appear on the electoral register. The electorate was still biased in favour of the wealthy through plural voting. A man with property in two or more constituencies would be entitled to a vote in each of them. The university constituencies were retained, and in these the electorate was composed of graduates – who, at that date, were mainly people of means. There was no guarantee that the popular vote would correspond even approximately with the number of MPs returned in the various party interests: a problem which remains to this day.

The great reduction in the number of two member constituencies may have exerted a considerable effect on the character of the Liberal representation. It had often been the practice to run a Whig and a Radical in double harness – anticipating, no doubt, that most Liberals who favoured one of the two would cast their second vote for the other. This practice could not be operated when the great majority of constituencies only returned a single MP. By the 1880s, Whigs (despite their persistence in ministerial office) were a diminishing force inside Liberalism, and the changes of 1884 probably accelerated their decline, and eventually their virtual departure from Liberal politics.

Although Ireland, imperial concerns in Africa, and questions of electoral reform had been the chief topics of public interest during the main period of Gladstone's second government, a number of legislative and administrative changes of a less dramatic character had also taken effect. Chamberlain, though well down in the Cabinet hierarchy, was the instigator of a surprising number of these changes. In 1880, he had been responsible for a measure governing the payment of merchant seamen's wages. In 1881, he brought forward the first Bill to entitle local authorities to adopt electric lighting without recourse to a private Act of Parliament. In 1883, he secured major changes in the law of bankruptcy and in patent law. In 1884, he was actively involved in preparing legislation to control the notorious 'coffin ships' which were insured far beyond their value, in the evident hope that they would founder. In a chilling speech on the subject, Chamberlain revealed that one in every sixty seamen had come to a premature death in the previous year. To Chamberlain's fury, pressure on the parliamentary timetable compelled withdrawal of the Bill; but he was able to secure appointment of a Royal Commission which foreshadowed legislation achieving most of the original proposals.

Other government measures removed a wide range of grievances. An Act of 1880 pleased nonconformists by authorising the burial of non-Anglicans in Church of England churchyards, according to their own rites. The Ground Game Act of the same year dealt with a long-standing complaint of tenant farmers. Hitherto, agricultural tenancies had frequently reserved shooting rights to the landowner. Thus 'ground game' – hares and rabbits – fed on the tenant's crops, but only the landowner was permitted to cull them. The new Act overrode such terms in tenancy agreements, authorising the farmer to shoot such pests himself. An Act of 1881 abolished the ancient barbarity of flogging in the army and navy. The Married Women's Property Act of 1882, introduced by the Lord Chancellor Lord Selborne, gave wives the clear right to own property separate from their husbands, with full title to their own income, earnings or inheritance. The Corrupt Practices Act of 1883 was a complex measure designed to deal with various kinds of bribery and undue influence at elections.

By the late spring of 1885, there were signs of deep tensions in the government. The most immediately acute problems affected Ireland; but there were three separate Irish issues involved. The Coercion legislation had been passed in 1882, at a time when the country was much more troubled, and would expire automatically after three years unless it was renewed. The Viceroy of Ireland pressed for renewal of some, though not necessarily all, of the Coercion legislation. The Cabinet hesitated, and the two 'Radicals' Chamberlain and Dilke made it known that they would resign if this were implemented. The government decided in principle to re-enact the Coercion legislation, though the details were not fully worked out and, for the time being, resignations were withheld. The second Irish issue was the Radicals' demand for measures of Irish local government reform. These included the proposal to set up a central board with administrative functions for the whole of Ireland. The Cabinet was deeply split. The commoners, except Hartington, supported it; the peers, except Granville, opposed it. The proposal was abandoned. At the end of the critical Cabinet meeting, Gladstone reflected to a colleague, 'Within six years, if it please God to spare their lives, they will be repenting in sackcloth and ashes'.[15] The repentance would require a good deal less than six years. A third Irish controversy concerned the proposal to enact an Irish Land Purchase Bill. On this question, too, there were threats of ministerial resignations, though these also were withheld.

While the various discussions over Ireland were proceeding, tentative approaches were made to Parnell both by Chamberlain on the Liberal side and by Lord Randolph Churchill on the Conservative side. Lord Randolph was coming to adopt a position in his own party in many ways comparable with that of Chamberlain. Both were intensely ambitious and relatively young men, closely linked to the 'official' hierarchy in some ways, yet for other purposes in a semi–independent position. Many people guessed – wrongly, as it proved – that Chamberlain would soon succeed Gladstone and Churchill would succeed Sir Stafford Northcote – who was nine years younger than Gladstone, but less well-preserved. Parnell was glad enough to play off the British parties against each other, but was coming to the view that, for the time being at least, the Conservatives might prove the more helpful to his interest. Churchill was glad enough to encourage him in that view.

The 1880 Liberal Government was brought to an end by a debate on the 1885 Budget. In 1882, Gladstone had found the two jobs of Prime Minister and Chancellor of the Exchequer more than even he could manage. Hugh Childers was appointed Chancellor. When preparing his 1885 Budget, Childers was required to meet the considerable military expenditure of the previous year. Among his proposals were additional taxes on beer and spirits, and an increased duty on real property. These touched on sensitive nerves, and in the course of the Budget debates a critical amendment was moved by the opposition and carried by 264 to 252. Thirty-nine Home Rulers and six Liberals – three of them representing Irish constituencies – voted with the Conservatives, and 76 Liberals were absent – many of them unpaired. The Cabinet took the news of the defeat with almost visible relief: at least it would avert splits on better-defined issues, which otherwise seemed inevitable.

In ordinary circumstances, either the government would have called a General Election, or it would have made way for the Opposition to form an administration and then call an election once it had done so. An immediate election, however, was out of the question, for the new registers were not yet ready, and a House of Commons elected on the old registers would have had no moral authority. On 12 June the Ministry resigned, and the Conservatives were forced to make two important decisions: whether to take office at all and, if so, under whom. Nearly a fortnight of discussions followed. The eventual decision was to accept office, with Salisbury as Prime Minister. The Liberals retained their nominal, if fissile, majority in the House of Commons, and an understanding was reached to the effect that the Conservatives would be permitted to remain in office without serious harassment until the new registers were ready, whereupon Parliament would be dissolved.

'Not with a bang, but a whimper.' The demise of the government may be regarded as an act of euthanasia. Thus ended an administration which had taken office five years earlier in an atmosphere of high enthusiasm. Its fate, however, must be seen in the context of events and ideas which were developing rapidly, and were largely outside the control of any government. Until the 1870s, there was something to be said for the view that Free Trade in the narrow sense of the term would do about as much as could possibly be done to improve the lot of the people as a whole, and of the poorer classes in particular, without much positive intervention by governments or local authorities. In the preceding quarter of a century, free external trade and minimal taxation had been accompanied by a great increase in the material

well being of nearly everybody. But soon many people soon came round to
the view that public authorities had an important part to play in improving
the quality of life.

Not long before the Liberals took office in 1880, there were signs that the
prosperity of the mid-century had come to an end. The trouble began with
the agricultural distress at the end of the 1870s. Farmers' incomes, estimated
to total £43 million in 1876, were down to £13 million in the fearfully wet
year of 1879.[16] Then they recovered a little; but for the duration of the Liberal
government they never totalled £30 million. The difficulties of people
dependent on agriculture had parallels among the industrial classes. Unemployment, which is usually a good inverse measure both of working-class
prosperity and of the general state of trade, has been estimated at 10.7 per
cent in 1879. It then dropped rapidly to 2.3 per cent in 1882, whereafter it
rose again just as steeply, reaching 9.3 per cent in 1885.

The Irish 'land war' drew attention to problems connected with the ownership of land in other parts of the British Isles. By coincidence, the crucial
year 1879 witnessed publication of a book by an American which would have
a great influence on ideas about land on both sides of the Atlantic, and was
to have a profound long-term effect on Liberal thinking. Henry George's
Progress and Poverty drew attention to the persistence of gross poverty,
despite the great technological progress of the previous century or so.
George contended that the root of poverty, in urban as well as rural areas,
was the fact that a minority of people had contrived to control the 'land' –
a term which he used as more or less synonymous with 'natural resources'
– to the exclusion of the large majority of mankind. As 'land' is indispensable for all human activities, landless people were compelled to pay a
'ransom' to the others, which was the ultimate source of poverty. *Progress
and Poverty* was very widely read, and George paid several visits to Britain,
which popularised his ideas further. One author has claimed that in the early
1880s he was the most discussed man in Britain after Gladstone himself.[17]
George's ideas were intensely controversial, and many people who started
from his standpoint later went off in very different directions; but he certainly played a major part in persuading people that the existing social and
economic order was not fixed by immutable laws, but could be altered
dramatically.

At the same time as George was making his first impact on political
thought, Chamberlain was emerging as the epitome of a new 'radical'
approach to contemporary problems. His views on specific questions
attracted much attention in the early 1880s, and a broad summary of those
views appeared in 1885 under the title *The Radical Programme*. Chamberlain
had evidently been influenced to an extent by George, although in places he

sharply criticised Georgeist teachings. All kinds of ideas which were interesting 'advanced' Liberals of the period tumble out of *The Radical
Programme* in profusion: slum clearance; free education; disestablishment of
the Church of England; reform of local government, particularly in rural
areas; opportunities for agricultural workers to acquire smallholdings; establishment of National Councils for Ireland, Scotland and possibly Wales and
many others. In the much freer attitude to public debate which prevailed at
the time, it was possible for a Cabinet Minister to propose reforms which
were visibly unwelcome to many of his colleagues.

One matter which Chamberlain did not develop strongly in *The Radical
Programme*, but which was already exercising his mind – and the minds of
many other people active in politics – was the question of Empire. Traditionally, Liberals had viewed imperial expansion with distaste, as a luxury
expensive in blood and money, bringing few positive returns. In the 1870s
there were signs that attitudes were changing, and in the last quarter of the
century Britain participated in a general European scramble for colonies,
particularly in Africa. Many Liberals remained hostile to the new imperialism, but Chamberlain would prove a notable exception.

A remarkable meeting in Birmingham at the end of January 1885 high-
lighted the change. Joseph Chamberlain and John Bright were both local
MPs, and both were accounted 'Radicals'. Their speeches did not exactly
contradict each other; but commentators immediately noted a very marked
difference of tone. Chamberlain argued for reforms very much in the spirit
of what would soon be published as *The Radical Programme*. Bright was
deeply critical of existing pressure for increased naval and military expenditure, and also condemned 'the constant cry of certain sections of the press
for colonies' – advocating instead freedom for existing colonies. Old Radicals and new Radicals within the Liberal Party were looking in very different
directions.

Both kinds of Radicals were thinking on different lines from traditional
Whigs, of whom Hartington was generally seen as the clearest example, and
Conservative literature frequently emphasised that point. So who in the
world would have guessed that in 1886 Chamberlain, Bright and Hartington
would find themselves together in a new political association, closely and (it
would prove) permanently linked with the Conservatives, while Gladstone
and most of the Liberal Party remained in the other camp? For the time
being there were few hints that matters could develop in that way.

5

Schism

Mr Gladstone was very much hated, but he was very much loved. Does anyone love Mr Chamberlain?

Lord Salisbury

When the Conservative Government was formed in 1885, the Irish policies of the new administration attracted especial attention. The idea of renewing coercion was dropped. The Liberal proposal to introduce land purchase was brought to fruition in Lord Ashbourne's Act, which provided government loans of up to 100 per cent when landlords were prepared to sell and tenants were willing to buy Irish land. The money was repayable by the tenant at a rate which was usually less than the rent paid hitherto. There was also an Act to improve the housing of Irish agricultural labourers. Discussions between the Irish leaders and the new Lord Lieutenant, Lord Carnarvon, also suggested that it was possible that the Conservatives might move towards Home Rule. In these circumstances, good relations began to develop between Parnell and the government.

By November, the new registers were ready for a General Election. The great changes both in electorate and in constituencies made it much more open than usual. Parnell threw an important weight into the scales by urging those of his compatriots who had votes in British constituencies to cast them in favour of the Conservatives. How far this advice affected actual results has long been a matter of debate. It seems likely that the outcome in a some constituencies with many Irish immigrants, particularly in Lancashire, was determined by this advice; but the most important consequence was to antagonise many Liberals who might otherwise have been persuaded to act sympathetically towards the Home Rule cause: a result which did not take full effect until some months after the election.

The Liberals won 335 seats, which exactly balanced the Conservatives with 249, plus the Nationalists with 86. When the results are seen in more detail, an astonishing picture is revealed. Contests were much more general than ever before, with the Whips playing an important part in raising funds to support candidates who could not, or would not, afford the expenses of a campaign personally.[1] Only 43 candidates, 19 of them Irish Nationalists, were returned unopposed. The Liberals led the Conservatives by only 29 seats in England, but by more than seven to one in Scotland and Wales.

The English results were irregular. Broadly speaking, the Liberals did unexpectedly well in rural areas, winning well over half of the county constituencies, where they had usually fared badly. There can be little doubt that the change was related to the recent enfranchisement of agricultural workers, and the sudden realisation that it lay within their power to upset the domination of the rural aristocracy that had survived the 1832 and 1867 Reform Acts almost unchanged. The attitude of the newly enfranchised voters is often, though unprovably, attributed to the influence of Chamberlain's Radical Programme and particularly the idea of rural smallholdings, sometimes described as 'three acres and a cow'.[2] Results in the English towns varied enormously. At one extreme, eight of the nine Liverpool constituencies were won by Conservatives. The ninth, an area of huge Irish immigration, was won by an Irish Nationalist, who contrived to hold it right down to his death in 1929. At the other extreme, every one of the seven Birmingham seats was won by a Liberal. Results from the other great towns fell in between. On the whole, however, the Liberals did badly in the English boroughs, falling back a little behind the Conservatives whom they had led by a huge margin in 1880. It is odd that the Liberals fared badly in the towns, where they were generally well-organised, yet did well in the county constituencies where their organisation was poor. Around a dozen working men, all of them Liberals, were elected. The former Oxfordshire stonemason Henry Broadhurst, was to accept junior ministerial office a few weeks later: the first working man ever to do so. Another important newcomer was Joseph Arch, who had played a major part in organising a trade union of agricultural workers.

But the most astonishing results were in Ireland. The increase in electorate was proportionally much greater than in Britain, because so many 'rural poor', who had been missed by the old franchise, now received the vote. The British electorate had grown by rather less than 80 per cent since 1880; the Irish electorate had much more than trebled. The Nationalists, or Home Rulers, won 85 of the 101 territorial seats. The Irish Liberals were wiped out to a man, and none of their candidates came anywhere near to victory. The Irish Conservatives held sixteen territorial seats, all of them in Protestant areas of what is today Northern Ireland, plus the two Dublin University seats. Throughout Ireland, the correspondence between religion and politics was almost complete, though Parnell himself was the great exception. There could be little doubt that the influence of the parochial Catholic clergy had been of massive importance in making the Nationalist victory so overwhelming.

Unlike the three previous General Elections, the polling of 1885 did not produce a clear party victory. The whole political outlook was immensely fluid and uncertain. A writer who had been a Liberal MP at the time reflected, a quarter of a century later, that 'in December 1885, those who speculated on the future considered it by no means "off the cards" that a few months would see an understanding arrived at between Mr Chamberlain and the extreme Radicals, Lord Randolph Churchill and his Tory Democrats, and Mr Parnell and his Nationalist followers'.[3] Later events would make such a forecast seem preposterous; but matters did not appear that way at the time. The one reasonable certainty was that Irish affairs would dominate politics. For the time being, Salisbury remained in office.

Until the middle 1880s, Gladstone believed in the merits of the Union, and sought to 'pacify Ireland' within its fabric of the Union. Even before the Liberals left office in 1885, he was beginning to have grave doubts on the matter. Reading a speech of one of the Home Rulers in March 1885, he 'saw then that there never was and never could be any moral obligation to the Irish race in the Act of Union'.[4] In his diary of 18 September 1885, he noted that the Union established in 1800 was 'a gigantic, though excusable, mistake'.[5] His address to the Midlothian voters in the same month declared that component parts of the United Kingdom should receive 'enlarged powers for the management of their own affairs', considering that these would be 'not a source of danger, but a means of averting it'.[6] The 1885 election results must have persuaded him that immediate action was necessary. For the first time, there was clear proof that the overwhelming majority of Irishmen really wanted Home Rule, and it was not just a dream of middle-class romantics. How could Gladstone, who had supported national independence in Italy, Bulgaria, Afghanistan and the Sudan so staunchly, deny similar rights to the people of Ireland, once their wishes were certain? Either Ireland must be held down indefinitely by force, or Home Rule would come sooner or later.

In Gladstone's view, by far the best way of resolving the matter would be for the existing Conservative Government to bring in a Bill designed to deal with the Irish constitutional question, which he would then support if possible. The Conservatives were in a much better position to make some advance in the direction of Home Rule than a Liberal government would be, if for no other reason than because they commanded a large majority in the House of Lords. Gladstone developed the idea in some detail with Salisbury's nephew and eventual successor A. J. Balfour.[7] doubtless in expectation that the matter would soon reach the ears of his uncle.

Whether or not there had ever been much chance that this idea would become a reality, hopes were largely dashed soon afterwards by what became known as the 'Hawarden Kite' (though Gladstone's Flintshire home was not the site of the critical discussions). Gladstone's third, and most political, son (popularly known as 'young Herbert' long after the adjective ceased to be appropriate), who had just been elected to Parliament, was also acting as his father's secretary. Many years later, Lloyd George would describe him as 'the greatest living embodiment of the Liberal doctrine that quality is not hered-itary'. This was less than fair, for Herbert Gladstone inherited his father's principles, though his political judgement would prove woefully inadequate on several important occasions, of which this was but the first.

In mid-December, Herbert Gladstone met several journalists. He spoke confidentially, to give them an idea of the way his father's mind was run-ning.[8] The confidences were broken. It was revealed in the press that the elder Gladstone 'has definitely adopted the policy of Home Rule for Ireland, and there are well-founded hopes that he will win over the chief represen-tatives of the moderate section of the party for his views'.[9] The 'Hawarden Kite' could hardly have been more damaging. It looked to the world like a deliberate bid by Gladstone to persuade Parnell to join forces to throw out the Conservative Government and install a Liberal administration which would try to enact Home Rule. Any faint hope that Gladstone's real wish would take effect, and the Conservatives would bring forward their own Home Rule Bill, was effectively extinguished.

Immediately after the General Election, Salisbury's Cabinet was deeply divided whether to resume a policy of Irish coercion or not, but the Prime Minister eventually prevailed upon his colleagues to do so. The decision announced early in the New Year ended the semi-alliance between Conser-vatives and Irish. The moment had arrived for the Liberals to challenge the government, and the natural reaction of the Irish made it certain that they would receive enough help from that quarter to enable them to succeed.

In the second half of January, Gladstone met the Liberal MPs, and coun-selled them to keep temporary silence on Irish matters. Most of those present, whatever their sympathies on the Home Rule question, agreed with that view, but a young and very rich MP named Albert Grey, heir-presumptive to the third Earl Grey, took issue with his leader and called on men more eminent than himself to declare themselves against Home Rule.[10] Thereafter he spent considerable energy, and probably money, in encouraging others to adopt a similar approach.

The fate of the government was finally sealed by a debate over the Queen's speech, towards the end of January. The critical issue was a somewhat sur-prising one, for it involved giving official party support to one of the proposals contained in the Radical Programme – which critics had often called the 'unauthorised programme'. A new Liberal MP, Jesse Collings, moved the so-called 'three acres and a cow' amendment. The celebrated expression was not included in the amendment, which expressed regret at the absence of provision for smallholdings and allotments for agricultural labourers. On 25 January, it was carried by 331 to 252, with Nationalist support. A number of Liberals disliked the 'three acres' idea, and there was a substantial revolt. Eighteen Liberals, including Hartington, Goschen and Gladstone's former Attorney-General Sir Henry James, voted with the government. Many more, including John Bright and C. P. Villiers, were absent from the division. But Salisbury resigned, and Gladstone was invited to form a third administration.

Gladstone had considerable difficulty in constructing his ministry. As the constitutional future of Ireland was bound to be a matter of major importance in its deliberations, he prepared a memorandum to show to those whom he invited to join the Cabinet. This indicated that the government would examine the possibility of setting up a legislative body in Dublin to deal with Irish affairs.[11] No plan was proposed, even in outline, but it was too much for Hartington, Goschen and James, who were intransigent opponents of Home Rule in any form, who all refused to join. Gladstone also had difficulties with Radicals. The *mores* of the time made it impossible to include Dilke, who was involved in a much-publicised divorce action. There were problems of a very different kind with Chamberlain. A few months earlier, he had declared himself in favour of 'the concession to Ireland of the right to govern itself in the matter of its purely domestic business',[12] but on another occasion he expressed doubts over Home Rule almost as sharp as those of Hartington.[13] When Gladstone invited him to join the government, Chamberlain made reservations over the Home Rule question. He eventually accepted Dilke's old post as President of the Local Government Board, which seemed to offer scope for his plans to set up elective public authorities in rural areas. In other directions, Gladstone had less difficulty. Another Radical, G. O. Trevelyan, who also felt doubts about Home Rule, became Secretary of State for Scotland. John Morley, also counted as a Radical and one of the few really enthusiastic Home Rulers, was appointed Chief Secretary for Ireland. The faithful Lord Granville accepted the unfamiliar post of Colonial Secretary, while his usual office as Foreign Secretary was filled by the young Lord Rosebery.

There was considerable scepticism on the Home Rule question even among some of those who were prepared to join a Gladstone government. Sir William Harcourt, who became Chancellor of the Exchequer, declared in private that he would join 'not because he believed in the possibility of the scheme ever succeeding but because he believed that in order to make a strong government of Ireland possible the scheme must be discussed and if possible tried'.[14] Apart from the absence of Hartington, the new Ministry did not appear significantly weaker than Gladstone's second government had been towards the end of its period of office, while Nationalist goodwill opened up some prospect that it might survive for a long time.

On 13 March 1886, when Gladstone submitted the outline of his Irish proposals to the Cabinet, the inherent difficulties immediately became apparent. His recommendations fell in two parts.[15] There would be a land purchase scheme to buy out Irish landlords at 20 years' purchase of their existing rents, at a cost of 120 million pounds. This remarkable plan never went beyond its First Reading in the House of Commons,[16] and interest in its contents was largely subsumed by the second recommendation, which was to set up 'a separate Parliament for Ireland with full powers to deal with all Irish affairs'. At that point, Chamberlain warned his colleagues that he could not remain a member of the government unless the scheme was substantially modified. A couple of days later he tendered his resignation, but Gladstone persuaded him to withhold it until the Home Rule proposals had been advanced in detail.

The Prime Minister set forth his Home Rule recommendations at the Cabinet meeting of 26 March. In answer to questions by Chamberlain, Gladstone made it plain that, under his scheme, an Irish Parliament would receive powers to tax, and also to appoint the judiciary, while Ireland would no longer be represented at Westminster. One second-hand account suggests that there were bitter altercations between Gladstone and Chamberlain.[17] At all events, Chamberlain, and also Trevelyan, resigned shortly afterwards.

On 8 April, Gladstone introduced his Home Rule Bill in the House of Commons. At this point, Liberal opponents of Home Rule were bound to declare their hand. Hartington, who had a strong admiration for Gladstone and close personal ties as well, had been particularly reluctant to do so. It was one thing to refuse office; it was a very different thing to declare war on the government. But on 14 April the die was cast. A cross-party meeting of protest was chaired by Earl Cowper, who had been Viceroy of Ireland in the previous Liberal administration. It was addressed by Salisbury and by W. H. Smith, who had been briefly Chief Secretary for Ireland in the Conservative Government, and also by Hartington and Goschen for the dissident Liberals. Here was an early expression of the new political concept of 'Unionism': the coming together of Conservatives and dissident Liberals (soon to be called 'Liberal Unionists') in a common front against Home Rule. Remarkably, two men who were to play major parts in the Unionist cause – Chamberlain on the Liberal side and Lord Randolph Churchill on the Conservative – were absent, and did not choose to send approbatory messages to the chairman.

Meanwhile, intense debates on the Home Rule question proceeded in Parliament and elsewhere. The views of the National Liberal Federation were important, because they were likely to influence the local branches, which in turn would exert strong pressure on MPs.[18] At first there was much uncertainty about popular Liberal opinion, not least because of the conflict between Gladstone and Chamberlain, both of whom were immensely influential with rank-and-file activists. Two days before Gladstone introduced the First Reading, the NLF sent a circular to the local 'hundreds', inviting them to determine their members' views. On 5 May, a Federation meeting was convened – perhaps significantly in London and not in Birmingham, where the Federation headquarters were located. The officers of the Federation prepared a resolution expressing confidence in Gladstone, but also asking him to consider modifying the Bill to allow Irish MPs to continue to sit at Westminster. An amendment expressing unabated confidence in Gladstone was carried with an overwhelming majority, whereupon several leading members of the Federation, including Chamberlain, resigned. These departures, however, were more than balanced by the affiliation within a month of fifty Liberal Associations which had not previously belonged, and the adherence of some seventy MPs who had not been connected with the NLF. The struggle continued in the constituency associations. A modern study led to 'a reasonable guess ... that 5–10 per cent of the Liberal militants disliked Home Rule enough to desert the party: a small number but probably disastrous under the British electoral system.'[19] No association disaffiliated from the Federation. The great majority of Liberal agents also remained in place. This looks like a great victory for the Gladstonians and a great defeat for Chamberlain, who lost his power base in the NLF. Perhaps, however, the victory was Pyrrhic in character, for Chamberlain became disposed to fight his campaign outside the 'official' party rather than within it. Thus the prospect of a mutually acceptable compromise being achieved was significantly reduced.

The other side organised as well. There were frequent meetings of Liberal Unionist MPs at Hartington's London home, Devonshire House. In the course of April, they began to establish a regular organisation and set up a committee which soon opened permanent offices. At first those attending were mostly what were loosely called 'Whigs', but at the meeting of 14 May, Chamberlain and Trevelyan were also present.[20] This was highly significant. Although Chamberlain's disquiet with Home Rule was universally known, he and Trevelyan had hitherto kept aloof from Hartington's brand of Liberal

Unionism, which had looked very much like a revolt of Whigs – many of whom could be expected soon to drop off from the Liberal Party, Home Rule or no Home Rule. Henceforth the Home Rule split began to appear more like a fundamental division of the party, cutting across old lines of cleavage.

On 22 May, the Liberal Unionists adopted a constitution, and decided to set up branch committees. A few local organisations, indeed, had already come into existence.[21] By early June, the Liberal Unionists were said to have a fund of £30,000[22] – considerably more than a million in modern money. Chamberlain and his associates set up a body called the Radical Union, with headquarters in Birmingham and branches elsewhere, evidently as a rival to the NLF.

Everything was moving towards a climax. On 27 May, Gladstone called a meeting of 280 Liberals, from which those opposed to Home Rule were deliberately excluded. The Prime Minister urged support for the Second Reading of the government's Bill, but it was made clear that that this would declare support for the principle of Home Rule rather than the detail of the proposals. Thereafter, the Bill could be amended in committee, or (as he would prefer) it could be reintroduced in a modified form later in the year. Gladstone also indicated that he was prepared to reconstruct the Bill to permit Irish Members to continue sitting at Westminster. This was a major concession to moderate Unionist opinion in the Liberal Party, and seemed designed to meet the requirements of those who had submitted the original resolution to the NLF. Perhaps if that concession had been offered a couple of months earlier, it would have been enough to keep most of the Radicals within the Gladstonian ranks; but public attitudes had now been struck, and it was too late.

On the following day, a meeting of Liberal Unionists convened by Hartington learnt some very important news. The Conservative Chief Whip, Aretas Akers-Douglas, had intimated that his party would not contest the seat of any Liberal who opposed the Home Rule Bill.[23] Thus Liberals in vulnerable constituencies whose minds were not firmly made up on the merits or otherwise of Home Rule had a powerful incentive to vote against the government.

All eyes turned to Chamberlain. On 31 May, he met 54 of his associates, and declared that he hoped they would agree to abstain on the Second Reading – though, whatever happened, they should act together. But a letter from John Bright was read, at which the veteran Radical indicated his own intention to vote against the government. This may well have turned the meeting, and the great majority of those present decided to do the same, although a few resolved either to abstain or to support the government.[24]

The crucial division on the Second Reading of the Bill took place in the early hours of 8 June. Winding up the debate, Gladstone made what seems by all accounts to have been one of the greatest speeches of his life, concluding with the prescient advice which rings down the years: 'Think, I beseech you, think well, think wisely, think not for the moment but for the years to come, before you reject this Bill.'[25] He made a passionate appeal for generosity: 'Ireland stands at your bar expectant, hopeful, almost suppliant.' In vain. By 343 votes to 313, the House of Commons chose to ignore this advice. It was one of the fullest divisions ever recorded, for only thirteen MPs were absent.[26] Ninety-three Liberals voted against the Bill, 267 in favour. Hartington and Goschen found themselves in the same lobby as Chamberlain, Trevelyan and Bright, while Gladstone, who was backed in the Lords by Whig peers like Granville and Spencer, was supported in the Commons by Radicals like Dilke, Morley and Bradlaugh. Later in the same day, the Cabinet decided to recommend an immediate dissolution of Parliament.

It is widely considered that the role of Chamberlain had been decisive. In his biography, J. L. Garvin reckoned that 46 – almost half – of the dissident Liberals belonged to 'Chamberlain's battalion'. On that assessment, if they had voted the other way, or even if they had abstained from voting, the Second Reading would have been carried. This would not have saved the Home Rule Bill: nothing could have done that, for it would assuredly have been destroyed by the Lords even if it had scraped past the Commons. But it would have given everybody time to reflect, and perhaps devise some other kind of measure with which most Liberals could live, which would also meet the national aspirations of Ireland. Garvin reflected that 'In the sight of the rank and file of Unionists [Chamberlain] was the hero of the decision; in the sight of others he was the enemy for ever, pursued by a spirit of vengeance to his last hour and after'.[27]

But was Chamberlain's belated decision to vote against the Second Reading really decisive? The Liberal Chief Whip Arnold Morley (no relative of John) apparently did not think so. After what he described as a 'careful analysis' of the 93 dissident Liberal MPs, he told Gladstone that 67 were 'against the principle' of Home Rule, 21 were 'mainly influenced by considerations connected with their seats – such as provision of no opposition, etc.' and only five were 'Chamberlainites'.[28] These figures should be taken with some reserve, not least because the categories were not mutually exclusive, and no doubt many MPs had been influenced by more than one consideration; nevertheless, they warn about the danger of accepting too uncritically the common judgement.

Throughout the long public debate over Home Rule, Gladstone's overriding aim had been to achieve a permanent solution of the 'Irish Problem' which would satisfy the aspirations of the great majority of Irish people. The main Unionist concern was expressed by Chamberlain in an address to the Birmingham Liberals, now known as the 'Two Thousand' rather than the 'Six Hundred'. If Gladstone's judgement proved wrong, he contended, 'We shall have taken a step that we cannot retrace … which may be disastrous to the interests of the United Kingdom, and which may lessen, if it does not destroy, the power and influence of that mighty Empire'.[29] This was an early illustration of Chamberlain's personal interest in the idea of imperialism, which was to prove of massive importance both for his own career and for Britain for many years to come.

In the later stages of the great public debate, a new factor began to acquire importance: the special problem of Protestants, who formed something like half the population of Ulster, and a large majority in much of the north-eastern section of that Province. Even in 1885, it was not certain what attitude some Ulster Protestants would take on the Home Rule issue. The Nationalist victor in the desperately marginal constituency of South Tyrone noted that a voter had spoiled his ballot paper by marking 'No landlord!' against the name of the Conservative candidate, and 'No Pope!' against his own. This, the candidate reflected, was 'a perfect picture of the mentality of the Ulster Presbyterian farmer'.[30] But as the Home Rule controversy deepened, it soon became apparent that the vast majority of Ulster Protestants, Presbyterian as well as Church of Ireland, were as deeply opposed to Home Rule as the majority of Catholics were in favour. One of the great paradoxes of the Home Rule controversy, not just in 1886 but for many years to come, was that British Liberals, a large proportion of whom were English or Welsh nonconformists, or Scottish Presbyterians, found themselves sundered from Ulstermen whose outlook in most religious and social matters was very similar to their own.

Perhaps the most significant achievement of the Parliament elected in 1885 was the 'Crofters' Act' promoted by the Radical Unionist Trevelyan. Throughout most of the 1880s, there was an agitation in the Hebrides and some parts of the Scottish mainland which had some parallels with the Irish 'Land War', although the attendant violence was much more moderate. It was enough, however, to persuade the authorities to use gunboats, marines and even soldiers.[31] Four of the Scottish MPs elected in 1885, who are often described as Liberals, are sometimes considered to be members of a distinct 'Crofters' Party'. The 1886 legislation in some ways emulated the Irish Land Act of 1881, but it had special features of its own.

When a new General Election was entered in the middle of 1886, it was generally seen essentially as a national referendum on Home Rule. Gladstonian Liberals and Irish Nationalists established a concordat. The official Liberals did not attack Nationalist seats; conversely, Irish voters in British constituencies were encouraged to support Gladstonians. Whether this was an important factor in the campaign is doubtful. The Annual Register[32] reflected that the expatriate Irish vote 'could scarcely exceed 40,000 persons, of whom three fourths were resident in London, Liverpool and Glasgow'. On the other side of the divide, the Conservative Chief Whip's undertaking not to oppose Liberal Unionists, and the tacit Liberal Unionist disposition to reciprocate, created a similar common front.

The Gladstonian Liberals approached the 1886 General Election in a remarkably hopeful mood. The great NLF organiser Schnadhorst remained with the Federation after Chamberlain's departure. His judgement at the beginning of the campaign was that 'we shall win more seats from the Tories than they will win from us, but the results as between ourselves and the [Liberal] Unionists ... are doubtful.'[33] The Chief Whip was disposed to take an even more sanguine view of election prospects. But the 1886 results were far less encouraging than these early forecasts indicated. In 1885, the Liberals had won 335 seats; a little over half a year later the Gladstonians retained only 192, while the Liberal Unionists – despite their arrangements with the Conservatives – received only 77, as against the 93 Liberals who had voted against Gladstone early in June. Even if the two Liberal groups could be reunited, they had still lost a good deal of ground. The Conservatives, with 316 MPs against 249 in 1885, had done well, but they nevertheless failed to win an overall majority. The Irish Nationalists slipped very slightly, from 86 seats to 85.

Seen in more detail, the 1886 results reveal some remarkable local variations. There were far more unopposed returns than in 1885: 224 as against 43. Gladstonian Liberals remained the dominant party in Wales and Scotland, though in both they lost a certain amount of ground. In England, they fared very badly, their representation being nearly halved, from 242 to 122, out of 456 seats in all. In some places results were appalling. In 1885, the Liberals had won every seat in Birmingham, and had proudly proclaimed 'We are seven!' In 1886, five of the Liberal MPs stood as Liberal Unionists, and all were unopposed. The other two remained Gladstonians. One, a local alderman, defended his seat and was defeated by a Conservative – at the instance, it seems, of Chamberlain. The other, the 'Lib-Lab' Henry Broadhurst, decamped to a more hopeful constituency in Nottingham, while his place in Birmingham was taken by Jesse Collings, standing as a Liberal Unionist. Collings was a friend of Chamberlain, and the two men were to remain closely associated for many years to come. Sympathisers compared their relationship with that subsisting between *fidus Achates* and Aeneas; to hostile critics they more closely resembled Sancho Panza and Don Quixote, or even the March Hare and the Mad Hatter.

Liberal results in London was nearly as bad as those in Birmingham. In 1885 the Metropolitan area returned 25 Liberals; in 1886 only eleven Gladstonians scraped home. There were a few Gladstonian triumphs elsewhere to counter these disasters. Conservative MPs were unseated in Cockermouth, Lancaster and one of the Liverpool constituencies. These results may be attributed to the large numbers of Irish immigrants who had followed Parnell in one direction in 1885, but the opposite direction in the following year. A few other Liberal gains from Conservatives are less easily explained. Liberal Unionists had varied experiences. Of the ninety-three Liberal MPs who voted against the Second Reading of the Home Rule Bill in June, sixteen stood down at the ensuing General Election. At least four of them appear to have been forced to retire because of local Liberal pressure.[34] Twenty-five of the remaining seventy-seven were unopposed. Thirteen were defeated by Gladstonian Liberals. They included three important casualties: Goschen, who was heavily defeated in Edinburgh, Trevelyan who lost Hawick Burghs and Grey who lost Tyneside. In Rossendale, Hartington was rejected by the local '300', and was opposed by a Gladstonian; nevertheless, he held the constituency by a comfortable margin. Despite the Conservative Chief Whip's promise, three of the 93 were opposed by Conservatives, and two lost their seats to Conservatives. Those two included the one Liberal Unionist who was opposed by a Gladstonian Liberal as well, who finished bottom of the poll.[35]

There was no doubt that the Liberal government must resign; but who should take over? On 20 July, Gladstone recommended the Queen to call Salisbury, who seemed the natural successor. But a Conservative government could only survive with Liberal Unionist support, which was by no means a foregone conclusion. Salisbury tried to persuade Hartington to head the government. Leading Liberal Unionists were split as to whether he should accept,[36] but in the end he refused. Nor could Salisbury prevail on Liberal Unionists to serve in his own government. It is a fair guess that neither Hartington nor Salisbury really wanted the premiership, on personal as well as public grounds. In the end Salisbury drew the short straw, and formed a purely Conservative Government.

6

Reconstruction

'He thinks like á Tory and talks like a Radical, and that's so important
nowadays.'

Oscar Wilde, *Lady Windermere's Fan* (1892)

The Conservative government which Lord Salisbury formed in July 1886
would last for six years; but that outcome would have seemed highly
unlikely at the time. The Liberals took defeat as an appropriate moment for
a hard, cold look at the workings of its electoral machine, and acted with
considerable speed. Chamberlain had departed, but Schnadhorst remained,
and this gave the party leaders and organisers the opportunity to change the
role and relationships of the National Liberal Federation and the Liberal
Central Association.[1] The London-based LCA had long been essentially the
office of the Chief Whip, who was himself an appointee of the Leader. The
Birmingham-based NLF had been busily encouraging the formation of
Liberal Associations with democratic structures, and had a strong tradition
of policy-making. Until the Home Rule crisis, it had served as a power base
for Chamberlain.

Because of the Home Rule debate, if for no other reason, it had become
a matter of some urgency that this dichotomy should be resolved. In September 1886 the NLF resolved to move its headquarters to London, where it
positioned itself next door to the offices of the LCA. Francis Schnadhorst,
secretary of the NLF, was offered the same post in the LCA. He refused, but
accepted the office of honorary secretary. Thereafter he proceeded with
alacrity to establish democratic Liberal Associations throughout the country. A year later the Chief Whip Arnold Morley was reporting to Gladstone
that Schnadhorst had 'revolutionised' the conduct of elections.[2] By this time
nearly all major areas of England and Wales were covered by the NLF. In
1887, the Liberal Publication Department was set up as a joint NLF-LCA
venture, and its pamphlets and leaflets were regarded as official party productions. Scotland had its own Liberal organisations. Matters there followed
a somewhat different course from England and Wales, but the upshot was
similar. The English LCA was paralleled by the Scottish Liberal Association,
while the National Liberal Federation of Scotland resembled its English

namesake. In 1886 the Association had inclined against Home Rule, while the Federation supported it. Later in the year, however, Gladstonians contrived to take over the Association, and the two bodies were amalgamated.[3] Schnadhorst became to a considerable extent an independent force in the Liberal Party. Thus, in 1891 he received a subscription of £5000 from the arch-imperialist Cecil Rhodes, with important strings attached. The money seems to have been passed into the account of the NLF, not the LCA, and was therefore kept secret from the Chief Whip. There was even a slight suspicion that Schnadhorst might – in Sir Henry Campbell-Bannerman's word – have 'trousered' it.[4]

The split of 1886 produced another consequence for the Liberal Party which was less tangible, but nevertheless real. On the whole, those Liberals who seceded from local associations because of Unionist sympathies were their wealthier, less radical, members. Just what made a man a 'radical' is perhaps a matter of dispute; but one analysis based on the behaviour of MPs in parliamentary divisions, employing a statistical method known as multiple discriminant analysis, has indicated that the radicals, who had been just short of a majority of the Liberal MPs in the 1885 Parliament, came to constitute a majority in 1886.[5]

This process of radicalisation of the MPs was paralleled by a growing eagerness of the NLF to incorporate new elements of policy in its proposals. Nobody claimed that such resolutions were binding on Liberal parliamentarians, but their persuasive force could not be denied. A sort of steering committee would draw up policy statements which would be accepted with little demur by delegates at the annual meetings, leaving aside issues which were seen as 'unripe' – in other words, where there was no substantial unanimity of opinion. The NLF had long been campaigning for religious equality, temperance reform, land reform and non-sectarian education. In the later 1880s it added disestablishment of the Welsh and Scottish churches; taxation of ground rents and mining royalties; the principle of 'one man, one vote'; abolition of food taxes; improved working class housing; payment of MPs and 'local option' as to the licensing of public houses.

But the overriding urgency of Irish Home Rule was not denied. Whatever harm the Home Rule debate may have done to the Liberals in some ways, in one respect the party was strengthened. There was a single clear issue which united all Gladstonian Liberals and divided them sharply from their opponents.[6] Addressing a group of MPs in March 1887, Gladstone drew the vivid analogy of a railway accident, with halted trains accumulating on both sides of the wreckage. 'You must clear the line. You must dispose of the Irish question', he told them.[7] The parallel was very good. Rank-and-file Liberals, as well as the leader, had taken the idea of Home Rule much to heart, and in many places seem to have taken the initiative themselves to suppress Liberals who had doubts on the matter. The party's original commitment to Home Rule was due overwhelmingly to Gladstone's personal influence; but, once that commitment had been made, nobody, not even Gladstone himself, could set any of the waiting trains moving until the Home Rule question had been resolved.

On the other side of the divide, the Liberal Unionists were in a curious position after the 1886 General Election. They soon constituted themselves a separate party, with Hartington as their leader; yet they sat on Opposition Liberal benches, and – at their own request – even continued to receive the Liberal whip, at least until the spring of 1887.[8] On the face of it, they were in a very strong position. If they were prepared to vote regularly with the Conservatives, they could keep the government in office for a long time; if they were not prepared to do so, they could put it out at any moment. In another sense, their position was much weaker. Unless they could somehow win back the Liberal Party to a Unionist position, they might be compared with the traditional mule: without pride in ancestry or hope of posterity. In an oft-quoted letter of September 1886, Chamberlain suggested to Hartington a general strategy, not wanting in cynicism, which the Liberal Unionists might adopt:

> Our real policy is never to vote with the Tories unless they are in danger and to vote against them whenever we can safely do so ... Our great difficulty is that in order to preserve the Union we are forced to keep a Tory government in power. But every time we vote with them we give a shock to the ordinary Liberal politician outside, and if we do it too often, we shall be completely identified with the Tories and shall lose all chance of recovering the lead of the Liberal Party.[9]

This view was predicated to the assumption that the long-term aim of the Liberal Unionists was to return to the Liberal Party, which they would then proceed to lead in a Unionist direction. Whether Hartington fully accepted that objective at the time is not clear; but before the Salisbury government had run its course neither man would have agreed with it.

One Liberal Unionist soon made his own decision for the future. Of all leading members of the new Party, Goschen was closest to contemporary Conservatism in his outlook. His opportunity came suddenly and unexpectedly. When the new Conservative government was formed, the brilliant but erratic Lord Randolph Churchill became Chancellor of the Exchequer. Towards the end of 1886 he resigned on a question related to naval expenditure, evidently believing himself indispensable – for the administration was conspicuously low on first-rank talent. He presumably hoped later to return on his own terms. As with many other politicians who have tried the same gambit, Churchill's action was counter-productive. For a moment, the possibility of Salisbury standing down in favour of Hartington was again bruited; but Hartington again refused, and Salisbury remained in office.

Goschen, whom Churchill had famously 'forgotten', was offered, and accepted, the post of Chancellor, and thus became the first Liberal Union-ist recruit to the Conservative ministry. His capacity as a financier was never in doubt, and he was a considerable buttress for a weak administration. That, however, was not the end of the story. As Goschen had been defeated at the General Election, he needed to find a new seat in the House of Com-mons in order to discharge the duties of his office. His first attempt, in a Liverpool constituency, resulted in another defeat, though by an exceedingly narrow margin. On his second try, in a Conservative London constituency with no Liberal tradition at all, Goschen was duly returned to Parliament, still clinging to the label of 'Liberal Unionist'.

Just two days after Churchill's resignation, Joseph Chamberlain faced some of his own West Birmingham constituents.[10] Many of them were clearly unhappy about the Liberal Unionists' relations with the Conservative ministry. Chamberlain spoke in a most conciliatory way about the prospect of reunion with Gladstonian Liberals. 'We Liberals are agreed', he told them on 23 December, 'upon ninety-nine points of our programme; we only dis-agree upon one. Even upon Irish matters', he continued, 'I am more surprised at the number of points upon which we are agreed than at the remainder upon which for the present we must be content to differ ... Sit-ting round a table, and coming together in a spirit of compromise and conciliation', he declared, 'almost any three men, leaders of the Liberal Party', would be able to arrange a mutually acceptable scheme.

In the early part of 1887, it was five men rather than three who met at a 'Round Table Conference'. Gladstone gave his approval, Hartington did not commit himself. There was a certain difficulty in selecting suitable negotia-tors from the Gladstonian side. H. H. Fowler, later Viscount Wolverhamp-ton, was proposed, but the Chief Whip considered him 'inclined perhaps to sacrifice too much for the sake of reconciliation'.[11] In the end, Harcourt and John Morley represented the Gladstonian view. Chamberlain and Trevelyan (who had by this time succeeded to his father's baronetcy, becoming Sir George) represented the view of the Radical Liberal Unionists, though not necessarily the view of the rest of their party. Lord Herschell, Lord Chancellor in the recent Liberal government, acted as a sort of chairman.

The discussions continued for some weeks, and at one point seemed close to success. But in an article of late February 1887, Chamberlain contended that the Liberal party 'will ... remain shattered and impotent' while the majority of Liberals remained committed to current Home Rule proposals. For practical purposes, the Round Table Conference collapsed, although there were still contacts between Chamberlain and Gladstone for several weeks to come. What is surely remarkable is not that Chamberlain took the stand he eventually did, which was more or less the position he had taken nearly a year before, but that he offered the olive branch in December 1886, and apparently remained eager for reunion for a month to come. Neither Chamberlain nor the Gladstonians can have had much doubt at any stage where the other stood on Home Rule, and so mystery surrounds the whole episode. Did Chamberlain receive some sort of inducement, perhaps from Hartington, perhaps from the Conservatives, to remain where he was? One can only guess. Trevelyan, however, eventually returned to the Gladstonian party.

Soon after the 1886 General Election, events in Ireland took a new twist, which had a considerable effect on both groups of Liberals. When 'Fair Rents' (or 'Judicial Rents' as they were often called) were fixed, under provisions of the Irish Land Act of 1881, nobody had anticipated the sudden and dramatic fall in agricultural prices which took place in the middle 1880s. Irish tenants complained bitterly that they could not meet the rents demanded of them. There followed a renewed land war – the so-called 'Plan of Campaign'. Towards the end of 1886, Arthur Balfour was appointed Chief Secretary for Ireland, In the first few weeks of 1887, the Conservative government developed a two-pronged strategy for the country. 'Coercion' would be restored; but this time it would be quasi-permanent, not subject to periodic review, as previous 'Coercion' legislation had been. At the same time, the government proposed to deal with some of the perceived economic grievances of Ireland, evidently believing that this would undermine Irish objections to political Union – 'killing Home Rule with kindness', as the policy was sometimes dubbed. The first instalment of this policy was a Land Bill, designed, among other things, to give relief to tenants who owed rent through no fault of their own.

The Coercion proposals caused a major furore. Some of the Liberal Unionists were deeply alienated. Four of their MPs transferred to the Gladstonians.[12] Coercion was duly passed nevertheless, and in August 1887 the government resolved to use its new powers to 'proclaim' – that is, to suppress – the Irish National Land League, the body through which most of the current agitation was being conducted. The Gladstonians moved a critical resolution. Chamberlain and five other Liberal Unionists supported it, forty-seven followed Hartington's recommendation and voted with the government, and seventeen abstained. The land legislation also ran into trouble, both in the Lords and in its later stages in the Commons. Even a Conservative government was not in complete control of the House of Lords, and some of the peers resented the proposed concessions to tenants. In the Commons, the Liberal Unionists (against Hartington's advice) were able to force through an amendment giving the courts certain powers to revise judicial rents.

A second instalment of the government's Irish land policy followed in the next year. By 1888, the sum allocated for Irish land purchase under the Ashbourne Act of 1885 had been taken up – indeed, it had been exceeded – and new legislation advanced further money for the purpose. The government, however, was considerably embarrassed by some Irish landlords who continued to act in a thoroughly oppressive manner towards their tenants. The most notorious case was the Marquis of Clanricarde ('Lord Clan Rack-rent'). He had been MP for Galway (as a Liberal!) from 1867 to 1871, when he resigned in protest against the Irish Land Act of the previous year. Clanricarde's estates were subject to considerable turbulence, requiring heavy expenditure to maintain order. The Prime Minister and the Chief Secretary visited him, urging some relaxation of behaviour – but without success.

Chamberlain continued to occupy a pivotal position in politics. He was, in a sense, fighting a personal war on at least three fronts. He attacked the Gladstonians with renewed vigour after the failure of the Round Table Conference; his dislike of Conservatism remained: and he was never fully at ease with his nominal leader Hartington, whom he had once compared with Rip Van Winkle. In 1887–88, he paid a prolonged visit to North America, acting as a sort of government agent to resolve a fishing dispute between Canada and the United States. On his return, Chamberlain discovered that the Gladstonians had captured control of the Birmingham Liberal Association, while there was also pressure from local Conservatives, who were avid for a substantial increase in representation both in Parliament and on the City Council.[13] He promptly established his own very effective political machine, the Birmingham Liberal Unionist Association. This action was of national as well as local importance, for it restored Chamberlain's local power base, and thus enabled him to continue exerting influence on both the Conservatives and the Liberal Unionists.

The complex arguments over Irish Coercion and land reform which occupied much parliamentary time in the late 1880s overlapped a series of controversies which centred on the person of Parnell, but which had deep implications for British politics. In April 1887, while the Coercion debate was still in full flood, *The Times* published what was claimed to be a facsimile of a letter from Parnell, giving tacit approval to one of the sensational

Irish murders of 1882. Other incriminating letters, also attributed to Parnell, were cited in the course of a libel action brought by an Irish MP against *The Times* in the course of the following year. Eventually Parnell managed to get a special commission of three judges set up, which investigated the authorship of all the disputed letters. Nearly two years after the original publication, it was proved that the letters had been forged by a disreputable journalist (who soon committed suicide), from whom they had been bought by *The Times*, and published in good faith. There was a strong public reaction of sympathy for Parnell.

Up to this point, events which touched on Ireland seemed to be moving strongly in favour of the Gladstonians. Neither Coercion nor 'kindness' had brought peace to Ireland, and there seemed little sign that either would do so in the foreseeable future. The only alternative policy, it seemed, was Home Rule. The personal character of Parnell, who had been widely execrated not long before, had been completely vindicated. But at the end of that year the Parnell saga took another turn, which had even stronger repercussions on British politics. For a long time, Parnell (who was a bachelor) had had a not very secret adulterous relationship with Kitty O'Shea, wife of Captain W. H. O'Shea, who had sat very briefly as a Nationalist MP. Then O'Shea petitioned for a divorce, citing Parnell as co-respondent. The petition was not defended, but the proceedings dragged on for most of 1890. Today it is difficult to imagine a politician being ruined by such a matter, but things were different in late-Victorian times, and not only some of Parnell's Catholic followers but also many British Liberals became deeply distressed by the whole business. The cynic might suggest that, in some cases at least, what upset people was not so much the existence of the liaison – Hartington, for example, had a well-known affair with the Duchess of Manchester – but the fact that the matter was brought in front of the courts.

Gladstone firmly refused to cast personal judgement on the matter. 'What!' he cried, 'because a man is what is called leader of a party, does that constitute him a censor and a judge of faith and morals? I will not accept it. It would make life intolerable.'[14] But he was firmly conscious of the impact which the whole business would have on his own political following. 'I have been for four years,' Mr Gladstone justly argued, 'endeavouring to persuade voters to support Irish autonomy. Now the voter says to me, "If [Parnell remains leader] – I will not support Irish autonomy." How can I go on with the work?'[15]

Before the O'Shea divorce case, by-election results and other pointers had suggested that the Liberals and their Nationalist allies would win the next General Election, and Gladstone would then be able to carry Home Rule.

Now everything turned on whether Parnell was prepared to perform an act of self-abnegation. This need not even be a permanent withdrawal from politics. A telegram sent by Cecil Rhodes, of all people, encapsulated the best advice: 'Resign. Marry. Return.'

Gladstone drew up a letter for John Morley to show to Parnell. Framed in amicable and courteous terms, it urged the Irish leader to withdraw, pointing out that if he remained this 'would render my retention of the leadership of the Liberal Party, based as it has been mainly on the prosecution of the Irish cause, almost a nullity.' Parnell refused flatly to stand down. With Parnell in place, there was no serious prospect of the Liberals winning the next General Election and achieving Home Rule within the foreseeable future. Gladstone, who was nearly seventy-nine, must have realised that this was the last chance he would have of leading the Liberals to victory, and that nobody else would be likely to push through Home Rule once he had gone. So he had little choice but to release the letter to the press. In the circumstances, this looked like an ultimatum rather than a friendly remonstrance.

The Irish now had to decide whether to reject Parnell's leadership, at least for the time being. Eventually they split into two bitterly hostile groups. Twenty-six remained with Parnell, forty-four, headed by Justin McCarthy, repudiated his leadership. The dénouement was both dramatic and pathetic. In June 1891, after her divorce decree had been made absolute, Parnell married his mistress. In October of the same year, still only forty-five, he suddenly died. The internecine Nationalist war continued unabated, and the party which he had led remained shattered for nearly a decade to come. It is not difficult to visualise the political capital which Unionists made to the dispute, to the disadvantage of the Nationalists and indirectly of the Liberals.

Meanwhile, the policy of agrarian reform in Ireland continued. Legislation of 1890–91 further extended land purchase, and also dealt with a problem which, in the judgement of one of their number, was unfamiliar even to the large majority of Nationalist MPs.[16] In the 'Congested Districts' of the west of Ireland, the tenants' problem was not so much over-renting, but rather that their holdings were far too small, while much of the best land had been taken for cattle ranches. The new legislation made a start in the reclamation of that land for the peasantry.

There were also important measures in various non-Irish matters, and a lot of this legislation could be called Liberal in spirit. Much appears to have been the result of strong Liberal Unionist pressure. Local government had always been an especial interest of Chamberlain, and legislation of 1888 went a long way in the direction he wished. Until that time, the English and Welsh counties were still administered largely by non-elected JPs (who were frequently landowners) meeting in Quarter Sessions. The new measure set up elected County Councils. It also established the County Boroughs, and set up a new London County Council. The importance attached to this new authority was signalled by the fact that Lord Rosebery, who had already been Gladstone's Foreign Secretary and was later to be Prime Minister, became first Chairman of the LCC. An unexpected feature in Goschen's Budget of 1891 made elementary education free throughout Great Britain. Another important government measure, the Factory Act of 1891, was much in the Disraeli tradition, reducing maximum hours of employment for women and raising the minimum age at which children could be employed.

Early in 1891, a by-election arose in Aston Manor – today part of Birmingham, but at that time a separate borough.[17] The constituency had been Liberal in 1885, but was captured by the Conservatives with a modest majority in the following year. If the Liberals took it back, this would prove a high embarrassment to Chamberlain. So he resolved to give maximum assistance to the Conservative defender. There was no longer anything to be said for the view that the Home Rule issue was a sort of family quarrel among Liberals, who (as Chamberlain himself had put it so recently) agreed on 99 per cent of policy and merely disagreed on 1 per cent. In the course of the Aston campaign, Chamberlain raised – rather tentatively – an issue which had not been bruited before by any major politician in any party: the proposal that Old Age Pensions should be granted to those too old for active work.[18] This, of course, was in no way a promise which could be held to bind the government, yet here was an 'Unauthorised Programme' with a vengeance. In the end, the Conservative held Aston with a comfortable majority.

Any remote chance of Liberal reunion which still remained was extinguished by Chamberlain at a luncheon in Birmingham on 25 November 1891. Speaking alongside Salisbury, he declared that 'I neither look for nor desire reunion.' He went on to speak warmly of his new associates, adding that his early fears that Conservatives and Liberal Unionists would 'fail to find a common ground in foreign policy and above all in domestic constructive legislation' had been dispelled by recent experience.[19]

Not long before the end of 1891, the seventh Duke of Devonshire died, and Hartington succeeded to the peerage. That removed him from leadership of his party in the Commons. His Rossendale constituency was lost to the Liberals in the supervening by-election: a very different result from Aston Manor a year earlier. The only credible successor to the Liberal Unionist leadership was Chamberlain. In his new capacity Chamberlain appeared no longer as captain of a rather small contingent of Radical Unionist MPs, mainly hailing from a small area in the west midlands, but as the most authoritative spokesman of an important party.

Meanwhile, the Liberal Unionists had been busily accumulating money which would prove very useful not only to help their own candidates but also as a bargaining counter with the Conservatives. By May 1890, Hartington was in process of building up a fighting fund aimed at a target of £60,000.[20] In the upshot this sum was more than doubled – largely, it seems, through Hartington's own efforts. Considerable details are preserved in the Devonshire archives. These show that the Duke of Bedford was good for £5500, Lord Rothschild and Horace Farquhar for £5000 each, two other Rothschilds for £5000 between them, the Earl of Derby for £3000 and the Duke of Westminster for £2000. There were also three donations, much larger than any of these, from anonymous 'Friends'. These seem to be linked with three baronetcies which materialised in due course.

In the Liberal Party, a curious condition prevailed. Gladstone's personal authority was supreme and unchallenged, and there was no 'heir apparent'. Everybody agreed that the next major measure which a future Liberal government must attempt was Home Rule. But, despite his current vigour, it was certain that Gladstone could not remain leader for much longer. Liberals in the second rank of the party gave increasing attention to the policies which must be followed once the Home Rule question was resolved and Gladstone was no longer in charge. The so-called 'Newcastle Programme', adopted at the NLF Conference of 1891, largely recapitulated proposals carried at earlier conferences. It acquired, however, a special authority from Gladstone himself, who gave personal endorsement to a large part of it in a speech delivered at the end of the conference. The 'Newcastle Programme' set Home Rule as the first of necessary reforms, but laid down no priorities among the remainder. Its proposals would certainly be enough to keep a Liberal government busy for years to come. The disadvantage of the 'Programme' was that these proposals were not closely linked to any single theme, and people attracted to one Newcastle policy might well be repelled by another.

So stood matters when Parliament was dissolved in June 1892, and a new General Election campaign began. The issues which interested candidates, and probably the issues which interested electors as well, varied considerably from place to place. Gladstone's personal preoccupation with Irish Home Rule seemed to dominate the debate in the larger towns, while in some industrial areas there was much interest in the 'Eight Hours Question' – the proposal that there should be a statutory limit on the hours of employment. In agricultural areas, the idea of making allotments available for farm workers was widely discussed. In both Scotland and Wales there was considerable interest in church disestablishment; in Wales there was also a

1. William Ewart Gladstone (1809–1898), four times Liberal Prime Minister.

2. Sir Henry Campbell-Bannerman, Prime Minister 1905–8.

3. Herbert Henry Asquith, 1st Earl of Oxford and Asquith, Prime Minister 1908–16.

4. David Lloyd-George, 1st Earl Lloyd-George, Prime Minister 1916–22

5. Sir Herbert Samuel, 1st Viscount Samuel, Liberal Leader 1931–35. (*Lib Dem News*)

6. Sir Archibald Sinclair, Liberal Leader 1935–45. (*Lib Dem News*)

7. Clement Davies, Liberal Leader 1945–56, at a Liberal meeting. (*Lib Dem News*)

8. Jo Grimond, Liberal Leader 1956–67, opens the new Liberal Party headquarters in Smith Square, London, in 1965. (*Lib Dem News*)

substantial demand that the real or imagined benefits of Home Rule should be extended to the principality. Outside the official policies of either the Liberal Party or its opponents, two very different ideas which evoked little interest a couple of decades earlier were coming to have wide influence. 'Imperialism', meaning both the acquisition and the development of Empire, was affecting the outlook of many people, not least of them Joseph Chamberlain. The much more radical idea that it was possible greatly to alter the existing economic order in a way which would substantially improve the lot of the poor was becoming widely discussed, though there was no sort of general agreement as to the measures which might be required in order to do this.

The overall results of the General Election of 1892 were far from satisfactory for any party. Liberals, including a few Labour men of varying degrees of independence, mustered 273: a substantial increase, but well short of an overall majority. The Conservatives lost ground, finishing with 268 seats. The Irish Nationalists were deeply split between Parnellites and anti-Parnellites, but together they held 81 seats – a small drop from 1886, attributable in one or two cases to a split vote between Nationalist candidates. The Liberal Unionists dropped to a mere 45. Patterns were by no means consistent everywhere. Gladstonian Liberals gained 57 seats from the Conservatives and 23 from Liberal Unionists, but lost sixteen to Conservatives and five to Liberal Unionists. In the West Midlands, the Chamberlain influence appears to have shifted some constituencies in favour of Conservative candidates.[21] Liberals also fared less well than had been expected in Scotland. Gladstone's own seat of Midlothian was held by a reduced majority.

As there was no clear overall majority, Salisbury's government remained in office until the new Parliament met in August. A general motion of no confidence in the government, not related to any specific issue of policy, was moved from the Liberal benches by Herbert Asquith, the future Prime Minister, who was then a young MP who had recently won his second electoral contest. The motion was carried by 350 votes to 310, on strict party lines. Salisbury resigned on 12 August. On the following day the Queen's secretary communicated to Gladstone her formal (though visibly regretful) commission to form a government.

THE BUCKING MULE.

In this Conservative cartoon of 1899, various riders seek without success to ride
the 'bucking mule', the Liberal Party, in the direction of 'Progress'. Harcourt
sits exhausted on the ground. Labouchere, Rosebery and Grey are in the
foreground; in the distance Morley, Asquith and Campbell-Bannerman
regard the animal with trepidation.

7

End of an Era

Your life has been grand – the noblest and best I have ever known. It has been an inspiration and a triumph; fruitful in untold benefits to millions of men and women.

Thomas Burt MP, former coal miner,
to Gladstone, on his retirement, 6 March 1894[1]

The chapter in John Morley's *Life of Gladstone* which deals with the Ministry of 1892 is headed by an epigraph from Gladstone's beloved Homer. The poet, speaking of the aged Nestor, declared that (in Morley's translation): 'Two generations of mortal men had he already seen pass away, who with him of old had been born and bred in sacred Pylos, and among the third generation he held rule.'[2] The parallel was strong. Gladstone commenced his fourth Ministry at eighty-two: a greater age than any Prime Minister before or since. By general agreement, the government's immediate responsibility was to prepare legislation for Home Rule, which would complete the 'mission ... to pacify Ireland' which Gladstone has assumed at the commencement of his first Ministry, nearly twenty-four years earlier.

The task of forming a Ministry was a good deal more difficult than it had been even in 1886. Granville was dead, Chamberlain had apostatised. Sir William Harcourt and Lord Rosebery, both notoriously prickly men, and both perhaps playing hard-to-get, posed difficulties, though they were both eventually accommodated in their 1886 roles as Chancellor of the Exchequer and Foreign Secretary. John Morley became Secretary for Ireland again. Earl Spencer became First Lord of the Admiralty. The major newcomer was Herbert Asquith, a young barrister who had the unusual experience of accepting the senior post of Home Secretary as his first ministerial appointment. Arnold Morley, who had been Chief Whip in the old Parliament, had long expressed the wish to resign that post, and did not wish to accept ministerial office,[3] but was eventually persuaded to become Postmaster-General, with a seat in the Cabinet.

In February 1893, Gladstone submitted his second Home Rule Bill. This was in some ways similar to the Bill of 1886, but in other respects markedly different. There would be a bicameral Irish legislature, with authority to make laws on purely Irish affairs. Several matters would be specifically excluded from the Irish Parliament's authority, including questions of peace and war, and external trade. It would also be precluded from interfering with matters touching on religious or personal freedom. Irish MPs would continue to sit at Westminster, but their numbers would be reduced.

Perhaps nobody expected such a Bill to pass into law without important changes, and there was a certain air of unreality from the start. It was a foregone conclusion that the overwhelmingly Unionist House of Lords (which still had, in strict law, unlimited power to throw out a Bill from the House of Commons) would resist it. The best that Home Rulers could hope was that some compromise might emerge (as with the Reform legislation of 1884–85), or that a long struggle between the two Houses would be resolved many months later in their favour (as with the Reform legislation of 1830–32). Initial reactions were muted, and many grudged the time which it would certainly take to produce any result at all. It is perhaps fair to say that a lot of people on both sides of the great divide were getting bored with the whole Home Rule question, and wanted it resolved quickly one way or the other, so that they could give attention to other matters.

In April 1893, the Second Reading passed the Commons by the exceptionally high vote of 347 to 304, with nobody breaking ranks on either side. Thereafter the Bill's opponents, and not least of these the Liberal Unionists, did everything in their power to stir up excitement. Special play was made of the problems of 'Ulster'. In practice, 'Ulster' was usually understood to mean the overwhelmingly Protestant north east alone. Unionist strategy was designed not to achieve some sort of compromise which would satisfy the Nationalist aspirations of the Irish majority and allay the honest apprehensions of the minority, but rather to use the fears of the minority to frustrate Home Rule altogether.

The Committee stage of the Home Rule Bill began in May, and both sides showed all signs of mounting bad temper. The government applied the closure frequently, to the great anger of the Opposition. At one point a Conservative MP physically assaulted a Liberal in the House of Commons, and for some time pandemonium broke out. There were also signs of fragmentation on the Home Rulers' side. An amendment was moved from Conservative benches to the effect that the new Irish Parliament should not be permitted to legislate on the matter of aliens. The government decided to accept this, to the fury of the Nationalists.

The Third Reading debate began at the end of August. Perceptible differences appeared among the Nationalists themselves. 'Official' Nationalist spokesmen like Justin McCarthy and John Dillon welcomed the Bill as it stood. John Redmond, a young Parnellite who would later play a very important part in politics, declared that he was only prepared to vote for it at all because he assumed that it was essentially provisional in character. Both attitudes, one suspects, were rooted in factional questions. In the end the Third Reading, like the Second, was carried by a comfortable majority: 301 votes against 267. The majority of 34 was slightly smaller than on the Second Reading. Gladstone explained to the Queen that 'two or three members of the Liberal Party abstained themselves or even voted against the Bill on account of considering it defective from the democratic point of view'.[4]

Earl Spencer introduced the Bill in the Lords in September, but Rosebery was seen as the principal Government spokesman. His support was somewhat muted, for he declared himself 'a witness [but] not an enthusiastic witness' in favour of Home Rule. He confessed that for him 'it was a question of policy, and Home Rule had to be adopted because all other policies had been tried and failed'. This was not dissimilar to the argument which had persuaded the Lords to carry the Irish Land Act twelve years earlier. But the upshot in the House of Lords was an overwhelming defeat for the Bill. On 8 September, out of a complete roll of 560 peers excluding princes of the blood, 419 voted against the Bill, and only 41 in favour. It had been generally anticipated for weeks that the Lords would throw out the Bill; the one feature which did cause surprise was the enormous majority by which they did so.

Few people today would deny that the vote was to have the most tragic consequences both for Britain and for Ireland. The immediate aftermath, however, was a strange anticlimax. Defeat by the Lords of a measure which had been the principal topic of debate at the General Election a year earlier might be expected to produce some dramatic reaction. *The Times* considered that 'three courses are open to the Premier. He may dissolve Parliament, or, without dissolution, he may start an agitation against the Peers, or he may acquiesce in his defeat.'[5] In this period, *The Times* was savagely hostile to the Government, and any advice it gave was doubtless tinged with malice; but there is much to be said for the newspaper's view that 'it would appear to be both the duty and the policy of the Government to give effect to their beliefs by appealing to the country'.

Nothing of the kind happened. It has sometimes been said that Gladstone wanted a dissolution, but was overridden by his colleagues. This view, for which there seems to be no contemporary evidence, may be based on a misreading of John Morley's biography of Gladstone.[6] The Cabinet, whatever its opinions on the matter might have been, did not meet again until November. On the other hand, one must assume that Ministers had been widely discussing among themselves the idea of a dissolution, both before and after the Lords' vote. The main difficulty in the way of such an action was the problem of raising enthusiasm among the British electorate.

It is likely that some Ministers, at any rate, already contemplated what soon became known as 'filling the cup' – that is, sustaining a series of defeats at the hands of the Lords without requiring a dissolution, in the hope that when a General Election at last took place so many people would be aggrieved at the behaviour of the Upper House that the Liberals would be returned triumphant to deal with the offending Chamber. The trouble with that strategy was that the Lords showed at least equal cunning. They were disposed to throw out, or mutilate, government measures only when (as with Home Rule) the electorate might well support their Lordships' view, or when the issue was so unimportant, or had such a narrow appeal, that the government would hesitate to dissolve Parliament.

Whether there was any general government strategy of 'filling the cup' seems doubtful; but even if such a strategy existed, new events soon blew everything off course. Just before the end of 1893, great pressure was suddenly mounted for a large increase in naval expenditure. Sir Edward Hamilton, Assistant Financial Secretary to the Treasury, was in close contact with Gladstone during the period, and his diaries throw much light on the politics of the period. Hamilton's private judgement that this pressure was attributable to 'the Sea Lords at the Admiralty, egged on by the *Times* and the rest of the press' seems a likely explanation.[7] The subject of the apprehension at that time was not Germany, but Germany's enemies France and Russia. Lord Spencer echoed the naval view. Sir William Harcourt did not accept the validity of that view on its merits, and was also naturally apprehensive about the likely effect of increased spending on the next Budget. Later, however, he began to look at the matter more from the eyes of a politician:

> But what was the alternative? The resignation not only of Lord Spencer and the whole of his Board (with the probability that no Admirals would be forthcoming to form a new Board) but also of Rosebery. This would infallibly break up the Government, and the huge expenditure would go on all the same, if not at a more excessive rate.[8]

Gladstone reacted more strongly and more consistently to the proposal, perceiving clearly its wider implications: 'It was, he said, a step taken by this country for the first time to join in the race of Europe for huge armaments. It was a grossly exaggerated scare. Has the country gone mad? he was tempted to ask.'[9] He began to mull over the possibility of resigning if his colleagues overrode him on the matter.

At this point, another worry began to enter the minds of political *cognoscenti.* The consequences if Gladstone resigned, and openly declared what the issue was, could be baleful indeed. Nobody would then be left in doubt that the contemplated rearmament was a hostile move against France and Russia, which Gladstone had opposed. This might have major international repercussions. At the lower level of domestic politics, it would further destabilise a government which was already weak, for Gladstone's personal prestige with the Liberal rank-and-file was incomparable. And who would become Prime Minister? There was no heir apparent, and many names were bandied about.

At that point Gladstone withdrew from the scene for a time, departing for Biarritz. This was not only a wise decision for an old man who had been under very heavy pressure, and whose health might be expected to benefit by a short escape from an English winter; but it also gave him the chance to review the political situation quietly, away from the imperious pressure of colleagues. The Prime Minister being the man he was, his sojourn in southern France was certainly not likely to be spent in sybaritic idleness. Sir Algernon West, Gladstone's private secretary, made a couple of rapid return visits from Biarritz to London. The first message from the Prime Minister indicated that he proposed to resign, and probably explain the real reason.[10] This, one may guess, was greeted with general consternation by his colleagues. The Chief Whip, Edward Marjoribanks, spelled out a mixture of political apprehension and personal affection in a letter to Gladstone:

> I need not repeat how greatly I grieve at that decision and with what anxiety it fills me for the future, not only of the government but the party. You once described one of your chief functions to me as being that of darning and patching up the holes that were worn day by day. I see no one to perform this duty in the future, or indeed to keep together the threads of the fabric even where it does not show signs of wear.[11]

A few days later another proposal emerged from Biarritz. Parliament should be dissolved, on the grounds that the government was being thwarted by the House of Lords.[12] In that event, presumably, Gladstone would have no cause to resign immediately. This would focus attention on a completely different issue from naval rearmament. Very likely it would have been the best (or the least worst) solution of all for the Liberals at that moment.

A good opportunity for implementing Gladstone's suggestion was just about to arise. Two Bills had been lumbering their way through Parliament at the time of the Lords' defeat of the Home Rule Bill, and both were still being considered by the House of Lords at the beginning of 1894. A Local Government Bill proposed to set up parish councils, whose most numerous electors would in many places be farm labourers. These bodies, it was

originally contemplated, would be quite powerful. Various hostile amendments were carried by the Conservative majority in the House of Lords, and
these had to be reported to the House of Commons. At this point the government received help from a rather unexpected quarter. In mid-February,
the Liberal Unionists decided to abstain from factious opposition to the
Bill. Compromises were eventually worked out which did not wholly please
the government, but left the measure a good deal closer to the original
intentions than the Conservative peers had wished.

The other contentious government measure was an Employers' Liability
Bill, which had been moved by Asquith in the previous year. It contained
two main proposals. The existing legal doctrine of 'common employment'
should be abolished. The effect of that rule had been to excuse an employer
from liability for injury sustained by an employee when the culprit had been
another employee. The second change was that employers should no longer
be permitted to contract out of their obligation to compensate employees
for industrial injuries. The Bill passed the Commons, but in February 1894
it was so mauled by the Lords that the government saw fit to withdraw it.

Home Rule, Local Government and Employers' Liability between them
might appear to have made the Lords' cup quite full, and to justify a dissolution if the government wanted one. There was a good chance of
persuading Gladstone to remain Prime Minister until the election was over,
and then allow (or encourage) him to resign in the aftermath. Pointers, such
as they were, did not suggest that an early General Election would be a disaster. The best indication of public feeling at the time was probably the
by-elections. Contests of 1893, and the one by-election held in January 1894,
indicated a slight, but only a slight, swing against the government. It was by
no means impossible that it would survive the contest. If so, it would have
acquired a much clearer mandate than it had received in 1892. At worst, the
Conservatives would be returned, probably with a small majority, which
would give the Liberals a chance to regroup themselves, select new leaders
in their own time, and prepare to fight new battles.

But it requires courage to jump into icy water, even when the ship is sink-
ing slowly, and there is no other hope of escaping drowning. Most Ministers
were in no mood for courage, even the courage of desperation. John Morley, who probably knew what was happening as well as anybody who has
written on the subject, later recorded Gladstone's assessment of the situation: '"I suggested dissolution to my colleagues in London, where half, or
more than half, were found at the moment. I received by telegraph a hope-
lessly adverse reply." Reluctantly he let the idea drop, always maintaining,
however, that a signal opportunity had been lost.'[13] There was now no
remaining doubt that Gladstone would soon resign. Yet two important

questions remained unanswered: whether Gladstone's resignation would be publicly linked with the ministerial disagreement over naval rearmament and who the successor should be.

On 27 February, Gladstone wrote to the Queen, indicating his intention soon to resign on 'physical grounds'.[14] The 'physical grounds' were certainly present. He was suffering from cataract in both eyes, and increasing deafness. These afflictions provided a better excuse than his eighty-four years; for his vigour remained remarkable for a man of any age. This announcement got his colleagues off the hook of a visible dispute about naval rearmament. On 1 March, Gladstone held his last Cabinet, which accepted under protest the Lords' amendments to the Local Government Bill. It was more famous, however, for a maladroit valedictory address to the Prime Minister, read by Harcourt from a 'well-thumbed' paper – as Asquith later described it. Some members were so overcome by the sense of occasion that Gladstone would call it the 'blubbering Cabinet'.

It is difficult to overstate the loss which the Liberals were about to sustain. A bare record of Gladstone's political achievements from the days of Peel, through his periods as Chancellor of the Exchequer and his four Premierships, provides little sense of his prestige, and the profound respect and admiration in which he was held by followers and by many who were by no means his followers. A few days after the resignation, Joseph Chamberlain – no less – told an audience in Birmingham that 'although to my deep regret … I have felt it my duty to oppose to the uttermost Mr Gladstone's policy, I have never, in private or in public, said one single word derogatory to his transcendent abilities and to his personal worth'.[15] Gladstone brought to political affairs a vision and a sense of duty which few men, if any, have imparted before or since. Anybody who followed Gladstone would inevitably be an anticlimax.

A successor had, nevertheless, to be selected. When Gladstone attended the Queen to present his formal resignation, he was prepared – if asked – to propose Spencer. The Liberal MPs – if asked – would probably have preferred Harcourt, whom they saw as a good political bruiser, but whose abrasive character as a colleague they knew less well. It is far from certain whom the Cabinet would have chosen. Perhaps Rosebery would have been selected, with the barest of majorities over Harcourt.[16] But the Queen did not ask anybody, and of her own volition invited Rosebery to form a government.

Rosebery's 'paper qualifications' were very good. He had acquired an excellent reputation as Chairman of the London County Council and he was generally approved by 'Labour' members. Against that, as we have seen, he was far from eager to take the job, and this reluctance appears to have been sincere. At forty-six, he was twenty years younger than Harcourt, his most serious challenger, who could hardly fail to resent the royal preference. Yet the outcome was not wholly unbearable for the disappointed Harcourt, for he could comfort himself with the reflection that his own authority, as principal government spokesman in the House of Commons, was almost as great as – in some ways greater than – that of the Prime Minister.

But the strained relations between the two men are signalled in a reported conversation between Harcourt and Marjoribanks, in which the Chancellor told the Chief Whip 'that he does not see that any personal communication would be necessary between a Prime Minister in the Lords and the Leader of the House of Commons, as the Leader would act on all occasions on his own initiative and responsibility'.[17] John Morley, who remained at the Irish Office, was even more intransigent, writing to Rosebery that 'I propose to confine myself strictly and absolutely to the business of my department, *plus* attendance at Cabinet councils, *plus* steady obedience to the calls of the whips for my vote'.[18] The new Prime Minister was – in his own words – 'deeply pained' by this letter – adding 'Had I known that this was to be your definite attitude I certainly would not have undertaken the Government, and if I could honourably now, I would give it up.'[19]

There were other problems even more serious than the palpable disapproval of colleagues. Rosebery did not sit in the more powerful Chamber of Parliament, and had never done so. In those days a peerage was not an insuperable obstacle to the Premiership – Salisbury still had another long Ministry ahead of him – but it was very difficult for a Liberal to manage affairs from a Chamber where his party's strength was almost negligible. About a dozen MPs, claiming the support of many more, waited on Marjoribanks to complain about the appointment. As would soon transpire, there were also temperamental, and perhaps medical, reasons why Rosebery was not the appropriate man to become Prime Minister. Not a very propitious start for a new Prime Minister who had a small and composite majority in one House, and was in a tiny minority in the other.

Rosebery's Cabinet followed as closely as possible the pattern of its predecessor. The new Prime Minister relinquished the Foreign Office to Lord Kimberley. Appointment of a peer for that post was another cause of friction among the Liberals. While the new Ministry was in process of construction, the Chief Whip's father died unexpectedly, and Marjoribanks succeeded to the peerage, as Lord Tweedmouth. He was too useful to lose, and Rosebery gave him a seat in the Cabinet, with the non-departmental post of Lord Privy Seal. The new Chief Whip, Thomas Ellis, was not included in the Cabinet. Ellis was widely regarded by those who knew him as a man of quite exceptional talents. He was the son of a tenant farmer who had been badly treated by his landlord, and was related to four farmers who had been evicted for refusing to vote for a Conservative candidate.[20]

A few days after accepting the Premiership, Rosebery made a remarkable statement on the Home Rule question. England, he declared, 'as the predominant member of the partnership of the three Kingdoms, will have to be convinced of its justice and equity'.[21] This looked very much like postponing the issue until the Greek Kalends. It caused predictable concern among the Irish and among those Liberals particularly committed to Home Rule. The Parnellites, though much the smaller group among the Nationalists, treated this announcement as effectively the end of the Liberal alliance. The main Irish body, headed by John Dillon, did not go as far as that, but was far from pleased.[22]

Perhaps Rosebery was considering another political possibility. If Home Rule was dead, or at least in suspended animation, the nominal cause for the Liberal Unionist secession had disappeared. Might the dissidents be brought back into the Party? But the theoretical possibility did not correspond with any political reality. Liberal Unionists of the Devonshire or Goschen sort were much closer in outlook to contemporary Conservatives than they were to Gladstonian Liberals. The wonder is not that they departed in 1886, but that they remained in the Liberal Party as long as they did. 'Radical Unionists' like Chamberlain had effectively cut their links with their past Liberalism. There was no fatted calf on offer. Those whom Chamberlain had once led would never forgive him. The division was irreversible.

By a curious paradox, far the most important achievement of the Rosebery government was wrought by Harcourt. The Budget which he introduced in April 1894 had already been the subject of astringent discussions between Prime Minister and Chancellor. Harcourt had to meet a jump in expenditure of a little over £4 million, well over £3 million of which was attributable to the increased naval spending. Granted his own views on that matter, he made the best of a bad job, and – like Lloyd George fifteen years later – used increased defence expenditure as excuse for a major exercise in fiscal engineering. Income Tax would be increased from 7d. to 8d. in the pound, and there would be increased taxes on alcoholic drinks; but the most remarkable change was in estate duties. These would be graduated from 1 per cent at the lowest taxable level to 8 per cent on legacies in excess of £1 million. The existing differences between duties payable on different kinds of estates, and particularly the difference between personal and real estate, would be abolished. Harcourt had originally contemplated graduating Income Tax as well, but had been dissuaded from so doing by strong opposition from the Board of Inland Revenue.

The attendant Finance Bill, predictably, passed the Commons, and – also predictably – ran into rough water in the Lords. The erstwhile Liberal Dukes of Devonshire and Argyll were among the strongest critics. In the end, however, their Lordships accepted the Bill. They may have been influenced by an ingenious argument from Salisbury – 'to reject a Finance Bill and leave the Executive Government in its place' means to create a deadlock from which there is no escape'. The effective bar to the Lords' right to alter Money Bills came from their incapacity to change the government. Maybe, however, the Upper House decided that it would be unwise to challenge the government for more cynical reasons. Rejection of a Budget would precipitate a General Election, in which public opinion might well be on the government's side. The 1894 Finance Act did not produce immediate and dramatic effects, but its long-term consequences make it one of the most important finance measures of the century. The progressive taxation which it included provided a very significant precedent. Still more important, perhaps, was the removal of special provisions for bequests of land. This would play a substantial part in the gradual erosion of great landholdings, and in undermining the economic and social position of their owners.

Soon the Prime Minister ran into trouble from various quarters. At its conference in June 1894, the National Liberal Federation had carried a resolution highly critical of the House of Lords. In October, Rosebery, addressing a large audience at Bradford, took up the theme, but pushed it further. He forecast that the next General Election 'would be fought not upon the question of Disestablishment, or Home Rule, or Local Option, but upon the question which included and represented them all, the question of the House of Lords'. Rosebery noted the absurdity that the Lords should have a vast, unassailable, Unionist majority, whatever the composition of the House of Commons might be. He described the Upper House as 'a permanent party organisation controlled for party purposes'. Rosebery, while in many ways a figure well to the 'right' of the Liberal Party, had his occasional moments of real radicalism.

The Queen reacted sharply, recording that she was 'deeply concerned at the policy', and 'still more is she pained to think that without consulting her, not to speak of not obtaining her sanction, Lord Rosebery should have announced the government's intended plan'.[23] For good measure, she wrote to Salisbury, indicating that 'she thinks a dissolution should be pressed before the agitation can be got up', asking whether the Unionist leaders 'would all agree to her insisting upon it'.[24] Rosebery had wished to begin his campaign against the Lords by getting a resolution tabled in the House of Commons. A rule existed to the effect that no resolution of such a kind could be moved in the Commons without concurrence of the sovereign, and the Queen declared that she would not consent to this without a General Election. Gladstone was not the only Liberal Prime Minister to have cause for regarding Victoria as 'the Leader of the Opposition'.

After trouble with the Queen, Rosebery might perhaps have hoped for help from his colleagues. Far from it. A Cabinet meeting in November was evidently in a critical mood. Exactly how the argument ran does not seem wholly clear, but the point appears to have been not so much that members dissented about the need to reform the Lords, but rather that they questioned the Prime Minister's strategy in setting the issue in the forefront of party policy.

There were difficulties in a different direction which are less famous today, but which could have proved very serious. Not long after his appointment, the Chief Whip Tom Ellis faced a serious threat in his native Wales. Shortly after Rosebery took office, a new statement of the government's programme gave Welsh disestablishment a lower priority than some MPs were prepared to accept. Ellis himself was under pressure to lead a national revolt on the subject. Instead he successfully put pressure on the Prime Minister to give a firm commitment on Welsh disestablishment. Soon the rebels fell out among themselves, while the government did what it could to redeem its promise to Ellis.[25]

The Queen's Speech in February 1895 promised a substantial spate of legislation, much in the spirit of the Newcastle Programme. Bills would be introduced dealing with the Anglican establishment in Wales, and (perhaps a concession to Harcourt) the liquor trade. There would be measures to promote conciliation in trade disputes, amendments to the Factory Acts, and various other reforms. Some of this legislation was soon set in motion, notably a Bill promoting the cause of Local Option, in which Harcourt was specially interested, and another for disestablishment of the Welsh Church. None of these proposals proceeded to enactment. The one major measure passed in the new Session was Harcourt's Finance Act. Unlike its counterpart of the previous year, this was more or less non-contentious and generated no excitement.

Various signs of tension appeared as the year advanced. Rosebery had long been prone to insomnia, which for most sufferers is a distressing, but tolerable, condition. In the Prime Minister's case it was so severe and protracted that at one point his physician feared a fatal termination.[26] Later in the spring, the deep-seated problem of imperial policy vexed the Cabinet. The immediate question concerned construction of a railway in Uganda Protectorate, which Rosebery and the other imperialists favoured but Harcourt and John Morley opposed.

In the middle of June, the Ministry ran into one of those bad periods which occasionally beset all governments. When the decision to continue construction of the Uganda railway was announced, Chamberlain was able to remind the House that Harcourt had once declared that the work would require forced labour, and the presence of armed men at hundred yard intervals. Harcourt blandly retorted that his views were unchanged. Soon a great wrangle began over a proposal to erect a statue of Oliver Cromwell by the Palace of Westminster. The government's Irish allies reminded the House of the atrocities with which Cromwell had been associated in their own country, and the proposal was withdrawn. This was followed by a defeat in the committee stage of the Factory Bill, and then by a small majority on an important Opposition amendment to the Welsh Church Bill.[27]

The government's *coup de grâce* was associated with one of its most popular and effective members, the Secretary for War, Henry (soon to become Sir Henry) Campbell-Bannerman. On 21 June, everything started well, for he was able to report the resignation of the army's aged and not very luminous Commander-in-Chief, the Duke of Cambridge, cousin of the Queen. This announcement was widely approved; but later in the day the Opposition moved a critical motion concerning the supply of cordite and other small arms ammunition to the army. The motion was carried against the government by a majority of seven on a snap vote in a rather thin House. Neither the Ministry nor the Conservatives appear to have anticipated that the division would prove of critical importance. Only the Liberal Unionists seem to have taken it seriously and ensured that all their MPs were either present or paired.[28]

In the ordinary way, an adverse vote of such a kind would be reversed a few days later, and would be recollected only as a minor irritation. This time, however, the government was generally demoralised, and took matters far more seriously. On the following day, 22 June, the Cabinet met to consider action. By lunch time, there were four Ministers favouring resignation, though most preferred dissolution of Parliament;[29] but in the afternoon the advocates of resignation prevailed. The same evening the Prime Minister reported the government's resignation to the Queen. Four years later, Rosebery reflected that 'there are two supreme pleasures in life. One is ideal, the other real. The ideal is when a man receives the seals of office from his Sovereign. The real pleasure comes when he hands them back.'[30] Seldom has a government perished so ignominiously. None of the three available courses, one may reflect, was a very attractive one; but the eventual decision was the worst of the three. The 'cup' was not full; the Ministry had not resigned on a great issue of principle; rather, it had confessed to the world that it was unfit, or perhaps just unwilling, to govern.

Shortly after Rosebery resigned, it was announced that Salisbury had accepted the Queen's commission to form a new government. The Ministry was different from his government of 1886–92 in one vital respect, because for the first time the Liberal Unionists as a whole were included. Like the Peelites of old, they had an influence far in excess of their numerical strength. Devonshire took the prestigious office of Lord President of the Council. Goschen was again included, but as First Lord of the Admiralty – the office he had held in the latter period of Gladstone's first government. Lord James of Hereford – formerly Sir Henry James – became Chancellor of the Duchy of Lancaster. The most remarkable Liberal Unionist appointment was Joseph Chamberlain, who became Colonial Secretary. That post did not normally rank high in the Ministerial hierarchy, but Chamberlain's willingness to accept it suggested that he had developed a very strong interest in the future, and probably the territorial expansion, of the British Empire.

An early General Election was inevitable. The first major Liberal speech of the campaign was delivered by Rosebery, who proclaimed the need to reduce the power of the House of Lords. Yet he made a strange qualification of his own authority in the matter: 'I do not speak as a leader but as an individual and as a Liberal'. Harcourt campaigned on the completely different issue of the Local Veto. John Morley concentrated on Home Rule.

In a sense, all this was consistent with the spirit of the Newcastle Programme, which Rosebery loathed,[31] but with which – for the time being – he was saddled. The Liberal Party had many policies to deal with many different problems, and a Liberal government would seek to implement those policies so far as possible. It was not unreasonable, one might say, that each candidate should give principal attention to those elements of the agreed policy which seemed most important to him, or to his constituents. But (then as now) voters seem to like a single overriding and clear-cut issue – or, at most, a small number of issues – on which they can support one side or the other. The overall effect of different Liberal leaders concentrating on different fields was a confusion of voices. 'Our weak spot is the want of one leader and one policy to conjure by', wrote Tweedmouth.[32] One may reflect that Rosebery's own selection of the House of Lords question as the one for special attention was probably the wisest choice, for most of the other issues about which different Liberals felt special enthusiasm were unlikely to pass into law while the Upper House was unreformed.

Not surprisingly, the Liberals suffered disaster. In 1892, they held 274 seats; this time they were down to 177. The Conservatives increased their representation from 268 to 340, the Liberal Unionist from 47 to 71. The combined representation of the two Irish Nationalist groups was practically unchanged: 81 seats in 1892, 82 in 1895. In 124 British seats there was no Liberal candidate; only in ten was there no Unionist. Four members of the

Rosebery Cabinet lost their seats – Sir William Harcourt, John Morley, Arnold Morley, G. J. Shaw Lefevre. The first two of these men were soon returned to Parliament for different constituencies; the others never stood again. On the face of it, the figures at the 1895 General Election were not wildly different from those of 1886, but in practice the position was far worse. In 1886, the Liberal Unionists were sitting very loose, and there appeared a serious chance that some of them, at least, would soon rejoin the main body of the party. In 1895 they were indissolubly joined to a predominantly Conservative Ministry. In 1886, the Liberal Party had a man whose leadership was universally acknowledged and a clear sense of priorities; in 1895 it had neither.

If the Liberal Party had much cause for complaint about the antics of its leading politicians, it was served better by the less conspicuous men who operated its organisation. The Chief Whip Tom Ellis not only had the modern parliamentary duties of a Whip, but still retained general charge of the party's organisation. One man who knew him well reflected, 'Had anyone asked us in those days what Welshman would one day be Prime Minister, we should have answered without a moment's hesitation, Tom'.[33] This observation refers to a time when David Lloyd George was already a well-known MP, after winning a spectacular by-election in 1890.

Francis Schnadhorst, prematurely aged and very deaf, resigned his offices in the NLF and LCA towards the end of Gladstone's last Ministry. He was succeeded in both offices by the twenty-nine year old Robert Hudson, who later acquired a great reputation as a stabilising force in the party. Propaganda was not neglected, and a major innovation was Liberal Magazine, which first appeared in 1893 and served as a constant source of information for party activists.[34] Hudson's brother-in-law Charles Geake soon became editor of the new periodical, which acquired an exceptional reputation for accuracy. Other professional workers who joined in the middle 1890s, who were to give long years of invaluable service, included R. Humphrey Davies and Jesse Herbert. Such men, and the professional organisers in other parts of the country, played a major part in saving the party from total destruction in the few years which followed.

8

Collapse and Recovery

... Linked in friendly Federation.
Freedom for our trade and nation!
That's the Liberal aspiration,
On to victory!

Election song, early twentieth century
(Tune, 'Men of Harlech')

The recent Prime Minister was relieved at the electors' verdict. 'I expected this overthrow and think it a great blessing to the Liberal Party', Rosebery wrote to Lord Ripon.[1] Lord Spencer tried to produce the cohesion which Rosebery failed to encourage, offering his own house for a meeting of the former Cabinet. Rosebery replied to the invitation to the effect that his connection with Harcourt had ended with the defeat of the Liberal government. He even sent a copy of the reply to Harcourt, who reacted 'with equal surprise and pain'.[2] 'The firm of Rosebery and Harcourt was a fraud on the public', Rosebery wrote to Gladstone.[3] 'And if cooperation between us was impracticable when we were bound by the strictest official ties and living under the same roof in Downing Street, it was obviously impossible in opposition when every man is too apt to be a law unto himself.' Nevertheless, Asquith and others did what they could to bring Rosebery and Harcourt together.[4] With the former Prime Minister in his existing frame of mind, the best and most dignified course would have been an early renunciation of the Party leadership. But Rosebery found it almost as difficult to resign as to address himself to the tasks of running the Party.

This state of affairs continued far into 1896. The crunch came over the Armenian issue, which was in some ways redolent of the 'Bulgarian horrors' of twenty years earlier, but in others very different.[5] The Armenians, most of whom lived in eastern Anatolia, were Christian subjects of the Ottoman Empire, and also extended into parts of the Russian and Persian Empires. Unlike the Christian peoples of the Balkans, they did not form a majority in any Ottoman province, but they constituted a substantial minority in six vilayets of eastern Anatolia. In 1894, and again in 1895 and 1896, there were sporadic massacres of Armenians in the Ottoman Empire. One account suggests that some 20,000 eventually perished,[6] although – at the time – there was no warning of the genocide which would take place in 1915.

The Armenian massacres did not produce a sharp split between the British parties as the Bulgarian atrocities had done twenty years earlier, for on this occasion Liberals and Conservatives alike reacted sharply against the Turks.[7] Under both the Rosebery government and its Conservative successor, various attempts were made to devise some effective scheme of intervention: possibly by the 'Concert' of European Great Powers, possibly by Britain alone. In the late summer of 1896, thousands of Armenians were massacred in the Ottoman capital itself by a mob who – in the words of the British *Chargé d'Affaires* – 'were organized and armed by the government, for the purpose of killing Armenians'. A month later Gladstone, now nearly 87 years of age, emerged from retirement to deliver to a Liverpool audience what would prove to be his last great speech, recommending a policy of intervention. Britain should break diplomatic relations with Turkey, and then issue a 'self-denying ordinance', undertaking to derive no private advantage from any action which would follow. According to recognised diplomatic practice, Britain could withdraw without loss of face in the highly unlikely event of any other European Power threatening her with war. If no such threat was made, Britain would be free to coerce Turkey: a course of action which, in Gladstone's view, would be likely to avert, rather than to cause, war.

It seemed at first that Rosebery was in general agreement with Gladstone's outlook, the difference being that Gladstone was proposing a specific policy, while Rosebery had spoken in generalities. There was, therefore, widespread astonishment when Rosebery took the Liverpool speech as occasion for resigning the Liberal leadership. The resignation, contained in a letter to the Chief Whip Tom Ellis, was published on 8 October 1896. Rosebery admitted 'some conflict of opinion with Mr Gladstone, who must necessarily always exercise a matchless authority in the Party, while scarcely from any quarter do I receive explicit support'. Yet a speech which he delivered in Edinburgh a few days later appeared fully compatible with what Gladstone had said, and furthermore the two former Prime Ministers remained on excellent personal terms, unsullied by the astonishing incident. It is easy to understand why Rosebery decided to abandon the Liberal leadership; it is much more difficult to see why Gladstone's speech should have constituted the nominal cause of the resignation. There is some irony in the fact that Harcourt had made a speech on the Armenian issue a very few days earlier, in which he took a line more or less identical with that of Rosebery.

As at the time of Gladstone's temporary withdrawal from the leadership in 1875. it was accepted that the Liberals in each House of Parliament should

choose their own leader, or chairman, but there was no immediate requirement to appoint an overall leader for the party. Indeed, there was no
acknowledged mechanism by which such an appointment could be made.
There was a brief, but scarcely serious, suggestion that Gladstone himself
might be recalled to the leadership, despite his age, and whatever precedent
might say. Soon, however, the 1875 example was followed. Harcourt, already
leader in the Commons, remained in place. In January of the following year,
the Earl of Kimberley was appointed Liberal leader in the Lords. There was
no presumption as to who should be invited to become Prime Minister in
the increasingly unlikely event of the Liberals forming a government in the
foreseeable future. Meanwhile, Rosebery was visible in the wings. An ex-
Prime Minister who is still of an age to accept political office is always a
loose cannon on the decks, much more likely to damage the vessel and
injure members of the crew than to harm the enemy.

The great question of 'imperialism' was at its zenith as the end of the century approached. Rosebery inclined towards the 'imperialist' side, Harcourt
to the other. Soon Harcourt found internal party tensions as wearing as
Rosebery had done, and began to meditate relinquishing the thankless burden of leadership in the Commons. This time he was actively associated with
John Morley, another anti-imperialist, though (such are the paradoxes of
political life) Morley had played a substantial part in the elevation of Rosebery to the Premiership in 1894. In December 1898 an exchange of
correspondence between the two men was published. Harcourt resigned
leadership of the MPs. Morley concurred in the decision, thereby effectively
relinquishing any claim he might have had on the succession.

Bad as the Liberals' position had been at the end of 1893, it was vastly
worse five years later. Gladstone, the one man whom all the party venerated,
had died earlier in 1898. Three senior members of the last Liberal Cabinet
had withdrawn noisily and polemically. There was no obvious heir to the
effective leadership. Nor was there any great question of policy which held
Liberals together and distinguished them from supporters of the Conservative (or, technically, 'Unionist') government. Liberals were visibly divided
on imperialism, the dominant issue of the day. Whether, and how far,
they were still interested in Irish Home Rule was doubtful. Their erstwhile
Irish Nationalist allies were even more noisily and savagely divided than the
Liberals themselves.

Leadership of the Liberal Party in the House of Commons looked like an
hereditas damnosa. Who might take the job? Three names were seriously
canvassed: Herbert Asquith, Sir Henry Campbell-Bannerman and Sir Henry
Fowler. The claims of Fowler were weakest of the three, and he soon
dropped from the running. Asquith might well have been chosen, but his

financial position was still not wholly secure, and he felt that it would be wiser to continue building up his practice at the Bar. Besides, the forty-six year old Asquith could afford to defer to the sixty-two year old Campbell-Bannerman, in full expectation that he would have another chance later. On top of that, Campbell-Bannerman had a special claim, for he was not seen to be closely associated with either wing of the party. And so, in February 1899, Campbell-Bannerman became leader of the Liberal MPs without a contest.

Two months later, the Liberal Party sustained a new disaster which – for once – could not be regarded as a self-inflicted wound. The Chief Whip, Tom Ellis died, still less than forty years of age. Campbell-Bannerman promptly sought the Grand Old Man's son Herbert Gladstone as successor. The younger Gladstone felt some concern about accepting the post,[8] but after receiving reassurances he complied with the request. Herbert Gladstone has been the subject of far more scholarly attention than most of his predecessors and successors.[9] This casts valuable light not only on his own influence on events, but on the workings of the Liberal machine and the functions of a Chief Whip.

Herbert Gladstone's first problem was with finances.[10] When he took over, he inherited about £15,000 from his predecessor, but there were few or no 'automatic' sources of income. Ordinary running expenses of headquarters were around £15,000 to £16,000 a year, and in the two General Elections over which he presided much greater sums were required. In the seven years during which he held office, around £272,000 passed through his hands, and he eventually left £20,000 to his successor. Many of the wealthiest subscribers had seceded with the Liberal Unionists in 1886, and the general state of the party at the turn of the century did not encourage those who remained to be particularly generous. Herbert Gladstone needed to write innumerable begging letters, and on two occasions had to borrow £5000 from his brother to make ends meet. He sternly resisted any temptation to offer the prospect of public honours to potential contributors. As for the other duties of his office, he had little to offer by way of either threats or inducements. Until 1902 or 1903, there were powerful siren voices from influential men who disputed his authority, and that of Campbell-Bannerman too. Nor was placement of candidates an easy task, particularly in the first few years. Local Liberal Associations usually expected candidates to make substantial contributions, yet mostly could offer no realistic prospect of election.

As the year 1899 advanced, imperial problems became increasingly acute, and set further strains on the Liberal Party. The arrangements which the Liberal government had concluded with the Transvaal in 1882 did not prove final. Discovery of vast mineral resources led to growing pressure for more complete imperial control. The 'Jameson Raid' of 1896 had been a spectacular, but hare-brained, attempt to stage an imperial *coup d'état* in the Transvaal, with no official British support whatever. During the course of 1899, confrontation became increasingly sharp between two very obstinate men: Sir Alfred Milner, British High Commissioner in South Africa, and Paul Kruger, President of the Transvaal. In September 1899, conflict between Britain and the Transvaal began to appear likely. John Morley adopted a very clear stand against the prospect on moral grounds:

> Such a war of the strongest Government in the world against this weak little Republic will bring you no glory. It will bring you no profit but mischief, and it will be wrong. You may make thousands of women widows and thousands of children fatherless. It will be wrong. You may add a new province to your Empire. It will still be wrong ... You may send the price of Mr Rhodes's Chartereds up to a point beyond the dream of avarice. Yes, even then it will be wrong.[11]

On 4 October, a conference of members of the old Liberal Cabinet was held. There was remarkable agreement. They concurred in the view that no *casus belli* existed; that the government should be urged to continue negotiations with the Boers, while Kruger should be urged to take a more conciliatory stand.[12] By then, however, the balance had been tilted strongly towards war. Yet British forces in South Africa were completely unprepared for such a war. 'If the Government meant war', wrote Herbert Gladstone to Campbell-Bannerman, 'or if they were persuaded that the Boers meant it from the first, they have blundered horribly in bringing it on before they were ready.'[13] Speaking at Maidstone on 6 October, Campbell-Bannerman expressed considerable alarm. 'No one could tell what we were going to war about', he declared. Even if the Boer republics were defeated, he accurately prophesied, the war would leave behind it racial enmity and anger which would take generations to overcome. The Transvaal, no doubt calculating that the British intended war, decided to gets its blow in first. On 10 October it issued an ultimatum demanding *inter alia* the withdrawal of British troops from its own borders. On the following day Transvaal forces crossed into Natal, and the Orange Free State also declared war against Britain. Soon Boer troops had occupied several important British bases.

Most Liberals considered that the government, or at least its representative in South Africa, were largely to blame for the circumstances leading to the war; but what should be the Liberal attitude, now that fighting had definitely commenced? Rosebery was clear. In a letter to the press,[14] he declared that 'the nation will, I doubt not, close its ranks' to face the Boer attack. Even Harcourt accepted the 'immediate duty to support the Executive government in maintaining the dominions of the Queen'.[15] Such views did not preclude Liberals from vigorously criticising the government for its policy in the run-up to war. An amendment to that effect was moved in the House of Commons by a Liberal MP, Philip Stanhope. Campbell-Bannerman recommended abstention; but ninety-four Liberals, or almost exactly half the full tally, supported the amendment, while fifteen voted with the government. Both sides, and the abstainers too, included celebrities. Among past or future members of Liberal Cabinets, Harcourt, Lloyd George, Augustine Birrell, Reginald McKenna, John Morley and Sir Robert Reid supported the amendment; Sir Henry Fowler, Sir Edward Grey and R. B. Haldane voted against it; while Campbell-Bannerman, Asquith and Herbert Gladstone pointedly abstained. Here was clear warning of further Liberal divisions to come.

In the next phase of the war, British troops were rushed to South Africa, and Boer forces were quickly cleared from British possessions. Now the argument for the need to defend 'the dominions of the Queen', which had persuaded even Harcourt, no longer applied. Meanwhile, the Liberal divisions in no way abated. The Imperialist section of the party began to organise, and in March 1900 set up the Imperial Liberal Council. A few months later what was effectively a motion of censure on the Colonial Secretary was moved by Sir Wilfrid Lawson. 31 Liberals, including Lloyd George and Henry Labouchere, supported him; 35, including Asquith and Campbell-Bannerman, abstained; 40, including Sir Edward Grey and R. B. Haldane, supported the government.[16] By the summer of 1900, the Boer armies had been defeated. Towards the end of May, annexation of the Orange Free State was formally proclaimed – 'almost without protest from any one at home'.[17] Annexation of the Transvaal was announced on 1 September. In truth the war was very far from over; but on 18 September the government decided to cash in on its apparent victory, and the division of the Opposition, by calling a new General Election. At the very beginning of the campaign, Herbert Gladstone publicly 'admitted the Opposition were not in a position to furnish a strong Government, and ... the result of the election ... could not be such as to put Liberals in the position of offering an alternative Government.'[18] Such words from a Chief Whip can hardly have given much encouragement to Liberals fighting in difficult constituencies, or to wealthy Liberals considering making donations to the campaign.

The contest which followed was, to all appearances, a particularly dirty one, in which every effort was made by government supporters to represent Liberals as eager supporters of the enemy. A cartoon issued from Conservative headquarters showed Kruger, encouraged by Harcourt, John Morley,

Lloyd George and Labouchere, waiting to ambush the advancing British troops, while treacherously flying the white flag of surrender. In Central Leeds, the voters were told that 'To vote for a Liberal is a vote for the Boer'. To reinforce the point of this illiterate poster, an unauthorised picture of Field-Marshal Lord Roberts accompanied the text, implying that the British Commander endorsed these political sentiments. In Newmarket, where the Liberal candidate had lost two sons in South Africa while a third was still fighting there, a crudely-drawn cartoon showed him assisting Kruger to pull down the Union Jack.[19] There were many other comparable examples. In this atmosphere, the Chief Whip had great difficulty in raising the money necessary for the campaign. In the end he was able to secure £60,000, but that only enabled him to field 397 candidates for 567 British seats.

In such a contest the Liberals were bound to be defeated; the astonishing thing is that, overall, they performed marginally better than they had done five years earlier. There is reason for thinking that the government was somewhat disappointed at the result.[20] With remarkable perception, the newly-elected young Conservative MP Winston Churchill wrote to Rosebery that 'this election, fought by the Liberals as a soldiers' battle, without plan or leaders or enthusiasm, has shown ... the strength, not the weakness, of Liberalism in the country'.[21]

Credit for the Liberals' ability to hold the line in such circumstances must be given overwhelmingly to the professional organisers and voluntary work-ers, who managed to persuade large numbers of ordinary men to continue regarding the Liberal Party as their friend. With usual reservations about classification of a few maverick MPs, the Conservatives returned 334 and the Liberal Unionists 68, against 184 Liberals, 82 Irish Nationalists and two MPs supported by the new Labour Representation Committee (LRC). There was considerable variation between swings in different constituencies; but, very broadly, the Liberals performed rather worse in the boroughs and rather better in the counties than in 1895. They also did better in Wales, though worse in Scotland. Among Liberals, the imperialist wing appears to have fared slightly better than the others. Different authorities have given markedly different numbers for the imperialists returned in 1900, ranging from 53 to 81.[22] Much, no doubt, depends on exact definitions of 'imperialists'.

There were soon many signs that the South African conflict was by no means over, and Boers maintained a very effective guerrilla struggle. The renewed ferocity of the war was reflected in an increasingly bitter internecine struggle among the Liberals. Around the turn of 1900–01, both leading Liberal newspapers changed hands. The *Daily News*, which had inclined to the imperialist side, was captured by 'pro-Boers' who included

Lloyd George; the *Daily Chronicle*, which had inclined to the anti-war side, was almost simultaneously captured by imperialists. The editors of both newspapers were duly dismissed. The British military were no longer dealing with an organised army – the sort of fighting with which they were familiar – but with men living on isolated farms who spent most of their time in peaceful activities, while they would attack the invaders when appropriate. Today such people would be called either 'freedom fighters' or 'terrorists', according to whether or not one approved of their cause. The army's counter to this development was to burn Boer farms and villages, and to set up 'concentration camps' for Boer families. The expression 'concentration camps', which was to acquire such infamy in the twentieth century, was not then linked with wilful cruelty; but as time went on it became clear that there was a great deal of suffering and death in the camps, largely through military incompetence and the rampant spread of disease.

The official Liberal Opposition, following the lead of Campbell-Bannerman and the NLF, began to argue with increasing vehemence that the overriding reason why the war was continuing at all was the current British demand for unconditional surrender from the Boers. Meanwhile, the horrors of the concentration camps began to dawn on many Liberals. In a famous, and unwontedly pungent, speech at the National Reform Union in June 1901, Campbell-Bannerman declared that the current policy involved 'methods of barbarism'. In a parliamentary debate three days later, David Lloyd George again raised the matter of the atrocious manner in which Boer civilians were being treated. Campbell-Bannerman backed the criticism; but when the House divided on the question some fifty Liberal MPs, including Asquith, Grey and Haldane, abstained from voting. Almost immediately there commenced what Henry Lucy famously described as 'war to the knife and fork' – a series of dinners in which pro- and anti-imperialist Liberal MPs publicly criticised each other's viewpoint.

Soon Rosebery returned to an active political role. On 15 December 1901, he addressed a large Liberal meeting at Chesterfield, supported by Fowler, Grey and Asquith. Choice of a town whose most famous feature is the twisted spire of its church seems curiously appropriate. The Chesterfield speech was a strange mixture. On the South African question, Rosebery did not entirely please either extreme. While criticising the 'methods of barbarism' view, he called for negotiations rather than unconditional surrender, declaring that 'I want to bind, to heal, not to keep open the mortal wound which is being caused by the war'. In an indirect knock at the Newcastle Programme, he condemned the 'fly-blown phylacteries of obsolete policies': an extraordinary metaphor, as Campbell-Bannerman observed.[23] He urged Liberals to 'clean their slates' of old policies and not to dissociate themselves from imperialism. Rosebery went on to invite Liberals to adopt the new watchword 'efficiency', which had various implications for commerce, industry, education, housing and temperance questions. The rhetoric was impressive; but what did it mean in practice?

There were mixed reactions among the 'official' Liberals. Herbert Gladstone waxed enthusiastic – 'on the whole one of the best bits of political work he has ever done'.[24] Campbell-Bannerman was a good deal more sceptical. 'All that he said about the clean slate and efficiency was an affront to Liberalism and was mere claptrap. Who is against it? This is all a *rechauffé* of Mr Sydney Webb.'[25] Speaking at Leicester in February 1902, Campbell-Bannerman repudiated the doctrine of the 'clean slate'. 'Who is to decide what is to be written on the clean slate?' he mused. A good question. He was also puzzled about the erstwhile Prime Minister's current position in relation to the Liberal Party. 'I do not know ... whether Lord Rosebery speaks to us from the interior of our tabernacle or from some vantage ground outside', he reflected. Rosebery had to answer that one, and in a letter to *The Times* replied that 'our views on the war and its methods are more or less discordant. I remain, therefore, outside his tabernacle but not, I think, in solitude'.[26]

On 3 March 1902, the Liberal Imperialists reconstituted their organisation as the Liberal League, with Rosebery as President, and Fowler, Asquith and Grey as Vice-Presidents. The Liberal League was not to be separate from the Liberal Party, but would be a pressure group within it, in support of the ideas expressed at Chesterfield. The Vice-Presidents continued to act in the House of Commons in their familiar roles as front-bench spokesmen for the Opposition. Apart from imperial questions, there was only one major issue of policy about which Chesterfield raised new uncertainty, and that was Irish Home Rule. Asquith, as usual, was the most moderate and clear-headed member of the Roseberyite section of the party, and soon declared a view from which few active Liberals would dissent: 'that the Irish problem was neither settled nor shelved, but that British opinion must be won by "step-by-step" methods'.[27]

The principal professional organiser of the Liberal League was William Allard, who had joined the League's predecessor, the Liberal Imperial Council, a few months earlier. Before that he had been regarded by the Chief Whip as 'our best man' at the party headquarters.[28] Herbert Gladstone was deeply upset, regarding the move as a kind of treachery. Rosebery still had no personal *locus standi* in the Liberal Party, and probably aspired to none. When Kimberley died in April 1902, Spencer succeeded him as Liberal leader in the Lords without Rosebery making any attempt to challenge the succession.

Much attention has been given to the struggles between Liberal titans like Rosebery, Harcourt and Campbell-Bannerman, and to the part played by rising men like Asquith, Grey and Herbert Gladstone. At the same time, however, a new factor was beginning to influence some elements of the party rank-and-file: what Herbert Samuel, the future Liberal leader, described in 1895 as 'the New Liberalism'.[29] A year or so earlier an eclectic group of young men had begun to meet in the Rainbow Tavern in Fleet Street, and became known as the Rainbow Circle. This group included Samuel, Ramsay MacDonald, future Labour Prime Minister, C. P. Trevelyan, and several active members of the Fabian Society. The link with MacDonald and Fabians was not in any sense compromising at that date: MacDonald still ranked as a Liberal, while the Fabian Society then had no party affiliation. They came to agree on such matters as the need for government intervention to promote social reform, the need for close relations between Liberalism and working-class organisations, and opposition to imperialism. The Rainbow Circle, as such, was not a particularly important body; but it was symptomatic of a much wider attitude to policies which the Liberal government adopted from 1906 onwards.

But in the early spring of 1902, the Liberals appeared to be making no headway at all. The only by-election change since the General Election had been a Liberal defeat in North East Lanarkshire, a constituency which they had held since 1885. The Liberal League posed a challenge to the whole purpose and structure of the party. And then, with astonishing speed, everything changed. The Boer War, which had been so divisive, ended in May 1902. Almost at the same moment, a major new issue arose on which nearly all Liberals were united. A. J. Balfour introduced a Bill dealing with education in England and Wales. The Bill proposed to bring primary, secondary and technical education under a single authority, which would normally be the local County or County Borough Council. The sticking point for nonconformists was that denominational schools – usually, but not invariably, belonging to the Church of England – would be largely supported from local rates. Doubts about this aspect of Balfour's Bill were shared by many of the Liberal Unionists. On the Second Reading, three of them, and even two Conservatives, went to the point of voting against the Bill. The only notable Liberal recalcitrant was R. B. Haldane, who abstained. As in 1870, both sides in the controversy seemed far more concerned about denominational aspects than about the likely effects of the measure on secular education.

In July 1902, Salisbury resigned the premiership, which devolved on his nephew Arthur Balfour. At the same time Sir Michael Hicks Beach, the Chancellor of the Exchequer, retired, and was succeeded by C. T. Ritchie, an eager Free Trader. Then, towards the end of the year, Chamberlain departed for a lengthy on-the-spot study of the situation in South Africa: a tour that would have momentous consequences. The 1903 Budget was prepared by Ritchie while Chamberlain was still out of the country, and included abolition of the small corn duty which had been introduced in the previous year.

In May 1903, not long after his return from South Africa, Chamberlain suddenly announced his conversion to imperial preference, and also his willingness to apply tariffs in certain other circumstances. Chamberlain had given earlier hints on the subject, and some of his Unionist colleagues were known to be Protectionists; but this was the first clear stand by a major political figure.[30] There followed intense discussions on the whole question of Free Trade versus Protection in all political circles, not least in the Cabinet itself.

In September 1903, three strong Free Traders in the Cabinet resigned. Ritchie, who was one of them, had been effectively dismissed. At the other end of the controversy, Joseph Chamberlain resigned as well, but his son Austen succeeded Ritchie at the Exchequer. Soon a fourth Free Trade minister, the venerable Duke of Devonshire, also resigned. There was widespread suspicion that Balfour, who tended to take a rather laid-back view of the whole fiscal controversy and steered away from firm commitment either way, was not sorry to lose the leading enthusiasts on both sides. For the remainder of his Ministry, he ensured that no serious measures were taken which would firmly commit the government either way. Meanwhile, Joseph Chamberlain commenced a nationwide campaign in favour of Protection and Imperial Preference, calling his programme 'Tariff Reform': a term which hitherto had been used in almost exactly the opposite sense.

A considerable number of MPs on the government side, both Conservatives and Liberal Unionists, were Free Traders. Classification is sometimes difficulty, but at various dates no fewer than 83 Unionist Free Trader MPs were listed: 60 Conservatives and 23 Liberal Unionists.[31] Eleven, including Winston Churchill, were so deeply alienated from the Tariff Reformers that they migrated to the Liberal side. Against these new Liberal recruits, one obscure backbencher, Sir Edward Reed of Cardiff, crossed the floor in the opposite direction. In the great public debate, the Liberals were nearly unanimous in their eager support for Free Trade – members of the Liberal League (including Rosebery), as much as Campbell-Bannerman and his closest adherents. Asquith soon acquired a great reputation as the most effective and penetrating critic of Chamberlain's policies.

By-elections provide some indication of the current of public opinion. In 1902 the Liberals gained three seats from the Unionists, but also lost one to the Unionists and one to the Labour Representation Committee (LRC). In

1903 there were four Liberal gains from Unionists, plus one LRC gain from a Unionist and another from a Liberal. In 1904, by which time the 'Tariff Reform' debate was in full swing, the Liberals took seven Unionist seats. In 1905 a further seven Unionist seats fell to Liberals. Men like the Duke of Devonshire, Lord James of Hereford, and Goschen – now a Viscount – who had been Liberals long ago, but of whom most contemporary Liberals had long despaired, took a strong stand on the Free Trade side.

Although the tide was running strongly for the Liberals, there was no guarantee that the next government would be Liberal, still less that the Liberals would obtain an adequate majority. They certainly had no wish to be dependent on the Irish Party for support, and did not make much effort to woo Irish Nationalist opinion. Any attempt to do so would probably damage their position with the British electorate. There were two very different directions in which they might look for assistance: the Unionist Free Traders and 'Labour'.

If any arrangement was made with Unionist Free Traders, this was most likely to be some kind of 'non-aggression pact', by which Liberals left their constituencies uncontested – just as the Conservatives had done with the Liberal Unionists in 1886. There were various difficulties here. In a large proportion of those cases, Liberal candidates were already in the field, and it would be very difficult to persuade them to withdraw now that many of them saw a good chance of winning. There were other problems too. Radical Liberals, or Liberals who were staunch supporters of particular causes like Home Rule, or undenominational education, or temperance, or radical land reform. would be strongly averse to the idea of giving a free run to Unionists who, on almost every issue but Free Trade, were sworn enemies.[32] Some of the Unionist Free Traders, like Lord Hugh Cecil, stood very much to the 'right' of the Conservative Party. No doubt many Unionist Free Traders had their own reservations about any deal with Liberals.

'Labour' was a different matter; and it is significant to note that negotiations with 'Labour' were already well advanced before the Tariff Reform question was raised in a clear form.[33] The nineteenth century Lib-Labs had never been very numerous – around a dozen at the most at any one time – although their influence was considerably greater than such numbers suggest. In the 1890s there had been several major strikes, and also a number of court cases which showed that the legal rights of Trade Unions were substantially less than most people had long believed to be the case. Remedial legislation was required.[34] There was everything to be said for the election of many more working men to Parliament, where they would be able to speak on such matters with authority.

In 1899, the Trade Union Congress passed a resolution calling for the establishment of a body which would secure more 'Labour' MPs. In pursuance of this resolution, a meeting was called in London early in 1900, at which the Labour Representation Committee was formed. The LRC was a loose alliance of some (though by no means all) Trade Unions and some Socialist Societies. The immediate objective was – as the TUC had suggested – to secure the election of more working-class MPs, without necessary reference to whether they were Liberals, Conservatives, Socialists or none of those things.

At the General Election of 1900, two candidates who had been supported by the LRC were elected, both in two-member constituencies, and both in exceptional circumstances. In Merthyr Tydfil, the two sitting Liberal MPs, D. A. Thomas and Pritchard Morgan, held opposing views of the Boer War. Thomas, a wealthy and popular coalowner, opposed the war; Morgan supported it. Keir Hardie appeared late in the campaign as an anti-war LRC candidate. Thomas urged his own supporters to give their second vote to Hardie, and the two were elected. In Derby, two Conservative MPs had been elected in 1895. This time, the local Liberals put forward Sir Thomas Roe, who had sat there previously, and Richard Bell, a lifelong Liberal and a local railway Trade Union official. His Trade Union was only prepared to support Bell if he stood under the LRC banner. The Liberals accepted this, and he was elected along with Roe: an unusual double victory in the dire circumstances of 1900. There was no reason, one might say, why a thoroughgoing Liberal was compromising his principles by supporting either Hardie or Bell.

After the 1900 General Election, a series of by-elections gave the LRC a much firmer foothold in the House of Commons. In 1902, the Liberal MP for Clitheroe, Lancashire, was elevated to the peerage, and a vacancy arose.[35] Clitheroe had a truly representative Liberal 'Six Hundred'. The LRC announced that it would be prepared to support a local Trade Union official, David Shackleton, if he stood as an LRC candidate, but not if he stood as a 'Lib-Lab'. Representatives of the Liberal Association met Campbell-Bannerman and Herbert Gladstone in London, and were urged to support Shackleton. They submitted this proposal to the 'Six Hundred', but it was rejected by an overwhelming majority. With great speed, and before the Clitheroe Liberals had time to find a candidate of their own, one of the Liberal Whips moved the by-election writ. The Conservatives also had not yet chosen a candidate, and Shackleton was returned unopposed. Not surprisingly, local Liberal morale was shattered, and the Liberals never represented Clitheroe thereafter. The thinking behind this almost incredible behaviour by the Liberal officials appears to have been the view that self-abnegation would in some way encourage goodwill in the LRC.

Soon any possible doubt about the political stand of the LRC was removed. In February 1903, a resolution was carried at its conference, requiring candidates and MPs 'to abstain strictly from identifying them-selves with ... any section of the Liberal or Conservative Parties'. As MPs were at the time unpaid, a parliamentary fund was set up by the LRC, out of which its MPs would receive a small salary. In spite of the unambiguous declaration of independence, Liberal headquarters continued to woo the LRC. Jesse Herbert, political secretary to Herbert Gladstone, played a major part in the arrangements which followed. To set Herbert's position in con-text, it should be noted that George Cadbury, the Quaker philanthropist and proprietor of the *Daily News*, was paying half of his salary, and also con-tributing to the LRC. At Cadbury's prompting, Herbert met Ramsay MacDonald, who by this time had abandoned his earlier Liberal links and had become secretary of the LRC. There was something cloak-and-dagger about the meeting. MacDonald urged that it should be 'on neutral ground and presumably to avoid the comments of those members of his party who are ill-disposed towards the Liberal Party'.[36] MacDonald assured Herbert that the LRC would have a fighting fund of £120,000 if the General Election were postponed for eighteen months. Herbert accepted this figure with-out question, and also took at face value the assertion that the LRC could influence the votes of around a million men.

After further discussions, in which the LRC's Chairman Keir Hardie was also involved, lists of constituencies were prepared by the LRC. Some were single-member constituencies (most, but not quite all, Unionist), in which it was proposed that the Liberals should not oppose the LRC; others were two-Member constituencies in which the two parties should run in double harness. Supporters contended that the scheme would benefit both sides. Some Unionist seats would be taken by the LRC; the Liberals would gain goodwill from LRC supporters elsewhere; and the LRC would acquire an increased foothold in Parliament. Herbert Gladstone does not seem to have queried the validity of this advice. In the end, the general principle of Lib-erals allowing the LRC a considerable number of unopposed returns was accepted, although neither Liberal nor LRC officials could be certain that they would be able to restrain local organisations eager for a contest. It was a fair guess that if the arrangement had been given publicity there would have been furious reactions in both quarters. In Scotland, a body known as the Scottish Workers' Representation Committee paralleled the LRC, but no corresponding pact was made with the Liberals there.

The outline of the 'Herbert Gladstone-MacDonald Pact' was drawn up in the course of 1903. While this was happening, two more critical by-elections took place. Woolwich was a London Conservative seat, whose Liberal

Association was more or less defunct. The LRC advanced a candidate, Will Crooks. The Liberals left the constituency unfought. Many Liberals actively supported Crooks, who (rather unexpectedly) was comfortably victorious.

The situation in Barnard Castle, County Durham, was more complex. Early in 1903, Sir Joseph Pease, the Liberal MP, announced that he would not contest the constituency again. The Liberals found a prospective candidate, Hubert Beaumont, who had already fought twice as a Liberal in other constituencies. In the early summer Pease died, and the LRC advanced Arthur Henderson, who had long been Pease's agent, as their candidate. The Conservatives put forward a candidate of their own. Unsuccessful attempts were made by Liberal headquarters to persuade Beaumont to withdraw. Liberal sympathies were deeply divided, some influential men supporting Beaumont and others Henderson. When the constituency polled in July, Henderson was elected with a tiny majority over the Conservative, with Beaumont third. A letter from Samuel Storey, a former Liberal MP, appeared in the *Daily News* in the course of the Barnard Castle contest, deploring 'the process by which some of the Liberal leaders and Whips are nursing into life a serpent which will sting their Party to death'.[37] That forecast would very nearly be fulfilled.

It was undeniable that working people were grossly under-represented in Parliament at the turn of the century, and that Liberal organisers had not exerted themselves sufficiently strongly in the past to persuade local associations to adopt working-class candidates. But it was fatal to foster a separate organisation. Even if Storey's baleful forecast was not fulfilled, it was certain that encouragement of the LRC would result in some radicals operating in one camp and others in the other, which could not fail to weaken their collective effect, to the benefit of their opponents. The older Gladstone had played a greater part than any other man in rallying working people to the Liberal Party. It is a strange paradox that his son, loyal in many ways to his father's principles and in most respects a hard-working and efficient Chief Whip, should have played a major part in demolishing that work.

In 1905 the question of land reform was becoming increasingly important
in politics. Cartoon by 'F.C.G.' (Francis Carruthers-Gould)
in the *Westminster Gazette*.

9

Triumph and After

Lugeamus igitur
'Unionists' qui sumus!
Nostrae heus! auctoritatis
Nostrae et majoritatis
Finis ecce – Fumus! ...

Let us therefore weep/ who are Unionists!/ Hark! for of our authority/
and of our majority/ behold the end – smoke! ...

Unionist parody on *Gaudeamus igitur*, February 1906[1]

From 1903 onwards, Liberals were benefiting enormously from the great
debate between Free Traders and Tariff Reformers. At a time when many
working-class budgets were close to the margin of subsistence, the increase
in food prices which would necessarily result from a Protectionist policy was
likely to result in real hunger. 'Labour' – whether the Lib-Labs or the LRC
– was as keen on Free Trade as were the mainstream Liberals. The Unionists were deeply split. Among their MPs were scores of enthusiasts on each
side of the controversy. In such circumstances, the Liberals could hardly fail
to make headway.

Although it was becoming increasingly likely that a Liberal Government
would soon take office, it was for a long time uncertain who would be the
Prime Minister. Campbell-Bannerman who led in the Commons and Earl
Spencer who led in the Lords were both widely considered. Then, in
October 1905, Spencer suffered a disabling stroke.

In the course of the following month, people active in politics were coming to the conclusion that Balfour would very soon resign or dissolve
Parliament, in either event precipitating an early General Election. There
was considerable discussion in high Liberal circles as to whether the Liberals
ought to accept office in the first event, or whether they should act as the
Conservatives had done under Disraeli's guidance in 1873, and refuse,
thereby forcing an unwilling and unpopular administration to continue in
office. Rosebery and Morley inclined to the first view, Herbert Gladstone,
Asquith and Grey to the second.[2]

The best hope of the Conservative government was that the Liberals

would start some great dispute among themselves which would check their
progress, as they had so often done in the past. Balfour therefore was disposed to bide his time. At last it looked as if the Prime Minister's patience
might be rewarded. On 23 November 1905, Campbell-Bannerman made a
speech in his own constituency of Stirling, in which he echoed the 'step-by-
step' view of Irish Home Rule to which the party seemed now committed.
At that moment, Rosebery was engaged on a speaking tour in Cornwall. On
the day after the Stirling speech he expressed misgivings at Campbell-Bannerman's statement in a speech at Truro. The following night, at Bodmin,
he declared 'emphatically and explicitly and once and for all that I cannot
serve under that banner'.

This seemed to the Prime Minister as good a moment as any to leave
office. But Unionists, like Liberals, were deeply divided over tactics, and the
Cabinet could not reach anything like a unanimous decision whether to
resign or not. Eventually Balfour's view prevailed.[3] On 4 December, he tendered his resignation. The King promptly invited Campbell-Bannerman
to form a government. Like Balfour, he made up his party's mind for it,
accepting office on the following day.

By this time, Liberal patience with Lord Rosebery was wearing very thin,
and his Cornish speeches did him no good with anybody, least of all his
Liberal League followers, who were angered at his evident willingness gra-
tuitously to open old wounds.[4] But although Rosebery had made it clear that
he would have no place in a Campbell-Bannerman government, to his credit
he did not allow his differences from others in the party to hamper his general support for the new administration, and he made it clear that he wished
it success at the forthcoming General Election. To give his government cred-
ibility, Campbell-Bannerman sought to include the widest possible range of
party members.

Sir William Harcourt, the other great figure from the Gladstonian past,
had died in the previous year. The Prime Minister's biggest problem was the
so-called 'Relugas Compact', an arrangement which had been concluded in
September between Asquith, Grey and Haldane.[5] The arrangement may be
regarded, according to taste, as a dark conspiracy, or as a reasonable measure of mutual self-defence between three Liberal Imperialist friends. Under
the compact, the three men agreed not to accept office under Campbell-
Bannerman unless he consented to withdraw to the Lords. If he did so, then
Asquith was to become Chancellor of the Exchequer and leader of the Commons, Grey would be either Foreign Secretary or Colonial Secretary, while
Haldane would become Lord Chancellor. Significantly, although the three
men were all Vice-Presidents of the Liberal League, Rosebery was not
included in the arrangements.

Of the Relugas trio, Asquith was in far the strongest position. He was the only one who had previously held Cabinet office; and in the last ten years had won golden opinions all round, not least for the skill with which he trounced Chamberlain's Tariff Reform campaign. Neither Grey nor Haldane had many enthusiastic followers, but it would be exceedingly difficult to construct a credible Liberal Government without Asquith. On 13 November – that is, more than a week before the Stirling speech – Campbell-Bannerman had met Asquith and offered him the Exchequer in a future Liberal Government. Asquith tacitly accepted. He argued in favour of the claims of Grey and Haldane, but did not present any kind of ultimatum, nor did he urge strongly the idea of Campbell-Bannerman going to the Lords.

When Campbell-Bannerman began to construct his government, immediate action was necessary under the Relugas arrangements. At that point Asquith did urge the Prime Minister to go to the Lords. There was a strong argument for this, not least because of Campbell-Bannerman's frail health, but he eventually refused – encouraged in that stand, it was said, by his wife. Asquith again did not press an ultimatum, but accepted the Exchequer. The Lord Chancellorship was already bespoke for the 'pro-Boer' Sir Robert Reid (who became Lord Loreburn), and so Haldane had to content himself with Campbell-Bannerman's old job of Secretary for War. Grey was offered the Foreign Office, though Campbell-Bannerman's first choice for the post had been Lord Cromer. At first Grey baulked; but, after much pressure from his friends, he accepted.

Had Asquith let his friends down? The 'Relugas Compact' had been concluded on the unspoken assumption that formation of a Liberal Government would follow, and not precede, a General Election. A certain amount of visible jockeying among the Liberals might then be permissible; but, as the new government was constituted before the election, it was essential that the appearance of unity should be maintained. In view of Campbell-Bannerman's obduracy, this necessitated breaking the Relugas arrangement. Neither Grey nor Haldane seems to have entertained serious resentment about Asquith's behaviour.

Other appointments were fairly straightforward. John Morley became Secretary of State for India and Herbert Gladstone Home Secretary. James Bryce, an undoubted Home Ruler, but also a man willing to approach such matters on a step-by-step basis, became Chief Secretary for Ireland. Among the high-sounding, but more or less non-departmental, offices usually listed high among Cabinet appointments, Lord Rosebery's son-in-law, Lord Crewe, became Lord President of the Council, while the veteran Marquis of Ripon, who succeeded Spencer as Liberal leader in the Lords, was made Lord Privy Seal. At a very different place in the social scale was John Burns of Battersea, leader of a famous dockers' strike of 1889. Burns, a 'Lib-Lab' and a proclaimed Socialist, became President of the Local Government Board. David Lloyd George entered office for the first time, joining the Cabinet as President of the Board of Trade. The recent convert Winston Churchill became a junior Minister. Apart from Rosebery, every major politician who could lay some claim to being a Liberal *sans phrase* was incorporated in the government.

Shortly before the end of 1905, Campbell-Bannerman delivered a speech aimed essentially at party enthusiasts, which might be regarded as a sort of oral manifesto. This contained reference to most of the ideas which were generally endorsed by Liberals of the time, much in the spirit of the New-castle Programme, with adjustments for changed times. The new Prime Minister called for arbitration in international disputes; for Ireland to receive control of her domestic affairs; for site value rating; for something like 'local option' with the sale of alcoholic drink; for educational reform; for new Trade Union legislation; and for measures to mitigate unemployment. Campbell-Bannerman also raised another important question. In the aftermath of the South African war, a great many Chinese labourers had been recruited to work in in the Transvaal mines, in conditions uncomfortably close to slavery. 14,000 new licences for recruitment of 'coolies' had been issued just before the change of government.[6] The Prime Minister promised to end the existing state of affairs as quickly as possible.

A General Election was bound to follow the change of government, and at the beginning of 1906 the campaign began in earnest. The question of Free Trade versus Tariff Reform dominated the contest.[7] 'Chinese slavery' occupied a significant, but secondary, place. A famous Liberal poster showed a hideous and anguished Chinese face, without any words at all. No doubt many Liberal enthusiasts gave eager support to the Newcastle Programme, some to Rosebery's 'Liberal Imperialism' and some to the social reform ideas of the 'New Liberalism'; but what was most likely to win new votes was none of those things, but rather Free Trade, stated in terms which would have warmed the heart of Cobden.

At an early point in the campaign, the Unionist Free Traders published a letter from the Duke of Devonshire, in which his Grace proclaimed the dangers of Tariff Reform, while acknowledging that the new government was unlikely to introduce Home Rule in the foreseeable future. This seemed to carry a broad hint that Unionist Free Traders, faced with a conflict between a Chamberlainite Tariff Reformer and a Liberal, might reasonably vote for the latter. This time, the Liberals had little difficulty in finding either money or candidates. £100,000 was raised, and 518 Liberal candidates were fielded.[8] In every British constituency there was a Free Trader of one kind or another.

The result of the election was a huge swing to the Liberals, who secured a very comfortable majority over all other parties combined. As usual there were a few MPs who defied easy classification, but roughly there were 376 Liberals of the traditional type and 24 Lib-Labs. The Unionists held 158 seats. The Irish Nationalists broke more or less even, with 83, a few of which belonged to a splinter group headed by William O'Brien. The LRC won 29 seats, the great majority of these attributable to the workings of the Herbert Gladstone – MacDonald Pact. When nearly all of the LRC victories had been registered, Herbert Gladstone told Campbell-Bannerman that all but two had received Liberal support.[9]

There were spectacular casualties, including six members of the old Cabinet. Balfour was heavily defeated in Manchester East, which he had held since the constituency was created in 1885. Soon, however, he was able to return to Parliament through a by-election in the City of London. Some areas of the country were particularly savage in their treatment of Unionists. They did not retain a single seat in Wales, and only ten of the seventy seats in Scotland. The only town whose results wholly pleased them was Birmingham, where they still held all seven seats. Liverpool, where they retained six seats out of nine, and Sheffield, with three out of five, were the only other large towns where they still predominated. In London, where the Conservatives had been dominant since 1885, they were now down to nineteen seats out of 61. Not a single Unionist seat remained in Manchester, Leeds or Bradford, and only one in Bristol.

The General Election produced a great change in the character of the Unionist Party. In the days of the Balfour Government, Unionist Free Traders and Tariff Reformers had been represented in comparable numbers. In 1906, there were only about 23 Unionist Free Traders; some writers suggest lower figures.[10] Against the Unionist Free Traders could be set a little over a hundred Tariff Reformers, and around 36 'Balfourites' who sat on the fence.

Predictably, Chamberlain set great pressure on Balfour to move decisively towards Tariff Reform. On 14 February, the 'Valentine Letters' were published, in which Balfour seemed to accede. The prospect of Balfour and Chamberlain providing joint leadership for the Unionists in the direction of Tariff Reform was suddenly destroyed a few months later. Early in July, Chamberlain's seventieth birthday was the subject of great celebrations in Birmingham. A few days later he had a severe stroke and was never again able to take much part in politics. But the legacy remained. Just as the Liberals had long been compelled to accept responsibility for Home Rule without the guidance of Gladstone who had inspired and led them, so now were the Unionists compelled to defend Tariff Reform without Chamberlain.

In the immediate aftermath of the election, several other changes took place. By far the most important of these was the decision of the 29 LRC members, plus one 'Lib-Lab' who had been omitted from the LRC list for technical reasons, to constitute themselves the Labour Party, with its own whips. Other changes concerned the party affiliations of two Unionist Free Traders, both of whom had been elected in curious circumstances. Robert Glendinning of Antrim North stood as a Liberal Unionist and defeated the sitting Conservative MP in a straight fight: a most unusual kind of contest. He joined the Liberals shortly after the election. More acrimony centred on Austin Taylor, who had been returned as Conservative MP for the East Tox-teth division of Liverpool at a by-election in 1902, some time before the Tariff Reform controversy began. His Free Trade views were well known, and the local Conservative Association had refused to support him, though it did not put up a candidate against him. Taylor's nomination papers were signed by Liberals as well as Conservatives, and he was returned unopposed. A week after the 'Valentine Letters' were published, he joined the Liberals.[11]

Some elements of the programme indicted at the General Election could take effect without new legislation. Free Trade could be preserved by simply avoiding enactment of protective duties. Asquith's budget of 1906, and sub-sequent finance Bills, demonstrated that necessary public revenue could be raised successfully in that manner. The 'Chinese slavery' question proved more difficult, because labourers' indentures could not be cancelled without breach of contract. Nevertheless, such contracts were not renewed, and in 1910 the last Chinese labourers left the Rand.

The legacy of the South African war presented further difficulties. Early in February 1906, the former Boer General Jan Smuts met several members of the Government, including Campbell-Bannerman, whom he convinced that it was necessary to take immediate steps to grant self-government to the Transvaal. The Prime Minister, who was already demonstrating consider-able (and rather unexpected) powers of leadership, persuaded the Cabinet to comply as soon as possible.[12] There followed furious parliamentary debates, but in December 1906 a new constitution was put into effect under Letters Patent, thereby avoiding any direct appeal to Parliament which might risk veto by the House of Lords. In June 1907 similar provisions were made for the Orange River Colony, formerly the Orange Free State.[13] This was by no means the end of the story of South Africa under the Liberals, but it was an important start, and did not produce any serious split between members of the party who had taken radically different views of South African affairs a few years earlier.

Where legislation was necessary to give effect to Liberal policies, the posi-tion was very different. The Unionist minority in the Commons could easily be overridden, but the House of Lords, with its immense Unionist majority, proceeded to act in a thoroughly partisan manner. Its behaviour, however, was marked by considerable subtlety. The fate of different Government Bills submitted to Parliament in 1906 brought that point out with great clarity. Reforming legislation which did not cut deeply across those vested interests that were strongly represented in the Lords, most particularly landed interests, was allowed a fairly easy passage. Thus, Lloyd George's Merchant Shipping Bill of 1906 was allowed to proceed without gratuitous obstruction.

When a Government Bill ran palpably against the wishes of the House of Lords, their Lordships weighed carefully the likely effects of obstruction on the general interests of the Conservative Party. This point is well illustrated by attitudes adopted to some important Bills introduced by the government in 1906. The Education Bill of 1906 was designed to remedy nonconformist objections to the Act of 1902, which had been voiced strongly in the intervening period, and for which the government could reasonably claim an electoral 'mandate'. The Lords proposed wrecking amendments. In the Prime Minister's judgement, the Bill 'has been not only altered but reversed in several of its main principles'.[14] An attempt was made to secure a compromise, but this failed and the government abandoned the Bill. No doubt that Lords had calculated that people who objected to the support of Anglican teaching from public funds had nearly all voted Liberal, and would continue to do so whatever happened; therefore, that there were no Conservative votes to be lost by opposing the Education Bill.

Another similar instance was the Scottish Land Values Bill of 1906. In Scotland, interest in land reform was even stronger than in England, and the overwhelming majority of Scottish MPs in the new Parliament had given public support to the idea of the taxation of land values. This could be applied to Scotland without necessary application to England as well, for Scottish land law was markedly different from English, and the revenues from such a tax might well be applied, at least in the first instance, for purposes of local rather than central government. An essential preliminary to land value taxation must be valuation. As the intended taxation was anathema to the landed interests which dominated the House of Lords, the government's Bill of 1906 was rejected, and a similar Bill in the following year was wrecked. The Lords' thinking was similar to their thinking about the Education Bill. No doubt supporters of the taxation of land values would be angered; but such people did not vote Conservative, and so no harm would be done to Conservative interests.

These cases must be contrasted with the Lords' behaviour towards the Trade Disputes Bill of 1906. Uncertainties about Trade Union law had led to establishment of a Royal Commission during the lifetime of the previous government, and the commission reported while the General Election was in progress. No party, therefore, had time to devise a fully-considered policy for submission to the electors. The Liberal government prepared a Bill on the general lines of the commission's recommendations, though some members evidently preferred more drastic measures.[15] The government indicated its willingness to consider changes. One of the Labour Party MPs proposed a different measure, which included exemption of Trade Unions from actions in tort. The Prime Minister gave his personal support to the new proposal, which was eventually carried by the Commons. It was then remitted to the Lords. There was no sort of electoral 'mandate' for such a change, and it must have been clear to careful observers that the government was itself deeply divided. No doubt many peers viewed the Bill with considerable distaste for various reasons. Yet rejection would be sure to antagonise Trade Unionists, and some Trade Unionists still voted Conservative. Thus the interest of the Conservative Party prescribed that the Bill should not be opposed, and the Lords acted accordingly.

If they could keep their heads, and only frustrate the government's wishes on issues where no harm would be done to Conservative interests, the Lords could continue indefinitely to make life difficult for a Liberal administration. George Whiteley, who had succeeded Herbert Gladstone as Chief Whip, was disposed to accept the challenge, contending that 'the whole question of our relations with the House of Lords will have to be immediately tackled' – otherwise 'we shall rapidly lose ground and our hold upon the country'.[16]

Liberal morale must have been low at the end of 1906. The government had done much for the Transvaal, but – then as now – most voters' interests centred on domestic matters. Liberals accepted the Trade Disputes Act, but with less than universal enthusiasm. The Merchant Shipping Act was important, but could scarcely stir the Liberals to their depths. Loss of the Education Bill was a deep disappointment for nonconformists. Yet the Unionists were in no better position. They might or might not now believe in 'Tariff Reform', but – with gloomy recollections of the General Election, and without Joseph Chamberlain to inspire them – they could hardly be expected to take up the question very eagerly.

The year 1907 was a mixed one for the Liberal government. A renewed attempt to carry an Education Bill ended in failure, but there were some legislative achievements. Haldane had little difficulty with a measure establishing the Territorial Army. Lloyd George carried an important Patents Bill. Always the man to interpret the scope of his office in the broadest possible way, he also scored a palpable success in ending a railway dispute, thereby setting an important precedent for government intervention in industrial questions. The only other important government measure was a Small-holdings and Allotments Act. Various Bills which excited deeper concern – including government Bills dealing with Scottish land questions, Irish devolution and licensing – fell by the wayside for various reasons. Not least of the problems for party managers was the difficulty of fitting the various Bills they wished to carry into the parliamentary timetable, especially without invoking the highly unpopular expedient of an autumn session of Parliament.[17]

The record of by-elections in 1907 was poor. In March, the Liberals lost Brigg. Early in July they lost Jarrow to Labour and a fortnight later they lost Colne Valley to an independent Socialist. In both cases they could console themselves with the argument that intervention of extra candidates had complicated matters, and both constituencies were in fact recaptured by Liberals at the next General Election. But it would be difficult to deny that the various by-election defeats signalled widespread disappointment at the government's limited record of achievements to date. The disparate character of the victors, however, suggested that there was a general feeling of dissatisfaction rather than a clear conviction that some particular alternative policy was required.

Private sorrow may have had a substantial and adverse effect on the Prime Minister's conduct of affairs. His wife, to whom he was deeply attached, had been in poor health for a number of years. In the spring of 1906 her condition deteriorated, and until her death in August Campbell-Bannerman was effectively acting as her nurse. Thereafter, he probably had little real zest for life, though he followed to the best of his ability the duties of his office. The Prime Minister's own health, not robust for many years, began to decline. In February 1908 he developed influenza – or was it a heart seizure, or both? Thereafter his health never fully recovered, and soon commentators were discussing the likely successor. Towards the end of March, the Prime Minister himself realised that he could not live much longer, and he told Asquith as much. The King had been anxious to avoid an immediate change of Prime Minister, and Campbell-Bannerman probably hoped to die in office, but on 3 April he resigned, whereafter he lingered for rather less than three more weeks.

Various names of possible successors were bandied around in the last period of Campbell-Bannerman's premiership, but there was never real doubt on the subject. When the King accepted Campbell-Bannerman's resignation, he summoned Asquith as the natural successor. Nobody questioned the wisdom of the decision, though some felt uneasy at the appointment of a former Liberal Imperialist. When he came to form a government, Asquith made as few changes as possible. His old post of

Chancellor of the Exchequer went to Lloyd George, whose record of achievement was perhaps the most spectacular of all the Ministers to date. In time, a splendid and highly productive partnership would develop between the two men. Lloyd George would supply imagination and vision in exceptional measure. Asquith would provide solid chairmanship of the Cabinet which in practice ensured that the Chancellor got what he wanted more often than not, without ruffling too many Liberal feathers in the process. Lloyd George's replacement at the Board of Trade was Winston Churchill, who entered the Cabinet for the first time.

The most impressive government achievement in the first year of Asquith's Ministry was the introduction of Old Age Pensions. The idea had been bruited long before by various people, particularly Joseph Chamberlain. As Lloyd George noted, however, every shell exploded in the Boer War was a lost Old Age Pension, and thereafter the matter was pushed aside while politicians and public attended to other business. The Liberal government eventually set up a committee to examine the question, and in May 1908 the Cabinet accepted its essential proposals.[18] Asquith told the King, accurately enough, that the proposals were 'of a modest and tentative character'. People over seventy whose income over the previous year had been less than £26, and who were not aliens, lunatics, paupers or criminals, would be entitled to a pension of five shillings a week, with reductions for married couples. In 1908 money values, the new pension probably represented something like subsistence for an elderly person. The pension, which would be of a non-contributory character, was not expected to impose an annual burden in excess of £6.5 million. It would not come into effect before the commencement of 1909, and so this required only about £1.5 million for the current financial year, against an estimated revenue surplus of £4 million.

The government's proposals were soon set out in a Bill which, predictably, attracted criticisms from various sides during its passage through the House of Commons, and some of its provisions were modified in the process. Few cared to challenge the principle of the Bill, and the most interesting division was on the Third Reading. The official Unionist line was to abstain, but twelve Unionists, including Jesse Collings, voted with the Government. Twelve MPs voted against it: eleven Unionists and the maverick Liberal Harold Cox, far more Cobdenite than Cobden, who resisted it on extreme Free Trade grounds. The Bill went to the Lords, where further amendments were proposed. Lord Rosebery expressed 'not hostility to the measure, but deep, solemn disquietude', describing it as 'Socialism pure and simple', and suspecting that it was 'dealing a blow to the Empire which may be almost mortal'.[19] The Lords proposed amendments, but these were rejected by the Commons. Thereupon the Lords – consistent with their established strategy – allowed the Bill to pass without further trouble. Thus was enacted the first instalment of the modern Welfare State. The original Bill had been drafted by Asquith, but it was Lloyd George who piloted it through the Commons, and whom the public perceived as its true author. This added greatly to his prestige. Right down to the 1950s, there were parts of the country where a person about to draw his pension would declare that he would be collecting 'my Lloyd George'. Some simple people, it is said, were unable to credit that such a boon could be the work of a mere commoner, and referred to their benefactor as 'Lord George'.

Another significant piece of social legislation also marked 1908: a government measure to limit the daily hours of employment in coal mines to eight. Herbert Gladstone, as Home Secretary, was set in charge of the Bill, but at one point he began to falter. It took the intervention of old Ripon, a good deal more radical and determined than some of his much younger and less high-born colleagues, to persuade the Prime Minister 'to infuse a little firmness into Herbert Gladstone'.[20] Another dispute with the Home Secretary later in the year was the real cause of Ripon's resignation from the Government,[21] though this was officially attributed to reasons of age and health.

With Ripon, the last link with a remote past disappeared. He had been born in 1827, during the brief Premiership of his Tory father Viscount Goderich, *alias* 'Prosperity Robinson',[22] and served in Cabinet under no fewer than six Prime Ministers: Palmerston, Russell, Gladstone, Rosebery, Campbell-Bannerman and finally Asquith. Ripon's considerable achievements were often ignored or forgotten. His social class caused him sometimes to be labelled a Whig, but his views were strikingly radical. His outlook was deeply humanitarian, and he proved his administrative skill as an imaginative and effective Viceroy of India.[23] As with Gladstone, religion was a major motivating force in Ripon's life, and he scandalised many contemporaries by converting to Roman Catholicism. On more than one occasion when the Liberals had been troubled to find a suitable leader, they would have been well advised to consider Ripon.

Apart from the Old Age Pensions legislation, 1908 was a worse year for the Liberal government than 1907 had been. A Licensing Bill, designed to placate the government's more moderate temperance supporters, was destroyed by the Lords. On the economic front, matters were bad indeed, for there was a serious trade recession. No official figures for unemployment yet existed; but returns from Trade Unions showed a huge jump, from 3.7 per cent in 1907 to 7.8 per cent in 1908.[24] In such circumstances, it was not surprising that by-elections went against the Government. The Chief Whip was 'terribly distressed' over the unexpected loss of Ashburton to the

Conservatives in January.[25] In the same month the Liberals lost Ross-on-Wye to a Liberal Unionist. As the year proceeded, there were further by-election losses. In March, Peckham returned a Conservative, with a huge swing of votes. When Winston Churchill joined the Cabinet, he was compelled to fight a by-election in Manchester North West, and lost the seat. The Liberals later found him a safer place in Dundee. When George Whiteley took a peerage, there was another Liberal defeat at Pudsey. In August Liberals lost Haggerston, and in the following month they encountered yet another defeat in Newcastle-upon-Tyne.

If the Unionists were making great headway against the Liberals in the by-elections of 1908, the same year witnessed a Liberal loss of a much more durable kind in a different direction. Coal-mining was an enormously important occupation in the early twentieth century. The 1911 census showed over 1.2 million men engaged in mining and quarrying – the vast majority of those in the coal industry. This represented nearly 10 per cent of the total male labour force. Hitherto, coal miners had generally been Liberal supporters. The Lancashire and Cheshire area was an exception, for many of the miners had traditionally been Conservative, and in 1903 they gave support to the LRC. Relations with local Liberal Associations varied wildly from place: some were glad to adopt miners or ex-miners as candidates; others were much less willing to do so.[26] This, however, did not usually upset the miners' general loyalty to the Liberal Party. At first the LRC had few attractions for miners in most places, for there was little that outsiders could do help them increase their parliamentary representation. When the LRC constituted itself the Labour Party in 1906, some of the Lib-Labs were disposed to dispute its right to the name.

When the Mineworkers' Federation held a ballot in 1906, a majority opposed affiliation to the Labour Party. In another ballot two years later, just under 56 per cent of the miners voted the other way. Was this in part a reaction, one may ask, to the relatively limited achievements of the government thus far? Perhaps; but the decision would have been unthinkable if the Herbert Gladstone-MacDonald pact had not given the incipient Labour Party a substantial foothold in the House of Commons. After complex negotiations, it was decided that the 'Lib-Lab' miners would continue to accept the Liberal whip throughout the current Parliament, but at the next General Election they would stand in the Labour interest. In the event of a by-election arising in a 'Lib-Lab' mining seat during the interval, the new candidate would stand as Labour. Many miners were far from satisfied with this arrangement. The two most distinguished veterans of all, Thomas Burt of Morpeth and Charles Fenwick of Wansbeck, continued to sit as Liberals throughout their careers, with evident support from the local rank-and-file.

Miners in various parts of the midlands, who had voted strongly against affiliation to the Labour Party, soon made their doubts felt. This was first brought out at a by-election in Mid-Derbyshire in 1909 – though a number of examples would follow later. The MP whose death occasioned the contest was not a 'Lib-Lab' but a Liberal of the traditional type. The local miners recommended the name of one of their number, J. G. Hancock, to the Liberal Association. Hancock had signed the Labour Party's constitution, but declared that he was, and remained, a Liberal. The Liberal Association accordingly adopted Hancock as its candidate. Shortly afterwards, the Labour Party also endorsed him, and he was returned with a comfortable majority over a Conservative opponent.

Many events of 1908 provided a powerful warning which the Liberals could only ignore at their peril. If they were to remain the government – indeed, if they were to remain the dominant party of political and social change – they must somehow capture the minds and imaginations of people who were convinced that there was something fundamentally wrong with the existing social and political order, which a Liberal government should be able to remedy, but had thus far failed to remedy. Unless that happened, many middle-class voters would be likely to revert to the Unionists, while radical working men would transfer to the Labour Party.

THE NEST EGG.

[*From the* "WESTMINSTER GAZETTE."]

The Squire: *I don't approve of these Old Age Pensions— people who have saved nothing should get nothing.*

Old Labourer: *Beggin' your pardon, squire, but what's been the use of the likes o' we trying to save when we knew we never couldn't save enough to live on? Now, these yur Old Age Pensions 'll be a zort o' nest egg as 'll put a little 'eart into folk an' make it worth while trying to put aside a bit.*

[The Tories pretend to be afraid that the result of Old Age Pensions to old people of 70 and over will be to get rid of thrift altogether.]

Cartoon from *Westminster Gazette* criticising Tory opposition to the old age pension introduced by Lloyd George in 1908.

10

Climax

> The two schemes [National Insurance and Unemployment Insurance],
> taken together with the Old Age Pensions Act, will, in the opinion of
> the Cabinet, form the largest and most beneficent measure of social
> reform yet achieved in any country.
>
> Asquith to George V, 5 April 1911[1]

Old Age Pensions were not the only important new item of expenditure for
which the Government would need to provide in its 1909 Budget. In October 1908, the Cabinet resolved to embark on schemes of public works and
other matters, designed to ameliorate what the Prime Minister described as
the 'exceptional and widespread though by no means universal distress'
which accompanied the trade depression of that year.[2] Soon, however, a
much bigger item of government expenditure appeared on the horizon.
Germany was busily engaged in a programme of naval rearmament, which
the Admiralty saw as a challenge. At the end of 1908, Reginald McKenna, the
First Lord, proposed a net increase of £2.9 million in net expenditure on the
Navy for the forthcoming year, the most conspicuous requirement being to
commence construction of six battleships of a new kind, known as Dread-
noughts.[3] Long Cabinet discussions followed, while advocates of the new
programme mounted an intense public campaign. Eleven weeks after the
matter had first been raised, the Cabinet at last reached agreement, to the
effect that four should be laid down in 1909, but another four should be laid
down in the following year if this appeared necessary. It did so appear.[4] In
Churchill's a well-known words, 'The Admiralty had demanded six ships,
the economists offered four: and we finally compromised on eight'.[5] The
government of New Zealand soon offered to be responsible for the cost of
one, and if necessary two, of these ships.[6]

The full eventual cost of naval rearmament was still not clear in the early
spring of 1909, but it was quite certain that the Chancellor of the Exchequer
would need to bring forward a Budget involving expenditure and taxation
on an exceptional scale. The new Budget would be Lloyd George's first one,
for the Budget of 1908, which had been prepared by Asquith as Chancellor
of the Exchequer, was introduced by him after he had become Prime

Minister. A Budget proposing massive new taxation would not be welcome, whatever the reasons for the increase; and on this occasion the political diffi- culty was compounded because the Government was passing through a period of marked unpopularity.

Lloyd George, like Churchill, was always seen at his best in a crisis where, to all appearances, the odds were stacked heavily against him. At first the extra money required was estimated to be in the region of £13.6 million – an enormous sum, by the standards of the time – though eventually it was recognised that this figure would need to be increased substantially. The Chancellor contemplated raising £6 millions from tobacco and drink (including liquor licences). £3.5 million would come from Income Tax, and a new Super Tax – later called Surtax – on high incomes. Estate Duties on bequests would produce an extra £2.85 million. Smaller sums would be drawn from revenue stamps required for certain documents.[7] There was also a relatively tiny item, which would become the epicentre of most of the argument over the Budget: around £500,000 from land taxes.

To understand the excitement which these land taxes were to generate, it is necessary to look back over the previous thirty years. The Irish Land War which began in 1879 attracted immense interest throughout the British Isles. It sparked off a Land War in the Hebrides and adjacent parts of the Scottish mainland, which ran through most of the 1880s, and received much atten- tion in all parts of Scotland, where the tradition of the Highland Clearances a century earlier was well remembered. The 1880s also witnessed a Land War in Wales, which was eventually deflected into a campaign against church tithes, in which the young Lloyd George had played a prominent part. As these rural land campaigns died down, a new kind of land agitation devel- oped in the towns – notably in Glasgow and London. Local authorities sought the right to collect rates on the basis of site values alone, rather than the total value of a hereditament. These ideas were taken up in the National Liberal Federation's proposals of the 1880s and 1890s. Not long after his famous Budget of 1894, Sir William Harcourt received a memorial signed by 94 MPs to the same effect. In the Balfour Parliament, various land rating Bills were proposed by Liberal MPs, and secured widespread support, some of that support even coming from Unionists. Early in 1906, it was reported that no fewer than 518 local authorities had petitioned the Chancellor for permission to levy rates on the basis of site values.[8]

Some Liberals wished to go a great deal further than this, and wanted a tax on land values to form the principal, or even the exclusive, source of public revenue.[9] Many, and probably the large majority, of Liberal MPs were willing to see land values assessed, and a measure of taxation applied to them. Thus when Lloyd George began to consider some kind of land taxing as a feature of his 1909 Budget, the underlying idea was already well understood and widely supported among Liberals, and many others as well. In Scotland, there was continuing resentment at the Lords' behaviour towards the Valuation Bills which had received overwhelming support from the Commons so recently.

Lloyd George had strong sympathy with this agitation, and the natural course would seem to be to introduce valuation proposals into the 1909 Budget, and to commence taxation on that basis at a later date. That course, however, was open to serious objections. It would not help meet the immediate financial requirements. More serious, there was considerable doubt whether the Speaker of the House of Commons would permit valuation proposals to come within the ambit of an annual Finance Bill unless they were linked to revenue proposals for the current year.[10] Even if these difficulties could be met, the Lords would probably feel free to block the legislation if it strayed beyond simple revenue-raising. At this date, it was generally thought that the Lords would pass a taxation Bill even though they disliked it, while they would be free to block a valuation Bill.

Lloyd George proposed three land taxes which would come immediately into effect, as the excuse for valuation. There would be a tax on land value increments, payable when land was transferred; a tax on undeveloped land and a tax on leasehold reversions. Those taxes were conceived not as the *casus belli* for an immense struggle with the House of Lords, but as a way of slipping valuation into the Budget, in the hope that it would be acceptable to the Speaker and would not be rejected by the Lords. When Lloyd George put his Budget proposals before the Cabinet, he encountered great difficulty, and on some matters was forced to make concessions.[11] Lewis Harcourt, son of Sir William, and generally known as 'Loulou', was a particularly strong opponent. When the proposals were submitted, he passed a card to a colleague, foretelling that the Budget 'will ensure the triumph of Tariff Reform'.[12] In the long discussions which followed, Asquith gave quiet, but vital, support to the Chancellor, which eventually ensured that the Budget proposals overcame that first obstacle.

When the Budget was introduced in the Commons, late in April, there was remarkably little immediate excitement. But as time went on the parliamentary struggle became increasingly intense. Until well into the summer, however, it looked like being little more than a party contest of the traditional kind. The Opposition would try to win a few changes in the Budget, and would certainly try to make every available ounce of political capital, which might prove useful at a later date. The Budget would, nevertheless, pass the Commons essentially in the form the Chancellor wished, and would then go to the Lords. The Upper House would grumble furiously, but it would eventually allow the Budget to pass, just as it had allowed Sir William Harcourt's Budget of 1894 to pass.

Both sides began to appeal with growing zest to the gallery. A Budget Protest League was set up under Walter Long, a prominent Conservative landowner. This was countered by a Budget League led by Winston Churchill, who was currently in the most radical phase of his career. In the House of Commons, some concessions on the land taxes were extracted from the government.[13] But although the deepest controversy centred on land, this was by no means the only point in dispute. The drink taxes were strongly opposed by Conservatives, and by Irish as well – not least, perhaps, because distillers were major contributors to Nationalist funds. 'Beer up, baccy up – and they call this a "People's Budget"', complained a working man on a Conservative poster. Perhaps the Opposition would have been wise to concentrate its main fire on such matters, and hint darkly that the Budget was the work of a temperance, or kill-joy, conspiracy. Some of the Unionist critics looked like very rich men whose wealth derived mainly from the ownership of land who were prepared to cause the maximum possible dislocation of public business in order to protect their own interests.

Meanwhile, the government received an important piece of evidence which suggested that the Budget might actually prove popular. The bad Liberal by-election performance of 1908 had continued into the early part of 1909, when they lost three seats: two to the Unionists, one to Labour. Then came the Budget, and soon Oswald Partington, MP for the High Peak Division of Derbyshire, was appointed a Lord Commissioner of the Treasury. As the law then stood, this required him to submit to a by-election. His constituency was highly marginal. In the previous six contests, it had returned a Conservative on four occasions, a Liberal on two. None of the victors had ever secured a majority running into four figures. Partington centred his own campaign on the Budget, and in July was duly returned with a majority only slightly reduced from that which he had received in the *annus mirabilis* 1906. Liberals must have greeted the news with a huge sight of relief.

The fight over the Budget continued. Just over a week after High Peak polled, Lloyd George made a famous speech at Limehouse, in the East End of London. When that speech is read today, it seems to contain nothing more objectionable than a little gentle satire and a good deal of cogent argument. Yet there was furious indignation in the Conservative press and among their supporters. One duke declared that he would 'like to see Winston Churchill and Lloyd George in the middle of twenty couple of dog hounds'. Other magnates proposed to cancel regular gifts to charity, because they were about to be impoverished. Even the King was held to be 'seriously annoyed' by the Chancellor's utterance.[14]

As the year advanced, the Bill continued on its slow, but inevitable, course through the Commons. Meanwhile, evidence began to accumulate showing that the Lords might decide to throw out the Finance Bill. They would be within their legal rights in so doing; but such action would run contrary to all recent precedent. By this time, Lloyd George had decided to reverse his original strategy. He no longer sought to slip the Budget past the Lords; he taunted them in the expectation and hope that they would throw it out. A speech he delivered at Newcastle in October was a spectacular example. It was a good deal more alarming than anything delivered at Limehouse. The Lords, he declared, 'are forcing a revolution. But the Lords may decree a revolution which the people will direct. Who made ten thousand people owners of the soil and the rest of us trespassers in the land of our birth?' Early in November, Asquith thought it necessary to warn the King that rejection of the Bill by the Lords was 'probable'.[15] If that happened, whatever the eventual upshot, there would be considerable dislocation of public finances. Not only would it be impossible to collect the extra taxation required, but two important taxes – income tax and the tax on tea – were technically 'temporary' in character, and could not be collected at all unless special arrangements were made. There was much anxious discussion in Cabinet as to how suitable provisions could be made.[16] The Marquis of Lansdowne, who in 1880 had been the first Whig to defect from Gladstone's second Government, was currently leader of the Unionist peers. In that capacity he moved a resolution refusing assent to the Finance Bill 'until it has been submitted to the judgement of the country.' On 30 November 1909, the Lords threw out the Government's proposals by 350 to 75.

One side-effect of the Budget was to clarify the position of Lord Rosebery. He was still President of the not-very-active Liberal League, of which Asquith, Grey and Haldane were Vice-Presidents. Rosebery made no secret of his dislike for the Budget (although, in the final division, he abstained from voting). Asquith wrote to him in September, indicating that he and his colleagues could not continue to serve under Rosebery's Presidency. Effectively, this was the end of any link between Rosebery and the Liberal Party, though the Liberal League was not formally dissolved until the following year. There were a few other defections. Carlyon Bellairs, Liberal MP for King's Lynn, crossed the floor and joined the Liberal Unionists. Two Liberals, Julius Bertram and Samuel Whitbread, voted against the Third Reading of the Finance Bill. Neither defended his seat at the forthcoming General Election. Ten Liberals were absent unpaired. One Unionist, T. H. Sloan, supported the Bill.

For most of 1909, the attention of politicians had centred on the Budget proposals, but one very important piece of Imperial legislation passed through Parliament in the same year. The grant of self-government to the two former Boer republics in 1907 was followed by moves aimed at establishing a federation which would also include Cape Colony and Natal, forming what would become known as the Union of South Africa. Negotiations were not easy, and one feature of the new arrangements presented particularly serious difficulties. The new constitution proposed that membership of the Union's Senate should be confined to persons 'of European descent'. This colour bar immediately raised the hackles of many Liberal like Sir Charles Dilke and Labour MPs like Keir Hardie. An amendment to delete it was proposed from Labour benches. Asquith made it clear that he disliked the colour bar as much as anybody, but pressed Parliament not to insist on the amendment, for the colour bar provision had been accepted by the four colonial legislatures as part of a very uneasy compromise, and the alternative would be to vitiate all the arrangements. The Prime Minister went on to express the hope that the South Africans themselves would soon remove the offending provision.[17] The amendment was rejected, and the Bill then proceeded to eventual enactment, without difficulty in either House. In the following year, the Union of South Africa came into existence. For many years, the governing legislation was generally regarded – despite the colour bar – as an enlightened measure which had largely removed the tensions between British and Boers in South Africa. Nobody appears to have guessed what baleful consequences would follow many years later.

The main attention of politicians and public alike was focused not on South Africa but on the Budget. Very soon after the Lords rejected the Finance Bill, a resolution was moved in the Commons, declaring their action to be 'a breach of the Constitution and an usurpation of the rights of the Commons'. Parliament was first prorogued, then dissolved. The proximity of Christmas and the difficulty of completing a new electoral register made early polling unacceptable, and so voting was postponed until January 1910.

Various inter-party electoral arrangements were made, particularly between Liberals and Labour. In the large majority of cases, care was taken to ensure that the two parties did not fight each other in places where the Conservative was likely to emerge as the *tertius gaudens*. The few Lib-Lab miners' MPs who remained loyal to the Liberals were unopposed by Labour. Conversely, with only one exception, the Lib-Lab miners who had turned to Labour faced no Liberal opposition. The Liberals did not attempt to regain a Sheffield seat which they had lost to Labour at a by-election in 1909, but they sought to recapture the by-election losses of Jarrow which had passed to Labour, and also Colne Valley which had been captured by an independent Socialist. In Balfour's old seat of Manchester East, which the Liberals had taken so unexpectedly in 1906, they even stood down in favour of Labour.

The result which emerged when polling was complete cannot have given much satisfaction to any of the British parties. The Liberals held 275 seats. Overall, they had lost heavily, but the pattern varied widely from place to place. In some parts of the country, they more or less broke even. In Scotland, they made five gains to five losses; in Wales no gains and two losses; in the four northern English industrial counties Northumberland, Durham, Yorkshire and Lancashire, nine gains and eleven losses. By contrast, in the seventeen English counties lying roughly to the south of the latitude of Bristol, there were only two gains against 67 losses. Labour, with forty seats, appeared to have improved its position substantially; but the gain is attributable exclusively to the transfer of the Lib-Lab miners, and not a single Labour candidate anywhere was victorious against Liberal opposition. The by-election losses of Jarrow and Colne Valley were avenged. John Johnson of Gateshead, the one former Lib-Lab miner who had joined the Labour Party and whom the Liberals decided to oppose, was heavily defeated. On polling day, 8000 miners demonstrated in favour of the Liberals. In most matters of immediate importance, however, the Labour Party could be regarded as a close ally of the Liberals. The Unionists, with 273 seats, had improved their position considerably, but they were a very long way from the overall majority which had seemed to lie within their grasp a year earlier. The Irish Nationalists, with 83 seats, held the balance of power.

The Nationalists could certainly not be regarded as assured allies of the Liberals in the new Parliament. Very soon after the elections, they threatened to vote against the Budget unless the government could assure them that the wider question of reducing the power of the House of Lords would be dealt with in he current year.[18] They had good reason for so doing. There was little prospect of securing Home Rule while the Lords' power remained unchanged. Many Liberals and Labour people, even those who were not particularly enthusiastic for Home Rule, could readily share the Irish anxiety on that score. Unless the current position of the House of Lords was changed, radical legislation of almost any kind was likely to be hindered, or even blocked entirely, by an unelected House whose members were overwhelmingly Conservative. On top of that, the Nationalists had difficulties of their own. As the Prime Minister perceived, John Redmond 'is not altogether his own master, as the Budget is extremely unpopular in Ireland, and the O'Brien party are on his flank'.[19] The 'O'Brienites' to whom he referred were a group of twelve Irish MPs who looked to William O'Brien, who had been a major figure in the Irish land troubles of the 1880s, rather than Redmond, as their leader.[20]

Three separate, but linked, questions faced the new Parliament. Should the Budget be accepted? Should the power of the House of Lords to interfere with future legislative proposals approved by the House of Commons be reduced? And should the composition of the House of Lords be changed, so that possession of a peerage should not automatically qualify a person for membership? All of those issues had been widely discussed at the General Election, and the great majority of Liberals would have given a resounding affirmative answer to all three; but a great deal would depend on the relative priorities which the Government gave them.

The Cabinet deliberated long on the matter. Cabinet Letters – that is, the communications reporting its discussions which were sent regularly by the Prime Minister of the day to the sovereign – are usually anodyne documents; but those which Asquith despatched to Edward VII in February 1910 leave the reader in little doubt that there was much disagreement, and probably no small measure of confusion. The fact that the Government eventually extracted itself from the muddle with no serious damage done is due overwhelmingly to one man: Alexander Murray, generally known as the Master of Elibank, MP for Gladstone's old constituency of Midlothian, whom Asquith had recently appointed Liberal Chief Whip. 'The Master' would only hold his new post for a little over two years; but in that time he would prove one of the greatest – perhaps the very greatest – Chief Whip the Liberals ever had.[21] His private observations about the situation at the highest level of government are positively sulphurous:

> There is no doubt that the Cabinet in these early days was absolutely discredited. It was well known that they were wrangling among themselves, because some of them were indiscreet enough to give hints to their friends as to what was occurring round the table. The Prime Minister ... had lost his nerve, he had no grip of the situation, and at any moment the secession of important Ministers would have brought down the whole fabric.[22]

This anger and frustration is understandable, but allowance must be made for the immense strain under which everybody in the Cabinet had been working for a long time: tension much greater and more protracted than the normal strain of a General Election. Meanwhile, Elibank was in close contact with the Irish and Labour Parties, whose attitudes were of critical importance. On 21 February 1910, the new Parliament met, and Asquith was able to announce the Government's plan of campaign, agreed by his colleagues. It was a compromise between the 'vetoists' like 'Loulou' Harcourt, whose main aim was to reduce the veto powers of the House of Lords, and the 'reformists' like Sir Edward Grey, whose main aim was to reform its composition. The Government proposed to bring forward resolutions dealing with the Lords, which would be taken alongside the Budget. The resolutions would eventually be embodied in a Bill.

Asquith in particular was in the firing line. In a major speech delivered at the Albert Hall in London on 10 December 1909, he had declared that 'We shall not assume office and we shall not hold office unless we can secure the safeguards which experience shows us to be necessary for the legislative utility and honour of the party of progress'.[23] Just what were the 'safeguards' to which the Prime Minister referred? Many people took his words to mean that he would require a promise from the King that he would be prepared, should need arise, to create enough pro-Government peers to swamp the Conservative majority in the Lords, though there was little reason for reading this into Asquith's Albert Hall speech. In the debate of 21 January 1910, Asquith stated emphatically 'that I have received no such guarantee, and that I have asked for no such guarantee'.[24] But the statement was not well received. Elibank described the speech in which it was contained as 'the very worst I have ever heard him make' – adding that 'the Prime Minister's prestige fell to so low an ebb that at one point I despaired of his ever recovering it.'[25] Some members of the Cabinet favoured immediate resignation. If the Liberals' resignation in 1895 had been folly, resignation in such circumstances in 1910 would surely have been even worse folly. Three days later, however, the Cabinet unanimously rejected the idea of voluntary resignation.[26]

Having recovered both courage and wisdom, the Cabinet gradually worked out a plan which offered a much brighter prospect for the future. On 21 March, Asquith submitted three resolutions to the House of Commons. The first proposed that the Lords should be disabled from blocking a measure certified by the Speaker to be a Money Bill. The second proposed that the Lords should lose the power to veto other Bills for more than two Sessions of Parliament. The third proposed to reduce the maximum duration of Parliament from seven years to five. In the following month, the three resolutions were duly carried with very comfortable majorities. Without making any wild promises to the Irish, the Government had effectively assured them, and any sceptics on the Liberal and Labour benches, of its intention to deal with the veto question. Any lingering doubts were removed by the Prime Minister on 14 April. Unless the Government found itself able of give statutory effect to its policy in the current Parliament, he promised, 'we shall either resign our offices or recommend the dissolution of Parliament'. He further promised that 'in no case will we recommend a dissolution except under such conditions as will ensure that in the new

Parliament the judgement of the people as expressed in the elections will be carried into law.'[27] The Chief Whip was immensely relieved, recording 'a great Parliamentary triumph for the Prime Minister. All his lost prestige has been recovered'.[28]

This unambiguous assurance removed any remaining hesitation on the part of the official Irish Party, the Labour Party and the more rebellious Liberal backbenchers. The Government was able to bring the suspended Finance Bill of the previous year before Parliament with confidence. The Liberal and Labour Parties naturally supported it. On the Second Reading, the Irish Nationalists split: 62 supporting it, eight of the O'Brienites opposing it, and eleven MPs being absent. The Bill accordingly passed that division by 330 to 244. It encountered no further serious trouble, and – as Lansdowne had more or less promised – was accepted by the Lords without a division. On 29 April 1910, it received royal assent.

While these debates about the Budget and the power of the House of Lords were taking place, an important cross-current was generated by Rosebery. On 14 March, he brought forward resolutions in the House of Lords, including a proposal that possession of a peerage should not confer an automatic right to sit in the House of Lords. These 'reform' proposals were accepted. Attractive though they might appear when taken in isolation, they would certainly not satisfy the 'vetoists', whose overwhelming concern was to reduce the power of the House of Lords rather than to reform its composition. It would be difficult to envisage any sort of Second Chamber, particularly one in which the hereditary principle played an important part, which would not be 'conservative-with-a-small-c' in outlook.

Everything was now being prepared for submission of the constitutional proposals outlined in the Prime Minister's resolutions. Then, on 6 May, suddenly and unexpectedly, King Edward VII died, and was succeeded by his son, who became George V. Four days later, the first Cabinet of the new reign agreed that the Easter recess, which was almost at an end, should be prolonged for a further month.[29] This decision was evidently taken with a view partly to relieving the new and inexperienced monarch of the burden of an immediate constitutional crisis, and partly in the hope that the hiatus would provide an opportunity of achieving a solution which would be generally acceptable. Towards the end of the extended recess, the Cabinet sought formal permission from the King to enter into communication with the Opposition leaders, and to set up a Constitutional Conference to try to resolve the dispute.[30] The King agreed, the Opposition agreed, and towards the end of June a Constitutional Conference was set up, consisting of four Liberals and four Unionists, without very closely defined terms of reference.

While the conference was sitting, Lloyd George (who else?) broached a much more radical idea. In a memorandum of August 1910,[31] he argued that 'some of the most urgent problems ... can only be successfully coped with by the active cooperation of the great Parties of the State'. Among those problems he listed not only constitutional reform (including the 'Irish Question'), but also matters like defence; international disarmament agreements; trade policy; working-class housing; national insurance against sickness, unemployment and invalidity; the poor law; the future of agriculture; denominational questions, including the status of the Welsh Church; imperial questions; and a wide range of problems connected with public finance. Tackling such problems, the Chancellor argued, was likely to incur temporary unpopularity. With two large parties evenly balanced, the defection of a few voters would produce defeat; therefore, in practice, such problems were commonly shelved. Lloyd George's mind was plainly turning towards the idea of a coalition. Superficially attractive though that idea might seem, it came to nothing in 1910; but it would be worked out much more fully some years later, in very different conditions.

Far from producing a general coalition, the Constitutional Conference failed to reach an agreed solution on the relatively narrow issues which it had sought to resolve, and finally collapsed on 10 November. At first the Cabinet recoiled from demanding an immediate General Election, fearing that an appeal to the country on a stale electoral register spelt doom for the Liberals.[32] Then Elibank persuaded them to change their minds. On 15 November the Cabinet recommended the dissolution of Parliament as soon as certain urgent non-contentious business had been disposed of. That advice, however, was contingent on the King agreeing, if necessary, to create the necessary peers. Next day, Asquith and Crewe met the King, and advised him to that effect.

The King was, not unreasonably, reluctant to give a firm guarantee. If the Government returned victorious from the General Election, its majority might be huge and convincing, or it could be wafer-thin. It would not be reasonable in the latter case to invite him to take dramatic action which would have a permanent effect, yet would be resented by a large and formidable Opposition. The Ministers took that point, appreciating that any indication of royal intent which might be given must be contingent on an adequate Government majority being recorded.[33] If the King were to refuse assurances over the creation of peers, the only remaining option was for the Government to resign. It was far from certain that Balfour would accept office in that event. The royal response was not made public at the time, but several months later Asquith reported that the King 'felt that he had no alternative but to assent to the advice of the Cabinet.'[34] On 18 November, Asquith announced the dissolution of Parliament.

A few days later, the Lords considered Opposition counter-proposals for their own reform; but these did not much alter things. Parliament was dissolved on 28 November and the General Election campaign began in earnest. At an early stage, Balfour observed that there were three principal issues before the electorate: the Lords' veto; Irish Home Rule and Tariff Reform. On all of these matters, most people's minds had probably been made up long before. The election was unexciting, and its importance was probably eclipsed in most minds by the imminent approach of Christmas.

Polling ran through much of December. A substantial number of seats changed hands in various directions, but the general upshot was almost the same as in January. This time, the Liberal and Unionist Parties were exactly equal, with 272 seats each: an overall loss of three seats by the Liberals and one by the Unionists. Labour, with 42 seats and the Irish Nationalists with 84, had each picked up two seats overall. The poll was lower than in January, though much higher than is usual today: 81.1 per cent of the electorate against 86.6 per cent. Some writers have suggested that this drop is attributable largely to apathy; but it seems that the deaths and removals which would be expected on an old register afford at least as likely an explanation.

In the new Parliament, priority had to be given to the Government's Parliament Bill, which sought to regulate relations between the two Houses. Predictably, it passed the Commons without difficulty. The real problem was what would happen in the House of Lords. The first important move there was a Bill moved by Lansdowne, which proposed radical changes in the composition of the House of Lords.[35] The large majority of hereditary peers would cease to sit. 120 members would be elected by the House of Commons, and 100 would be appointed by the Crown, in proportion to the strengths of parties in the Commons. Some bishops and senior judges would continue to sit. These proposals, Asquith considered, 'go considerably further than any that has hitherto been put forward from the same quarter'.[36] Two distinguished authors have even noted that 'it was said at the time that if the Peers had been asked to choose between the Parliament Bill and the Lansdowne Bill, and a vote had been taken by ballot, an actual majority would have accepted the former as the lesser evil.'[37]

The Lansdowne Bill touched on the royal prerogative, and the sovereign's assent was therefore required before it could be considered. The Cabinet did not propose that this assent should be refused, nor that the Bill should be resisted.[38] On the other hand, there was no question of withdrawing the Government's own Bill. Lansdowne's proposal advanced to its Second Reading in the Lords, whereafter it was dropped, and all attention focussed on the Government Bill.

The Unionists, with their huge majority in the Lords, were in a position to throw out the Bill entirely if they so chose. Instead, they elected to propose drastic amendments, which, in the Cabinet's judgement, were 'destructive of its principle and purpose, both in regard to finance and to general legislation'.[39] The Commons were certain to reject some, at least, of those amendments. The operative question would then be whether the Lords would insist on them, in which case the Government would be compelled to advise the King to create enough peers to swamp the Opposition majority in the Lords. A very substantial list of potential creations was drawn up.[40] The Government's majority, which had been far over 100 in critical divisions, would be more than adequate to overcome the King's initial hesitation. On 20 July 1910, and with the King's approval, Asquith wrote to Balfour and Lansdowne, intimating that, should need arise, he would advise the King to take the appropriate action, and the King would act on that advice. Both Unionist leaders could see that the game was up, and were prepared to advise their followers in the Lords not to insist on the proposed amendments.

This wise advice was by no means universally accepted. By this time, a substantial number of 'diehards' had appeared, prepared to oppose the Parliament Bill to the very limit. Their leader was the famous jurist and former Lord Chancellor, the Earl of Halsbury, almost 88 years of age; but he had many supporters. What made the situation peculiarly open was the fact that there were a great many peers who seldom participated in parliamentary business, and whose political judgement might not be very balanced. If Halsbury and his friends could rally such people, then the Lords' eventual vote was very open indeed.

When Asquith first sought to explain the Government's position in the Commons, he was howled down by infuriated Unionists led by Lord Hugh Cecil, son of the Prime Minister Lord Salisbury – the 'Hughligans', as they were rather appropriately nicknamed. Eventually, on 8 August, the House had calmed down sufficiently to deal with the Lords' amendments. One of these, which would prove of importance in both world wars, was accepted. It provided that a Bill to extend the life of Parliament beyond the normal limit of five years would still require the assent of both Houses. One or two smaller changes were also accepted, but most of the amendments were rejected. Preparations were now made to return the Bill to the Lords, and leave them to decide whether to insist on the remaining amendments.

The Unionist leaders advised abstention. The Government had its own list of Liberal peers who would support the Bill; but were they sufficient to overcome the 'diehards'? Massive pressure was set on moderate Unionists actually to vote in the Government lobby, in order the avert the mass creation of peers. On 10 August, the Lords decided not to insist on their own amendments by 131 votes to 114. The Government majority included 37 Unionists and thirteen Bishops. Nobody in the whole field of public life was more relieved at this result than the King.

Some of the Unionists, however, greeted the news with unbridled fury, blaming betrayal by 'the bishops and the rats'. Balfour's position was seriously undermined, and in November he resigned the Unionist leadership. There was no obvious successor, but the choice eventually fell on Andrew Bonar Law, a dour man with few intellectual pretensions, but a hard political fighter, a strong Tariff Reformer and a particularly bitter opponent of Home Rule, especially in its possible application to Ulster. Perhaps as a result of Bonar Law's influence, the distinction between Conservatives and Liberal Unionists was removed in May 1912, and the two groups were formally joined together as 'Unionists'. For many years, the distinction between them had been nominal rather than real, though 'Liberal Unionism' had served as a convenient power-base for the Chamberlain family.

During the long struggle between the Liberal Government and the Lords, much important legislation was held up. One major domestic measure nevertheless proceeded to enactment: the National Insurance Bill proposed by Lloyd George. This provided for a scheme of insurance, under which workers, employers and Government were all required to make contributions to a fund, from which insured persons and their dependents – some 17 million people in all[41] – would be entitled to draw benefits. These proposals were linked with a scheme for unemployment insurance in certain trades. There was considerable opposition, ranging from private insurance collectors (most of whom, by repute, were Liberals) who feared for their livelihoods, to doctors who considered that some aspects of the Bill would vitiate their professional relationship with patients, and people who objected to the contributory principle. The Unionists tabled a resolution, which was of course defeated, approving the principle but sharply criticising the application. In the end all opposition was either mollified or beaten down. On the Third Reading the Government was victorious by a huge majority, but the hostile vote was curiously mixed. Most Unionists abstained, but a nine voted for the Bill and eleven against. The Labour Party was also split. 32 Labour MPs supported the Government while five of the socialistic wing of the Party voted against. 58 'Redmondite' Irish voted with the Government, seven O'Brienites against it. Without enthusiasm, the Lords decided to let the Bill through, and shortly before the end of 1911 it received royal assent, Another important and controversial change which took place about the same time was the payment of MPs, who received an annual salary of £400.

As in the theatre of ancient Athens, serious and cerebral drama was followed by a delightful farce, When the time approached for the new National

Insurance Act to take effect, various tax resisters appeared. The most colour-ful element was a body of domestic servants who (with obvious prodding from their employers) constituted a 'Servants' Tax Resisters' Association', and held two demonstrations at the Albert Hall. Insurance stamps had to be stuck on cards as evidence of payment, and much resentment was expressed at the idea of 'licking stamps for Lloyd George', who was the special target of the meetings. The nursery rhyme 'Taffy was a Welshman, Taffy was a thief' was sung with enthusiasm. Soon, however, the measure was univer-sally accepted, and stamps were licked with no visible ill-effects.

Liberal leaflet produced for the General Election of January 1910.
It refers to the land clauses in Lloyd George's 1909 Budget.

11

When Troubles Come

Hark! The sound is spreading from the east and from the west,
Why should we beg work and let the landlord take the best?
Make him pay his taxes on the land – we'll risk the rest!
God gave the land to the people!

From Liberal Land Song

The story of the Liberal Government from the conclusion of the struggle with the Lords in August 1911 to the outbreak of war three years later is a good deal more complex than that of the previous period, because several currents of events were running side by side. Sometimes those currents interacted with each other.

The big majorities which had accompanied the Liberal legislation of 1908–11 made the government's position appear stronger than was really the case. From 1910, the Irish Nationalists and the Labour Party between them held the balance of power. Through most of 1911, both had little choice but to support the main items of Liberal legislation. Thereafter, each of those parties had formidable demands to make. The main immediate demand of the Labour Party seemed fairly easy to satisfy.[1] When the January 1910 election campaign had already begun, a judgement of great political importance was pronounced by the House of Lords, sitting not as a chamber of Parliament but as a court of law. A trade unionist, W. V. Osborne, disputed the legal right of his trade union, the Amalgamated Society of Railway Servants, to make contributions to the Labour Party. For many years similar contributions had been made by various trade unions, and it had been generally assumed that they were legal. They formed the principal source of finance of the Labour Party. Within a short time, people in other trade unions began to obtain injunctions to restrain their own organisations from making political contributions. This had little effect on the General Election of January 1910, but by December the Labour Party was very short of money, and was compelled to reduce the number of its candidates from the January figure of 78 to 56. It seems unlikely that Labour would have secured more MPs if it had fought on a broader front in December; but the danger for the future was plain.

At the beginning of the second 1910 campaign, Asquith made an explicit promise that a Liberal Government would initiate legislation to empower trade unions to provide funds for political purposes.[2] The simplest way of doing this seemed to be by introducing a short Bill reversing the 'Osborne Judgement', and establishing what most people had long assumed to be the law. But many Liberals had considerable qualms about so doing. Why should a person who objected to giving a contribution, via his trade union, to a political party of which he disapproved, be compelled to do so? Membership of a particular trade union, while theoretically voluntary, was in many cases not voluntary at all, for 'closed shop' policies made it impossible for a person who did not belong to that union to get a job in the field where he was most qualified.

The government sought to meet the difficulty by a Bill introduced in 1911. This proposed that a trade union should be authorised to set up a political fund which should be kept separate from the ordinary funds of the union. Any member who objected to paying into that fund should be permitted to contract out of such contributions, without losing any rights of membership. The Bill advanced as far as its Second Reading, but was then withdrawn, apparently because of the over full Parliamentary timetable. In 1911, however, the government did take one important step to enable men of modest means to sit in Parliament, by making provision in the Budget for payment of Members. The sum originally contemplated was £300 a year, but it was eventually advanced to £400.[3] This was a good deal more than most working men could expect to earn in their ordinary employment, and compared with the £200 which the Labour Party had hitherto paid to its MPs. That payment was promptly terminated.

In 1912 the Trade Union Bill was introduced again. At one moment there seemed to be a chance that it would be defeated by a combination of Conservatives who objected to any kind of political fund and Labour people who objected to the principle of contracting out. Eventually, however, both objections were withdrawn, and the measure proceeded to enactment as the Trade Unions Act of 1913. Nobody seems to have guessed at the time that the requirement that political funds should be kept separate from ordinary Trade Union funds, with facilities for 'contracting out', would eventually prove vastly more beneficial to the Labour Party, and correspondingly more harmful to the Liberals, than a simple reversal of the 'Osborne Judgement' would have been. To that point it will be necessary to return later.

The relationship between the Liberal and Labour Parties was a complex one. In critical parliamentary divisions, they usually voted in the same lobby. *Liberal Magazine*, which may be regarded as the official voice of the party, approved of that relationship and wished it to continue. In its reports of events, the word 'Ministerialists' is often used to comprehend members of both parties. Yet at other levels the relationship was far less close. At parliamentary by-elections, the two parties would often oppose each other. As the Parliament aged, and by-elections became more common, so also did contests of that kind become more frequent.[4] Three of the most remarkable by-election contests involving the two parties arose in constituencies held by 'Lib-Lab' miners, originally elected as Liberals, who had transferred to the Labour Party under the more or less collusive arrangements of 1908–9. In 1912, Enoch Edwards, MP for Hanley, died. The claim of the Mineworkers' Federation to Hanley was dubious, for there were not a great many miners in the constituency. There appears to have been some kind of understanding between the two party headquarters, but the local Liberals, neither knowing nor caring about any such arrangement, chose R. L. Outhwaite, a noted enthusiast for land taxing, as candidate, and brushed aside an effort by headquarters to persuade him to withdraw. The Liberal campaign, which centred on the land question, began at once, before the Labour Party had even chosen a candidate.[5] Many observers thought that the Conservative would win on the split vote, but in fact Outhwaite was triumphant, and the Labour candidate languished at the bottom of the poll. If Hanley was remarkable, the contest in Chesterfield in 1913 was no less so. James Haslam's career as the constituency's MP followed a similar course to that of Edwards in Hanley. When Haslam announced his intention not to contest the next election, both Liberals and Labour selected candidates. On his death in the summer of 1913, the Liberal announced that he would not stand. So the local Liberal Association decided to adopt the Labour nominee, Barnet Kenyon, as their own candidate. It soon appeared that Kenyon proposed, if elected, to take the Liberal whip. Labour then repudiated him, but did not offer a candidate of its own. An independent Socialist candidate, John Scurr, then appeared. Kenyon was victorious, far ahead of the Unionist, and Scurr's vote was derisory. When William Harvey, MP for North-east Derbyshire and yet another former 'Lib-Lab' miner, died in 1914, all three Parties advanced candidates for the ensuing by-election. This time the upshot was different. The Unionist captured the seat with a small majority over the Liberal, with the Labour defender far behind. As one historian summarised the position, 'The stubborn Liberal loyalties of the ordinary miners dominated the electoral picture ... Labour candidates backed by the Miners' leadership were repudiated by the membership and finished at the bottom of the poll.'[6]

These three by-elections were by no means the only signs that traditionally working-class constituencies, and politicians of working-class origin – most particularly miners' representatives – were in the process of transferring allegiance from Labour back to the Liberals. In the course of 1914, William Johnson, MP for Nuneaton, was thrown out of the Labour Party for continuing to address Liberal meetings, and refusing to form Labour organisations in his constituency. By the outbreak of war, three other Labour MPs with special miners' backing also appeared to be in the process of either being expelled from the Labour Party, or defecting to the Liberals of their own volition, or both.[7]

A by-election contest held in very different conditions from Hanley, Chesterfield or North East Derbyshire illustrated a danger of another kind which confronted both Labour and the Liberals. Leicester was one of the two-member constituencies which had contrived to return a Liberal and a Labour man in double harness in 1910. In 1913, the Liberal retired. Should Labour contest the vacancy? If it did so, not only was a three-cornered contest likely, but in all probability Labour would do badly. It would be very difficult thereafter to restore the old arrangements with the Liberals, who would probably contest both seats at the next General Election. In the end, the local Labour Party decided to fight, but the central organisation refused to endorse its candidate. The Liberal was victorious over the Unionist, and the 'rebel' Labour man finished, predictably, at the bottom of the poll.

The disposition of Labour and Liberal candidates to oppose each other in by-elections had wider implications than these particular contests. By the outbreak of war, there had been five by-elections in constituencies which were Liberal in 1910, where Labour candidates intervened, and the Unionist won the seat on a minority vote, and one by-election where a Liberal had intervened in a Labour seat with a similar result. *Liberal Magazine*, expressing a semi-official view on the matter, pleaded plaintively for 'a policy of accommodation between liberal and labour which will produce in the constituencies the cooperation which obtains at Westminster'.[8] Would such a policy be produced, or would local enthusiasts for the two parties render it impossible? The matter would never be properly tested, for not many more by-elections were held before the war produced a three-party truce; while the next General Election would be held in wholly unpredictable conditions.

The early rise of the LRC and the Labour Party was due, overwhelmingly, to three considerations. First, it was difficult for a politically ambitious, and otherwise suitable, working man to obtain nomination as a Liberal candidate for financial reasons, though a wealthy and powerful Trade Union might well be able to provide money on his behalf. Secondly, at the beginning of the century, and again from 1906 down to 1908, there was real doubt about the capacity of a Liberal Government to deliver the radical, though not socialist, legislation which many working men demanded. Thirdly, the Liberal leaders and Headquarters organisation seemed willing – indeed, eager – to encourage the growth of a separate Labour Party, often in the teeth of resistance by rank-and-file Liberals. But once the Liberal Government began to adopt a truly radical programme, and also arranged for the payment of MPs, the Labour Party began to wither away. It still had a considerable 'nuisance value', for a Labour candidate could often expect to draw enough votes from a Liberal to enable the Unionist to win the constituency.

If Labour, in a party sense, presented considerable problems for the Liberals, Labour, in an industrial sense, created difficulties of a different kind. There was, however, remarkably little relationship between the strategies of the two kinds of 'Labour', and the fortunes of 'political' Labour were not much affected, one way or the other, by the industrial disputes of the period. Several of them were accompanied by considerable disturbances. Most famous of these disputes was one of the earliest, at Ton-y-Pandy, Glamorganishire, in November 1910, where there were riots, and many shops were destroyed.[9] The Chief Constable requested troops. As soon as he discovered that troops were being sent, Winston Churchill, the Home Secretary, ordered them to be halted, but also ordered outside police to the scene. He successfully urged the strikers to accept arbitration, but more riots soon followed. In the end troops were despatched, but they were not used, even though there was fighting between rioters and police, in course of which six policemen were seriously injured. The real irony of Ton-y-Pandy is that contemporary criticism of Churchill turned largely on his failure to use troops, while subsequent critics invented the myth of troops sent by Churchill firing on rioters.

The wave of industrial disputes continued, reaching a peak in 1912, when more than 40 million working days were lost in that manner. Mining, textiles and transport were the industries most seriously affected. The government began to intervene in such disputes in a novel manner. In August 1911, at the very height of the crisis over the Parliament Bill, it set up a small commission to investigate grounds of conflict. Early in the following year, the Cabinet gave serious study to possible action to avert a threatened coal strike. A few months later, a transport strike was described as the 'principal subject' of Cabinet discussions.[10] Today, active government intervention at times of major industrial action would be expected; but such action had a considerable element of novelty in the early twentieth century.

The 'Irish Question' was the most difficult of all the essentially party-political problems facing the Government. Now that the House of Lords had lost the power permanently to block Bills from the Commons, the Irish parliamentarians insistently demanded Home Rule. Left to its own devices, the Liberal government might well have acted rather as Bryce had sought to act in 1906, and set up an elected Irish body with limited powers, so that all could see how matters were faring, and decide whether or not to proceed later to full Home Rule. But the government was not a free agent. Without support, or at least toleration, from the Irish Nationalists, it could not govern at all. Nor, for that matter, were Redmond's Nationalists free agents. Whatever they might have thought privately about the merits of a pilot scheme on the lines of an Irish Council with limited powers, they could not possibly give public support to anything short of Home Rule. They faced an immediate threat from the O'Brienites. William O'Brien's claim to be a doughty fighter for Irish causes was every bit as good as that of Redmond, and probably better. The Redmondites also faced a long-term threat from Irishmen who would not be satisfied with Home Rule, but wanted Ireland to become a sovereign republic, completely independent of Great Britain. Superficially, Redmond's position seemed enormously strong, and wherever he went in Ireland he was greeted with great enthusiasm; but unless he could deliver Home Rule soon his authority might crumble away with great suddenness.

The biggest difference between the parliamentary debates on Home Rule in the nineteenth century and the debates after 1911 was that it was no longer possible for the Lords to block it in the peremptory way they had blocked it in 1893. If a Home Rule Bill passed the Commons in three successive Sessions, it would proceed to royal assent whether the Lords approved or not. On 11 April 1912, Asquith introduced the government's Home Rule Bill, which was rather like Gladstone's Bill of 1893. A separate Irish Parliament would be set up for dealing with exclusively Irish business, formally reserving foreign policy, and a large component of financial policy, for decision by the Parliament at Westminster. Various safeguards were proposed to protect the interests of minorities, particularly religious minorities. The Bill was open to amendment, and there had already been discussion in Cabinet about special treatment for those parts of Ulster which were hostile to Home Rule.[11] This represented an important departure from the nineteenth century assumption, by Home Rulers and Unionists alike, that Ireland was indivisible. Yet there was an element of unreality about the Home Rule Bill of 1912. Everybody knew that there would be a huge fight in the Commons, but that the Bill would eventually pass, and then proceed to the Lords, who would reject it. The predictable rejection duly took place in January 1913, by the crashing majority of 326 to 69. The solemn charade was repeated when the government re-introduced the Bill soon afterwards. In July 1913, the Lords rejected it by 302 to 64.

The longer the Home Rule debate continued, the uglier the question became, and both sides became increasingly disposed to resort to violent measures, In 1912, the 'Ulster Covenant' was produced, by which signatories pledged – often in blood – 'to use all means which may be proved necessary to defeat the present conspiracy to set up a Home Rule Parliament in Ireland'. The Covenant was organised under the auspices of Sir Edward Carson, soon to be known as the 'Uncrowned King of Ulster'. Oddly, Carson was not an Ulsterman at all. He was born in Leinster, lived much of his time in London and his Parliamentary constituency was Dublin University.

The 'Ulster Covenant' suggested that events in the province were moving in one direction; but almost immediately an exciting by-election in what was then generally known as Londonderry City pointed the other way. A Unionist had held the 'Maiden City' in the two 1910 General Elections with tiny majorities. He succeeded to a peerage, and the seat became vacant. A Liberal – a Protestant and a Home Ruler – challenged the controlling party, and was elected by a margin of 57. By this event, a numerical majority of one gave the principal representation of Ulster constituencies to Home Rulers.

Signs that the two sides were contemplating violence increased. In November 1913, Chief Secretary Augustine Birrell told the Cabinet that about 50,000 'Ulster Volunteers' had been enrolled, and had at their disposal a conjectural figure of five thousand rifles. Later in the month he reported that Nationalists were also beginning to arm and drill.[12] All this was taking place at a time when the government's Bill was still blocked by the Lords. But the government was bound to introduce a new Home Rule Bill in 1914, by which time the House of Lords would have lost its power to reject the Bill, though not its power to debate it. The Bill would, therefore, be introduced 'for real', and there was an adequate majority to force it into law. The Government's overwhelming concern, however, was to avert violence in any part of Ireland. As Morley put it, 'to start Home Rule with a baptism of bloodshed would be fatal to its prospects'.[13]

There were protracted and anguished Cabinet discussions as to how violence might be averted. Everything was likely to turn on what special provisions – if any – could be made for 'Ulster'. 'Ulster' could mean at least three very different things, and it is often far from clear which of these things contemporaries meant when they discussed it. At one extreme, 'Ulster' might mean the historic province of nine counties. In religion, and in parliamentary representation, the province was almost equally divided. At the other extreme, 'Ulster' might mean the four counties in which Protestants formed a large majority. In between was 'Ulster of the Six Counties' – modern Northern Ireland – which also included Fermanagh and Tyrone, where the two religions were fairly evenly balanced.

However 'Ulster' might be defined, any kind of special treatment would present great difficulties. No dividing line could be drawn which did not leave great numbers both of Catholics and of Protestants on the wrong side.

Birrell told the Cabinet that exclusion of Ulster, whether in whole or in part, was 'opposed by all sections of Irish opinion as a bad and unworkable expedient'.[14] Voters without strong party affiliations, but with general sympathy for the Liberals' economic and social policies, might have been ready to heave a huge sigh of relief if the government could somehow contrive to drop Home Rule, or at least to make special provisions for the Protestant parts of Ulster; but the same was not true for Liberal activists at any level of the party. In November 1913, Asquith reported to the King that 'All the Cabinet were agreed that the temper of the Party outside was actively and growingly opposed to any form of compromise, largely, no doubt because the rank-and-file wholly disbelieve in the reality of the Ulster threat'.[15]

No happy solution was possible; the best thing that could be hoped was that somehow an arrangement might be made which would enable the bulk of Ireland to enjoy Home Rule, without driving the Protestants of Ulster to acts of violence. But time was running out, and soon the government must re-present its Home Rule Bill. Birrell and Lloyd George were able to offer their colleagues just one glimmer of hope.[16] Early in 1914, they had conversations with the Nationalist leaders, whom they persuaded to agree to a plan by which the counties of Ulster would be authorised, if they so desired, to exclude themselves for a period of years from a Home Rule Ireland. It is not difficult to see that Redmond and his colleagues were taking their political lives in their hands by preparing to acquiesce in such a compromise.

When Asquith moved the Second Reading of the Home Rule Bill in March 1914, he made a vital concession on these lines. Amendments might be considered later authorising any Ulster county to exclude itself from the operation of Home Rule for six years, whereafter inclusion would be automatic unless Parliament decreed otherwise. Ulstermen would have a chance of judging for themselves whether Home Rule presented the terrors they had feared. This, as the Prime Minister pointed out, would probably allow two General Elections to take place in the intervening period. A cynic might have added that the ordinary pattern of British politics suggested that one of those elections would result in a Unionist majority, and the baby would pass, kicking and screaming, into somebody else's lap.

Responses were very mixed. Carson told the House of Commons that, from the point of view of Ulster Protestants, the sentence of death would remain, though with six years' stay of execution. On the Liberal side of the House, two Cornish MPs, Sir Clifford Cory and T. C. Agar-Robartes, found themselves voting against the government. The Irish Nationalists split more severely. Redmond urged acceptance of the proposals, as the extreme limit of concessions; O'Brien condemned a policy of 'chopping an ancient nation into a thing of shreds and patches'.

During the spring of 1914, two new incidents cut across the ordinary debates on Home Rule, though both served to emphasise the seriousness of Ulster Protestant opposition. In March, attention was suddenly given to the possibility that orders might one day be given to soldiers in Ireland to take action against militant Protestants, with whom many officers stationed in Ireland were likely to have sympathy. John Seely, Secretary for War, indicated to Irish military authorities that, in event of serious trouble, officers domiciled in Ulster might be allowed to 'disappear'. Other officers would be expected to obey orders; but any who considered that they might have difficulty in so doing should resign their commissions at once. Without authority from the Cabinet, Seely later added a rider in the form of an assurance that the government did not propose to use the army 'to crush political opposition to the policy or principles of the Home Rule Bill'. As soon as the gravity of the matter became apparent, Seely offered to resign. At first the Cabinet rejected the offer,[17] but a couple of days later it was accepted. Asquith himself assumed the vacant office: a matter which would later prove of considerable importance.

One of the considerations which had led to close discussions between Seely and the military authorities had been fear that Ulstermen might attempt to seize army equipment in order, if necessary, to resist Home Rule by force. In fact, they obtained weapons in a different manner. During the night of 24–25 April, 35,000 rifles and three million cartridges were landed at Larne, and were rapidly distributed throughout the province. This was obviously a well-planned operation, and it is said that 12,000 men were engaged in it. Yet, incredibly, the 'establishment' headquarters at Dublin Castle knew nothing of it until all was over.

Meanwhile, the Home Rule Bill was lumbering through Parliament. Was it possible to avert violence? An Army Council memorandum early in July 1914 reported that 'the two opposing forces, with approximately a total strength of 200,000 men are being systematically raised, trained, equipped and organised on a military basis in Ireland ... In the event of a conflagration in Ireland, the whole of the Expeditionary Force may be required to restore order, not only in Ireland but in Great Britain as well.'[18] With a little prompting from the Prime Minister,[19] the King intervened in a last-ditch attempt to moderate the situation. A Conference was summoned to Buckingham Palace, with representatives from the Government, the British Opposition, the Ulster Unionists and the Irish Nationalists. It met on 21 July. On 24 July, it collapsed in failure. A couple of days after the Conference, a gun-running incident in the South paralleled the Larne landings of three months earlier. This time, however, most of the weapons were seized by the authorities, though three people were killed in the disturbances which followed. At the very brink of world war, it was anybody's guess whether part, or all, of Ireland would soon be plunged in civil conflict, and – if so – what effect this might have on the British mainland too.

A less dramatic measure followed a rather similar course of parliamentary treatment to Home Rule. The Church of Wales ranked as part of the Church of England, and enjoyed a similar establishment in the principality. Yet figures produced by a Royal Commission late in 1911 revealed that Welsh nonconformists outnumbered Anglicans by more than five to two. Twenty years earlier, Welsh disestablishment had been widely seen as a Liberal cause second only to Irish Home Rule in its importance. By the early twentieth century, interest in the question through most of Britain had declined greatly, but it was still a matter of real and widespread concern in Wales. As with Home Rule, the House of Lords was intransigently opposed to the idea, but after passage of the Parliament Act of 1911, it became possible eventually to override such opposition. A Disestablishment Bill was introduced in the spring of 1912. There was predictable opposition in the House of Commons, particularly from Conservative Anglicans. As this was spearheaded by Lords Hugh and Robert Cecil, sons of the 3rd. Marquis of Salisbury, it elicited from Lloyd George one of his best pieces of rhetoric, in which he reflected on the deeds of their sixteenth century ancestors:

> Look at the whole story of the pillage of the Reformation. They robbed the Catholic Church, they robbed the monasteries, they robbed the poor, and they robbed the dead. Then they come here when we are trying to seek at any rate to recover part of this pillaged property for the poor, and they venture, with hands dripping with the fat of sacrilege, to accuse us of robbery of God.[20]

One can almost hear Lloyd George saying this, and imagine the excited responses from all sides.

The Welsh Disestablishment Bill followed its predestined course: passage through the House of Commons with substantial majorities; rejection by the House of Lords. Like the Home Rule Bill, it was reintroduced in the Commons in 1913, and again rejected by the Lords. In 1914, the Bill again passed the Commons, but the Lords had by this time lost their power of veto. Like the Home Rule Bill, it was in the queue of measures awaiting formal royal assent, when war changed everything.

More general interest attended the possibility of a further instalment of parliamentary 'Reform'. The 1885 franchise had extended to nearly all male householders, but pressure was growing rapidly for further changes in various directions. There was still a good deal of plural voting. Another cause of complaint was the limited character of the household franchise. Why not make the franchise universal for adult males? There was also a widespread demand that women should receive the parliamentary vote, as well as the local government votes which those who happened to be ratepayers already enjoyed. It was difficult to defend a system under which an illiterate male drunkard could vote, while a female graduate, working as a doctor or a teacher, was denied a vote through the accident of her sex. Other people were beginning to question the functioning of the electoral system, and groping towards some form of Proportional Representation. A major over-haul of electoral boundaries was also needed. In Romford, 57,882 electors returned one MP; in Kilkenny only 1676 did the same. Even in England, there were fewer than 4000 voters in Durham, and in Bury St Edmunds.[21]

Rectification of all, or any, of these anomalies was likely to have impor-tant political implications.[22] Abolition of plural voting would help the Liberals, because most plural voters were fairly wealthy and voted Conser-vative. Extension of the franchise to all adult males would probably have a similar effect, for the younger men were more likely to have radical opin-ions. In some places, it might well benefit the Labour Party. Female voting would be likely to operate in the opposite way, for it was widely believed that women tended to be less radical in their opinions than men. If that was so, then extending the franchise to women was likely to favour the Conservatives. That could prove particularly important in places like south-west England, where many constituencies were held by Liberals with small majorities. One of the curiosities of the debate about enfranchisement of women was that – while it cut across both major parties – Conservatives, who might be expected to benefit, were noticeably more hostile than Liberals, who might be expected to lose.

No government could attempt to rectify this tangle of electoral anomalies without the near certainty that the Opposition would cry foul. If a Liberal Government was in office, trouble with the Lords was certain. It was also a fair guess that many MPs of all parties would view any kind of major change, particularly one which substantially altered constituency bound-aries, with apprehension. If an MP's seat was likely to disappear, or undergo adverse changes, he might encounter serious difficulties in finding another place where he had a good chance of being elected. And so it happened that past Governments of different parties had been disposed to leave the can of worms undisturbed, and the various efforts which were made from time to time to improve the situation ran into the sands for one reason or another.

Advocates of women's suffrage were particularly determined to force that issue on public attention. A Bill to extend the franchise to women passed its Second Reading with a substantial majority on a free vote in July 1910, but the government's programme for the session was over-full, and no further progress was made with the Bill. Some supporters of women's suffrage,

popularly known as 'suffragettes', were resorting to unlawful and often violent behaviour in order to attract attention to their cause. As far back as
1906, they had been disturbing public meetings; soon they began breaking
windows; later they turned to blowing up houses, burning churches, physically assaulting Ministers, slashing pictures and chaining themselves to
railings. Such antics were largely counter-productive, and support for
women's franchise was beginning to drop away.[23] When convicted,
suffragettes often went on hunger strike. Forcible feeding was tried, but
this was a messy, painful, unpleasant and sometimes dangerous procedure.
The nearest the Government got to success in dealing with imprisoned
suffragettes was through Home Secretary Reginald McKenna's much-
criticised 'Cat and Mouse Act' of 1913, under which hunger strikers could be
released so that they did not die, and then be taken back to prison.

Attempts, none of them ultimately successful, were made to rectify some
of the electoral anomalies. A government Bill to deal with plural voting was
accepted by the House of Commons in 1906, and promptly rejected by the
Lords. A Franchise Bill with a wider scope, which also sought to simplify
electoral registration, was introduced in 1912. As the discussion proceeded,
amendments were proposed, designed to introduce an element of women's
suffrage. The Cabinet, like the front Opposition bench, was split on the merits of those amendments, and there was formal agreement that Ministers
would be free to speak and vote on either side.[24] Then, suddenly, in January
1913, the Speaker threw the question into disarray by declaring that these
amendments, if carried, would render the whole Bill unacceptable. If MPs
were to have a chance of voting on the matter, it would be necessary to withdraw the Bill and replace it by a different one. The Prime Minister, no
supporter of women's suffrage himself, nevertheless reported to the King
that, in his view, the Speaker's judgement was 'utterly wrong' and 'in flat
contradiction of the assumptions upon which all parties in the House have
hitherto treated the Bill'.[25] There was no effective way of challenging the
Speaker's ruling, and the Bill was accordingly withdrawn, but time was
allowed for a Private Member's Bill for women's suffrage to be proposed. A
Liberal MP, Willoughby Dickinson, accordingly did so, with support from
MPs from all three British parties.

Dickinson's Bill was somewhat odd, for it did not recommend that
women should be enfranchised on the same terms as men. A minimum age
of 25, not 21, was proposed. Subject to that, women householders would be
entitled to registration, and so also would the wives of male householders.
The Bill was lost by 268 to 221 on the Second Reading. The Liberals split 146
to 74 in favour, the Unionists split 159 to 40 against and the Irish Nationalists 54 to 13 against. All 34 Labour votes supported the Bill, but three Labour

MPs were absent unpaired. The line-up was remarkable. Most of the leading Liberals, including Grey, Lloyd George, Rufus Isaacs, Runciman and John Simon supported it; so also did rather unexpected Unionists like the Cecil brothers; while Asquith, Churchill, 'Loulou' Harcourt and Herbert Samuel were among the opponents.[26] Pressure continued, however, and in 1914 the National Liberal Federation called unambiguously for women's suffrage. Abolition of plural voting also remained a very live issue. When the Franchise Bill of 1912–13 failed, a government Bill was introduced, designed to abolish more than half a million plural votes. It passed the Commons with substantial majorities, but again the Lords rejected it.

Pressure was also generated in support of further land reform. In May 1911, 173 Liberal and Labour MPs signed a memorial supporting Land Value Taxation,[27] and a deputation met the Prime Minister and Lloyd George. They were told that it was anticipated that the valuation would be complete within five years of passage of the Budget – that is, by 1915. This extreme delay was explained many years later by Sir Edgar Harper, who had been Chief Valuer of the Board of Inland Revenue in 1910.[28] Many questions were asked of landowners which were, no doubt, of interest, but had little to do with proposed taxation. Thus a matter which should have been simple for a valuer became unnecessarily complex. Until the valuation was complete, the main scheme for Land Value Taxation could not be set into effect. The determination of land taxers to keep up the pressure may be seen as one of the reasons behind the remarkable course of the Hanley by-election of 1912. The much smaller number of Liberal opponents of land taxing were also active, and in November 1912 forty of them presented a memorandum to Asquith to the contrary effect.[29]

Other aspects of the land problem began to attract ministerial attention. A new Land Campaign was inaugurated late in 1913. This was concerned essentially with rural problems, and proposed, among other things, greater security for tenant-farmers and minimum wages for farm labourers. There was an eager response. The Government's proposals, wrote Lloyd George to Asquith, 'seem to have been responsible for a great revival in the rural villages. Liberal Members and candidates state that their meetings are better attended than they have been since the General Election'.[30] The towns were no less enthusiastic. 'Swindon was electric,' he wrote to Percy Illingworth, who by this time had succeeded the Master of Elibank as Liberal Chief Whip.

> I have rarely addressed such an enthusiastic audience. The land has caught on. Winston found the same thing at Manchester. But we must not flag. The Tory Press have evidently received instructions from headquarters to talk

Ulster to the exclusion of land. If they succeed we are 'beat', and beat by superior generalship.[31]

Illingworth's experience was similar. 'The Prime Minister's speech last night' – that is, at the National Liberal Federation meeting in Leeds – he wrote, 'was I think the best I ever heard him make. "Land" went like hot cakes at the delegates' meeting.'[32]

By the spring of 1914, the government was ready to take further steps in the direction of land taxing. These were linked with the 1914 Budget, which – like its 1909 predecessor – was required to provide for naval rearmament and also a substantial programme for education, poor law provisions, police, health and roads. Lloyd George proposed various tax increases at the upper end of the scale. The Budget proposed Treasury grants in relief of rates, contingent on legislation to encourage site value rating. A 'cave' of Liberal critics developed, who objected to various features of the Budget for very disparate reasons. The Finance Bill encountered a good deal more trouble than is usual, and received its Third Reading just over a week before the outbreak of war.[33]

As often happens, allegations of what would today be called 'sleaze' arose at a time of intense political controversy, and there can be little doubt that many people were disposed to believe the 'sleaze' allegations not on the basis of any evidence advanced, but because they disliked the government party for completely different reasons.[34] The Imperial Conference of 1911 had urged the establishment of a chain of state-owned wireless telegraphy stations throughout the Empire. Tenders were sought, and in March 1912 that of the Marconi Company was accepted by the Postmaster-General, Herbert Samuel, subject to a final contract being laid before the House of Commons. The Company's Managing Director was Godfrey Isaacs, brother of Sir Rufus Isaacs, the Attorney General. An obscure periodical with an anti-Semitic bias alleged that Samuel had improperly recommended the contract because of the link between the Isaacs brothers. Samuel considered suing for libel, and sought advice from Sir Rufus, who referred him to Asquith. The Prime Minister advised Samuel to ignore the matter. Another, and quite different, charge soon received publicity, to the effect that Sir Rufus, Lloyd George and the Master of Elibank had all traded in Marconi shares at a great profit, making use of 'insider' knowledge.

In October 1912, the Government set up a Select Committee (appointed, as usual, on an all-party basis), to investigate all charges. The allegations against Samuel were soon shown to be completely unfounded. Isaacs, Lloyd George and Elibank had indeed bought shares in an American Marconi Company, but only after satisfying themselves that it had no financial interest in the British company, or in any contracts which the British company might make with the British Government; and that its operations were confined to working Marconi patents in the United States. In the Parliamentary debates leading to the appointment of the Select Committee, Isaacs and Lloyd George had correctly denied that they had any interest, direct or indirect, in the British company, but had not referred to their dealings with shares in the American Company.

In June 1913, the Select Committee published two reports. They both agreed that the Ministers were innocent of the charges alleged. The minority report, however, held that there was 'grave impropriety' in the American share transactions. A motion of censure on the Ministers was moved by the Opposition, and rejected by a vote which followed. In the end, however, a resolution was carried unanimously, indicating that the House of Commons 'acquits them of acting otherwise than in good faith, and reprobates the charges of corruption brought against Ministers which have proved to be wholly false'.

A well-known monograph on the history of the Liberal Government in this period takes as its sub-title 'Unfinished Business'. What went wrong? The government had not worked itself out of a job, like the government of 1868; it had not been swept off course by largely unpredictable events like the government of 1880; it had not been defeated on a major issue, as in 1886; it had not succumbed to general demoralisation, like Rosebery's government in 1895. There was a majority, though a composite one, for most of the things it wanted to do. A major part of the trouble, of course, was the sudden arrival of war in August 1914, which threw all political calculations to the winds. Without that catastrophe, there is good reason for thinking that Irish Home Rule and Welsh Disestablishment would have taken effect, and perhaps a substantial measure of franchise reform as well. There was a chance that land valuation would have been complete in time for the first instalment of Land Value Taxation to appear in the Budget of 1915. Another serious difficulty was the continuing power of the House of Lords. The Upper House had presented problems to earlier Liberal Governments, and occasionally even to Conservative governments; but, before 1906, it had never shown the consistent partisan opposition which it currently demonstrated towards the Liberals.

Yet, taking its whole period of office together, the pre-1914 Liberal government must rank as one of the greatest, perhaps as the very greatest, British reforming government of all time. It perceived, much more clearly than any previous administration (or most later ones, for that matter), that the vast existing gap between wealth and poverty was iniquitous, and that statesmen had a great duty to narrow that gap. This necessarily involved public spending on a much larger scale than hitherto. In 1906, income and expenditure balanced at around £125 millions; in the last year of peace they balanced at around £195 millions. Some of the increase was due to extra defence costs, particularly of the navy, but most of it was due to spending on items like Old Age Pensions, National Insurance and education. Many people have suggested that all this was a repudiation of Gladstonian ideas of retrenchment. That is to misunderstand both Gladstone and his twentieth century successors. In Gladstone's heyday, hardly anybody contemplated spending large sums of state money on 'welfare'. The expenditure on which Liberals of that period sought to retrench was of a completely different kind. When people began to take up the idea that organs of government could, and should, take positive action to rectify the imbalance between wealth and poverty, Liberals rapidly set themselves in the vanguard of that movement. Yet they remained true to the Gladstonian notion that they had a duty to treat public money as a trust which the statesman should dispense with more care than he would dispense his own resources. Like Gladstone, too, they saw Free Trade not only as an economic expedient but also as a great moral cause.

12

Catastrophe

Honour, Duty, Humanity all unite in my protest against this wanton war.

John Burns, 3 August 1914[1]

In the 1890s, there existed two Alliances of European Great Powers: the Dual Alliance of France and Russia, and the Triple Alliance of Germany and Austria-Hungary, with Italy loosely attached. Both Alliances were, in form at least, purely defensive. Britain, priding herself in 'splendid isolation', and determined to pursue a policy of 'friendship with all, alliance with none', was not committed to either group. In 1904, while the Unionist Government was still in office, the *Entente Cordiale* with France was concluded. Various points of disagreement, mainly affecting 'spheres of influence' overseas, were resolved; but Britain was under no sort of duty, stated or implied, to go to war in support of France in any circumstances, even if France were victim of an unprovoked attack. Yet the arrangements were not wholly innocuous. Britain and France undertook to afford each other 'diplomatic support' in disputes affecting Egypt (which fell in the British sphere), and Morocco (which fell in the French sphere).[2]

When the Liberals took office in December 1905, a major international dispute which had considerable bearing on the *Entente* had already been in operation for a long time. The French had begun to put pressure on the Sultan of Morocco to introduce 'reforms' which would operate in their favour. In March 1905, the German Emperor descended on Tangier, and proclaimed the independence of the Sultan. It was widely considered that this dramatic action was not prompted by any perceived German interest in Morocco, and still less by any deep concern for the Sultan of Morocco, but rather in order to test the Anglo-French *Entente*. By the time Sir Edward Grey became Foreign Secretary, plans were already afoot for an international conference at Algeciras, in southern Spain, to attempt a resolution of the dispute.

On 10 January 1906, while the General Election was still in progress, Grey had an interview with the French Ambassador, Paul Cambon, who sought to determine how the new Government would react to issues at stake between France and Germany.[3] Cambon asked whether Britain would go to war in France's defence, if she were attacked by Germany. This, of course, went far beyond the terms of the *Entente*. Grey replied that the Prime Minister and Cabinet were dispersed, and that he could not answer without their authority; but that, in his view, public opinion would support France.

When the General Election was over and the new Ministers were able to assemble again, there was no doubt about their general concurrence with Grey's attitude. Secret military and naval conversations between British and French experts began almost immediately. At the Algeciras Conference, a compromise agreement was reached by which, on the face of things, nobody got their own way entirely; but the general disposition of the British representatives to support France was noted. The change of government had not resulted in any perceptible shift in foreign policy.

The French were eager that the *Entente* should be followed by a British *rapprochement* with their ally Russia. That was difficult for various reasons. There had been intermittent hostility between Britain and Russia for many years. There were also large doubts about the efficiency of Russia's armed forces, particularly after the massive defeat she had sustained at the hand of Japan in 1905. There was also a widespread loathing for the Tsar's autocracy, most particularly among radical supporters of the government.[4] As with France, however, hostility was followed by diplomatic understanding, and in 1907 what is sometimes called an Anglo-Russian *Entente* was concluded.

But removal of tensions with France and Russia was accompanied by increasing tensions with Germany. These turned in particular on fears of Germany's growing naval strength. By 1908, a major 'naval race' between Britain and Germany was in operation, and the link between this contest and the celebrated Budget of 1909 has already been noted. In July 1910, Lord Loreburn, still Lord Chancellor, raised in Cabinet 'the possibility of a close political understanding between this country and Germany'.[5] If an *Entente* with France and Russia was useful for the cause of peace, why not a similar *Entente* with Germany? Grey's response was not encouraging. 'He pointed out the inexpediency of entering into any engagements with Germany which would be of such a character as to lead to misunderstanding, and perhaps the loss of friendship, with France and Russia.' This seems to mean that the Foreign Secretary had decided to support the Dual Alliance countries, and tacitly accepted that this implied reserve towards Germany.

Early in 1911, there were nevertheless some signs that serious negotiations with Germany might begin. But Asquith had to admit to the King 'the impossibility of France openly abandoning as against Germany, the policy of "*revanche*"'.[6] Not to put too fine a point on it, no French diplomat or statesman could publicly repudiate the intention of ultimately avenging the French defeat in the Franco-Prussian war of 1870–71, and particularly of recovering the lost provinces of Alsace and Lorraine. Such aspirations could only be satisfied through war.

As the year 1911 advanced, serious international tension developed. France began to interfere increasingly with the internal affairs of Morocco, pleading the familiar excuse that she was acting 'to restore order in an oriental [*sic*] state falling into chaos and civil war'.[7] Fez and Alcazar were occupied – action which, in the German view, constituted a breach of both the letter and the spirit of the Algeciras agreements.[8] Germany sought 'compensation' in the form of a large chunk of the French Congo. Early in July the German government despatched the gunboat *Panther* to the Moroccan port Agadir.

Grey recommended to the Cabinet that Britain should propose a conference to deal with the situation, with the veiled threat that, in the event of Germany refusing to join, 'we should take steps to assert and protect British interests'.[9] This produced a shocked response from Lord Loreburn, 'on the ground that our direct interest in the matter was insignificant, and that, as a result of such a communication, we might soon find ourselves drifting into war'. What was described as 'a long and animated discussion' followed. In the end it was agreed, on the one hand, that admission of Germany to Morocco would not necessarily constitute a *casus belli*, and on the other hand that Britain would 'aim to work in concert with French diplomacy'.

Before the Agadir crisis was quite over, a new issue was raised, which also bore on Britain's relations with France. Rather by accident, some of the more pacifist members of the government discovered that detailed talks had been taking place between the British and French General Staffs concerning possible military operations against Germany. At the beginning of November, Morley protested in Cabinet that these discussions had taken place 'without the previous knowledge and directions of the Cabinet'.[10] Haldane, still Secretary for War at this time, blandly informed his colleagues that 'the communications in question [had] been initiated as far back as 1906 with Sir H. Campbell-Bannerman's sanction, and resumed in more detail during the spring and summer of the present year'. In other words, not only Asquith but his predecessor had withheld these vital matters from Cabinet colleagues.

Early in 1912, the Cabinet learnt that the German Emperor was anxious that the Foreign Secretary should visit Berlin.[11] Following Grey's lead, they decided that such a visit would be 'premature', but that Haldane, who would be visiting Germany in any event, might meet the Kaiser 'to feel the way in the direction of a more definite understanding'. Haldane returned with a rather encouraging view of meetings he had had with the Emperor and some of his Ministers, but the aftermath was less encouraging. Grey concluded that 'the Germans were not really willing to give up the naval competition and ... they wanted a political formula that would in effect compromise our freedom of action. We could not fetter ourselves by a promise to be neutral in a European war'.[12] In spite of this grave setback, there were soon signs which suggested that the situation was easing. As late as January 1914, Winston Churchill, by this time First Lord of the Admiralty, submitted long-term naval estimates. He was faced by 'strong protests ... against this scale of expenditure' by several members of the Cabinet, including Lloyd George, and was forced to make some reductions.[13] Evidently there was no general sense of confrontation with Germany, still less any sense that war was likely in the near future.

War came suddenly in 1914. On 25 July, when Archduke Franz Ferdinand, heir presumptive to the throne of Austria-Hungary, had been dead for almost four weeks, the Cabinet met in an atmosphere of crisis. This was not prompted by the international situation but by failure of the Buckingham Palace Conference on Ireland, and current fears of civil war there. Later in the meeting, Grey reported the Austrian ultimatum to Serbia, which he described as 'the gravest event for many years past in European politics: as it may be the prelude to a war in which at least four of the Great Powers might be involved'.[14] The Serbian reply to the ultimatum was construed in Austria as rejection, and on 28 July war began between the two countries. It soon became apparent that Germany, Russia and France were also likely to be involved. Although no treaty obligation existed for Britain to go to war in defence of France, Grey considered that it would be necessary to do so for her own interest, and was prepared to resign if that view was not adopted.[15]

There was a further peril in the current situation. If war arose between Germany and France, it was highly likely that one of them – more probably Germany – would invade Belgium in order to strike at the other. Was Britain under an obligation, moral or strategic, to enter war in such circumstances in defence not of France but of Belgium? On 30 July, Asquith told the King that

> It is a doubtful point how far a single guaranteeing state is bound under the treaty of 1839 to maintain Belgian neutrality if the remainder abstain or refuse. The Cabinet considers that the matter if it arises will be rather one of policy than of legal obligation.[16]

What Asquith did not say, though doubtless the King guessed it, was that the Cabinet was profoundly split as to whether Britain should go to war in support of France, whether Belgium was invaded or not. A substantial section of the Liberal press was strongly anti-war at this stage. The lines of cleavage at all levels in the party were not sharp and clear; rather was there a continuum of opinions. As often happens in such circumstances, the upshot was worse than a decision either way:

> After much discussion it was agreed that Sir E. Grey should be authorised to inform the German and French Ambassadors that at this stage he was unable to pledge ourselves in advance, either under all conditions to stand aside, or in any conditions to join in.

No doubt the French and German Governments would put their own interpretations on likely British action, probably inspired in each case by a considerable amount of wishful thinking.

Events began to gather momentum, and on 1 August Germany declared war on both France and Russia. In the meantime, Grey was under huge pressure from his Foreign Office officials, who were eager for Britain to intervene in support of France. Of all Departments of State, the Foreign Office was perhaps the one in which the permanent officials' opinion was most influential. The Under-Secretary of State, Sir Arthur Nicolson (later Lord Carnock), wrote to Grey, with explicit advice that 'We should order mobilization today so that an expeditionary force may be on its way during next week'.[17] Nicolson's Assistant Under-Secretary and eventual successor Sir Eyre Crowe contended that 'the whole policy of the *Entente* can have no meaning if it does not signify that in a just quarrel England [*sic*] would stand by her friends.'[18] That explains very clearly the peril which doubters of the *Entente* had long feared. It was not simply a *quid pro quo* arrangement over imperial interests, or even a promise of mutual diplomatic support over Morocco and Egypt; in the last analysis, it could lead straight to war. But even Grey was forced to admit that opinion at all levels – in the government, in the House of Commons, in the country – was still profoundly divided, and that any attempt to force a clear decision would have been counter-productive.[19]

By the time that the Cabinet met on 2 August, the possibility of Germany invading Belgium was seen to be very strong.[20] The general, though far from unanimous, view was that infringement of Belgian neutrality would require Britain to intervene. Just after the Cabinet meeting, eight members who had greater or lesser doubts about intervention met.[21] Morley, who was one of the number, reflected afterwards that 'it wore all the look of an important gathering, but was in truth a very shallow affair'.[22]

On the following day, 3 August, Germany issued an ultimatum to Belgium, requiring free passage for troops, and on the next day Belgium was invaded. That altered everything. Whether or not Britain had a technical obligation to defend Belgium under a treaty already three-quarters of a century old, a majority of the Cabinet treated the invasion as the *casus belli*. Four members tendered their resignations: Morley, Burns, Lord Beauchamp and Sir John Simon.[23] Later in the day, the last two of these were persuaded to remain in place, but Morley and Burns persisted.[24] They were soon joined by a junior Minister, C. P. Trevelyan.

That evening, Grey delivered his famous speech in support of the government's policy. It was clear that Britain was on the verge of war. There is no doubt about the enormous effect which the Belgian invasion, and the determination of the Belgian King and government to resist that invasion, exerted not only on the government but also on British public opinion. Grey's speech received a remarkable parliamentary reception. Nobody was surprised that Bonar Law, for the Unionist Opposition, pledged support for the war. There was some astonishment when John Redmond did the same for the Irish Nationalists. Ramsay MacDonald, chairman of the Labour MPs, spoke against the war; but he was soon replaced in his office by Arthur Henderson who took the contrary view.

The three Liberal Ministers who resigned made remarkably little fuss. Burns issued no public statement. Incredibly, we find him writing to Asquith a few days later, urging that police recruiting should be stopped, in order to divert potential recruits into the army.[25] Morley also made no public statement at the time, but wrote privately that he had no place in a council of war 'not from a squeamishy conscience but because I should neither find much interest nor be of the slightest use to other people'.[26] Trevelyan sent a letter to his constituents in which his main concern seemed to be about the adverse economic effects which war would produce.[27] None of the three was taking what could be called a truly pacifist stance.

Other Liberals, though only a tiny minority in the parliamentary party, had grave doubts about the war. A. A. W. H. Ponsonby, the son of Queen Victoria's Private Secretary, and R. L. Outhwaite, the land-taxing victor at the Hanley by-election of 1912, were among them. Arnold Rowntree of York, and T. E. Harvey of West Leeds may perhaps be added to the little band. So may a few Liberal publicists like Norman Angell and E. D. Morel. Several of them would soon be linked closely with the anti-war minority in the Labour Party, through an organisation known as the Union for Democratic Control. No war can ever be waged successfully by liberal means. Inevitably, different Liberals baulked at different acts of illiberality which were necessary for its prosecution. The Liberal Party had nearly been torn to pieces by the Boer War, where the measure of national commitment was vastly less. It was sure to be shattered by the new conflict.

Asquith had held the War Office himself since the Seely fiasco earlier in the year. Now he gave the post to Field-Marshal Kitchener, who had recently been created an earl. All agreed that the appointment was a non-political one; but there was surely something anomalous about appointing the man who had been responsible for the Boer War concentration camps to what was otherwise still a Liberal Cabinet.

The domestic political crisis which had been subsumed in the greater international crisis at the end of July required urgent attention. The Irish Home Rule Bill and the Welsh Disestablishment Bill had both passed through all necessary stages and were awaiting royal assent, though an amending measure was expected which might take some heat out of the question of the six Ulster Protestant counties. Now that the Irish National-ists had rallied to support the war, would the Unionist Opposition be prepared to make some concessions? Not so. They demanded that the Home Rule Bill should be abandoned, and re-submitted at the end of the war. This, of course, would mean indefinite postponement, and perhaps eventual abandonment, of the whole matter. No agreement was reached between the parties, and the Government was compelled to act on its own. The Irish and Welsh Bills were to proceed to royal assent, but at the same time it was pro-posed that a Suspensory Bill should be passed, delaying operation of the two controversial measures for twelve months – or longer, if the war was still in progress. The Government proposed also that provision should be made for passage of an amending Bill affecting the Six Counties, and promised that force would not be used to coerce them. These over-generous concessions were received by the Unionists with the worst possible grace. Bonar Law made a savage speech, and his followers walked out of the House.

In some respects, however, there was considerable cooperation between the parties. An electoral truce was concluded between Liberals, Unionists and Labour, providing that any parliamentary seat which fell vacant should remain in the hands of the party which previously held it, and should not be contested by the others. The Parliamentary Recruiting Committee was established, with support from all three parties. By the end of the year, well over a million and a quarter men had either joined the forces or indicated their willingness to do so. A War Council was set up as the Cabinet's chief war policy committee, and included the former Unionist Prime Minister Arthur Balfour among its members.

At the turn of the year, an unforeseeable event occurred, which would have dire indirect consequences both for the Liberal Party and for the coun-try. The Liberal Chief Whip, Percy Illingworth, died of typhoid. Like the Master of Elibank before him, Illingworth was a man of exceptional ability, highly respected by both Asquith and Lloyd George. Asquith had consider-able difficulty in finding a successor, but eventually John Gulland, who had been nobody's first choice, was selected. In less tempestuous times, Gulland would probably have been accounted a good, though hardly an outstanding, Chief Whip; but in the turmoil of the war and its various political crises he played little part.[28]

Early in 1915, there were signs that the political situation in Britain was changing. The original assumption that the war would be a short one had been disproved. The Russian offensive in the east and the German offensive in the west had both failed to achieve decisive results. By the end of 1914, the land war was largely bogged down in mud. The Unionist opposition was frustrated because it was supporting the war, yet had little say in its management. Bonar Law was under increasing pressure from his own followers to try to bring about some kind of Coalition.[29] Lloyd George also began to warm to the idea of a Coalition.

The unexpected stagnation on the Western Front meant that shells became particularly important, and British supplies were inadequate. This necessarily reflected on the government, and criticism was acute. In the spring of 1915, while the shells crisis was developing, the Dardanelles campaign began. Landings were made at Gallipoli, not far from the Ottoman capital. Initial signs were encouraging, but it soon became apparent that the campaign had been badly mishandled, and a great many lives unnecessarily lost. Then the maverick, but very popular, First Sea Lord, 'Jackie' Fisher, resigned. The crunch came in the late spring. As recently as 12 May, Asquith had declared that the formation of a Coalition Government was 'not in contemplation'. On 17 May, Bonar Law wrote to Asquith, threatening a parliamentary debate. On the following day, to the astonishment of nearly everybody, an announcement was made to the effect that a Coalition Government was being set up. It appears that Asquith's Liberal colleagues were not consulted, and most of Bonar Law's Unionist colleagues did not approve of the idea.[30]

Formation of the new government proved very difficult, and the names of the new Cabinet were not announced for a further week. The change which may have distressed Asquith most was the removal of his friend Haldane from the Lord Chancellorship. Haldane, not the most popular Minister in the Government (long before, Campbell-Bannerman had nicknamed him 'Schopenhauer'), had been the victim of a scurrilous press campaign. There was no obvious candidate for the job. It was first offered to the Attorney-General Sir John Simon, who refused it.[31] The post was eventually given to the Solicitor-General, Sir Sidney (later Lord) Buckmaster. Churchill, who was widely blamed for the failures of the first part of the Dardanelles campaign, was shifted from the Admiralty to the more or less non-departmental post of Chancellor of the Duchy of Lancaster. The most remarkable Liberal change was the removal of Lloyd George from the Exchequer to a completely new post, as Minister of Munitions. His willingness to accept a technical demotion was typical of the man: he saw the production of weapons, most particularly of shells, as the most urgent need of the moment. Liberals were deeply opposed to the appointment of a Unionist to the Exchequer, fearing an attack on Free Trade, and so Reginald McKenna was moved in.

Space had to be found for Unionists, and so a number of Liberals were demoted from the Cabinet, or transferred to different posts. Most of the posts to which Unionists were appointed were not likely to prove central to public interest. Balfour, who became First Lord of the Admiralty, was the principal exception. Labour also entered the Coalition, Arthur Henderson becoming President of the Board of Education. Asquith tried hard to persuade Redmond to take a Cabinet post, but without success. The first Coalition Cabinet included twelve Liberals, eight Unionists, one Labour man and the non-party Kitchener. With the exception of Lloyd George's transfer to the Ministry of Munitions and Churchill's removal from the Admiralty, the changes had obviously been made for political rather than military reasons. There was no cause for thinking that the Unionist or Labour incomers would bring any special strategic insight, imaginative vision or administrative skills to the conduct of the war.

The new government soon ran into serious difficulties. McKenna's 1915 Budget, so far from being a vindication of Free Trade in wartime conditions, proved to be the first major attack on the whole principle. Inevitably, there was a massive general increase in taxation, direct and indirect. What drew the special attention of the keenest Free Traders was new duties on certain imported items, notably motor vehicles, cinema films, clocks and musical instruments. These so-called 'McKenna Duties' looked like devices for excluding foreign goods from British markets rather than devices for collecting wartime revenue or saving shipping space. One Liberal MP, 'Tommy' Lough of West Islington, described them as 'the price we are paying for a Coalition Government'; another called them 'simply the thin end of the wedge of Tariff Reform'. At the Committee Stage of the Finance Bill, some Liberals challenged various proposals of the Chancellor, but were – predictably – voted down. McKenna brushed aside such objections, urging that the new duties were merely temporary measures, designed to meet wartime needs. Time would show whose judgement was correct.

Nor was the Coalition particularly successful in its conduct of the war. Production of munitions, particularly shells, was the most significant exception, and the credit for this was widely accorded to Lloyd George. But the bloody stalemate on the Western Front continued; while, as 1915 advanced, it became increasingly apparent that the Dardanelles expedition was most unlikely to deliver the benefits which had initially been expected of it. The decision to evacuate Gallipoli was not taken until almost the end of the year, but the prestige of Churchill as chief author of the expedition continued to decline, and his resignation from the Government was announced in November.

The problem of army recruitment presented even more serious difficulties. When war came, the flood of eager volunteers was so great that it is doubtful whether the military leaders could have made much use of extra manpower, even if it had been available. As the war developed, however, matters began to change, and the demand for what cynics would later call 'cannon fodder' proved insatiable. In October 1915, the 'Derby Scheme' was considered by the Cabinet. It was proposed that men of military age should be invited, though not compelled, to attest their willingness to serve, and a promise would be given that married men would not be taken until unmarried men had been called up. Liberals and Conservatives were both split on the merits of the scheme.[32] In the end, the scheme was launched. It soon became clear, however, that not enough unmarried men had attested to meet requirements. By the end of the year, Asquith had come to accept the need for conscription of unmarried men.[33] In January 1916, the Government announced its intention to introduce legislation to that effect. One Liberal member of the Cabinet, Sir John Simon, resigned in protest. In a very short time it was clear that conscription of unmarried men would still not produce enough recruits. During the spring of 1916 legislation was passed which enabled married men to be taken as well. 28 Liberals voted against the measure on the Second Reading, 27 on the Third.[34]

The spring also witnessed the first signs that failure to apply Home Rule to Ireland would produce profound disaffection through most of the country. John Redmond – indeed, William O'Brien too – had taken immense political risks when they urged support for the British wartime cause. The Easter Week rising of April 1916 profoundly challenged not only the Government but also the authority of the traditional Nationalists. The rebels seized a number of important buildings in Dublin, proclaiming the 'Irish Republic'. They were roundly condemned by the Nationalist Party, and surrendered after about a week, while Dublin crowds turned out to jeer them after their arrest. Birrell, the Chief Secretary for Ireland, resigned. Soon captured rebels were court-martialled, and considerable numbers were shot. The Cabinet quickly decided that only leaders of the rising should be executed, and in no case women.[35] Already, however, enormous harm had been done to British prestige in Ireland. In a great many Irish minds, the executed rebels were rapidly included in the very long list of patriotic martyrs.

The rising may have been stimulated in part by the conscription proposals. Despite Redmond's encouragement, recruitment in southern Ireland had been slack from the very start of the war. Although the conscription legislation did not apply to Ireland, it was always open to Parliament to change its mind on the matter, and no doubt a great many young Irishmen who had no wish to fight at all would – if forced to do so – prefer to fight to drive the British from Ireland rather than fight to drive the Germans from Belgium. After a week viewing the Irish situation on the spot, Asquith decided that the only way of preserving what remained of Southern loyalty to some kind of British connection was by bringing Home Rule into operation. Lloyd George was charged to work out a plan, in close contact with both Redmond and Carson. The three men concluded that the suspended measure of 1914 must be brought into immediate effect, while an Amending Act should be passed, excluding the six Protestant Ulster counties for the duration of the war and for a limited period thereafter. Initial reactions were very encouraging. The Ulster Unionists accepted the plan, while a convention of Nationalists from the Six Counties did the same.

When the matter was referred to the Cabinet, however, serious difficulties began. Even before the Cabinet actually met, one Unionist, Lord Selborne, resigned in protest. The Liberals were unanimous in support. The Unionists, by contrast, were deeply split.[36] Bonar Law, Balfour and Carson favoured the proposals; most other Unionist members of the Cabinet were to a greater or lesser degree opposed. At one moment in the discussions, it looked as if the government would break up; but Lloyd George saved the situation temporarily by suggesting that a small Committee of the Cabinet should be set up, charged to devise plans for maintaining military and naval control in Ireland for the duration of the war. On that understanding, the Unionists who had contemplated resignation decided to remain in place. A few days later, an acceptable arrangement seemed to emerge from the Cabinet; but in truth the matter was far from settled.

On 11 July, Lansdowne, Unionist leader in the House of Lords and a senior member of the government, addressed their Lordships, and went far outside the agreed compromise. The implication of the speech was that exclusion of the Six Counties must be permanent. Stress was laid on coercive measures which, in his view, would need to be applied in Ireland. Redmond described the speech as 'a gross insult to Ireland'. Technically, however, the issue which finally broke down the compromise was Bonar Law's assertion, nearly three weeks later, that the number of Irish MPs sitting at Westminster should be reduced once the Home Rule Parliament was set up. The damage was done, and it was irrevocable. The Home Rule Act was not brought into effect, and within a short time Ireland was set on a course which would lead to complete alienation and eventually civil war.

Already, other great changes had taken place. Early in June 1916, Kitchener embarked for Russia, which was already showing early signs of the eventual collapse. The ship carrying him was torpedoed, and Kitchener, along with most of the ship's company, was drowned. For a month, Asquith again assumed control of the War Office himself. This was an enormous extra burden on the Prime Minister, who had been carrying the Irish Office as well since Birrell's resignation in May. In July, however, Asquith decided to relinquish the two extra offices. There was considerable doubt about the succession in both cases,[37] but eventually Lloyd George was transferred to the War Office, and was succeeded at the Ministry of Munitions by another Liberal, Edwin Montagu. The new Chief Secretary for Ireland was H. E. Duke, at the time a relatively obscure Unionist, though later (as Lord Merrivale) a famous judge.

Towards the end of 1916, it became increasingly evident that neither side was winning the war, while both were sustaining enormous numbers of pointless casualties. As usually happens when matters are developing badly, media and public looked for scapegoats, and Ministers – particularly Asquith – came in the line of fire. On 13 November, Lord Lansdowne submitted a memorandum to the Cabinet in which he appeared to think the unthinkable, and suggest that there might be merit in commencing peace negotiations.[38] But the war had acquired a momentum of its own, which nobody could control or stop. If peace negotiations were impractical, then the only other course which made sense was a much more vigorous prosecution of the war. A Liberal War Committee was already in existence, and had been campaigning for some time for action of that kind. Anything in between would be more damaging than either extreme course.

There followed several weeks of complex intrigues, involving most of the leading political personalities in various combinations. In some important cases, the motives of particular individuals admit of very different interpretations. What really matters, however, is not the behaviour and intentions of the various politicians, but the upshot. On 1 December, Lloyd George wrote to Asquith, arguing that the existing War Committee should be replaced by a much smaller and less cumbersome body. Asquith agreed with that point, but disagreed with Lloyd George's proposals for its composition. On 3 December, most of the leading Unionists met, and Bonar Law presented Asquith with an ultimatum: either the Prime Minister must resign, or they would do so. This looks like an attempt to break Asquith; but next day several of the men who had attended the meeting waited on the Prime Minister and assured him that they had no wish for him to retire, but sought to enable him to reconstruct his government, and return in a stronger position than before. Perhaps.

Whatever the intentions may have been, Asquith had no choice but to tender the government's resignation. He was immediately commissioned by the King to form a new administration, but soon reported failure. The King then invited Bonar Law to form a Ministry, and later Lloyd George, but both soon decided that they would be unable to do so. So on 6 December Asquith, Bonar Law, Lloyd George, Balfour and Henderson were invited together to Buckingham Palace. Again no clear decision emerged, but it appeared unlikely that either Bonar Law or Lloyd George would be prepared to serve under Asquith.

Later in the same day, a meeting was held, attended by most of the Liberal Ministers and also by Henderson from the Labour Party. All agreed that it was impossible for Asquith to form a new Government without support from Lloyd George or the Unionists. But should he join an administration formed by either Lloyd George or Bonar Law? Asquith's colleagues thought that he would have little influence on the course of events if he did so, and a new collision would probably follow soon. As Lord Crewe wrote a few weeks later,

> The creation therefore of a sober an responsible opposition (if that be the proper term) steadily supporting the government in the conduct of the war, criticising where necessary, and in the last resort offering an alternative Administration, was the best outcome of the crisis in the national interest.[39]

Most of the leading Liberals soon decided not only that Asquith should not join an alternative administration, but also that they would not themselves do so.

What did ordinary Liberal MPs think of the matter? Much attention has been focused on the account by Christopher Addison, a Liberal MP who canvassed colleagues extensively. At a late night meeting on 6 December, Addison assured Lloyd George, Bonar Law, Sir Edward Carson and the Unionist Chief Whip Lord Edmund Talbot that Lloyd George had 49 out-and-out supporters among the Liberal MPs, and that a further 126 would support him if the could form a government. Subsequent events would show that this was an exaggeration.[40] But it would be inordinately difficult for Bonar Law or any other Unionist to form a viable government without official Liberal support. That left Lloyd George, whom the King now invited to form an Administration. On the following day, 7 December, Lloyd George formally kissed hands as Prime Minister.

Next day, 8 December, Asquith gave an account of events to a meeting of Liberal MPs and peers at the Reform Club.[41] He began by explaining that, although he had resigned the premiership, he had not resigned leadership of the Liberal Party, 'though I am quite prepared to do that if I am asked'.

Asquith expressed goodwill towards the new government in unambiguous terms, but also gave a lucid explanation of his own refusal to serve. If he were to enter the government in a subordinate capacity, the attacks on him would continue, which would compel his new colleagues either to get rid of him or to be 'tarred with the same terrible brush'. He categorically denied having exercised any kind of pressure on his own colleagues to stay out of the new government.

> I have said to them collectively, and I have said to them individually, 'Exercise your own judgement; consider how you can best serve them. If you think you can serve them by going in, for God's sake go in; if you can best serve them by remaining with me outside, stay outside. I do not quarrel with your judgement or attempt to exercise any pressure upon you one way or another.'

13

The Era of Lloyd George

From your time among barbarians, you have become a barbarian.

Euripides, *Orestes*, 485

Lloyd George did not find the construction of a government easy, and several days elapsed before the full list of new Ministers was ready. The new Prime Minister had considerable difficulties with all three parties. In the end he was able to incorporate most of the leading Unionists, the conspicuous exception being Lansdowne, who appears not to have been invited. The Labour Party decided to join. But Lloyd George's greatest problem was with his fellow Liberals.

Grey was almost bound to follow his chief's example and refuse office – if, indeed, it was offered to him. In his case, there were considerations of health as well as political reasons.[1] Apart from the Prime Minister himself, no Liberal who had held Cabinet office under Asquith was included in the Government at the beginning. It is not clear in all cases whether they had been invited to serve, but refused, or whether they had not been invited. Churchill, who had left Asquith's Cabinet a year earlier, would probably have been pleased to serve under Lloyd George, but the Unionists appear to have interposed a veto. Those Liberals who had held junior ministerial office under Asquith, and who were prepared to continue, sometimes received considerable promotion.

As he indicated in December 1916, Asquith remained leader of the Liberal Party. Various Liberal bodies soon passed pointed resolutions of appreciation and continued confidence in his leadership. Asquith's Chief Whip, John Gulland, remained in control of the party organisation. Lloyd George, like his predecessor, appointed two Government Chief Whips, representing the two main parties. Lord Edmund Talbot continued as Chief Unionist Whip, but Neil Primrose, son of Lord Rosebery, was appointed Chief Government Liberal Whip. Primrose left his post for active service in the spring of 1917, and was later killed in action. His successor was Captain F. E. ('Freddie') Guest. Liberal MPs therefore received two Whips, while Unionists received just one.

When Asquith's Ministry fell, the Cabinet included thirteen Liberals, nine

Unionists and one Labour man. In the new Government (discounting the difference between members of the War Cabinet and other Ministers 'of Cabinet rank'), the leading figures were eight Liberals, twelve Unionists and two Labour men. The change from a Ministry in which most of the principal offices were still held by Liberals to one in which most were held by Unionists was obviously adverse for the Liberal Party; but there were even graver features in the new arrangements. The partnership of Asquith and Lloyd George had been extremely fruitful. Lloyd George was a man of great imagination and mercurial temperament. Asquith had a judicial mind which usually, though not always, led him to the same conclusions as Lloyd George, but by a very different route. Although the 1916 changes did not produce any immediate division between 'Asquithians' and 'Lloyd Georgeites', it broke the partnership. Neither man had wished this to happen. Lloyd George had sought control of the war effort, not the title or the other duties of Prime Minister, which he would have been glad enough to leave to Asquith. Asquith was willing to continue as Prime Minister provided that he retained the plenitude of powers traditionally associated with that office – but he was also willing to give up the job entirely. In the first week of December, he may well have been almost indifferent as to which of the two results should follow. Politics was by no means the totality of his life. He was sixty-four years of age, and was not wearing well physically; while he had recently lost his most talented son in the war.

It is not difficult to appreciate that Lloyd George must have felt very isolated in a Government dominated by Unionists, whose other Liberal members were relatively minor figures. In May 1917 he tried, though without success, to bring back his old chief in the role of Lord Chancellor. In July, however, the resourceful Prime Minister was able to bring in two Liberals with Cabinet experience into offices 'of Cabinet rank'. Winston Churchill was appointed Minister of Munitions. This prompted an explosive response from the National Union of Conservative Associations; but leading Unionists, including Bonar Law and Carson, were prepared to welcome him. At the same moment Lloyd George brought in Edwin Montagu as Secretary of State for India. Asquith's reaction to the appointment was less than enthusiastic, but he did not condemn Montagu's decision to accept.[2]

Unexpectedly, Montagu was the newcomer who had the greater immediate influence on events. Working closely with the Indian Viceroy Lord Chelmsford, and also with the Unionist Lord Curzon, himself a former Viceroy, Montagu was able to announce in the following month that the government's aim was 'increasing association of Indians in every branch of the administration and gradual development of self-governing institutions with a view to the progressive realisation of responsible government in India as an integral part of the British Empire.' This was the first case in which self-government by a non-white indigenous people had been set as the ultimate goal for the British government in any imperial territory. The announcement was soon followed by detailed proposals concocted by Montagu in collaboration with Chelmsford.

In another direction, however, Montagu was less successful. The Government, like its predecessor, was disposed to promise anything to anybody if this seemed to offer some prospect of helping the Allied cause in the war. At that time, Palestine was still part of the Ottoman Empire, but a substantial 'Zionist' movement existed among Jews, particularly in Russia and the United States, who sought a return to their traditional homeland. The Germans were seeking Zionist support, and in the course of October 1917 there was much discussion in the War Cabinet about means of outflanking them. This eventually led to the so-called 'Balfour Declaration', promising 'a National Home for the Jewish race'. Montagu, the one Jew who held senior office in the Government, was not a member of the inner War Cabinet, but he was invited to one or two of its meetings. Declaring himself to be a 'Jewish Englishman', he was a passionate opponent of the Zionist proposals. The War Cabinet, however, had an eye much more to the prospect of winning foreign support than of meeting the scruples of British Jews like Montagu. In so doing, it was storing up enormous trouble for its successors.

1917 was an immensely important year in the progress of the war. The Tsar fell in March and, by the time of the Bolshevik revolution in November, Russia was already for practical purposes out of the war. The United States entered the war on the Allied side in April. By the end of the year, Germany and her associates were triumphant in the East; on the Western Front stalemate continued, but there was now a prospect that the arrival of innumerable Americans would prove decisive.

Throughout 1917, the Lloyd George Coalition faced several domestic challenges, though none sufficiently serious to threaten its existence. In March, the new Indian cotton duties raised the hackles of the most staunch Free Traders. The National Liberal Federation passed a critical resolution, and in the crucial House of Commons division 46 Liberals voted against the government, though 59 followed the Coalition whip.[3] Meanwhile, Asquith and his principal followers sat on Opposition benches, but the influence of the chief was wholly in the direction of giving external support to the Government. There were, however, two political sensations, both of which would have indirect bearing on the fate of the Liberals. In the summer, the question arose whether the Labour Party and the Trade Union movement were to be represented at an international Socialist conference in Stockholm, where delegates from enemy countries were also likely to be present. At first the Cabinet favoured the idea that Henderson should attend,[4] but later changed its mind. Henderson did not back down. There was an angry meeting with Lloyd George – the 'doormat incident' – which led to Henderson's resignation from the Government. Thereafter he devoted his considerable skills to the reconstruction of the Labour Party.

The other political sensation of 1917 was caused by publication in November of a letter to the *Daily Telegraph*, in which Lord Lansdowne argued publicly for peace negotiations. The Lansdowne letter had no immediate effect on the war, but it may have encouraged some of the senior non-government Liberals to question the desirability of continuing the conflict. One member of Lloyd George's secretariat even suspected that the letter had been inspired by the former Lord Chancellor, Lord Loreburn.[5]

In Ireland there were abundant signs of a sea-change in opinion in 1917. There were four contested by-elections in traditional Nationalist seats during that year, and in each case the constituency was captured by a Sinn Féin candidate who sought to break in the British connection completely. Home Rule, in the sense in which the term had been understood by Butt, Parnell and Redmond, was no longer the issue; the question was when, and how, Ireland would become an independent state.

In March 1918, Russia formally withdrew from the war, and enormous tracts of land were occupied by Germany and Austria. The Germans then attacked on the Western Front, and at one moment seemed near to victory. In the end they were held; but it was a close thing. By the late spring of 1918, there were various political elements in Britain which were disposed to favour peace negotiations. The 'Lansdowne letter' of the previous year had suggested that there might be other people on the political 'right' who perceived that the war was undermining traditional society, and it was therefore imperative to call a halt. On the 'left' were members of the Independent Labour Party (ILP), still affiliated to the Labour Party in those days, who had pacifist proclivities, and were cooperating with like-minded Liberals in the Union for Democratic Control. Towards the end of April, a by-election in the traditionally Liberal constituency of Keighley gave an anti-war ILP challenger almost a third of the vote, even though he received no support from the official Labour Party. Keighley was the only place where the electors were really confronted with the peace issue, and it is difficult to decide just how widespread the anti-war feeling was; but it was a fair guess that a series of serious military reverses could easily create a huge groundswell in favour of peace negotiations.

Among the Liberals, there were deep doubts about the war. A few had opposed it from the beginning; but there were signs that some of the most senior men who had left the Government in 1916 were beginning to think on similar lines. As early as August 1917, McKenna asked privately whether possible benefits from victory warranted the human and material cost.[6] In May 1918, 'Loulou' Harcourt discussed the need for 'a man to make peace', proposing the somewhat unlikely name of Grey as the candidate.[7] McKenna and Harcourt had both expressed these views in correspondence with Walter Runciman, another former member of Asquith's Cabinet; one may guess that they considered that such opinions might fall on receptive ears. In August, 'Freddie' Guest wrote to his chief that 'the Asquithians (except Mr Asquith)' were disposed to enter peace negotiations.[8] The exclusion of Asquith is significant; but he was the sort of man who would support a particular point of view for intellectual rather than emotional reasons, and who might well be persuaded the other way by force of argument or evidence.

By the spring of 1918, considerable numbers of Liberal MPs were voting regularly against the government on issues relating to the conduct of the war. Twenty-four of them went into Opposition lobbies on seven or more important occasions. In April, an amendment seeking to reduce the maximum age limit for conscripts was supported by no fewer than 73 Liberal MPs.[9] All this was happening without any encouragement from Asquith, who must have wondered just how long he could maintain any kind of restraint on his followers.

The astonishing 'Maurice Debate' of 1918 would have enormous consequences for the whole future of the Liberal Party. On 7 May, a letter was published in *The Times*, over the signature of Major-General Sir Frederick Maurice, who, until recently, had been Director of Military Operations. Maurice disputed the truth of public statements by Lloyd George and Bonar Law relating to the numbers and distribution of British forces. Asquith asked in the House of Commons what the Government proposed to do to enable MPs to examine the truth or otherwise of these allegations. Bonar Law, for the government, proposed to set up a judicial enquiry. Asquith was not satisfied, and demanded a Select Committee to study the matter. Lloyd George replied by countering the actual charges made by Maurice, pointing out for good measure that the letter was a breach of military discipline. A division was taken: the only occasion in the lifetime of that Parliament on which Government Whips told one way and Asquithian Whips the other. Including tellers, 108 MPs voted for the inquiry, and 295 supported the Government. The parties split very unevenly. The Liberals divided 98 to 71, the majority supporting Asquith's motion. Only one Unionist supported the motion. The Labour Party divided 9 to 15, the majority supporting the government.

There is evidence to show that Maurice's figures were correct, and that

they had been sent to Lloyd George's office; but that an accidental omission
by his secretariat, followed by deliberate destruction of the document destined for the Prime Minister, ensured that he never saw it, and honestly
believed that the figures were wrong. It also seems likely that a number of
Unionists would have voted against the Government, but were persuaded by
the Prime Minister's concluding speech. On that view, the apparently convincing government majority was more or less accidental, and the vote
might easily have gone very differently.

Thus there was a certain jitteriness in government circles in the summer
of 1918, and a feeling that an early General Election might well become necessary while the war was still in progress. If that happened, no major
politician was likely to challenge the government on the issue of fighting the
war to a finish *versus* peace negotiations; but a government defeat at such
an election might well be followed by peace negotiations. Lloyd George and
his associates had plenty of reason to analyse closely just which Liberals
could be regarded as 'theirs' in such an event. On 20 July, Guest sent the
Prime Minister a list of Liberals who could, and another list of Liberals who
could not, be regarded as government supporters.[10] Where a Liberal MP had
voted in the Maurice debate, that vote usually determined on which list he
appeared; but a good many Liberals had been absent from the division – in
some cases because they were on war service – and these had been allocated
one way or the other. Similar lists were drawn up for members of the Labour
Party. A 'mushroom' party, the National Democratic Party, was also
included in the list of people who should receive Government support. The
prospect of an early General Election soon vanished, but Guest's lists would
prove of great importance later on.

Plans for radical changes in the electorate and in constituency boundaries,
largely worked out in 1917, were finalised early in 1918. Although these had
been a matter of great controversy before the war, much of the old dispute
was thrust aside in wartime conditions. A very large proportion of the soldiers were not 'householders'; but how could such men be denied the vote?
How could women be excluded merely by reason of their sex, when their
work had been of vital importance during the war? There was little opposition in any party either to universal franchise for adult males, or to the
principle that women should receive the vote. Under the arrangements
which were eventually enacted, most men received the vote at age 21, while
those who had been on war service received the vote at 19. Women received
the vote for the first time, but not on the same terms as men. The qualify-
ing age was 30, and a woman received the vote only when she was a local
government voter or the wife of one. It was fairly obvious, however, that this
disparity would be rectified at no very distant date. Plural voting was

abolished, save in the case of the university franchise. It was noted at the time that, whereas the Reform Act of 1832 had enfranchised a mere half million new voters, the Act of 1867 had enfranchised a million and the Act of 1884 had enfranchised two million, yet the 1918 Act enfranchised eight million, three-quarters of whom were women.

Another extremely important political development of 1918 affected the Labour Party. In pre-war elections, Labour had never advanced more than 81 candidates, and many of those (particularly in hopeful seats) had received more or less support from local Liberals. If pre-war Labour had a 'role-model', it was the Irish Party, which had no aspiration to form the government itself, but hoped to return a substantial contingent of MPs who would be able to influence a government, be it Liberal or Conservative, in the direction of changes which the party desired. Much has been written about wartime divisions among the Liberals; but it is important to remember that the Labour Party had been every bit as divided. They split at the very start into supporters and opponents of the war; they threw out their pre-war Chairman; at one point some Labour MPs were sitting on the Government side of the House and others on the Opposition. Even in the Maurice debate they were deeply divided.

But in the course of 1918, the Labour Party underwent a complete change, and in this the influence of Henderson was very strong. The Trade Union Act of 1913 had provided that a Trade Union could maintain a political fund. Members of the Union were free to 'contract out' of contributions to that fund, but ordinary inertia ensured that most did not do so, even when they were not supporters of the Labour Party. Henderson was able to draw Trade Union attention to these substantial funds, which had no virement with the ordinary funds of the union, and urged them to use the idle money to promote Labour Party candidates. This led to a huge increase in the number of such candidates. At the same time, the Labour Party ceased to see itself as a loose confederacy of groups with different ideas and interests, and came to regard itself as a political party with a distinctive policy and programme, which sought eventually to become the government of the country.

While the war continued, all politics was in a state of uncertainty. Was the Coalition to continue into peacetime? Lloyd George was in a truly anomalous position as a Prime Minister who was not leader of a party. No doubt the ideal condition, from his point of view, would be for the Coalition to continue indefinitely under his Premiership, with a number of substantial political groups operating, no one with an overall majority, who could by played off against each other. This would ensure that in nine cases out of ten Lloyd George would get his own way.

The most important group which was currently outside the Coalition was the 'official' Liberals, led by Asquith. The former Master of Elibank, by this time Lord Murray, was one of the few influential Liberals who were still on close terms with both Asquith and Lloyd George. Late in September, he met Lloyd George and 'left with the understanding that off my own bat I would propose to Mr Asquith a reconstituted Government in which he should hold the post of *Lord Chancellor and nominate two of the Principal Secretaries of State and six Under Secretaries*'.[11] The proposal also required an agreement by Asquith to support conscription of Ireland. Asquith rejected the whole idea, and Murray reflected ruefully that 'in these two conversations I have been present at the obsequies of the Liberal Party as I knew it'. Lloyd George, however, did not take the rejection as final, and several weeks later Guest was writing as if acceptance was still a possibility.[12] The Unionists, by contrast, were much more willing to contemplate extending the Coalition into the foreseeable future.

The end of the war was abrupt, and on 11 November an Armistice was concluded with Germany. Almost immediately, Lloyd George called a General Election. The Labour Party promptly decided, by a convincing majority, to withdraw from the Coalition, though several members of the party defied this call, and remained in the government. For the first time, all polling would take place on the same day, 14 December. Allowing for changes in electoral qualifications and for changes in the register over eight years, something like two-thirds of the 1918 electors had never had the opportunity of voting before. In many places, political organisations had largely disintegrated, as local agents, MPs and active party workers had been on active service. Many constituency boundaries had changed beyond recognition.

In the great majority of British constituencies there existed Liberal and Unionist organisations of some kind, and for the first time the Labour Party was preparing to fight in most of them. All these local bodies were anxious to promote candidates. But there was a Coalition in existence, and it would be strange if candidates purporting to support the same government regularly took the field against each other. In the summer, there had been considerable discussions between Liberal and Unionist leaders in the Coalition as to which candidates should be regarded as deserving their support. When the election came, Liberal attitudes ranged from one Welshman who described the Prime Minister as 'the greatest man since Jesus Christ' to the scepticism of Runciman, who asked pointedly whether a land reformer, a Free Trader, a supporter of temperance or a believer in reform of the House of Lords could feel confidence in the policy of a government endorsed by certain of the prominent Unionists.[13] Asquith gave no very clear lead one way or the other.

Liberal headquarters were bound to give candidates some kind of advice about how to act in relation to the Coalition. The National Liberal Federation, in a magnificent attempt to square the circle, decided that candidates

should be free to promise support for the Coalition Government so long as it exists for the purpose of:
(a) securing a clean and durable peace;
(b) of promoting such consequential measures of social and political reconstruction as do not contravene in any vital particulars the declared policy of the Liberal Party.

Just what did that mean in practice? One may well ask.

In the end, complex arrangements were reached between the central offices of Lloyd George's henchmen and the Unionists. On 20 November, letters were sent out over the signatures of the Prime Minister and Bonar Law to approved people, declaring the individual concerned to be 'the Coalition candidate' for the constituency and inviting voters to support him. These letters were nicknamed 'Coupons', to parallel the coupons used in wartime rationing, and the name has stuck. In a number of cases, the Coupon was given to, or withheld from, a candidate in what looks like a perverse manner. There were also some places where Coupons were not used, including most, and possibly all, of the Irish constituencies. A large majority of the recipients were Unionists, but around 159 were Liberals, seventeen were members of the National Democratic Party (NDP), and a few belonged to other groups. The place of Labour in these arrangements was anomalous. Those Labour men who remained in the government were repudiated by their party, but received the Coupon. More remarkably, the 'official' Labour candidates whose names had appeared on Guest's July list of supporters did not usually find the Coupon used for their opponents. Most Liberal recipients of the Coupon, unlike Unionists, were selected with reference to their past political behaviour, usually on the basis of Guest's July list. Where a Liberal MP destined for the Coupon was not standing again, the usual practice was to award it to his successor in the constituency.[14]

The overall result of the election was a huge majority for the Coalition. In Great Britain 480 candidates with the Coupon were elected, against a very mixed bag of 122 who had not received it: thirty Liberals, sixty Labour, twenty-five Unionists and seven members of other Parties.[15] 332 of the British Coalition MPs were Unionists, 132 were Liberals, ten were NDP, and six came from other groups. Every Liberal frontbencher who had not received the Coupon was defeated, including Asquith in whose constituency the Coupon was not used at all. Although sixty Labour MPs, 57 of them 'official' candidates, were returned, yet most of Labour's leading figures, including both MacDonald and Henderson, were defeated. Sir Leo Money and E. T. John, both of whom had sat as Liberal MPs in the old House, stood unsuccessfully as Labour candidates. The Labour numbers compare with 42 MPs elected in December 1910, of whom 36 remained at the dissolution. In Ireland, the real sensation was the slaughter of traditional Nationalists. Sinn Féin, whose MPs were pledged not to sit in Westminster at all, won 73 seats. The Nationalists held only six: five in Ulster, where rather special conditions prevailed, and just one south of the Boyne. They held a seventh seat in a Liverpool constituency where there had been massive Irish immigration. The Irish Unionists, with 23 MPs, were overwhelmingly strong in Protestant parts of Ulster; they also held a seat in a wealthy district of Dublin.

In most parts of Britain, the Coupon appears to have been a huge asset for the recipient. Sir Percy Harris, a former Liberal MP who found the Coupon used against him, declared that 'it was assumed that I must have done something wrong for a member of my own party, Lloyd George, to sign a letter supporting my opponent ... my friends melted away like snow in the night'.[16] Similar experiences were widespread. In a few places the Coupon was less effective. West Derbyshire had been held by a Unionist ever since the Liberal split of 1886. In 1918, the two candidates were the same as in 1910, and the Unionist received the Coupon; yet C. F. White, the Liberal, was able to capture the seat with a comfortable majority. The fact that the Unionist was the son of Lord Lansdowne may have helped this remarkable result.

Those Liberals who had taken an unpopular line about the war were blotted out. Trevelyan ran fourth in Elland, with a Coalition Unionist, an uncouponed Liberal and a Labour man all far ahead of him. Outhwaite in Hanley did somewhat better. The Coupon went to an NDP man, who was duly elected, with Labour close behind. Outhwaite was a bad third, with an official Liberal fourth. D. M. Mason in Coventry ran fifth, with Coalition Unionist, Labour, official Liberal and Independent all ahead.

Of course, the Prime Minister had to appear delighted with the election result, but privately he must have been appalled. The last thing he would wish was to be dependent on a vast Unionist majority in the House of Commons. But everything had turned against his original hopes. The Asquithians had refused to enter the government, and then had been almost blotted out at the election; Labour had seceded from the government and moved into opposition; the Irish Nationalists had been crushed. He did his best to give Liberals an important place in the government. The reconstituted Ministry was announced on 10 January 1919. Including the Prime Minister, nine of the new appointees were Liberals, eleven Unionists, one 'Coalition Labour' and one non-party.

In both the Liberal and the Unionist Party, some MPs had been elected with support of the Coalition, others without it, and a few in defiance of the Coalition, whose 'Coupon' had been awarded to a rival. Despite this superficial similarity, the two leading parties were in profoundly different positions. Bonar Law, the Unionist leader, was a senior member of the government, while Asquith was outside both government and Parliament. Yet he and his Chief Whip still controlled the very considerable central funds of the party and most of its organisation.

It was immediately obvious that some of the Liberal MPs could be regarded as government supporters, others emphatically not so. But – as Gulland wrote – 'It is very difficult to draw accurately a list of the free men and to differentiate between the Coalition Liberals and the others'.[17] Roughly, but not exactly, the division corresponded with receipt, or non-receipt, of the Coupon. One or two of the 'uncouponed' Liberals, like Sir Francis Blake and Hilton Young, were Coalitionists at heart who had been denied the Coupon for technical – or accidental – reasons. A few of the Liberals who had received the Coupon, like P. W. Raffan, Samuel Galbraith and Evan Hayward, had no liking at all for the Coalition. Some MPs from both groups changed sides during the course of the next few years. For convenience the non-Coalition Liberals may be called 'Asquithians' (they were often nicknamed 'Wee Frees', after a small and strict Scottish sect), but several of the little band who had scrambled home without Coalition support were long-standing rebels, who may have preferred Asquith to Lloyd George, but could certainly not be regarded as dutiful followers of the official Leader or anybody else. Coalitionists and 'Asquithians' alike included a wide range of opinions on most questions: people who (to use the objectionable modern terms) stood to the 'left' and to the 'right' of the party.

On 3 February 1919, at the beginning of the new Session, a meeting of 23 Liberal MPs who might very loosely be called 'Asquithians' was convened by Captain Wedgwood Benn, a former junior Whip (who would later become the father of Tony Benn).[18] Four of those present had actually received the Coupon,[19] though they do not appear all to have used it. Some Liberals elected without the Coupon were absent: whether because they were not invited or because they did not choose to attend seems unclear.

With some dissension, the group proceeded to constitute itself the Liberal Parliamentary Party, and to elect officers. Sir Donald Maclean was elected sessional Chairman. Maclean had been Chairman of Ways and Means and Deputy Speaker in the old House, and had performed important administrative work during the war, but had never held government office. Although the Labour Party had twice as many MPs as the 'Wee Frees', it was never wholly clear who was the official Opposition. The *Annual Register* declares that it was Labour; but there is some evidence that for practical purposes Maclean performed the rôle of Leader of the Opposition.[20]

Choice of a Chief Whip presented further difficulties. As Gulland had been defeated at the General Election, he certainly could not continue. Asquith had wanted Wedgwood Benn, but Benn would not accept the job, and the leader's second choice was G. R. Thorne. The meeting was in no mood to accept instructions from anybody, even Asquith, and (apparently at the instigation of Josiah Wedgwood, a radical and keen land reformer),[21] insisted on partnering Thorne with J. M. Hogge, a noted rebel of pre-war days, whom Maclean heartily detested.[22] In practice neither Thorne nor Hogge secured the overall control of the party machinery which Chief Whips had exercised in the past, which largely devolved on Maclean.[23] Thereafter Liberal headquarters were controlled largely by a triumvirate composed of Maclean, Viscount Gladstone and the party's chief salaried official, Sir Robert Hudson, all of whom were bitterly opposed to Lloyd George.

A couple of days after the Wee Frees met, a meeting was convened of all 'unofficial' Liberal MPs – that is, those who did not hold office in the government. George Lambert, who had defeated a 'Couponed' Unionist in South Molton, presided; the most notable absentee was Maclean. It was decided to establish a committee of eight MPs, four from each section, to promote unity. The Coalitionists at once appointed their delegates. When the 'Wee Frees' met on the following day to do the same, two at least of their number opposed the idea altogether; but eventually four were chosen.[24] The committee held several meetings, but broke down a month later. The occasion, if not the cause, of the breakdown was the first by-election to be contested by a Liberal in the new Parliament. At the General Election a 'Couponed' Unionist had defeated a Liberal in a straight fight at West Leyton. When the MP died, a Coupon was again used for the Unionist candidate, but on 1 March the Liberal, A. E. Newbould, was victorious, with a large swing of votes. At the meeting of Liberal MPs five days later, the non-Coalitionists invited the others to support a seemingly innocuous resolution to the effect that, when a Liberal candidate was selected by a Liberal Association, 'it is undesirable that a Liberal MP should oppose that choice'. This was a knock at the Prime Minister, and the Coalitionists could not possibly accept it.[25] That was the end of the joint committee; but another meeting of 'unofficial' Liberal MPs was summoned later in March. Lambert was elected sessional Chairman.[26] This annoyed the 'Wee Frees', who soon decided to withdraw their whip from him. 'Whipping' of Liberal MPs was already becoming a matter of serious controversy. At first, Guest had sent the Coalition Whip to all Liberal MPs; early in April the non-Coalitionists requested him to cease issuing it to them.

How far the deepening controversy between Liberal parliamentarians and leaders actually touched ordinary voters, or even rank-and-file Liberal activists, in the first half of 1919 is uncertain. At the end of March, a by-election in Hull Central resulted in a Liberal, Lieutenant-Commander J. M. Kenworthy, taking a seat which had been held by a 'Couponed' Unionist, with a huge overturn of votes. In April, another Liberal gain from a Coalition Unionist was recorded in Aberdeenshire Central. This time the Liberal had succeeded despite the intervention of a Labour candidate. These three successes, in widely scattered and very different constituencies, suggested that politics was reverting to a pre-war pattern. One wonders to what extent voters were turning actively against the Coalition, and to what extent they were merely ignoring the Coupon, and voting just as they would have done five years earlier. It is possible that Lloyd George himself did not wholly regret these developments, for they demonstrated to his Unionist colleagues that Liberalism remained a substantial force, which they could ignore only at their peril.

In the spring of 1919, there were other signs that Coalitionist, as well as Asquithian, Liberals had not forgotten where they had stood in the old battles. Some of the Coalition Liberal Ministers certainly exerted a marked influence in the Liberal direction. Christopher Addison's Housing Act required local authorities to submit plans for provision of new houses and for slum clearance to the Local Government Board; in default, the Board could act instead. There were also schemes to encourage urban home-ownership. Edwin Montagu was able to carry Government of India legislation which enshrined the idea of the Montagu-Chelmsford proposals, with the avowed object of eventually granting self-government to India.

A run of particularly important by-elections took place at the end of 1919 and in the early part of 1920. Spen Valley was a traditionally Liberal constituency which had been represented since 1892 by Sir Thomas Whittaker, who had received the Coupon in 1918. When he died, the local Liberal Association decided, by a majority, to seek a candidate from the Asquithian headquarters. When the name of Sir John Simon, Asquith's former Home Secretary, was proposed, he was unanimously adopted. Why Simon, one may ask. Why not Asquith himself, who had lived for much of his early life in the West Riding, close to the constituency? Lloyd George had a strong animus against Simon ('I don't care who wins if that blighter is last!' he snorted to one of the Unionists)[27] and the Coalition Liberals produced a certain Colonel A. C. Fairfax, who had never been a candidate anywhere before and never was again, who operated from the local Unionist offices. Some of the 'Coalies' showed visible disquiet at the decision to oppose Simon. One of them, A. R. Barrand, who sat for the nearby constituency of

Pudsey, even spoke in his favour; while Dr T. J. Macnamara, one of the Liberal Ministers, was sharply and publicly criticised by his local Association when he spoke in support of Fairfax. On 20 December the Labour candidate was elected, with Simon a close second and Fairfax running third. This was the first occasion since the General Election on which a Coalition Liberal opposed a candidate who had been nominated by a Liberal Association, and from that moment it was open warfare between the two Liberal groups.

In January 1920, Sir John McCallum, Liberal MP for Paisley, died. The by-election following his death was bound to be a very interesting one in any event. The local Liberals decided – though only after some hesitation – to offer the candidature to Asquith, and so excitement was intense. On 12 February, he was returned with a fairly comfortable majority over the Labour candidate. The Unionist, who appears to have been a highly unsuitable choice, ran a very bad third, forfeiting his deposit. But even in this moment of triumph, the Asquithians received sharp warning of danger from a different quarter. Nine men who had sat as Liberal MPs in the old House, and also Lord Haldane, gave public support to the Labour candidate.[28]

In the following month, the division between the Liberal groups became even sharper. Maclean, the most hawkish of the Asquithians, promised Headquarters assistance to independent Liberals wherever either the candidate or the local Liberal Association had made 'a compact or arrangement' with the Conservatives. A few days after Maclean spoke, a by-election was held in North-West Camberwell. The 'Coalie' Macnamara was opposed by a 'Wee Free' in a triangular contest. Macnamara was returned with a comfortable majority over Labour, with the other Liberal running third. Elsewhere, the Asquithians continued to make some progress. A Coalition Unionist seat fell to them in June, when Tom Wintringham captured Louth, in Lincolnshire.

If the Coalition Liberals' relations with the Asquithians were deteriorating so rapidly, just what sort of alternative political arrangements should they make? In the first half of 1919, a group of newly-elected Coalitionist MPs evinced interest in the idea that the Coalition should eventually turn into a 'Centre Party'. Most of the group were Unionists, but the Chairman was Oscar Guest, brother of the 'Coalie' Whip. These new MPs had little direct influence on events, but the idea of 'fusion' of the Coalition groups began gradually to attract attention from much more important public figures, including Addison and Churchill on the Liberal side and Balfour and Austen Chamberlain on the Unionist side. As time went on, Lloyd George and Bonar Law both seemed interested as well.

In March 1920, while the North-West Camberwell by-election was still being fought, the idea of 'fusion' was aired more generally. It was tested at a meeting of about 25 Coalition Liberal Ministers. The business was supposed to be secret, but an extensive report was published in *The Times* next day. Considerable shades of opinion could be discerned between those, like Addison, who favoured 'fusion', and others who were strongly against it. In the end Lloyd George, always adept at smart political footwork, explained that what he sought was merely closer cooperation between the two wings of the Coalition in the constituencies.[29] Any hope – or fear – that the 'Centre Party' idea still had life in it was effectively dispelled at a meeting of Liberal MPs (most of them Coalitionists) held a couple of days later.[30] Bonar Law, who was having trouble with some of his own followers on the same score, also reacted strongly against the idea of 'fusion'.

But what *were* the 'Coalies' to do? If fusion with the Unionists was out of the question, would other Liberals continue to acknowledge them as members of their own party – heretics perhaps, but Liberals nevertheless, with whom they would expect one day to reunite? They made their last major stand at the National Liberal Federation meeting at Leamington in May, where a considerable number of their MPs attended. They were hooted down, and finally withdrew *en masse*. The 'Coalies' did not wholly abandon their interest in the NLF,[31] but in most places outside Wales the principal party organisations were soon unambiguously in Asquithian hands. It was increasingly clear to many 'Coalies' – as Macnamara had discovered – that they could not even rely on continued support from their own constituency parties.

Their best option for the 'Coalies' seemed to be to establish their own central organisation, and await events. Many of the constituency organisations which had Coalition Liberal MPs remained loyal to them, and some regional bodies were set up. In October 1920, the first issue of *Lloyd George Liberal Magazine* appeared – a rather feeble retort to the much more impressive and long-established *Liberal Magazine*, which remained firmly in Asquithian hands. But the scope of the 'Coalies' was necessarily a very limited one. They could not set up organisations in Unionist constituencies without impugning the whole principle of the Coalition. At one time there was a rather perfunctory interest in persuading the Unionists to hand over traditional Liberal constituencies which they had won in the wholly exceptional circumstances of 1918 to Coalition Liberals,[32] but – not surprisingly – the Unionists were not amenable to the idea.

Important issues of principle were also appearing. In the spring of 1919, Austen Chamberlain's Budget proposed, predictably, a reduction of wartime taxes; but the Chancellor gave this taxpayers' boon a protectionist twist. He reduced the McKenna Duties in a selective manner, leaving a considerable measure of preference for imperial goods. In a vote on the committee stage of the Finance Bill, in which the 'Asquithians' voted against the government proposals, they were joined by sixteen Coalition Liberals. In 1920 the Coalition undermined another important item of Liberal faith. The land taxes which Lloyd George had introduced in 1909–10 were never conceived by their author as important fiscal measures in themselves, but as devices necessary to enable a valuation of land to take place, so that land values could eventually be taxed. As has been seen, the valuation was not quite complete when war broke out and it was suspended for the duration. By 1920, the valuation was obsolete, and the yield of the taxes microscopic. No doubt scenting danger to landed interests in the future if valuation remained on the statute book, the Unionists pressed successfully for abolition both of the taxes and of the valuation. People like Asquith who understood the principle of land taxing and realised what underlay the Government's action were severely critical.[33] Again the Coalition Liberals were deeply split.

Another infringement of traditional Free Trade principles was set before Parliament late in 1920, and became law in the following year. The Safeguarding of Industries Act 1921 authorised the Board of Trade to impose an *ad valorem* duty of one-third on imported goods produced by 'key industries'. The Bill's passage through the Commons produced another substantial split in Coalition Liberal ranks.[34] Even in some Cabinet circles – Unionist as well as Liberal – it generated little enthusiasm.[35]

By the autumn of 1920, division of the Liberal MPs was complete. The *Liberal Year Book* for 1921 lists the whip allocation at the end of the Parliamentary session. 33 MPs received the Asquithian Whip, between 126 and 129[36] received the Coalition Whip. Eight MPs who had been elected without the Coupon took the Coalition Whip,[37] but seven MPs who had received the Coupon took the Asquithian Whip, and one had defected to the Labour Party.[38]

Events in Ireland much deepened the controversy between different kinds of Liberals. In January 1919, the Sinn Féin MPs (or rather, most of those who were out of prison) met in Dublin to constitute the Dáil Éireann.[39] During 1919, the country drifted towards civil war, which became far more intense in the following year. The 'Volunteers' who had been established before the war to defend the cause of Home Rule metamorphosed into the Irish Republican Army, or IRA. On the other side, a sort of military police force, usually known by its nickname as the 'Black-and-Tans', was recruited to maintain government control. Atrocities and counter-atrocities became the rule of the day. The Dáil had little control over the IRA; the British Government did not have much control over the Black-and-Tans. Violence peaked on 'Bloody Sunday', 21 November 1920, when the IRA killed a dozen suspected British agents, some in front of their wives, and the Black-and-Tans opened fire on a football crowd, killing a similar number of spectators and wounding sixty more.

To make matters peculiarly difficult for Liberals, the *hereditas damnosa* of Irish administration was largely in 'Coalie' hands. Churchill, always the fire-eater, urged his colleagues to adopt a policy of reprisals.[40] Sir Hamar Greenwood, who by this time had become Irish Secretary, was another noted 'hawk'. By contrast, the Home Secretary Edward Shortt approached matters from a different angle. At one point he argued strenuously, though unsuccessfully, that a famous Irish prisoner should not be permitted to die when he went on hunger-strike.[41] On the Asquithian side, too, it was possible to discover substantial differences of emphasis and even of policy.[42] The overall impression left on the public was that the 'Coalies' were deeply implicated in a policy of active repression in Ireland, while the Asquithians were disposed to grant the country a large measure of independence.

Towards the end of 1920, the government proposed to set up two Irish Parliaments, one for the bulk of the country and the other for the Six Counties. Each would have limited powers, and a reduced number of MPs from both areas would continue to sit at Westminster. In the first part of 1921, violence somewhat abated, and in the spring elections were held for both Parliaments. In the North, a Parliament was duly established. In the South, Sinn Féin swept the board except for the four University seats. The members elected refused to attend the proposed Southern Parliament, and the result was treated as a new election to the Dáil. Eventually, both sides edged towards a different solution. Early in 1922, Southern Ireland became the Irish Free State, enjoying 'Dominion Home Rule'. The North remained an integral part of the United Kingdom, though with its own Parliament for provincial affairs. To some Liberals, Lloyd George was seen as the architect of Irish peace; to others he was remembered as 'the man who sent the Black-and-Tans to Ireland'.

Long before the Irish settlement was reached, British public interest in Irish matters had been largely pushed aside by concern over matters of more domestic importance. The years 1919 and 1920 had witnessed considerable industrial tensions, including several very serious strikes. During this period, the Labour Party began to make significant advances in by-elections, capturing five seats from the Coalition. In 1921, the wave of industrial turbulence continued, but at the same time the economy underwent a very serious downswing. As the year advanced, unemployment became an increasingly serious problem. According to National Insurance figures, it had stood at 3.9 per cent in 1920, but in 1921 it had reached 16.9 per cent. The 'Coalie' Dr Macnamara, who was Minister of Labour, was necessarily the target of much criticism. In several places there were serious riots. At a time when provisions for the unemployed were very sketchy indeed, the men and their families suffered fearfully. Local authorities, on whom the burden of unemployment payment largely fell, were threatened with insolvency. Expedients were introduced to mollify the difficulties of the unemployed; but by October Sir Robert Horne, Unionist and Chancellor of the Exchequer, was warning Parliament that unemployment was so severe that it might threaten the social fabric of the state.

Against the background of economic gloom, there were several remarkable political developments. In the course of 1921, a new movement, the 'Anti-Waste League', eagerly promoted by certain elements of the press, won three seats from the Coalition Unionists. This was an early sign that traditional Conservative voters as well as Liberals were beginning to feel disquiet about the Coalition. Labour gained four seats – one from a Coalition Unionist, two from Coalition Liberals, one from the Asquithian Liberals. They also lost a seat to the Unionists, though in highly exceptional conditions. Labour was beginning to establish itself as a very serious contestant for political power. The Asquithians had one encouraging result. After the death of Tom Wintringham, who had captured Louth in the previous year, his widow Margaret successfully defended the seat. This result was remarkable for two reasons. The Liberals had retained a seat which, even in pre-war days, had been marginal, and despite the intervention – for the first time – of a Labour candidate. It is also noteworthy that Mrs Wintringham was the first woman to be elected in the Liberal interest, and only the second to sit in the House of Commons.

In January 1922 'Coalies' constituted themselves the National Liberal Party. Meanwhile, the Asquithians were faring moderately well, though their progress was less than spectacular. In February, Isaac Foot was able to capture Bodmin, which had been won by a Coalition Unionist in 1918. But Bodmin, even more than Louth, was remote from the urban and industrial heartlands, where the running was being made by Labour. Should the Asquithians prepare an all-out attack on Coalition Liberal seats, many of which they could reasonably hope to capture, or should they regard Coalition Liberals as future allies who should be left alone? And how should they view the Labour Party? Might some concordat, perhaps, be achieved, by which Liberals would tacitly abandon their claim to most of the industrial seats which were currently in Coalition hands, in return for forbearance by Labour in places where they had little organisation or hope of victory? No doubt Conservatives and Labour supporters felt corresponding doubts and hesitations about their own futures. In practice, no party's leadership was in a position to devise much of an overall grand strategy. Matters were largely in the hands of local organisations, where local and personal considerations were paramount.

Overriding much of this was a consideration often neglected in political histories: money. In many places, though by no means all, Liberals still expected a candidate to make a very substantial personal contribution to his election campaign, and often to the ordinary funds of his political association as well. Suitable people were not likely to come forward as candidates in such circumstances unless they thought they had a sporting chance of victory.

Both groups of Liberals had considerable financial problems, though of different kinds. The Asquithians still had substantial funds accumulated during years of office, but this money was being dissipated rapidly and was not being replaced. The 'Coalies' had no call on Asquithian funds, and were compelled to devise new ways of raising the money they required. Some of that money, it later transpired, came from purveying public honours in a manner which looks suspiciously like sale in the open market, with little regard for the merits of the recipient. One report said that a knighthood was priced at £14,000; another that it could be obtained for £5000 as the 'inside price' for merit, and £10,000 without merit; while baronetcies ranged from £20,000 to £40,000.[43] No doubt the Unionist wing of the Coalition was also able to build up funds by such practices. After the scandal had attracted a good deal of public attention, a Royal Commission was set up to prepare guidelines for the future. By various means, most of them no doubt less objectionable than sale of honours, the Coalition Liberals were able to amass a very large sums of money, generally known as the 'Lloyd George Fund'. The money was subsequently invested skilfully and profitably. One apparently informed estimate set the eventual figure at £3 millions: an enormous sum in those days.[44]

Whatever the Government did, strains were set on the loyalty of Coalition Liberals and Coalition Unionists alike, and even more so on the support of ordinary voters. Liberals were becoming convinced that the Coalition was too Conservative, and Conservatives were becoming convinced that it was too Liberal; while Labour, which called for a plague on both houses, was making the running. In the context of the overwhelming problems of mass-unemployment, with the associated general downswing in the economy, the domestic situation was looking increasingly bleak for the Coalition.

Could the Coalition nevertheless survive for a long time to come, and – if not – what was the alternative? All kinds of ideas were bruited. One which attracted particular attention, notably from people who were generally considered to be ultra-loyal Asquithians, was that the reluctant and nearly blind

Edward Grey – by then Viscount Grey – should be recalled from retirement and pushed into the premiership, thrusting Asquith aside in the process.[45] Yet, whoever led the Liberals, so long as the Coalition leaders stuck together, there seemed no way of shifting them.

For a long time, relatively little happened to change the situation dramatically. By the late summer, the government was edging towards the view that the best strategy would be to call an election soon, with the Coalition intact. The only available Conservative leaders were members of the Government, and most of the Coalition Liberals were not likely to withdraw their support. Neither Labour nor the Asquithian Liberals, nor even a possible combination of the two of them, seemed to possess anything like the strength to offer the prospect of an alternative administration. The argument for an early General Election was suddenly countered by the discovery that no fewer than 184 constituency Conservative Associations proposed to run candidates outside the Coalition.

The Conservative leaders in the government needed a showdown with the rebels in their own party, and so a meeting of their parliamentarians was called at the Carlton Club on 19 October. The Ministers do not seem to have been unduly worried that this might turn against them. Well into October, the Cabinet was discussing legislative and administrative matters which would necessarily take a considerable time to put into effect, with no intimation that the government might suddenly fall. Everything turned on the variable health of Bonar Law, who – as Unionist leader – had been Lloyd George's right-hand man in the Coalition. Earlier in 1922 he had fallen ill. He had resigned both from the government and from leadership of his party, and had been succeeded by Austen Chamberlain. After some months his health improved, and attempts were made, unsuccessfully, to bring him back into the government. Conservative rebels realised that, if he could be persuaded to strike against the Coalition, he would be a convincing alternative Prime Minister. Bonar Law probably had no wish to assume that office, but he was a party loyalist, and was convinced that if the Coalition continued much longer the Conservatives would split as deeply as the Liberals had done. So he urged the Carlton Club meeting to reject the Coalition. By a remarkable accident, on the very day of the meeting the result of a by-election in Newport was announced. In 1918 it had been held by a Coalition Liberal. At the by-election, Conservatives, Liberals and Labour all advanced candidates, none of them committed to the Coalition. The Conservative was victorious. If an unattached Conservative could win a Welsh Liberal constituency, the world was the Tories' oyster. And so, to the amazement of most observers, the meeting followed Bonar Law's advice by a large majority. When he heard the news, Lloyd George resigned. Chamberlain, whose advice had been rejected so decisively, could not possibly retain the Conservative leadership. A day or two later he was replaced by Bonar Law, who was promptly summoned to the Palace to receive the King's commission to form a government.

The Liberals, one may reflect, had got the worst of all worlds during the previous four years. There was much to be said for them breaking the Coalition at the end of the war, and seeking election on their own policy. There was something to be said for continuing to support the Coalition as a united party, and seeking to influence its behaviour in a Liberal direction. There was nothing whatever to be said for some Liberals taking one course and other Liberals taking the other.

TAXATION OF LAND VALUES

WHAT IT MEANS.

The Taxation of Land Values does not mean an *additional* burden of taxation; it means a *redistribution and readjustment* of the burden of taxation, so as to make it easier to carry.

The proposal is to alter the method of calculating the amount of Rates and Taxes which a man has to pay on the property which he occupies or owns. At the present time the Rates and the Income Tax (Schedule " A ") are based on the rent actually received or paid. If a man improves his property by extending a shop-front, or by putting up sheds and starting a market-garden, his taxes are increased. On the other hand, if a man allows his land to lie idle, either for his own pleasure or in hopes of selling at an enhanced price later on, he is hardly taxed at all.

The proposal is that Rates and Taxes should be reckoned, not on the rent of the whole composite property (including buildings and other " improvements "), but on the value of the land alone, and *on its real selling-value*—whatever may be the use to which it is put at the moment.

This bare, original, " unimproved " value of land, sometimes called its " site-value," depends on the development and progress of the Community as a whole. It is not created by any individual, but by the general public. There is therefore **justice** in taking what is necessary for public purposes from this publicly created value.

WHAT IT WOULD DO.

If Rates and Taxes were calculated in this way on the real selling-value of the land alone, the chief results would be these :

(1) **We should cease to be taxed for our enterprise and industry.** Business development would be stimulated, because a man would know that the improvement of his premises or the cultivation of his land would not be penalised by heavier taxation.

(2) **Land would come more readily and cheaply into its best use,** because it would be rated and taxed on its value for this use (*i.e.,* on its real selling-value), even though the owner chose to keep it back for some private purpose. In other words, when land has to bear the share of taxation which is proportionate to its real value, the owner will usually want it to " earn " its taxes by coming into its best use.

These two things—*the unburdening of enterprise* and *the pressure of land into its best use*—are two powerful promoters of industry and progress; and they are the aims of the Taxation of Land Values.

Printed by LOXLEY BROS. LIMITED, Whitefriars House, Carmelite Street, London, E.C. 4; Published by the LIBERAL PUBLICATION DEPARTMENT, 42, Parliament Street, London, S.W. 1.
Leaflet No. 2628.1   [4s. per 1,000.

This Liberal leaflet of 1923 provides a clear thumbnail exposition of the idea of land value taxation (LVT).

14

Politics in Chaos

The future lies between honourable Members opposite [the Labour Party] and ourselves.

Stanley Baldwin, Debate on the Address, 21 January 1924

On 19 October 1922, the day on which Lloyd George resigned office, a public statement deploring the Carlton Club decision was issued by several leading Conservatives, including Balfour, Austen Chamberlain, Birkenhead and Horne. This naturally excluded them from participation in the new Ministry which Bonar Law formed a few days later. Such men were not given to empty gestures of defiance; plainly, they expected that no party would be able to form a viable government by itself, and so a new Coalition would have to be set up. It soon transpired that only four members of the Coalition Cabinet were prepared to serve under Bonar Law. The new Prime Minister sought to appoint the bitterly anti-Lloyd George Liberal Reginald McKenna as Chancellor of the Exchequer. Only when that approach failed did he turn to a member of his own party: Stanley Baldwin, who had been President of the Board of Trade in the closing period of the Coalition. A more junior appointment was Neville Chamberlain, who became Postmaster-General. The Chamberlains were a close family; but apparently Neville and his half-brother Austen did not see anything seriously amiss in the different attitudes which they adopted on this occasion.

The break-up of the Coalition was bound to precipitate a new General Election. This caught all parties unprepared. The Conservatives were visibly split. Furthermore, the Coalition arrangements which had prevailed until so recently meant that they did not have candidates ready in a number of places, particularly some of the National Liberal constituencies, which they might have hoped to win. Both groups of Liberals were uncertain about tactics. Should National Liberals attempt to make compacts with the Conservatives, with the Asquithians, or with neither? Should the Asquithians attempt to make arrangements with the Lloyd Georgeites; or should they try to come to terms with Labour, or should they salute the new Government as a welcome alternative to the Coalition? The Labour Party was in the least ambiguous position; but Labour was not yet in a position to fight everywhere. In practice, inter-party arrangements varied widely from place to place.

The line between Asquithian and Lloyd Georgeite Liberals was sharp in some constituencies but not all. Many Liberal Associations included people who had been supporters, and people who had been opponents, of the Coalition. Some Liberal candidates were glad to accept nomination by local Liberal Associations, but had no wish to indicate a strong preference for Asquith or Lloyd George – perhaps to avoid offending potential supporters, perhaps to keep their options open in the aftermath. The *Liberal Year Books* took an Asquithian view, and regarded as Liberals *sans phrase* all who were not firmly linked to the Lloyd George machine. This represents a clear, if partisan, view of classification, and the numbers the *Year Books* give may be taken as a general indication of where the parties stood, although some details are open to different interpretations. Following those figures, for the 615 constituencies in Britain and Northern Ireland, the Conservatives and Ulster Unionists advanced 491 candidates, Labour 411, the unqualified Liberals 331, the National Liberals 130, and various oddments 47. In about 65 seats, Liberals and National Liberals stood against each other. Every party was leaving well over a hundred seats unfought. About 200 seats had no Liberal of any description.[1]

The overall result came as a general surprise. The British Conservatives won 336 seats, and to these may be added eleven Ulster Unionists, who for many years to come could be regarded as Conservatives for all practical purposes. The unqualified Liberals took 64, the National Liberals 53, Labour 142, and the others nine. Two features of immense importance emerged. The Conservatives had a clear overall majority, so there was no question of any kind of Coalition being required. And Labour, for the first time, was the second party of the state, without argument the official Opposition, with more seats than the two Liberal groups combined. With his opponents split between three substantial parties, Bonar Law and the Conservatives appeared to be set in office for a very long time. Who would have guessed that Bonar Law would only remain Prime Minister for a few months, and his party would be defeated after not much more than a year?

Sheer accident had played a large part in some of the results. Lloyd George was returned unopposed in Carnarvon Boroughs, the one occasion in which he would have that experience in more than fifty years' representation of the constituency. Asquith held Paisley with a small majority over Labour in a straight fight. Among their respective henchmen, Winston Churchill and Captain F. E. Guest on one side, Sir Donald Maclean and Francis Acland on the other, were out of the House. One of the few Labour casualties was Arthur Henderson, who had won a remarkable by-election at

Widnes in 1919 but failed to hold the seat at the General Election. Yet Ramsay MacDonald, the one Labour man to lose a seat for his party at a by-election, was found a more hopeful place elsewhere, and was duly elected. With Henderson out of the running, leadership of the Labour Party, and eventual reversion of the Premiership, passed to MacDonald.

Thirteen Liberal MPs who had taken the Coalition whip in 1920 stood in 1922 as unqualified Liberals, and of these six were elected.[2] Dr Christopher Addison, who had resigned noisily from the Government in the previous year, unsuccessfully defended his Shoreditch constituency as an unqualified Liberal, but was turned out by a National Liberal. One 1920 recipient of the Asquithian whip, J. A. M. Macdonald, stood unsuccessfully as a National Liberal. The essentially defensive character of the National Liberal fight in 1922 was brought out by the fact that, of their 53 MPs, 31 had sat in the old House, and another fifteen were returned for constituencies which had been Coalition Liberal in 1918. One of the new National Liberal MPs would be particularly important for the Liberal Party's future. A young baronet, Sir Archibald Sinclair, defeated a Liberal *sans phrase* (who had been elected as a Coalitionist in 1918) in Caithness and Sutherland. Asquithians broke a substantial amount of new ground, and among their victories was the return of Simon in Spen Valley, avenging his defeat three years earlier.

A gloomy sign for the Liberals was the decision of a number of their former MPs to take the field under the Labour banner. The Buxton brothers, Charles and Noel, were both elected in the Labour interest. So was Edward Hemmerde, who had captured a Unionist seat for the Liberals in a by-election of 1912. H. B. Lees-Smith had been returned as a Liberal for the two-member constituency of Northampton in both 1910 Elections; in 1922 he was elected as the first Labour MP for Keighley. Charles Trevelyan, who had left the Liberal Government on the outbreak of war in 1914, was also now sitting as a Labour MP. Josiah Wedgwood, who had sat as Liberal MP for Newcastle-under-Lyme from 1906, transferred to Labour in 1919 and still represented the same constituency. It has been said that the persistent support he received from the *Staffordshire Sentinel* had something to do with the editor's belief that Wedgwood had saved his son's life.

Did all this mean that Labour had fought its way to Opposition leadership against a staunchly resistant Liberal Party? Had erstwhile Liberals become converts to a different ideology? Hardly so. There is little evidence that any of these notable adherents to the Labour Party were positively attracted by Labour policies. Rather should we say that they despaired of the quarrels and lack of collective purpose evinced by Liberals from the mid-war period onwards, and turned to Labour *faute de mieux*.

The position of both Liberal groups after the 1922 election was – to put it mildly – anomalous. The National Liberals, though still a substantial body in Parliament, plainly had no future as an independent party. They had, however, two very important assets: a considerable number of able and eminent men, some of them currently out of Parliament; and a large and growing 'Lloyd George Fund'. The 'Asquithians' performed substantially better at the General Election, winning about 43 new seats against about fourteen losses. The pattern of success and failure was a very irregular one. Some areas of traditional Liberal strength fared very badly. In December 1910, Liberals had held eight of the twelve seats in County Durham After the 1918 redistribution there were fourteen seats in the county.[3] In that year Coalition Liberals and uncouponed Liberals each held three. In 1922 only one Liberal remained. Yet there were also unexpected victories. Oxford and Bootle, both consistently Conservative since 1885, were captured by Liberals. Penistone, the one 'Asquithian' seat which had been lost in a by-election, was recaptured from Labour.

Neither Liberal group was even approximately homogeneous in an ideological sense. The National Liberals were, if anything, the more divided of the two. Some of them – like the three defeated candidates Churchill, Guest and Greenwood – had been moving rapidly towards the Conservatives during the Coalition period. Others – Lloyd George himself was a good example here – had viewed the Coalition as a useful device for achieving some Liberal objectives, and were prepared to make concessions to Conservatives as a *quid pro quo*. These people, one might say, were the most genuine Coalitionists of all. Other men, like Major-General Sir Robert Hutchison, appear to have been attracted to Coalition Liberalism by the evident skill with which Lloyd George discharged the role of wartime Prime Minister. Some of the Welsh contingent probably saw Lloyd George as the supreme example of local-boy-makes-good.

Although Labour was larger than the two Liberals groups together, the margin was not great, and it appeared possible that the disparity could be reversed. The two Liberal groups had every reason to seek reunion. George Lambert, whose ambivalent position has already been noted, and whose candidature in South Molton was unopposed in 1922, wrote to both leaders in that vein, and received encouraging replies from each of them.[4] Almost immediately after the 1922 election, a memorial in favour of reunion was signed by seventy MPs, including members of both Liberal groups.[5] When Captain Guest broke ranks with other National Liberals, and spoke in favour of the old 'Centre Party' idea of union with Conservatives 'to fight Socialism', he was explicitly repudiated by Lloyd George himself.[6] On the other side of the Liberal divide, Maclean told the National Liberal Federation at Buxton that letting 'bygones be bygones' was conditional on 'repentance' by former Coalitionists.[7] This was less than helpful to the cause of reunion. Perhaps the greater part of responsibility for the Liberal split lay with the Lloyd Georgeites, but by no means all did. In any event, very few politicians of any brand are capable of pronouncing the words, 'I was wrong'.

At by-elections which took place during the lifetime of the Conservative Government, at least the scandal of two proclaimed Liberals opposing each other was averted, and various degrees of actual cooperation ensued. In March 1923, Harcourt Johnstone captured Willesden East from the Conservatives in a straight fight; in April Sir R. J. Thomas won Anglesey, which had previously been represented by an Independent Labour man; in June Francis Acland won a Conservative seat at Tiverton. There were four places where candidates bearing the label National Liberal had stood in 1922. In none of those places did National Liberals stand under that designation in the by-election, but in all there was a Liberal. Those four by-elections cast light on the very different role which National Liberals had played in different constituencies at the previous General Election. A glance at the comparative figures suggests that in Newcastle-upon-Tyne East and in Berwick-upon-Tweed, where no Conservative had stood at the General Election, the former National Liberal votes passed almost entire to a Conservative at the by-election; yet in Anglesey and at Ludlow the National Liberal vote passed almost entire to a Liberal.

Whipping presented problems. If reunion was to take place, this implied that eventually all Liberal MPs would come under the same Whip. It was generally agreed, however, that matters had not yet advanced as far as that. A few Liberal MPs, including C. R. Dudgeon, who had been elected as Liberal *sans phrase* for Galloway, and H. K. Stephenson, who had been elected as National Liberal for a Sheffield constituency, jumped the gun and accepted both Whips. Both of the Asquithian Whips, Hogge and Thorne, continued in office, and for a time Sir Arthur Marshall, who had captured Huddersfield from a National Liberal, also served as a Whip. Soon Thorne resigned through ill-health, and Vivian Phillipps, who had been Asquith's Private Secretary, was appointed overall Whip for the Asquithians.

Meanwhile, important changes were taking place elsewhere. In May 1923, Bonar Law, already mortally ill (though he would linger for some months to come) resigned the Premiership. After a period of uncertainty, the Chancellor of the Exchequer, Stanley Baldwin, succeeded him. Like his predecessor, Baldwin turned to McKenna as first choice for Chancellor of the Exchequer. This time McKenna showed more interest, hoping to be returned as a non-party MP for the City of London, but the sitting MP for the constituency refused to stand down. So the embarrassment of a former Liberal Cabinet minister accepting senior office in a Conservative administration was averted, and the place went to Neville Chamberlain. It is striking to reflect that McKenna, who found the Lloyd George Coalition intolerable, was willing to contemplate membership of an otherwise purely Conservative Government.

Without McKenna's Free Trade influence (such as it was), Baldwin moved sharply in the opposite direction. In October he declared in favour of 'protecting the home market'. As in 1903, the issue of Free Trade *versus* Protection brought together all the Liberals, and Labour as well. Baldwin accepted the need for a General Election. Even those Liberals who in other respects were coming to look more and more like Conservatives were still Free Traders, and were glad to enter the fray in the traditional cause. Liberal divisions ended almost completely, and on 19 November a manifesto was issued over the signatures of Asquith and Lloyd George. Asquithian finances were by now in a poor condition, but a subvention was willingly given from the Lloyd George Fund, which ensured that the campaign could be fought on level terms with the other parties. Headquarters received £90,000 from that source. Lloyd Georgeite information suggested later that they had disbursed £160,000.[8] The disparity may perhaps be explained on the assumption that some grants were made directly to particular constituencies.

Nearly everywhere, Liberal candidates took the field without reference to antecedents. Cardiganshire, where the contest between different brands of Liberals had been intense for a considerable time, was the notable exception; but there Liberals so dominated other parties that rival Liberals could oppose each other without serious risk of anybody else capturing the seat in consequence. At a higher level of the party organisation, the old Liberal suspicions of the Coalition period were not completely stilled, though the two leaders were glad to work together. 'H.H.A. is not Ll.G. proof by any means ... We must not let L.G. alone with H.H.A. more than we can help,' wrote Sir Donald Maclean to Viscount Gladstone.[9]

Again all Parties left some seats unfought. The Conservatives, with 540 candidates for 615 places, came closest to a full ticket. Liberals ran 453, Labour 422 and others 31. When the results were declared, the Conservatives, with about 258 MPs, were still clearly the largest single party, but they had lost their overall majority. Labour, with 191, had improved their position substantially, but were well behind the Conservatives. The Liberals, with about 158, had also made substantial advances, but were still only the third party.

Many, but not all, of the principal Liberals were successful. Asquith retained Paisley in a four-cornered contest, but the figures did not suggest that his tenure was safe. Lloyd George had a very comfortable majority over a Conservative in Carnarvon Boroughs. Winston Churchill, defeated in

West Leicester, and Walter Runciman, defeated in Brighton, were the only members of Asquith's old Cabinet who sought election but were unsuccessful. There were other important defeats, however, including Sir Donald Maclean, C. A. McCurdy, Hilton Young and (if he is really entitled to be called a Liberal) Sir Hamar Greenwood.

The pattern of Liberal victories and defeats was remarkable. 67 seats were captured from Conservatives, against fourteen losses; thirteen seats were captured from Labour, against 22 losses. As in 1922, there were victories in places with no recent record of Liberal support, this time including Aylesbury, Basingstoke, Blackpool, Chelmsford, Chichester, Lonsdale and Shrewsbury. In Hemel Hempstead, which the Liberals had not contested since the war, Baldwin's chief lieutenant was unseated. In the Wavertree division of Liverpool, where no Liberal had stood since an appalling result in 1918, a Liberal was victorious in a triangular contest. In the Rusholme division of Manchester, Charles Masterman, sometimes called 'the unluckiest man in politics', was at last successful, winning a spectacular victory over Jeremy Thorpe's Conservative father.[10] South-west England was particularly impressive. Of 41 seats, rural and urban, in Cornwall, Devon, Dorset, Gloucestershire, Somerset and Wiltshire, Liberals took 24. The great towns varied wildly in their performance. Birmingham, Glasgow, Leeds and Sheffield did not return a single Liberal. Yet Manchester returned five Liberals for ten seats, Edinburgh three for five seats, while Newcastle-upon-Tyne, Bradford, Nottingham and Hull each returned two Liberals for four seats.

Polling had been on 6 December 1923, but the new House did not meet until early in the following year. In the meantime, Baldwin's Ministry continued in office. As no party had an overall majority, or anything near it, the Liberals were bound to play a decisive role in affairs. Because of the issue on which the election had been fought, they were more or less bound to join with Labour in throwing out the Conservative Government. Beyond that, there were several possibilities open. There are a few snippets of information as to how they viewed matters immediately after the election; but in several respects the position is still far from clear.

The first important meeting of leading Liberals was an informal gathering of Asquith, Vivian Phillipps, Simon and the great classicist Gilbert Murray, three days after the election. Asquith indicated that Labour was not yet ready for office. 'MacDonald, Snowden, Thomas and Arthur Henderson are all right, but for the rest the less said about them the better.'[11] There was a discussion about the possible composition of a Liberal Government. Should Lloyd George perhaps become Foreign Secretary? There were doubts. Simon was suggested as a possible Chancellor of the Exchequer – whereat, in Phillipps's delightful words, he 'began to purr like a contented cat.'

Not long after this, a more authoritative meeting was called. As C. P. Scott, the immensely influential editor of the Liberal *Manchester Guardian*,[12] recorded:

> The general view, adopted by Asquith and strongly urged by Simon, was that the Tories should first be turned out by a combination with Labour and Labour (if it formed a Government) as speedily as possible by a combination with the Tories, the Liberals then taking Labour's place.

Lloyd George dissented, and when the gathering met a few days later, they concurred in a policy of complete independence. But what did that mean in practice?

On 18 December 1923, Asquith met the Liberal MPs. Reflecting on the contest, he observed:

> What had been the main plank of the Tory platform? Protection. What was the main plank of the Labour platform? The Capital Levy with its Socialist adjuncts and accessories. Both have been rejected with overwhelming emphasis by the will of the country.

That could hardly be denied; but Asquith went on to express, and apparently to endorse, what he claimed was the general view – that 'as the second largest party in the House of Commons the Labour Party will be allowed to assume the responsibility of government' – adding that 'If a Labour Government is ever to be tried in this country, as it will sooner or later, it could hardly be tried under safer conditions'.

For the Liberals, however, the consequences were bound to be disastrous. It was evident to anyone surveying the Liberal benches that, while all were keen Free Traders, and the great majority would follow a Liberal Government on the issues which it would be likely to set before them, yet there were some who much preferred Conservative to Labour, others who much preferred Labour to Conservative, and others still who were more or less indifferent between them. If either of the other parties assumed office with tacit Liberal support, or even with Liberal toleration, it was humanly certain that many Liberals would disagree profoundly with the decision, and would drift away. Churchill took up in public the idea of first joining with Labour to throw out the Conservatives; then moving a resolution which the Conservatives would be bound to support, to throw out Labour.[13] He may or may not have known that a similar idea had been discussed some weeks earlier by the Liberal leaders. It would probably have been the wisest course to follow.

When the new Parliament met, an Amendment to the Address was moved from Labour benches, in the form of a simple motion of No Confidence in

Baldwin's government. The motion was carried by 330 to 258. The official
Liberal line was to support the Amendment; but ten Liberals voted with the
government, and seven were absent unpaired.[14] The great majority of the
seventeen recalcitrants had been linked with the Coalition. Here was the first
warning of great trouble to come for the Liberals. But the government defeat
was decisive, so Baldwin resigned and Ramsay MacDonald formed the first
Labour Government.

It became immediately apparent that both of the other parties were eager
to win support from individual Liberals. The new Labour Government had
several members with Liberal antecedents. The Lord Chancellor, Viscount
Haldane, had had a long career as a Liberal (and in some ways a rather
'right-wing' Liberal at that). Charles Trevelyan had been a junior member
of the pre-war Liberal Government. Noel Buxton and Josiah Wedgwood had
both been Liberal MPs. Lord Chelmsford, the former Viceroy of India, and
Lord Oliver were regarded as non-party men. One member of the Cabinet,
Lord Parmoor, had been a Conservative until not long before. The Conservatives also showed recognition of the need to muster Liberal support. At a
party meeting in February 1924, Baldwin promised not to submit the proposal for a general tariff again unless there was evidence of a large shift of
public opinion in that direction. Like Labour, the Conservatives guessed
that the Liberals would soon disintegrate, and it was important to prove into
as much as possible of their estate.

The Budget which Philip Snowden introduced in April was so close to
traditional Liberal views on finance that Asquith declared it failed to reveal
any difference between the two parties. Duties on sugar and tea, both of
which bore heavily on working-class incomes, would be drastically reduced,
and so also would several other indirect taxes. The McKenna Duties, which
had been introduced ostensibly for wartime purposes, but had been retained
by successive governments, would be permitted to expire later in the year.
Proposals for Imperial Preference which had been welcomed by the previous government, but had not yet been applied, would be dropped. In the
same month, a motion seeking leave to bring in a Bill providing for the valuation of land, and for rating on the basis of that valuation, was proposed
from Liberal benches. It received the unanimous support of Liberal and
Labour Members, and the unanimous opposition of Conservatives, and was
duly carried by a large majority.[15] Such measures seemed to point to the possibility of real cooperation between Liberals and Labour on an agreed
programme.

In the following month, however, matters began to change. The pattern
of three-party or even four-party politics which had been developing in
recent years threw into high relief the inadequacy of the existing electoral

system, which could very easily produce a House of Commons in which the relative strengths of the parties bore little relation to the popular vote they had received. Liberals were coming increasingly to advocate Proportional Representation as a means of rectifying the situation. Early in May, a Bill to that effect was submitted to the House of Commons. On a free vote on the Second Reading, all but one of the Liberals supported the measure, but substantial majorities of both Labour and Conservative Parties voted against it and the proposal was lost.[16] Defeat in such circumstances naturally disappointed the Liberals, but was not of itself an occasion for serious dispute with the government. But in the course of the debate, Labour's Arthur Henderson, with unnecessary spleen, defied the Liberals to put the Government out if they dared. From that point forward, relations between the two parties began to cool markedly.

What lay behind this apparent change of front by the government? The Labour Party had sought to show that it could govern responsibly, even in difficult conditions and that it was in no sense the revolutionary conventicle which many people had feared. That point had already been established by the spring of 1924. Thereafter, it was willing to face the electors at any moment, hoping either to win a decisive majority or to leave office and prepare for a return in less ambiguous conditions. The Conservatives were also coming to adopt a different strategy from the one they had adopted a few months earlier. They had jettisoned Protection, at least for the time being, and would now be able to face a new General Election at any time as the perceived alternative to 'Socialism'.

The Liberals, by contrast, were extremely anxious to avoid an election until internal difficulties had been resolved. Most acute of these difficulties was the party's financial problems. The subvention received from the 'Lloyd George Fund' at the 1923 General Election had been adequate for immediate purposes, but provided no long-term solution. Negotiations on that subject continued throughout much of 1924. Party Headquarters could not fix candidates without a financial guarantee.[17] Lloyd George was well aware of the personal dislike in which he was held by leading organisers at Liberal headquarters. That probably did not worry him very much. He had few, if any, dealings with Viscount Gladstone;[18] but he had many discussions with Sir Donald Maclean, and surviving reports suggest that these were conducted on a tolerably amicable business basis. What certainly did worry Lloyd George was doubt about the efficiency of the party's organisation.[19] He was not the only Liberal to feel such doubt; Viscount Gladstone himself had deep criticisms to offer.[20] But improvement in organisation necessitated close cooperation between leading Liberals. In July, efforts were made to effect some significant changes; but these seem to have run into the sands.

Repeated attempts were made to find a basis of agreement about finance. The precarious balance between the three parties made it more or less certain that a further General Election would not be long delayed, and the Asquithian organisers were agreed that £200,000 would be required, as well as running expenses of between £40,000 and £50,000 a year.[21] Lloyd George did not dispute the sum required, but left no doubt that his own Fund could not provide that sort of money. At first there were certain legal doubts; but the main trouble was that the Fund was largely sunk in the *Daily Chronicle*, and relatively little liquid capital was available. For a short time, the cost of the National Liberal headquarters imposed a major burden on available money. These, however, were wound up – 'with dramatic suddenness', as Maclean put it – early in 1924.[22] There was also a strange dispute over the Lloyd George Fund among the Lloyd Georgeites themselves, which resulted in substantial changes in its trusteeship – including the removal of Guest.[23]

The political problem was also unresolved. If the Conservatives decided that an early General Election would be to their advantage, they could force one at almost any moment unless the Liberals were prepared actually to vote with the government. Abstention was not enough; for Conservative MPs outnumbered Labour. For Liberals, with their uncertain finances, an early General Election was a recipe for disaster. On the other hand, continued support for the Labour Government was not only sure to alienate the Liberals' more 'right-wing' members, but was also proving uncomfortable for the party's radical element, who felt increasingly unhappy with the Government's poor record on matters like unemployment. Yet it was becoming increasingly difficult for the Liberals to avoid such an election. Even tactical cooperation between the two parties proved very difficult. Vivian Phillipps, the Chief Whip, fulminated against the sheer incompetence of his Labour counterparts in their management of parliamentary arrangements affecting the Liberals, and noted the irritation which many Liberals felt about 'ill-natured criticism and frequently abuse' which they encountered.[24]

Most of the important departures from the Liberal Party over the past decade had been towards Labour, but there were soon signs of shifts in a different direction. A by-election arose in the Abbey Division of Westminster – home of many MPs. Winston Churchill resolved to stand as an Independent candidate, hoping for support from both Liberals and Conservatives. In the view of his principal biographer, he aspired to lead 'some thirty Liberal MPs who disliked Asquith's support for Labour – "who wish to act with the Conservatives and whom the Cons are anxious to win as allies"'.[25] At one moment it seemed as if he would receive official Conservative backing; but the local Association decided to advance their own man instead. Labour and Liberals also put forward candidates. In the end, the Conservative defeated Churchill by the narrow margin of 43 votes.

The downfall of the Labour Government came later in the year on a series of issues related to the Soviet Union. Many people regarded Bolshevik Russia not so much as a Great Power with its own international agenda, but rather as a hotbed of conspiracy. which sought to bring down all other existing Governments in bloody revolution. Whether that was the case or not, the Russian government's financial reliability was certainly in doubt. In the summer of 1924 the Labour Government concluded a so-called 'Treaty' with Russia which was to include a British loan. Liberals and Conservatives both prepared to vote against the 'Treaty' when Parliament met again in the autumn. This would almost certainly have led to a General Election; but in fact the dénouement took place on a different issue.

A Communist periodical featured an article inviting soldiers, in certain highly hypothetical and unlikely circumstances, to rebel against their officers. The Government, through the Attorney-General, brought an action against the journalist responsible on a charge of incitement to mutiny. Then the charge was suddenly withdrawn. Whatever case there may have been for bringing the charge and sustaining it to a conclusion, there was no case whatever for bringing the case and then dropping it. The Conservatives prepared a motion of censure on the government for its handling of the matter. The Liberals, realising that the motion was likely to be carried, and would precipitate a General Election for which they were wholly unprepared, sought to avert that result by proposing an enquiry, which would get the government off the hook, and would permit the Liberals to vote down the Conservative motion. The plan, ingenious though it was, miscarried completely. The Conservatives decided to withdraw their own motion and support the Liberal one; while the government declared that its passage would constitute a motion of No Confidence, with the implication that a General Election would immediately follow. The only way in which the Liberals could avert a government defeat would be by voting against their own resolution. Twelve even did that,[26] though this was more than the majority could accept. In the full knowledge that they were heading for electoral disaster, most of the Liberals voted for the resolution, which was duly carried – with Conservative support – on 8 October, by 364 to 198. Parliament was dissolved, and a new General Election called.

The Liberals cast around desperately for the money and candidates required. In the end, they scratched together £50,000 from the Lloyd George Fund, £30,000 from their own resources, and £40,000 from a financial appeal.[27] 340 candidates were found, against more than 500 for each of the other Parties. On numbers alone, it was plain that the Liberals had no serious prospect of forming a Government in the aftermath.

Not long before Polling Day, another twist appeared in the Russian saga. A letter was published, which was said to have been written by Grigor Zinoviev, head of the Moscow-based 'Third International', to the British Communist Party, calling for violent overthrow of the organs of Government, and subversion of the armed forces. The letter is now known to have been a forgery, but it did express opinions compatible with those of which Zinoviev had delivered himself publicly not long before. It seems likely that the letter had some effect in stampeding timid Liberals into voting Conservative as the safer option.

The upshot of the election was a huge swing to the Conservatives, who won around 415 seats – a majority of two hundred over all others combined. Labour lost a considerable amount of ground; it was reduced to 152 seats. But the Liberals sustained complete disaster, obtaining only 42 MPs. Asquith himself was beaten at Paisley, although this time he had no Conservative opponent. Personal regrets at the defeat were by no means confined to Liberals. Rosslyn Mitchell, the victorious Labour candidate, was in tears when he received the congratulations of Asquith's daughter, replying 'I'm so sorry, so terribly sorry this has happened'. Baldwin wrote to Asquith expressing his 'real regret'. The King wrote that 'Nothing in connection with the General Election has caused me more regret' – adding that Asquith's absence from Parliament was 'a national loss'.[28] Vivian Phillipps and all the other Whips were defeated. J. M. Hogge was beaten by the first Labour candidate ever to stand in Edinburgh East. In Manchester, Edinburgh, Newcastle-upon-Tyne and Nottingham, where the Liberals had done so well a year earlier, not a single Liberal seat remained. Lloyd George and Simon both had a straight fight with Labour, and both were victorious. The only important Liberal to return after a substantial absence was Walter Runciman, who captured Swansea West from Labour in a triangular contest. Liberal victories in such circumstances were rare; only seven Liberals in the whole country were successful against both Conservative and Labour opponents,[29] while another six had been unopposed.

In a number of constituencies, there are clear signs of arrangements with Conservatives. In three double-member constituencies, a Liberal was returned in harness with a Conservative against two Labour candidates. Twenty-two of the victorious Liberals had had a straight fight against Labour; only two had had straight fights against Conservatives. In some places the cooperation between Liberals and Conservatives was particularly obvious. In the five Bristol constituencies, there were two places where no Liberal stood and three where no Conservative stood. In Bristol North,

'Freddie' Guest was adopted as candidate by the local Liberal Association, but then formally supported by the local Conservatives, while his campaign was directed by joint committees. This naturally caused high embarrassment to Liberals elsewhere. Winston Churchill and Sir Hamar Greenwood, who had been Liberal candidates at the previous General Election went even further than that, standing as 'Constitutionalists', with the active support of a local Conservative Association.

Stanley Baldwin proceeded to form another Conservative Government. This time he was able to incorporate several of the leading members of his party who had repudiated the Carlton Club decision two years earlier. The most remarkable appointment, however, was Winston Churchill, who became Chancellor of the Exchequer. This was not only clear indication that other Liberal converts would be welcome, it also underlined Baldwin's earlier assurance that Protection would not be introduced until when and if there was clear indication of a significant swing in public opinion. Churchill's political inconsistency is legendary; but at least on the issue of Free Trade he was consistent.

And so, in the closing week of 1924, it appeared that Baldwin's prophecy of less than a year earlier, which forms the epigraph of the present chapter, would be fulfilled earlier and more completely than even he had anticipated.

15

Recovery and Collapse

[Lloyd George's] rule was dynamic and sordid at the same time.

A. J. P. Taylor

Although he was out of Parliament, Asquith remained Liberal leader, and all the party notables, including Lloyd George, appeared willing, even anxious, that he should continue. There was no dispute when he exercised the leader's prerogative which had been contested in 1919, and appointed a Chief Whip, Sir Godfrey Collins, in succession to the defeated Vivian Phillipps. Nor was Asquith's position challenged when he was created Earl of Oxford and Asquith, early in 1925. In this book, to avoid confusion, he will continue to be referred to as 'Asquith'.

Lloyd George, however, was determined to secure effective control over the Liberal Party in the House of Commons. Just after the election, he was elected Chairman of the Liberal MPs, with seven dissenting votes and three abstentions. The Liberal MPs over whom he presided were a miscellaneous collection.[1] Lloyd George's seven opponents, plus three who had supported him, constituted themselves the 'Radical Group'[2] who might be regarded as the most orthodox Liberals in the pre-war sense of the term. Some MPs, including Captain Guest and Hilton Young, were already very close to Conservatives, on whose support they depended for their seats in Parliament. There were also a number of MPs, with Coalition antecedents, who would be likely to follow Lloyd George wherever he might lead.

Almost immediately after the election, Asquith appointed a small committee under the chairmanship of Maclean, to consider the reorganisation of the party.[3] At the end of January 1925, a National Convention of Liberals held in London adopted the essentials of the report. This proposed increasing emphasis on constituency organisation, with the aim that the party should contest all British constituencies; and it also introduced the idea of a Liberal Million Fund, designed to enable the party henceforth to meet its opponents on a footing of financial parity. Vivian Phillipps was set in charge of the fund. Within a month of the fund's inauguration, however, there were signs that it 'hasn't got going'.[4] In the judgement of at least one Liberal observer,[5] the Million Fund was vitiated from the start by the existence of the Lloyd George Fund, which seemed to be 'a sum of money sufficient for all present needs in the hands of one of the leaders'. The Lloyd Georgeists also had grounds for complaint over Million Fund arrangements. Outside Wales, the area federation treasurers and secretaries appointed to administer the fund were not 'our people'.[6] Perhaps many potential subscribers who were not firmly tied to either section felt unwilling to contribute the large sums required while the party remained in it existing chaotic condition.

But how much money *was* there in the Lloyd George Fund?[7] Vivian Phillipps claimed that the sum was 'something like £3,000,000'.[8] Some years later it was stated authoritatively that the capital sum in the Lloyd George Fund was £765,000, in addition to 279,000 *Daily Chronicle* ordinary shares which had never yielded a dividend.[9] It is not clear to what extent Lloyd George had free disposal of the money, and there is no reason for doubting his statement that it was used exclusively for public rather than personal purposes.[10] Much was used to finance a series of very important studies of the British economy, commencing with *Coal and Power* in 1924.

One of the Lloyd George Reports, entitled *Land and the Nation* – often known as the 'Green Book' – was published in October 1925. It proposed land nationalisation, and immediately stirred a huge controversy. A Party Conference to debate the proposals was planned for February 1926; but even before the Conference was held the great industrialist and Liberal MP Sir Alfred Mond took them as the cue to join the Conservatives. When the Conference was held, the offending points were deleted, and reference to the traditional policy of Land Value Taxation was strengthened. This did not persuade the apostate to return. Others soon followed Mond: another MP, Hilton Young, and at least two men who had recently sat as Liberal MPs: the Lloyd Georgeite H. C. Hogbin (whose defeat at Battersea North in 1924 resulted in the sole Communist victory); and the former 'Wee Free' C. F. Entwistle.

The controversy over the land proposals was followed by an even more acrimonious debate over the General Strike of May 1926. The Strike was the culmination of a long dispute in the coal industry, and most trade unionists were called out on strike in support of the miners. There was serious doubt – never really resolved – whether the General Strike was lawful or not. On 3 May, the first day of the strike, a meeting of the Liberal Shadow Cabinet was summoned. Lloyd George was among those present; and there was a decision – apparently unanimous – to support the government in resisting the strike. A further meeting of the Shadow Cabinet was called for 10 May. This time Lloyd George wrote to Collins, indicating that he would not join in condemning the strike without also criticising the government's behaviour which – in his view – was 'precipitate, unwarrantable and mischievous'. The immediate response of the Shadow Cabinet was very moderate. Collins sent Lloyd George a friendly letter expressing the 'general feeling' that he had 'probably overlooked, or had not the opportunity of reading, Lord Oxford's speech in the House of Lords, of which I enclose an extract'.[11]

Soon after this meeting, the strike collapsed. No doubt most people, Liberal or otherwise, were far more interested in the substantive result than in any disagreement between Lloyd George and his colleagues. All ordinary considerations of party interest prescribed that the dispute should be allowed to lapse into oblivion. But on 18 May, there was a gathering of prominent Liberals in Asquith's London home.[12] Those present were mostly men whose antipathy to Lloyd George long antedated the General Strike. The one noted Lloyd Georgeite present, Lord Beauchamp, had to leave the meeting early to catch a train. The others, evidently relieved at the departure, soon screwed up Asquith's resentment. On 20 May a letter was sent to Lloyd George which declared that his failure to attend the meeting ten days earlier was 'impossible to reconcile with ... the obligations of political comradeship'. 'I never thought [Asquith] would come right up to it but he has', wrote Maclean to Viscount Gladstone in unfeigned delight.[13]

There is nothing surprising about the attitude of Maclean and most of his colleagues; but the response of Asquith seems wholly out of character. Throughout the controversies of the previous decade, he had invariably resisted pressure from 'hawks' among his putative supporters who were attempting to engineer a permanent rupture with Lloyd George. A third-hand account sent to Lloyd George some months later provides a possible explanation of Asquith's behaviour. It claims that 'certain rich Liberals came to [him] and said, "We shall not give a shilling to the Liberal Fund until you have got rid of L.G."'. Asquith was 'completely hoodwinked', and finished up 'miserable about the whole business'.[14] Beauchamp wrote to Lloyd George that 'there never was any hope of any meeting nor any wish for compromise. I was alone.'[15] Inevitably, Lloyd George published a reply to Asquith, which added further fuel to the flames. A few days later, a group of Lloyd George's opponents, sometimes known as the 'Twelve Apostles', produced a further broadside, and the wrangling continued.

Lloyd George's Liberal 'power base' was the MPs, who had elected him their Chairman a year and a half earlier. As those of the Liberal MPs who were regarded as Lloyd George supporters were largely men to the 'right' of the party, who might be expected to oppose his views on the General Strike every bit as strongly as did 'Asquithians' in the Shadow Cabinet, his position even there seemed precarious. Then, suddenly, salvation came from an

unexpected quarter. On 1 June, Guest sent a letter to Lloyd George, expressing the view of 'several of my friends ... who form the Coalition Liberal
group'. Guest admitted that they were out of sympathy with Lloyd George's
attitude during the strike, 'but, be that as it may, we are not prepared to see
you censured ... so long as you can give us ... assurances ... that you have
no intention of allying yourself with the Labour or Socialist Party', or supporting 'a policy of Nationalisation of industry in any form'. Guest indicated
that this view had the support of nine Liberal MPs in addition to himself,
plus the likely support of a further ten.[16] Lloyd George gave the required
assurances, and received renewed support from the MPs.

On 12 June, Asquith, on whom the strain of all this must have been enormous, had a stroke. He had been due to speak to the National Liberal
Federation a few days later, but was unable to do so. In the new atmosphere
of uncertainty about the leader's health and political future, nobody wished
to press the controversy further. Thus the NLF meeting wore all the aspects
of anticlimax. A resolution of loyalty to Asquith's leadership was carried; but
nothing was done to make reconciliation with Lloyd George more difficult.
For a few months more, the uncertainty continued. Then, in October,
Asquith finally resigned leadership of the Party. His Chief Whip, Sir Godfrey Collins, also resigned, and was succeeded by the Lloyd Georgeite Sir
Robert Hutchison. Asquith survived, in declining health, until March 1928,
but played no further part in politics.

The first significant electoral contest which followed Asquith's retirement
was disastrous. J. M. Kenworthy, who had been victor in the Central Hull
by-election of 1919, had long favoured cooperation between Liberals and
Labour. He now joined the Labour Party, and fought a by-election in his
new interest. On 29 November he won a comfortable overall majority, and
the vote of the Liberal defender was so derisory that he forfeited his deposit.

But steps were already being taken which would lead to a profound
change in the fortunes of the Liberal Party. When the Liberal Million Fund
was launched, an Administrative Committee was formed, which served for
some purposes as the governing body of the party. From October 1926
onwards, it debated whether to accept an offer of a massive contribution
from the Lloyd George Fund. On 19 January 1927, by seventeen votes to eight
with several abstentions, the decision was taken to accept the offer. £300,000
would be provided for the next General Election, and a sum which would
be somewhere in the range £35,000 to £50,000 a year for ordinary expenses
of the party. By a smaller majority, the Administrative Committee decided
to call for the resignation of its sub-committee, known as the Organisation
Committee, over which Vivian Phillipps presided. Several important resignations ensued. Of the professional workers for the Party, Sir Robert

Hudson and R. Humphrey Davies (whom the present author remembers with considerable affection as a very helpful friend, still mentally alert in his late nineties) retired.[17] Soon afterwards a number of prominent Liberals who were sceptical about Lloyd George constituted themselves the Liberal Council, under the presidency of Viscount Grey.[18] The Liberal Council, however, did not seek to perpetuate old animosities, which largely died down.

Thereafter, a key role in the party's fortunes was played by Sir Herbert Samuel. Not long before his retirement, Asquith had concurred with Lloyd George in the idea that Samuel should receive overall responsibility for the organisation of the Liberal Party. As he had an impressive record of public service, had played no part in the recent controversies and was willing to work with all sections of the party, the choice was a very appropriate one. In February 1927, in the aftermath of the Administrative Committee crisis, Samuel was appointed Chairman of the Organization Committee of the party, with general approval.

About this time, however, there was another important resignation from the Liberal Party. Captain Wedgwood Benn, whose admiration for Asquith was great and whose opposition to Lloyd George was implacable, told Liberals in his constituency of Leith that he was seeking membership of the Labour Party; but that he recognised an 'honourable obligation' to resign his seat.[19] The by-election which ensued was of critical importance. The Liberal defender was Ernest Brown, a public speaker in the Liberal cause, famous for the power of his voice, whose selection appears to have been almost accidental. In March 1927, Brown was returned with a small majority in a triangular contest.

Thereafter, the by-elections ran strongly in the Liberals' favour. A few days after Leith polled, E. A. Strauss recaptured the London working-class constituency of Southwark North, which he had once held as a National Liberal, but which had fallen to Labour in 1923. In June, Sir William Edge was returned for the largely rural constituency of Bosworth. 1928 was an even more encouraging year for the Liberals. In February, Robert Tomlinson captured Lancaster. In March, two remarkable victories came on successive days. Walter Runciman, already an MP, had planned to transfer from Swansea to St Ives when the General Election came. A by-election suddenly arose in St Ives, and his wife – very much a personality in her own right – stood as candidate in his place. The Conservatives made fun of Hilda Runciman as 'the warming pan', and Samuel incurred the wrath of Lloyd George when he went down to Cornwall to speak on her behalf;[20] but she was duly elected. At Middlesbrough, Kingsley Griffith was victorious in a closely-fought triangular contest. Then followed a remarkable by-election in Carmarthen. When Sir Alfred Mond transferred to the Conservatives in

1925, he saw no reason to give the electors of that traditionally Liberal constituency an opportunity of deciding whether they still wanted him as their MP. A couple of years later, however, he received a peerage. This necessitated a by-election, and Lieutenant-Colonel W. N. Jones recaptured the seat in the Liberal interest. In the early part of 1929, the Liberal tide continued to run. On two successive days in March, R. J. Russell captured Eddisbury and James Blindell won Holland-with-Boston. With only one exception, these by-election victories had been recorded in three-cornered contests, and so there was no question of Liberals having been returned on the votes of supporters of other parties.

There were other signs of a Liberal upsurge. A very powerful committee was established to conduct a general enquiry into the condition of the British economy. This work was linked with a distinctively Liberal institution which was already well-established by this time: the annual Summer School. The enquiry included a number of the most famous economists of the day, including Maynard Keynes and Sir Walter Layton, plus several prominent Liberal politicians. Its conclusions were eventually published as *Britain's Industrial Future* – popularly known as the 'Liberal Yellow Book'. Not long before the 1929 Election, a policy was hammered out to confront the most urgent social problem of the time, and Liberals prepared to go to the country on the slogan 'We Can Conquer Unemployment'. Although some of the ideas advanced were new, considerable care was taken to reconcile them with traditional Liberal policies like Free Trade and the Taxation of Land Values. For the first time in many years, the Liberals were beginning to capture the imagination of young people with no previous party commitment.

Not all the signs pointed to a great Liberal upsurge. Three great Liberal newspapers were amalgamated. The *Westminster Gazette*, with a small but very influential readership, ceased publication in 1928. Two years later the traditionally Asquithian *Daily News* and the traditionally Lloyd Georgeite *Daily Chronicle* were amalgamated to form the *News Chronicle*. As time went on, Liberal speakers frequently found themselves vexed by awkward questions about how the party would respond if it found itself holding the balance of power between Conservatives and Labour.

The next General Election took place on 30 May 1929. The electorate had been somewhat enlarged by what was called the 'flapper vote', since for the first time women received the franchise at 21, on equal terms with men. For the first time, too, all three major parties fielded something near a full field of candidates for the 615 seats: 590 Conservatives, 570 Labour, 512 Liberals, plus 56 'others'. There was a remarkable mismatch between the votes cast for the parties and the number of seats they obtained. The Conservatives, with 8,656,225 votes, won 260 seats; the Labour Party, with 8,370,417 votes won 288; the Liberal Party, with 5,308,738 won only 59. Thus it required 33,000 votes to elect a Conservative MP, 29,000 votes to elect a Labour MP, and almost 90,000 votes to elect a Liberal MP.

Most of the seats which were captured or retained by Liberals were in more or less rural locations. In London, the only encouraging spot was Bethnal Green, where the Liberals took the North-East constituency from Labour and retained the South-West. The three other London seats were lost. Two seats were captured by the Liberals in Manchester, and one each in Newcastle-upon-Tyne and Nottingham; otherwise the Liberals recorded no victories at all in the large towns. They even lost the two Bristol seats they had held in rather dubious circumstances in 1924. They did better in somewhat smaller places like Middlesbrough, Wolverhampton and Norwich.

Sir Herbert Samuel's capture of Darwen was an impressive result. The Runcimans had curiously mixed fortunes. Walter was successful in St Ives, which his wife had captured on his behalf at the by-election. Hilda transferred to Tavistock, where she was narrowly defeated. Sir John Simon held Spen Valley; but – as in 1924 – he had no Conservative opponent. Sir Donald Maclean was at last returned to the House, representing North Cornwall. Lloyd George had the personal satisfaction of not only comfortably retaining Carnarvon Boroughs but also witnessing the election of his son Gwilym, his daughter Megan and a more distant relative, Goronwy Owen.

Some less famous Liberals made remarkable and unexpected gains. Ashford, which had been Conservative even in 1906, was captured by a nonconformist minister. the Reverend Roderick Kedward, with a 21 per cent swing of votes. Astonishing victories were recorded in several other places. Liberals captured the Eye division of Suffolk, Dorset East, Hereford, Dumfriesshire and Flintshire with swings of 10 per cent or more, and there were several other victories only a shade less impressive.[21]

Although there was a substantial increase in Liberal representation, the results were in truth a disaster for the party. The Liberals had exerted every possible effort, and yet they were far behind the other two parties. They had no excuses. They were not short of money; there had been no ructions in the party for a couple of years; they had shown imagination and skill in development both of policy and of organisation. Yet they were back in the balance-of-power position they had occupied with such disastrous consequences in 1924, and with far fewer MPs. Their position was really much worse than in 1924; for then many people still believed that a Liberal Government was a serious possibility within a measurable period, while after the 1929 General Election nobody could have had any illusions on the matter.

When the results were clear, Baldwin resigned and MacDonald formed a government, without either of them bothering to enquire what support, if any, the Liberals might give. Almost immediately, the Liberals sustained a further loss. William Jowitt, who had just captured one of the seats in the two-Member constituency of Preston (in harness with a Labour man), was offered the post of Solicitor-General in the new Labour Government, and accepted with alacrity. When Jowitt gave his electors the opportunity of deciding whether to continue supporting him in his new colours, the Liberal Party was in such a demoralised condition that it did not even advance a candidate against him. Very soon a number of prominent Liberals (though no more MPs) defected to the Labour Party, while others, including Guest, joined the Conservatives.[22]

From now on, it was hardly a question of whether the Liberal Party would break to pieces, but of how and when the rupture would take place. Substantial contributions from the Lloyd George Fund ceased soon after the General Election, and there was a good deal of Liberal resentment on that score. The Liberal Council, which had been anxious to avoid rocking the boat for the previous two years, became increasingly critical.[23] But disputes of a familiar kind were soon subsumed in a much graver debate over the Liberal Party's attitude to the Labour Government. Whether or not the Liberal Party had any long-term future, it certainly had the power to bring down the Government at any time, should it choose to vote with the Conservatives on a major issue.

The end nearly came within a few months of the Government's formation. The first really controversial measure was the Coal Bil, whose object was to reduce hours of work in the coal industry, to enable the state eventually to acquire mining royalties, and to establish schemes regulating output and sale of coal. The Bill, which looked very much like a compromise between different points of view and different interests, received both support and opposition from unexpected quarters. In December 1929, Lloyd George declared against the Bill's Second Reading. A small Liberal revolt saved the day for the government. A couple of months later another Liberal revolt again saved the government. Then, suddenly, Lloyd George announced that Liberal opposition to the Bill would cease. Clement Davies, one of the new MPs, who had been set in charge of drafting Liberal amendments to the Bill, was 'unrestrained in his indignation'.[24]

The first impact of the Great Depression on the British economy was felt in 1930. Almost every month, unemployment figures rose. By the end of the year they had nearly doubled, and something like one worker in five was without a job. Nobody, perhaps, could have averted a rise in unemployment, or sufferings in all classes of society; but there was little sign of any serious attempt by the government to cope with the economic problem.

The old question of Protection began to be raised again. As Snowden told the National Government Cabinet two years later, 'all the arguments for and against tariffs had been familiar to most of his colleagues for thirty years'.[25] Nobody seems to have confuted his assertion. The real change was the overwhelming gloom of the Great Depression. People who are – or who think they are – in a desperate situation are not disposed to view matters rationally, but clutch wildly for any 'solution' which may be offered

Meanwhile, the Liberals were beginning to ponder strategy. Three courses seemed possible. First, the party might maintain complete independence: view each issue on its merits and vote accordingly, without bothering whether by so doing it preserved the government or brought it down. The second course was to try to coerce the Labour Government to adopt Liberal policies, offering as an inducement general support in the House of Commons. This course might be pushed even further, and lead to incorporation of some Liberals in the government. The third possible course was to join with the Conservatives in putting the government out.

Each of these courses had its merits and demerits. Complete independence would probably produce the least internal damage to the party; but it was unlikely to generate tangible results in the form of legislation or changes in administrative policy. It was also likely to result in a General Election at a highly inopportune moment. Some sort of deal with the government might result in the application of specific Liberal policies, and to those Liberals who regarded Labour as a lesser evil than the Conservatives it had obvious attractions; but it would also mean keeping an incompetent government in office. A deal with the Conservatives might appeal to those Liberals who regarded them as the lesser evil, and the Conservatives indicated that any Liberal MP who joined with them in putting out the Labour government would be spared Conservative opposition at the ensuing General Election. But if the Conservatives became the government it was likely that they would follow a policy of Protection, and very likely other unwelcome policies as well. Cooperation either with Labour or with the Conservatives was likely to drive substantial numbers of Liberals into the other camp.

In September 1930, a wide-ranging discussion took place between Mac-Donald and Snowden for the government and Lloyd George and Lord Lothian for the Liberals.[26] Lloyd George expressed concern about the Liberals' current representation in Parliament, which was far less than the electoral support the party had received. The Liberal Party was committed both on ideological grounds and by considerations of self-interest to a policy of Proportional Representation (PR), and Lloyd George urged the government to put forward legislative proposals in that direction. This would encourage Liberals to resist the Conservative blandishments, and dispose them to give general support to the government. In reply, it was pointed out that, while Snowden personally supported PR, the Labour Party could not be persuaded to do the same; but the government would be prepared to introduce an Electoral Reform Bill providing for the Alternative Vote. When no candidate secured an overall majority of votes cast in a triangular contest, the second preference of voters supporting the candidate at the bottom of the poll would be considered.

Sir John Simon, however, favoured a radically different strategy. Late in October, he wrote to Lloyd George that 'If ... the question arises as to confidence in the Government, I shall feel obliged to vote in such a way as will show that I, at any rate, have no confidence in it'.[27] In other words, he favoured the Conservative counter-offer. But neither Lloyd George nor Simon could exercise complete control over the Liberal MPs. For the time being, neither strategy was adopted.

The complexity of the situation was brought out by some of the issues faced when Parliament met for a new Session in the autumn of 1930. Liberal members were highly critical of the King's Speech for its failure to advance schemes dealing with unemployment. They were bracing themselves to vote against the government on a hostile Conservative amendment; but Neville Chamberlain, who moved the amendment, chose to deal largely with fiscal questions, in a manner which was bound to antagonise Free Traders. After what was called 'a very frank discussion', the Liberal MPs decided to abstain. Five Liberals, however, eventually voted for the Conservative amendment, and four against it. The first group included the Chief Whip Hutchison – of Lloyd Georgeite antecedents – and the sternly Asquithian Sir John Simon. The second group was composed of the Lloyd Georgeite Sir William Edge and the Asquithians Maclean, Runciman and Collins. A day or two later, a division took place on the government's education proposals. 33 Liberals (including Simon and Hutchison) supported the government, three voted against, and 21 abstained from voting – three of them very pointedly so. Liberal MPs were still voting in a highly idiosyncratic manner without reference to either the Lloyd George or the Simon strategy. Sir Archibald Sinclair, who reluctantly agreed to act as Hutchison's successor, urged that the Liberals should henceforth behave less erratically. The new Chief Whip's advice was ignored. On 16 March, there was a government motion to abolish university constituencies. The official Liberal line was to support the government. Nineteen Liberals voted as required, ten voted the other way, and many abstained.[28] The net effect was that the motion was lost by four votes. That was too much for Sinclair, who promptly resigned.

In the following week, a particularly well-attended meeting of the Liberal MPs was held. Two separate issues were considered: whether Sinclair could be persuaded to return, and whether the Liberals should – on the whole – cooperate with the government. Nobody wanted Sinclair to depart, and he was induced to resume his position as Chief Whip. The question of future strategy, however, was not resolved in an equally satisfactory manner. A Declaration of Policy was proposed. It began with what seemed like an unambiguous statement that 'The Liberal Party is and will remain an independent party; it has made no pact and seeks no pact with any other party.' Closer examination, however, suggested that the 'small print' of the Declaration might involve Liberals cooperating with the government on a number of issues. In the end, it was approved by a majority of 33 to 17.[29] It is noteworthy that neither the supporters nor the opponents of the Declaration followed even approximately the old lines of 'Asquith-Lloyd George' cleavage; nor, for that matter, did they follow closely the lines of the new cleavage which would develop later in 1931.

This episode was indirectly related to the government's Electoral Reform Bill. As Snowden had envisaged, it included some 'second preference' voting, and would probably have operated to the Liberals' advantage. If it had been passed in the form originally proposed, the temptation for Liberals to come to terms with the Conservatives as Simon recommended would have been greatly reduced. The history of the Bill, however, was not encouraging. It passed through all stages in the Commons. In the summer it went to the Lords, who proposed amendments which largely defeated the original purpose. All that remained was the Alternative Vote, restricted to London and the larger boroughs. Even this small boon disappeared with the change of government later in the year.

An important move in a Liberal direction appeared in Snowden's Budget, which was introduced in April 1931. Snowden was a keen advocate of the Liberal policy of Land Value Taxation, and the difficulties the Labour Chancellor encountered on this score were remarkably similar to those which Lloyd George had met more than twenty years earlier. No doubt the simplest way of achieving LVT would have been by first passing a Valuation Bill, and then – when the valuation was complete – incorporating taxation proposals based on that valuation in an annual Finance Bill. Unfortunately the House of Lords was still, even in 1931, composed overwhelmingly of men with strong landed interests and Conservative proclivities. The Parliament Act of 1911 had removed its power to block a 'Money Bill', but it could still hold up a Valuation Bill for two or three years. Snowden, like Lloyd George, sought ways of circumventing the Lords. His method was to incorporate valuation proposals in the 1931 Finance Bill, along with proposals to tax land on the basis of that valuation two years later.[30] At first, the proposal was greeted with enthusiasm by Lloyd George, but soon a great difficulty was perceived. The combined effect of the new Land Value Tax and existing Income Tax arrangements would be to subject many taxpayers to double taxation. Discussions between Liberals and the government about possible ways of introducing Land Value Taxation without incurring double taxation proved difficult and acrimonious, and some Liberals developed a strong animus against Snowden for the way in which he handled the matter.

The muddle provided the pretext for a dramatic move in the Liberal Party. On 26 June, Sir John Simon, Sir Robert Hutchison and Ernest Brown took this as the occasion for formally renouncing the Liberal Whip. A glance at recent figures in their respective constituencies suggests that all three could reasonably hope to be re-elected if the Conservatives were kept out of the field, but would probably meet defeat in a triangular contest. A few days later, Lloyd George savagely attacked Simon's 'intolerant self-righteousness',[31] contrasting him with 'greater men' who had changed their opinions in the past – and adding, with considerable venom, 'They, at any rate, did not leave behind the slime of hypocrisy' – Lloyd George gestured the slimy trail of a slug – 'in passing from one side to another.'

When he resigned the Liberal Whip, Simon wrote to another MP, Leslie Hore-Belisha, who was also uncomfortable with Lloyd George's strategy, suggesting that he might do the same. Hore-Belisha contacted other like-minded Liberal MPs, who agreed that 'we could do more by staying inside the party, as in the end it might be that those who are now supporting Lloyd George will leave the party to join the Socialists'.[32] This may have been Hore-Belisha's expectation for some time. At the NLF Conference in the previous month, he had supported a resolution declaring 'the absolute and unfettered independence of the Liberal Party'.

Discussions between Lloyd George and Labour continued – perhaps encouraged rather than discouraged by the three departures. A memorandum written by Lloyd George late in July indicated that MacDonald was interested in the idea of an alliance, in which Lloyd George would be Leader of the House and also either Foreign Secretary or Chancellor of the Exchequer.[33] But almost immediately Lloyd George fell ill. An operation was necessary, and for some time his life was in danger. Thereafter he gradually recovered, but for several weeks was unable to play a full part in politics.

A few days after Lloyd George's illness began, Parliament rose for the summer recess, Soon afterwards, the government published the Report of an Inquiry into current revenue and expenditure, which had been set up some months earlier, largely as a result of Liberal pressure. The report revealed a Budget deficit of £120 millions: an enormous sum at a time when money values were very different from today, and state income and expenditure normally balanced at less than £900 millions. The greatest single cause of this deficit was a mismatch between receipts and benefits in respect of unemployment insurance. The state scheme, which was contributory in character, had been thrown completely out of kilter by the huge recent upsurge in unemployment.

The Cabinet debated possible economies for over three weeks, without reaching agreement on measures which would be adequate for the crisis. Various discussions about possible ways out of the problem took place, involving all three parties. As Lloyd George was still convalescent, his place in those discussion was taken by Sir Herbert Samuel, deputy Chairman of the MPs; but Lloyd George – sick or not – would not allow important business to be done without claiming a hand in the matter. On 24 August 1931, MacDonald astonished his Cabinet colleagues by informing them that he had agreed to set up a new National Government, which would include members of the three parties. In theory, it would not be a 'Coalition', but rather a gathering of individuals to deal with an immediate crisis. Once that crisis had been resolved – so MacDonald promised in a broadcast that evening – the National Government would be dissolved, parties would revert to their original independence, and a new General Election would be held, which 'will not be fought by the [National] Government'.

Choice of members of the new government was not easy. In all parties, there were special problems. Some of the Labour people who would have had a good claim for inclusion were not willing to serve. The Conservatives were still suffering from the aftermath of a gigantic internal dispute over India, which left Churchill at loggerheads with Baldwin, and therefore unavailable for office. Simon and his two rebel colleagues had cut themselves off from the Liberal Party, and therefore had no claim for preferment. The initial National Government Cabinet consisted of only ten members: four Labour, four Conservatives, two Liberals. Lloyd George was still out of commission, but Samuel's inclusion was predictable. He returned to the post of Home Secretary, which he had held under Asquith fifteen years earlier. The other Liberal inclusion in the Cabinet is puzzling. Lord Reading, the former Rufus Isaacs, who became Foreign Secretary, had held various important public offices, but had not been a front runner in Liberal politics for a long time, and his best current claim was that he was leader of the Liberal peers. Other Liberals incorporated in the government included Sinclair, Maclean and Lords Crewe and Lothian, plus several men in junior office. Most glaring of several omission was Runciman. He had held Cabinet office; he still sat in the House of Commons. If the great issue was soon going to be Free Trade versus Protection – as many guessed – then Runciman's Free

Trade credentials appeared at that moment impeccable. There were other very notable absentees, including Leslie Hore-Belisha and Sir Godfrey Collins. Lloyd George, so Samuel wrote much later,[34] 'raised strong objection to one or two of my suggestions for junior posts. As he was the leader and I was acting only as his deputy, I could not insist; those exclusions gave rise to difficulties afterwards.'[35] Unfortunately, Samuel did not amplify this very important point. One MP who had a fair claim on some Ministerial office reflected that his own omission 'was a bitter blow. I remember thinking at the time that this was my last chance of becoming a Member of the Government.'[36] Others, no doubt, felt the same. It is noteworthy, however, that Lloyd George was able to find a place for Maclean, despite the part he played in the Coalition period and afterwards. This is typical of Lloyd George. During the wrangles of the 1920s, he had little or no contact with 'Asquithians' like Viscount Gladstone and Vivian Phillipps, for whom he had little regard; but he was prepared to do business with Maclean (as, indeed, with Asquith himself), whom he respected.

Two days after the National Government was formed, a joint Conference of the TUC, the Labour Party's National Executive Committee and the Parliamentary Labour Party condemned Labour participation in the administration in unambiguous terms, and disowned the Ministers involved. It is easy to understand their anger; it is less easy to commend their wisdom. Labour Ministers were thereby cut off from their own party, and became effectively prisoners of the Conservatives. By contrast, the two other parties, whose leaders also had 'jumped the gun' in accepting office without formal authorisation, soon gave retrospective approval to the action taken. Liberal approval was signalled at a meeting of peers, MPs, prospective candidates and leading members of the NLF on 28 August, with only one dissident. The House of Commons soon carried an emergency Budget designed to meet the deficit, and gave a Vote of Confidence to the new government. This received support from Conservatives, Liberals, and a dozen or so people, originally elected as Labour MPs, who became known as 'National Labour'.

The National Government was soon able to raise loans to cover the Budget deficit, and so the most acute phase of the financial crisis was over. Matters, however, were still very far from resting on an even keel. The Conservatives, who had had every reason to wish to avoid an early General Election at the moment when the National Government was formed, now had no such reason. The National Labour members of the government, who had lost their power base outside, could no longer resist the demand effectively. The strongest remaining weapon in the hands of those who sought to avert an election was the evident wish of the Conservatives to preserve the form of a National Government. As late as 20 September, MacDonald wrote to Samuel that 'there is not even a theoretical justification for an Election now'.[37]

About this time, however, signs began to appear that the Conservatives were not only warming to the idea of an early General Election with the government intact, but were also contemplating the introduction of tariffs in the immediate future. There were also signs that some of the Liberals, most particularly people who had been omitted from the Ministry, were moving in the same direction. On 25 September, Leslie Hore-Belisha obtained the signatures of 27 Liberal MPs for a manifesto declaring support for Mac-Donald in whatever measures he thought necessary.[38] This was really an appeal over the heads of the party's Free Trade leadership, indicating that there were Liberals available to take places in the government, should the tariff pill prove too bitter for the existing Liberal Ministers to swallow. It is, surely, remarkable that the organiser of this petition had been such an ardent champion of Liberal independence four months earlier.

On 5 October 1931, two vital meetings were held simultaneously. First of these was a meeting of the Cabinet, which had been struggling to reach agreement on a policy relating to imports, but was eventually forced to admit defeat.[39] The possibility of the Government breaking up was considered, but rejected. Ministers then debated whether or not to call an immediate General Election. The eventual decision to do so was reached for an odd reason. As the Cabinet minutes record, 'If a decision were taken to remain in office it would be known that the real cause was failure to reach agreement.' General Elections have been called for many reasons, but never before or since have they been called for the primary reason that the Government did not wish the electorate to appreciate that it was divided on a fundamental question of policy.

Samuel resisted the proposal to call an election. It appears that Lord Reading and Snowden took the same view, but that point is not wholly clear. There are some hints on the matter in secondary literature, which are not all consistent. Unfortunately the Cabinet minutes, which might be expected to give an objective, if anodyne, account are silent on the matter. Samuel was, however, able to obtain one concession of substance. The National Government would not produce a comprehensive manifesto, which would probably have included proposals for tariffs. Instead, the Prime Minister would make a general statement to which everybody could assent (he was rather good at that sort of thing), and the parties would make their own separate appeals to the electorate. On that understanding, Samuel and Reading remained in the government.

The second meeting was a gathering of rather more than twenty dissident

Liberals,[40] headed by Simon, who resolved to set up a body to support the Prime Minister 'for the purpose of fighting a General Election'. This body subsequently became known as the Liberal Nationals. The similarity of name with the body formed in 1922 to support the Lloyd George Coalition has caused some confusion. The thinking behind the formation of the new organisation was clear. It was expected that Samuel and the other Liberals would withdraw from the government after defeat on the question of an immediate General Election at the Cabinet meeting. It would then be important for the government to incorporate other Liberals, or putative Liberals, to replace them, in order to continue the illusion of a genuine three-party administration.

The Liberal National secession was followed almost immediately by another split. Lloyd George had been exerting every pressure on Samuel to resist an election, and expected him to resign if he was unsuccessful. His anger when Samuel remained in the government knew no bounds. 'You have sold every pass that we held!' he exploded to Liberal MPs who visited him.[41] He probably never really forgave Samuel, though some contact between them continued. Liberals could expect no Lloyd George money at all for fighting the election. Gwilym Lloyd George and Goronwy Owen, who held junior office in the government, resigned a couple of days later; but most of the Liberals did not, and so no place was made for immediate incorporation of the Liberal Nationals.

Lloyd George was not yet well enough to make speeches, but he was well enough to condemn the decision to call an election in unmeasured terms: 'The election itself is the most wanton and unpatriotic into which this country has ever been plunged. In the midst of a grave financial emergency the Tory Party managers have forced upon the nation a political conflict.' Lieutenant-Colonel H. F. Tweed, who had long acted as Lloyd George's adviser and chief of staff, resigned his post as chief organiser of the Liberal Party's election machine. The determining factor, he explained, was the Liberal Election Committee's decision not to run candidates, and to seek withdrawal of those already in the field, in constituencies where Liberal intervention might result in a Labour victory.[42] No doubt Tweed was judging, as Lloyd George declared in a broadcast a week later, that it was unthinkable that the election would result in a Labour Government, but that the current danger was 'all in the direction of Protection'.

Many Liberals at a lower level of the party were evidently unhappy about Samuel's decision to remain in the government. A meeting of Liberal candidates was held a couple of days later. One speaker was loudly applauded when he asked whether it was, even then, possible for Samuel and his colleagues to withdraw from the Government. An apparently reliable report indicated 'that while opinion was clearly divided the trend of the meeting was markedly towards the attitude of Mr Lloyd George in disapproving of the election and the cooperation of Liberal Ministers with members of the National Government upon the terms indicated by Sir Herbert Samuel.'[43]

Samuel had been right to argue that there should have been a broader spectrum of Liberals when the National Government was formed. Men who were omitted, yet had a reasonable claim for inclusion, were under a very strong temptation to join with Simon, who might otherwise have been more or less isolated. On the other hand, Lloyd George had been right in condemning the failure of Samuel and Reading to leave the gvernment when the decision to call a General Election was taken, in defiance of the Prime Minister's earlier promise. If the Liberals had left the government, they would have been free to campaign actively for Free Trade, and to expose the National Government for what it had already become: an essentially Conservative administration, which was almost certain to embrace Protection in the aftermath of the election. As in 1906 and 1923, the great issue would have been seen as Protection versus Free Trade. It is unlikely that this would have averted a great victory for the National Government; but both the party as an institution and the causes in which its members believed would have had a much better chance of early recovery.

When the General Election came, three groups of Liberals could be discerned.[44] The Lloyd George group, which included not only Lloyd George's own family but also Frank Owen, who was defending his seat in Hereford, and perhaps one or two other candidates, could be regarded as unqualified opponents of the government. The 'official' Liberals, who remained in the government, whom one might call 'Samuelites', were not prepared to give it *carte blanche* on the issue of Protection. The Liberal Nationals, often called 'Simonites', had no reservations on the matter. During the election campaign, Samuel sought to act with both Simon and Lloyd George, but in both cases he was rebuffed.

However broadly the word 'Liberal' is used, there was a great shortfall of Liberal candidates. About 115 could be regarded as 'Samuelites', about 39 as Liberal Nationals, about six as 'Lloyd Georgeites': 160 in all, against well over three times that number a couple of years earlier. By contrast, Conservatives and Labour each fielded substantially over 500 candidates. The chief reason for the dramatic decline was lack of money; but general demoralisation may have played a large part as well. There was considerable confusion about the precise political location of a number of Liberal candidates, for neither the 'official' Liberals nor the Liberal Nationals were anxious to emphasise the differences existing between them. The 'Samuelites', recollecting past divisions and hoping that this one would eventually be followed by reconciliation, made no serious attack on the 'Simonites'. The Liberal Nationals, for their part, required Liberal as well as Conservative votes to see them safely home, and had no wish to antagonise traditional supporters. A few candidates, including Walter Runciman who was defending St Ives (where he was unopposed), and E. A. Strauss, who was seeking to regain Southwark North, appeared on both Liberal and Liberal National lists. In literature of the time, the words 'Liberal' and 'National' were sometimes used in conjunction to mean 'a Liberal who supports the National Government'. Thus Samuel in his own election address is described as 'the Liberal and National Candidate'.

The 59 MPs who had been elected as Liberals in 1929 were all still sitting at the time of the Dissolution in 1931. With reservations about some classifications,[45] they divide into 23 who defended their seats as 'Samuelite' Liberals, five who stood as 'Lloyd Georgeite' opponents of the government, and 26 who defended their seats as Liberal Nationals. The distinction between different kinds of Liberals was not always sharp. Nowhere did Liberal and Liberal National candidates oppose each other, and in four cases the allegiance of individual MPs was not clear until after the election.[46] Some – probably most – of the MPs on both sides had no sense that the division was permanent. Two Liberal MPs retired from the contest, and one 'Samuelite', E. D. Simon (no relation of Sir John), moved to a different constituency. C. R. Dudgeon of Galloway, who at first adhered to the Liberal Nationals, eventually defended his seat as a 'New Party' candidate. William Jowitt, who had accepted the lure of government office to leave the Liberals for Labour in 1929, succumbed to the attraction of membership of the National Government two years later, and stood as National Labour. Switching parties for the benefit of his career was quite a habit with Jowitt. By 1945 he was back in the Labour Party, and appeared in the third Labour Government as Lord Chancellor.

The Conservatives, though unambiguous in their support of the National Government, were more ambivalent in their attitude to Liberals. Samuel faced a three-cornered contest in the precarious constituency of Darwen, and may well have owed his eventual re-election to a public statement by Baldwin to the effect that it was 'not quite playing the game' to oppose the head of a party which was included in the National Government. Thirteen of the MPs defending their seats as 'Samuelite' Liberals had no Conservative against them; but Goronwy Owen, a declared opponent of the government, was also without Conservative opposition. Nine 'Samuelites', and four declared opponents of the government, encountered Conservative opposition. The Liberal Nationals were more fortunate in that respect, for 24 of their MPs had no Conservative opponent; nevertheless, three were opposed by Conservatives. Such matters were much in the hands of local parties, who often had their own ideas on the matter. An odd situation arose in Heywood and Radcliffe. Colonel England, who had been elected as a Liberal, became a Liberal National. In the end he did not defend the seat, and no other candidate using the word 'Liberal' appeared in the constituency.

It is not difficult to visualise how matters must have looked to rank-and-file Liberal voters. About three-quarters of them had no Liberal candidate, not even a nominal one, for whom to vote. Those who did have such a candidate would have required some perspicacity to appreciate just where he stood on what were obviously going to be the big issues of politics in the very near future. Other Liberal voters had to choose between a Protectionist Conservative and a Labour candidate who probably seemed sound on the Free Trade issue, but who also carried a good deal of unacceptable political lumber, and whose party did not seem to possess convincing credentials as an alternative government. Such a Liberal voter did not have much of a choice, and may well have stayed away from the polling station in a mixture of disgust and despair.

The upshot of the election was a landslide without parallel since the passage of the Great Reform Act almost a century earlier. At least 552 seats, and arguably several more, were won by supporters of the government, against only 58 who could be regarded as definite opponents. Government MPs divided into 471 Conservatives, 33 'Samuelite' Liberals, 35 Liberal Nationals, 13 National Labour and a few others. Against the government were ranged 46 official Labour, six unendorsed Labour, four Independent Liberals and two Irish Nationalists. Ironically, the Labour Party, which had been so reluctant to support Proportional Representation in the old Parliament, suffered much more sharply from the injustice of the existing electoral system than any other major party, Roughly speaking, it took 25,000 votes to elect a Conservative or Liberal National MP, 41,000 to elect a Liberal and 128,000 votes to elect a Labour MP.

The Conservative victory was almost as impressive as that of the National Government itself. They did not lose a single seat anywhere. Comparing the position after the election with that at the Dissolution,[47] they captured 182 seats from Labour, nine from the Liberals, three from Liberal Nationals. four from National Labour and seven from others. On a superficial view, Liberals seemed to perform moderately well. 'Samuelites' won 15 seats from Labour and one from National Labour, to compensate for their losses to the Conservatives. Liberal Nationals won ten seats from Labour. Four of the five 'Lloyd Georgeite' Liberals were returned. If all the MPs using the name Liberal could have been gathered in one body, they would have totalled 72, which would have made them the second largest group in the House of Commons, well ahead of Labour.

That assessment, however, bears little relation to political reality. Nor do the considerable gains which the Liberals made in municipal elections a few days after the General Election give any real indication of Liberal strength. Almost immediately after the election, a decision was taken to offer the Liberal whip to all MPs approved by local Liberal Associations, which would have meant almost or quite all of the 72. The Liberal Nationals promptly resolved not to accept the Liberal whip, but to place themselves under the Government whip, thereby claiming the status of a separate political party. Plainly, they aimed at incorporation in the government as soon as it was remodelled, on more or less equal terms with the 'Samuelites'. Lloyd George declared that he would not stand again for office, publicly deploring 'the disastrous course into which the party has been guided'. Samuel was elected chairman of those MPs who chose to attend the meeting. He did not accept either the Simonite or the Lloyd Georgeite rebuff as final, apparently believing that somehow all the Liberals would come together again, as in 1923. For several years, the *Liberal Year Books*, which were published under 'Samuelite' direction, continued to list MPs belonging to all three groups as 'Liberals', refusing to distinguish between them.

As in 1924, the experience of holding the balance of power proved an unqualified disaster for the Liberal Party. A slight inclination towards the Labour Party had proved catastrophic, just as the link with the Conservatives during the Coalition period had proved catastrophic. In 1931, however, the position was far, far worse than before. Until the election, the Liberals could claim, at worst, a certain negative role in politics. Weak as the Liberal Party was, its very existence meant that neither of the other parties could assume that the 'swing of the pendulum' would eventually give it power to act as it chose. The Labour Party could not safely embark on a policy of Socialism, and the Conservatives could not safely embark on a policy of tariffs, because in either case this would be likely to drive large numbers of supporters into the arms of the Liberals. After the 1931 General Election, the Labour Party was so shattered that the prospect of any Labour Government, Socialist or otherwise, could be discounted for the foreseeable future. Meanwhile, the Conservatives were avid for tariffs, and nobody was in a position to restrain them. The 'Samuelites' might put up a brave stand against Protection, but their defeat was certain, and it was difficult to see what function they could perform thereafter. As their old supporters died or retired, the Liberal Party would wither out of existence.

Or so it seemed; but politics is full of surprises.

16

Salvage

The tree of Protection and economic nationalism is in flower. Unless we cut it down it will bear fruit after its kind, and the fruit will be war.

Sir Archibald Sinclair, National Liberal Club, 12 February 1936

After the 1931 General Election, the National Government was drastically remodelled. The Conservatives were enormously stronger than in August. Liberal Nationals could claim to be a distinct group of government supporters, meriting inclusion in the Ministry. Chancellor of the Exchequer Snowden had not been a candidate, and could not retain an office whose duties presupposed membership of the House of Commons. Liberal 'elder statesmen' Lords Reading and Crewe, who had been useful to add *gravitas* to the government, could be permitted (or encouraged) to retire gracefully. MacDonald, despite the ludicrously small representation of the National Labour Party which he headed, remained Prime Minister, and nobody sought to shift him. Baldwin, who might have done so, was altogether too kindly a man to shoot his prisoner. It is likely, too, that Baldwin was well pleased to have men of Liberal and Labour origin in his government, since they formed a useful counterpoise to the more diehard members of his own party.

The small National Government Cabinet was expanded to a more normal size of twenty members. The Conservatives took eleven places. Baldwin was for practical purposes Deputy Prime Minister. That eager Protectionist Neville Chamberlain became Chancellor of the Exchequer in place of the staunch Free Trader Snowden, who moved to the far less influential office of Lord Privy Seal. Of the Liberals, Samuel remained in the dignified but somewhat unrewarding post of Home Secretary. Sinclair, the Secretary of State for Scotland, and Maclean, the President of the Board of Education, retained their old posts, but were now brought into the Cabinet. Of the Liberal Nationals, Simon became Foreign Secretary, and Runciman (whose party position was at last clarified) became President of the Board of Trade. Ministerial office outside the Cabinet was occupied by the Liberals Isaac Foot, Lord Lothian and Graham White, and by the Liberal Nationals Ernest Brown, Leslie Hore-Belisha and Percy Pybus. Pybus was the only member of the original National Government who transferred to the Liberal Nationals.

The Labour Opposition was forced to make changes even more radical than those of the Ministry. Some leading members had joined the National Government; most of the remainder had been defeated at the General Election. Half of the surviving MPs were nominees of a single trade union, the National Union of Mineworkers, and would in all normal times be regarded as diligent, but inconspicuous, supporters. Leadership devolved on George Lansbury, an old-style patrician Socialist with strong pacifist proclivities.

After the 1931 General Election, the Liberal and Labour Parties appear, superficially to have been in a rather similar situation. Both had suffered the departure of leading members, and a huge decline in popular support. There were, however, some very important differences, which would greatly affect their future progress. Although Labour had lost all of its principal members either to the National Government or to the ravages of the electors, this had had relatively little effect on the organisation at lower levels of the party. The Liberals had been split down the middle, with comparable numbers of MPs adhering to 'Samuelites' or 'Simonites'. An even more important difference concerned party funds. The Labour Party continued to enjoy the more or less automatic contribution of Trade Unions. The Liberals had long spent most of the reserves acquired in pre-war days, and were now deprived of Lloyd George money as well. If they were to revive – indeed, if they were to survive – they must find new ways of raising money.

The Tariff question was bound to be the most critical, and the most divisive, to face the National Government once the General Election was over. The first hurdle was the question of 'Abnormal Imports'. There was some evidence that certain foreign exporters, convinced that Britain would soon adopt a policy of tariffs, were sending goods into the country in unusual quantities in order to forestall any duties which might be imposed. Chamberlain, the convinced Protectionist Chancellor, and Runciman, the erstwhile Free Trader President of the Board of Trade, cooperated in devising legislation authorising the Government to impose duties of up to 100 per cent *ad valorem* on manufactured articles, designed to operate for a limited period. Labour voted against the proposal – more, perhaps, because it was the Opposition than because it deeply disagreed – but (incredibly) the large majority of Liberals of all kinds supported it.

Another matter which deeply interested Liberals also arose in the closing weeks of 1931. Snowden's land valuation was still on the statute book. Chamberlain submitted a memorandum to the Cabinet proposing to end it. The Liberals and Snowden were supporters of Land Value Taxation, and were bound to object. A compromise emerged. The valuation would be suspended, ostensibly on economy grounds; but, as the Cabinet Minutes declared, 'this decision was taken without reference to the merits of the scheme and did not involve its abandonment'.[1] It was not formally abandoned until 1934, by which time Snowden and the Liberals had left the National Government.

The second instalment of the Government's tariff policy was a great deal more divisive than the first. Late in 1931, a Cabinet Committee on the Balance of Trade was set up to deliberate the matter, and reported early in 1932.[2] Predictably, Conservative members of the Committee supported tariffs. Equally predictably, Samuel and Snowden opposed them. The Liberal Nationals Simon and Runciman were prepared to accept tariffs 'temporarily' – though nobody knew for how long that might prove to be. The issue was set before the Cabinet not in terms of the economics of national recovery, but of crude politics. As Simon told his colleagues, 'The crux was the Parliamentary position ... Whatever plan was produced must be a compromise solution ... designed to keep the Government together.' The Cabinet debated the matter at length. It proved impossible to reach a compromise policy which would be tolerable both to the Protectionists on one side and to the Samuelite Free Traders and Snowden on the other. It looked as if the Government would break up. Perhaps it would have been better for all concerned if it had done so. What emerged was an agreement to the effect that Ministers who disagreed with the Protectionist majority should be free to speak and vote as they saw fit.[3] The Protectionists were really conceding nothing. They knew that they had a huge, built-in, parliamentary majority. Did it matter that this majority was slightly reduced in order to appease the susceptible consciences of the Free Traders?

So the Government prepared to go ahead with its tariffs. If no compromise could be reached between Free Traders and Protectionists, at least an uneasy compromise was worked out between different brands of Protectionists. There would be a 10 per cent *ad valorem* tariff, subject to such exceptions as might be made by Act of Parliament. For the time being at least, goods from the British Empire would be exempt.

Samuel attacked the proposed tariffs on traditional Free Trade grounds. Poignantly, one of the strongest defences of the government proposals came from Runciman. It was noticed at the time, however, that there were considerable differences of emphasis between his arguments, which were based largely on the view that British tariffs could be used to induce foreign countries to reduce their tariffs on a reciprocal basis,[4] and those of Chamberlain, who perceived long-term advantages from a Protectionist policy.

The 'free list' of goods which were to be exempted from the 10 per cent duty was the subject of much parliamentary discussion. The old idea of a 'free breakfast table' still appealed to Liberals, and even to some of the Liberal Nationals. An amendment in the committee stage of the Government's Import Duties Bill to add 'foodstuffs for human consumption' to the free list secured support from the Samuelite Liberals, while the Liberal Nationals split almost evenly.[5] Inevitably, the amendment was defeated by the huge Conservative majority. In the end, of course, the Government's measure was carried, though with the 'Samuelites' voting against it. One of the Liberal Nationals, A. C. Curry, also voted against the Bill, while two of the putative 'Samuelites', J. A. Leckie and Dr J. Hunter, voted in favour. Thereafter, Curry could be regarded as a 'Samuelite', Leckie and Hunter as Liberal Nationals.

Liberals outside Parliament began to develop grave misgivings about their leaders' continued presence in the government.[6] At the NLF Conference in Clacton in April, a resolution was carried, declaring that 'Liberal Ministers ... must themselves be the judges of the extent to which their support of the government should be carried', but adding, rather pointedly, that 'it hopes that it will be able to count upon the united strength of the Party, free from all entanglements'. That went about as far as a loyal organisation could go in saying that patience was wearing thin, and that Liberals in the government should take the earliest decent opportunity of resigning. Meanwhile, the Liberal Nationals set up a council designed to give 'wholehearted support to the National Government', to coordinate relations with the Conservatives and to raise funds.[7]

The rupture with the Government came in the aftermath of the Imperial Economic Conference held at Ottawa in July and August 1932. This resulted in various trade agreements between Empire countries. Britain was required to continue the exemption of Empire goods from the Import Duties, and also to impose new duties on foreign imports. As the new arrangements, unlike the Import Duties Act, involved international obligations, and were to continue in existence for a period of years, this provided the Liberal Ministers with sufficient reason, or excuse, to leave the Government. On 28 September, the 'Samuelite' Liberals, and also Snowden, at last resigned, and were duly replaced by Conservatives and Liberal Nationals.

A few days earlier, when the resignation was already planned, Sir Geoffrey Shakespeare, LIberal National Chief Whip, had written to Simon, warning prophetically that

> our lines of communication with the Liberal Party will be cut for ever. Ottawa will be our Rubicon ... If we still parade the name of Liberal it will really only be by false pretences, because it must be clear to everybody that there is no future for us but ultimate absorption in the Conservative Party.[8]

Ottawa caused substantial disquiet in Liberal National ranks. Runciman, so

Viscount Grey told Samuel, 'is not in line with the Ottawa negotiations, but I assume as he is a party to the result he must adhere to the Government'.[9] Nor was the tariff question the only one to disturb some of the Liberal Nationals. Sir Geoffrey Shakespeare describes a secret meeting at his own London house about this time 'as we wanted to discuss frankly the conditions under which we would continue our support for the National Government. We were dissatisfied with the small number of progressive measures included in the Government's programme. We wanted more social reform.' Knowledge of the meeting soon leaked out, and Shakespeare 'got a severe reprimand from Simon'.[10]

By-elections in 1932 suggested that the Liberals still retained considerable public support. By far the most important of these contests was in North Cornwall, and followed the sudden death of Sir Donald Maclean. The constituency was a precarious one, where the issue always lay between Liberals and Conservatives, with Labour either not fighting at all or securing a negligible vote. In the supervening by-election, Sir Francis Acland was able to retain the seat, with a slightly increased majority. In September the Liberals retained the much safer territory of Cardiganshire. Liberals could also draw modest satisfaction from the Dulwich by-election in July. The Conservatives held the seat with their usual large majority, but the Liberal narrowly beat Labour for second place. In the first half of 1933, results in constituencies as diverse as Ashford, East Rhondda and Altrincham were moderately good.

Some Liberal Associations who had Liberal National MPs appear to have been more concerned to have a representative who included 'Liberal' in his designation than whether he was a government supporter or not. In Asquith's pre-war seat of East Fife, the constituency association had backed the Liberal National Duncan Millar. On his death, it decided to support another Liberal National, Henderson Stewart. A young Liberal, David Keir, entered the lists, but fared disastrously, despite public support from several prominent Liberals. A strange situation arose shortly afterwards in the Scottish Universities – the only three-member constituency in the country. In 1931, one Liberal and two Conservatives had been returned without a contest. The Liberal died, and another candidate, Dr G. A. Morrison, also declared to be a Liberal, was returned in his place. It soon became apparent that Morrison was in fact a Liberal National.

Although the NLF had urged Liberal Ministers to resign from the National Government in September 1932, Liberal MPs – apart from the Lloyd George 'family group' – continued to sit on Government benches in the House of Commons. In February 1933, Major H. L. Nathan MP for North-East Bethnal Green, crossed the floor to join the Opposition. Meanwhile active Liberals were becoming even more restive than they had been in the previous year. In May, the NLF Council, meeting at Scarborough, openly expressed the opinion that the proper place for Liberals was on Opposition benches. The process of persuading the Liberal MPs to go into opposition to the National Government was still a slow one. On 16 November 1933 they did at last formally join the Opposition. Even then, not all of the MPs were prepared to cross the floor. Three who had originally ranked as 'Samuelites' remained on the Government side of the House.[11] By contrast, all the principal organisations of the Liberal Party welcomed the move.[12] 'Liberal Nationalism' touched parliamentarians ('Liberal for the sake of their consciences; National for the sake of their seats'), and often the constituency organisations which supported them; but it had little influence on ordinary Liberals elsewhere.

The painfully slow process by which the Liberal leadership dissociated itself from the National Government, and the absence of a clear, defining, issue at the end wrought much damage. By late 1933 or early 1934, the Liberal position was considerably worse than it had been at the General Election. By contrast, the Labour Party was showing signs of revival. The Fulham East by-election of October 1933 evinced a particularly spectacular rise in Labour support. Local election results told the same story. In municipal elections held in principal towns of England and Wales in November 1933, Labour made many gains, while Liberals and Conservatives sustained heavy losses. In March 1934, Labour recorded a great victory at the London County Council elections, and the small Liberal representation was wiped out. In July of that year Major Nathan joined the Labour Party. Later in 1934, Frank Briant, Liberal MP for Lambeth North, died. In 1931, Briant had had nearly a two-to-one lead over Labour; but three years later the defending Liberal candidate secured only a shade over a quarter of the votes cast, and the seat passed to Labour with a substantial majority. At the end of 1934, Labour still did not look like a convincing alternative Government, but was making rapid progress in that direction, while with the Liberals it was downhill all the way.

The General Election of November 1935 confirmed this gloomy view of Liberal prospects. The government chose its moment rather well. Britain, like most other countries, was emerging from the Great Depression. Unemployment figures, and other indications of national prosperity, were improving substantially. In May, the Silver Jubilee of George V was the occasion of national excitement difficult to imagine today, and such events usually redound to the benefit of the government in office. In June, Ramsay MacDonald, already visibly senile, at last resigned the premiership, and Baldwin took over. One of the ministerial changes associated with the change-over was the removal of Simon from the Foreign Office to the less controversial Home Office. In October the Italian attack on Abyssinia

(Ethiopia) began, and the British government appeared to be demanding resolute League of Nations action.

The Liberal organisation was in a parlous condition. In November 1933, Ramsay Muir, President of the NLF, had assured the Glasgow Liberal Club that 'we at headquarters see our way to fighting at least 400 seats ... I should be happier if it were 500, and happiest if it were 615'.[13] This was wildly, ridiculously, optimistic. In the event, the Liberals fought 161 seats against 579 supporters of the National Government and 552 Labour. It is not at all surprising that the Liberals were only able to fight on a narrow front. They had neither the money nor the organisation to do much more. It is more surprising that they did not give more attention to Liberal National seats, for these were mostly places of traditional Liberal strength. Denbigh was the only constituency where a sitting Liberal National was faced with Liberal opposition.[14] A glance at election results show that a Liberal candidate could almost certainly have caused Simon to be unseated at Spen Valley (though Labour would probably have been elected) and several other Liberal Nationals were vulnerable. They could not rely on Conservative votes alone; they needed Liberal votes as well to be sure of election. Yet the opportunity was missed, probably through the pathetic hope that at some future date Liberal Nationals would reunite with the Liberal Party.

On what issues could the Liberals fight in 1935? In 1929, there had been an outside chance of a Liberal Government, and a realistic prospect that enough Liberals would be returned to influence the behaviour of a government of a different party strongly in a Liberal direction. This was completely out of the question in 1935. Even the Free Trade issue, the one question on which the man-in-the-street had a fairly clear idea of where Liberals stood, was a good deal less sharp than it had been a few years earlier. No doubt the 10 per cent tariffs of 1932 had an adverse effect on the economy, as the Free Traders had predicted; but the gradual and world wide recovery from the Great Depression had largely obscured that fact. The Protectionists, for their part, had not cared to push their policy further.

For the Liberals, disaster was humanly certain, and disaster duly supervened. Only 21 Liberal MPs were returned, against 428 supporters of the National Government, 154 Labour, and a few 'oddments'. Sir Herbert Samuel was defeated at Darwen, while other celebrities, including the Chief Whip Sir Walter Rea, Isaac Foot and Harcourt Johnstone also lost their seats. Twelve of the defending Liberal MPs were unseated, while just three seats were gained: all of them taken by small majorities after straight fights with Conservatives, all of them in scattered rural constituencies far from centres of population. Of the 21 Liberal MPs elected, six had had straight fights with Conservatives, seven had had Labour but not Conservative opponents, and one had had a straight fight with a Scottish Nationalist. Only seven had encountered opposition both from Labour and from supporters of the National Government. Embarrassingly, the Liberal Nationals, with 33 MPs, were more numerous than the official Liberals.

It is easy to blame the débâcle on Samuel's leadership, but that would be a hasty and unfair judgement. His devotion to the Liberal Party was complete and consistent. He acted with the caution of a thinking man who carefully weighed up arguments, rather than the flair of a man like Lloyd George or Churchill whose political instincts were sometimes brilliantly right, but at other times disastrously wrong. David Marquand's striking encomium perhaps overstates the position: 'Samuel does not have a high place in the pantheon of Liberal leaders. But if he had not deployed great skill in playing a weak hand in September 1931 and September 1932, it is doubtful if the Liberal Party would exist today.'[15]

Samuel's defeat made it necessary for the Liberal MPs to select a new leader, and the choice alighted on Sir Archibald Sinclair, one of the few MPs whose constituency appeared safe. At 45, Sinclair was still, by political standards, youthful, but he had sat in Parliament since 1922, and had had experience both as a Cabinet Minister and as Liberal Chief Whip. At first sight, Sinclair did not look like the sort of man who would give the Liberal Party a new, dynamic and radical character. A Scottish aristocrat – his grandfather had sat for Caithnessshire as a rather Whiggish Liberal until he was turned out in 1885 by a 'Crofters' Party' candidate – Sinclair's early career had been in the army. When he turned to politics, he was closely attached to Churchill, and a considerable bond remained between the two men. A very sympathetic observer noted that 'on Service subjects and foreign affairs he speaks effectively, but he is not so strong on social problems in which he lacks experience'.[16] Yet very soon after he became Leader, he proved a great inspiration to Liberals, particularly the young and radical among them.

As the Chief Whip had been defeated, he was replaced by Sir Percy Harris, the only surviving London Liberal MP. Sinclair and Harris both rendered great service to the Liberal Party, and played large parts in saving it from the threatened obliteration. Lloyd George and his family approved of the new leadership, and were regarded henceforth as full members of the Liberal Party, though the patriarch played little further role in party activities.

Almost immediately after the 1935 General Election, a Liberal Reconstruction Committee was set up, under the chairmanship of Lord Meston, a former Indian civil servant of high distinction. The committee had wide terms of reference, and its essential proposals were adopted by a Liberal Convention which met in London in June 1936. On their face, the proposals looked rather like a sledgehammer to crack a nut. The National Liberal Federation was to disappear, and a new body, the Liberal Party Organisation (LPO), would be set up, whose composition would be somewhat broader than that of the NLF. It would hold an annual Assembly, and quarterly meetings of a smaller Council. There seem to have been two overriding reasons for setting up a completely new body, instead of modifying the composition and functions of the old one. The name of the National Liberal Federation invited confusion with the Liberal Nationals. There was also much to be said for a fresh start, to avoid the risk of Liberal National infiltration, since disaffiliation of existing bodies which supported Liberal National MPs could prove difficult. Another feature of the new arrangements was centralisation of Headquarters funds, though the precedent of the 'Million Fund' did not suggest that a great increase in available money would necessarily follow.[17] The Secretary of the new LPO was W. R. Davies, cousin of R. H. Davies, who – like the older man – would give many years of loyal and effective work to the Liberal cause. Liberals often had good reason to complain about the behaviour of their politicians; they seldom had reason to complain about the devoted work rendered by their professional workers.

At almost the same moment as the Liberal Party prepared to draw lines which would clearly separate them from the Liberal Nationals, the other body was doing exactly the same thing. The first meeting of the Liberal National Convention was held in London in the same month as the Liberal Convention, and formally established a Liberal National Council. The Liberal Nationals were able to make some headway against the 'official' Liberals. In the period between the 1935 General Election and the outbreak of war in 1939, two Liberal MPs, R. H. Bernays of Bristol North and Herbert Holdsworth of Bradford South, defected to the Liberal Nationals. Both had had straight fights against Labour in 1935 in circumstances which strongly suggest that some kind of collusive arrangement had been reached with the local Conservatives.

The fact that the two parties were completely distinct by the mid-1930s must not be read back to 1931, and be taken to imply that from the very beginning Liberal Nationals had decided that their future lay in permanent alliance with the Conservatives. Very likely Simon had so decided, but – as Neville Chamberlain observed privately – Simon 'hasn't a friend even in his own party'.[18] Others saw matters very differently. Sir Geoffrey Shakespeare 'believed it better for Liberals to play their part in a National Government and to infuse Liberalism into that government ... rather than to criticise in opposition without any real prospect of securing a vestige of Liberalism in the government's programme'. Hore-Belisha warned in 1932 that 'if the Tories ... get on the back of us ... they will continue their pecking to the death'. Runciman, as late as March 1938, was pleading for 'pure, simple, strong Liberalism in order to save [the] country from disaster.'[19] But, whatever their different motives may have been, the Liberal Nationals had long been indistinguishable from Conservatives in their actual political behaviour.

The division of MPs into orthodox Liberals and Liberal Nationals did not correspond at all closely with either their past or their future political orientation. On the Liberal National side, Simon and Runciman had been Asquithians, but Hutchison had been a Lloyd Georgeite. On the Liberal side, Samuel and Harris had been Asquithians but Sinclair a Lloyd Georgeite. Looking into the future, the Liberal National Clement Davies would return to the Liberals, and would play an invaluable part in keeping the party in existence during its most desolate period. The Liberal National Edgar Granville would also return to the Liberals, but would eventually join Labour, while Hore-Belisha would become a Conservative. Most of the orthodox Liberals would remain in place, but Geoffrey Mander would join Labour. So would Megan Lloyd George; while her brother Gwilym would become a Minister in a Conservative government.

The Ross and Cromarty by-election of February 1936 was a disaster for the Liberals, who took fourth place and forfeited their deposit; but thereafter the Liberals performed moderately well in those by-elections which they fought. They avoided all contests in the larger towns, while Labour usually stood down in places where the Liberals could expect to do well. There were two agonising by-election 'near-misses', both in the summer of 1937. Walter Runciman went to the Lords, and the contest at St Ives was a straight fight between a Liberal National and the Liberal Isaac Foot. The defenders held the seat with a majority of 210. In North Dorset, in a straight fight with a Conservative defender, the Liberal was defeated by 543 votes. In other more or less rural constituencies which the Liberals contested, their candidate regularly did well, and improved his position; but nowhere did he come close to victory.

As the 1930s advanced, public attention was drawn increasingly to the baleful course of international affairs. By May 1937, when Prime Minister Stanley Baldwin retired and Neville Chamberlain took his place, it required no prophetic genius to see that a new major war was likely soon. All parties were divided as to the appropriate response. Some Conservatives like Winston Churchill blamed the National Government for its alleged pusillanimity. In the Labour Party, the pacifist George Lansbury was replaced as Leader in 1935 by Clement Attlee, whose attitude on such matters was very different from that of his predecessor. Many Liberals were drawn towards the idea of resistance to 'the dictators' – by force if necessary; but this response was not unanimous. By the late 1930s, there was not much difference between the approaches of Churchill, Attlee and Sinclair in these matters, for all were equally opposed to the 'Appeasement' policy linked with the name of Chamberlain.

After the German seizure of Austria in March 1938, it became apparent that the next great issue would probably concern Czechoslovakia and the real or imagined grievances of the German-speaking Sudetendeutsch who lived on the country's western fringes. Would those grievances provide the reason, or the excuse, for a German invasion of the country? If that happened, then existing international engagements seemed to require that France, and perhaps the Soviet Union as well, should go to Czechoslovakia's assistance. In that event other countries, including Britain, might soon be dragged in.

The ailing Viscount Runciman, most Liberal of the Liberal Nationals, was despatched, against his will, to act as British 'mediator', charged to attempt to bring the Czechoslovak government and the Sudetendeutsch to the conference table, to achieve an agreement between themselves which would de-fuse the whole crisis. The mission collapsed, and a major crisis followed, which many people thought would lead to a general war. The Munich Conference at the end of September resulted in an agreed plan for incorporation of the Sudetenland in Germany. A great reaction suddenly set in, and in the parliamentary debate which followed a few days later, all three parties showed deep divisions. In the end, voting took place, with three-line party whips. It is well known that a substantial number of Conservatives, including Churchill. abstained from voting in support of the government; it is not so often remembered that substantial numbers of Labour members abstained from following their own party recommendation to vote against it. The Liberals were openly divided: fourteen voted against the government, four voted in support.

Some senior members of the party, including Lord Crewe and J. A. Spender, perhaps the most prestigious of Liberal journalists, took a very different view from most of the MPs. But the most conspicuous Liberal supporter of the Munich settlement was Samuel, who by this time had become a Viscount. He wrote to Chamberlain indicating approval, and was offered a Cabinet post. Samuel refused, partly through continuing disagreement with the government's tariff policy, partly to avoid embarrassing Liberal colleagues.[20] We now know a great deal more about the highly confidential information which had come into Chamberlain's hands than most people did in 1938.[21] Perhaps Samuel was not so wrong after all.

In the aftermath of Munich, the various critics of Chamberlain's policy were drawn increasingly together. There had long been talk of a 'Popular Front' composed of various opponents of the National Government, who would sink their differences, at least temporarily, in a common cause. The

Liberal leadership gave qualified support to the idea, while the *News Chronicle* and the *Manchester Guardian* were enthusiastic for it; but the leadership of the Labour Party set its face firmly against anything which could be seen as a compromise of its own principles.

There was, nevertheless, a general disposition on the part of the two Opposition parties to avoid treading too much on each other's toes. In three important by-elections of late 1938, both parties stood down in favour of a non-Party candidate opposed to the government. At Oxford City in late October, the distinguished academic A. D. L. Lindsay stood as an Independent Progressive without opposition from either Liberals or Labour, but was rather narrowly defeated by the government candidate Quintin Hogg. In the following month another Independent Progressive, the *News Chronicle* journalist Vernon Bartlett, captured the government seat of Bridgwater. A remarkable contest arose in December in Kinross & West Perthshire. The sitting Conservative MP, the Duchess of Atholl, disagreed sharply with her party on various questions of foreign policy, and resigned in order to fight a by-election in support of her views. Predictably, an official Conservative candidate was nominated against her. Independent the Duchess may have been, but Progressive she wasn't, and the Liberal who had polled strongly in 1935, Mrs Coll Macdonald, was anxious to stand again. The Liberal leadership set great pressure on her to stand down, and she eventually complied; but, as Sinclair wrote privately,

> Whereas I wanted to make it clear that the whole object of Mrs Coll Macdonald standing down was to ensure an emphatic vote against Mr Chamberlain's foreign policy, the dominant consideration in Mrs Coll Macdonald's mind was obviously the defeat of the Duchess![22]

Mrs Coll Macdonald got her wish, but Sinclair did not, for the Duchess was defeated. Taken together, the by-elections suggested that there was a gentle swing of votes against the government, but no dramatic move towards Liberal, Labour or – except at Bridgwater – independent anti-government candidates.

The final extinction of Czechoslovakia in March 1939 was a complete violation of what had been agreed at Munich, and everybody, including Chamberlain, acknowledged that Appeasement was dead. It was equally clear that Hitler had by no means exhausted his territorial ambitions. Poland looked like being the next victim. A British 'guarantee' was given to Poland at the end of March. A glance at the map will show that there was no possible way of Britain rendering effective help to Poland in the event of a German attack; but the 'guarantee' was taken to mean that an attack on Poland would constitute a *casus belli*.

No important voices were raised against the 'guarantee', though Lloyd George expressed immediate concern that the Soviet Union was not involved in the arrangements. Thereafter, although there were many unsettled issues of foreign policy, the deep and fundamental split which had affected all parties at the beginning of the year was resolved.

As the international situation deteriorated during the 1930s, increased attention was necessarily given to questions of what all nations euphemistically call 'defence'. Here, too, sharp political lines were soon drawn; but these did not correspond closely with the lines drawn in diplomatic matters. In 1936 the British Government made a cautious beginning to a policy of rearmament by presenting Parliament with supplementary estimates for the three armed forces. The Liberals, despite their growing opposition to the government's foreign policy, supported those estimates, while the Labour Party resisted them.[23] Three years later, the government decided to introduce a small measure of military conscription. When the proposal was first introduced in the House of Commons in April 1939, the Liberals split deeply, six supporting the government, seven voting against, along with the Labour Opposition, and a number abstaining. The government's motion was, inevitably, adopted.[24] *Liberal Magazine* declares that this had a sudden effect on 'our friends in Europe', convincing them that 'Britain means business'. Not to put too fine a point on it, the result (and probably the main intention) was not to deter Hitler, or to add to Britain's military potential, but to keep France in line in a determination to go to war if Poland was attacked. When a Bill was introduced giving effect to the motion, five Liberals voted in support of the Second Reading and none against.[25]

In July 1939 Liberals fought the last really important peacetime by-election, following the death of Sir Francis Acland, Liberal MP for North Cornwall. The Liberal candidate, Tom Horabin, was a newcomer to the constituency, while the Conservative, who had run Acland close in 1935, was an established local personality. Labour did not advance a candidate. The gloomy international situation cast a heavy shadow over the election, and Horabin's nomination papers were signed by both Labour and dissident Conservatives.[26] The Liberals took the contest very seriously, and Sinclair was one of many speakers in Horabin's support. But not long before polling day, a letter appeared in *The Times*, over the signature of J. A. Spender. He did not exactly advise the voters to support the Conservative, but expressed his 'misgivings about the recent tendency of Liberal policy under the leadership in the House of Commons', and the letter was widely used by Horabin's opponent. The upshot of the by-election, however, was a Liberal victory, with a slightly increased majority.

On 23 August, the international situation changed radically with the announcement of a 'Non-Aggression Pact' between Germany and the Soviet Union, which meant that the Allies had no further hope of assistance from Russia. A week later, Germany attacked Poland. Two days after that, Britain and France declared war on Germany. As soon as the German attack on Poland began, and even before the British declaration of war, the government was broadened by incorporation of the great Conservative rebel Churchill, and the more dubious rebel Anthony Eden. Chamberlain made an attempt to include both Opposition parties in the government as well. Labour refused. In discussion with Sinclair, Chamberlain explained that he proposed to form a small inner War Cabinet. Sinclair was offered a post in the Cabinet, but not in the inner group. He then had discussions with some senior members of the party, most of whom considered that the offer should be refused, since the Liberals would not have a share in the big decisions of policy, and 'could best support the vigorous prosecution of the war from an independent basis'. There was later some discussion as to whether Samuel might join the government as an individual, without engaging the party, but this idea soon foundered.[27] One 'real' Liberal, Gwilym Lloyd George, was later taken into the government in a junior capacity. As in 1914, a party truce was quickly established, under which the three parties undertook not to oppose each other in wartime by-elections.

By the spring of 1940, a series of wartime disasters culminated in a highly successful German attack on Norway and a thoroughly unsuccessful attempt by Britain and France to drive the Germans out. Early in May there commenced a great parliamentary debate on the conduct of the war. On this occasion Lloyd George delivered his last great Parliamentary speech, concluding with the oft-quoted words,

> I say solemnly that the Prime Minister should give an example of sacrifice, because there is nothing which can contribute more to victory in this war than that he should sacrifice the seals of office.[28]

When the vote came, the government secured what would, in all ordinary circumstances, be regarded as a victory: 281 votes to 200 – but around forty MPs who would normally be considered government supporters voted with the Opposition, and about sixty did not vote. Those MPs who were members of the Ministry, including Churchill, voted with the government. Labour and the Liberals voted against it. So did a number of prominent Conservatives, including Leo Amery, Quintin Hogg, and the future Prime Minister Harold Macmillan.

There were some aberrant votes among both Liberals and Liberal Nationals. The Lloyd George family was split: Gwilym, as a Minister, was required to vote with the government, his father and sister voted against it. The future Liberal leader Clement Davies, who had already broken with the Liberal Nationals but had not yet rejoined the Liberals, voted against the government. So did four MPs who still ranked as Liberal Nationals.[29] Most interesting of the four was Leslie Hore-Belisha. He had been a highly innovative Secretary for War until January 1940, when he fell foul of some of the more hide bound military people, and was forced to resign.

The government majority was not adequate for an administration conducting a major war, and Chamberlain immediately considered ways of broadening his government. Labour, at any rate, would not serve under him, and so it was certain that he must resign. It was a good deal less certain who would be the successor, and at first the scales seemed weighted in favour of the Foreign Secretary, Viscount Halifax. There is strong evidence that Clement Davies played a crucial part in determining that the eventual choice would light on Churchill. On 10 May he formed an all-party Coalition. At the centre was a War Cabinet of five. No Liberals were formally incorporated in that War Cabinet, but Sir Archibald Sinclair was appointed Secretary of State for Air, and in practice attended most of the War Cabinet meetings. Other Liberals – Harcourt Johnstone, Gwilym Lloyd George and Dingle Foot – were included in more junior capacities. As the war proceeded, there were various changes in Liberal appointments.[30]

When Churchill's government was formed, Simon was appointed Lord Chancellor, taking a viscountcy. There was some irony in this, for Simon had refused the same job ('better the sack than the Woolsack') when it had been offered to him by Asquith a quarter of a century earlier. In those days Simon had not unrealistic aspirations for the eventual reversion of the Premiership; but that was out of the question by 1940. Labour had a particular animus against Simon, and was only prepared to endorse his continued presence in the Ministry at all because it was perceived that he would be politically innocuous in the new post.

Throughout the German war, Sinclair continued to hold the office of Secretary for Air. With responsibility for one of the most important offices of the state, he could not possibly devote much time to leadership of the political party which for five years had relied very largely on him for inspiration. Effectively, Liberal leadership devolved largely on Sir Percy Harris, who was Deputy Chairman of the MPs and also Chief Whip. Harris was a devoted MP, loved as well as respected in the tiny working-class constituency he represented.

For the remainder of 1940 and the first half of 1941, public attention centred on the war itself, and Britain's part in it. With the German attack on the Soviet Union in June 1941, and the Japanese attack on the United States in December, the whole character of the war changed. Britain was no longer alone, fighting desperately for survival, and it was possible for people to give attention to the sort of country and world they wished to establish in the aftermath. Meanwhile, however, the leaders of all three parties remained engrossed in the war itself. Initially, the new public concern received little encouragement from any of the party leaders, but all of them were eventually compelled to respond to it.

In 1941, a body originally called Liberal Action, but later renamed Radical Action was set up, with Lancelot Spicer, Honor Balfour and Sir Richard Acland MP, son of Sir Francis, as conspicuous members. Radical Action served as a ginger group which encouraged new thinking about both policy and party strategy. Acland's speeches disturbed many Liberals, and the Chief Whip was under some pressure to expel him. Harris resisted that pressure,[31] but Acland soon went off on a political frolic of his own, initially known as the Forward March and later as Common Wealth, and in 1942 seceded from the Liberal Party.

The by-election truce enabled the Liberals to return a number of MPs without opposition from the other parties. The two changes in Berwick-upon-Tweed were particularly important. In 1941 the Liberal MP, Sir Hugh Seely, accepted a peerage, and was succeeded by the 23-year old George Grey, a kinsman of the former Foreign Secretary, who had once represented the same constituency. Grey was immensely popular in the House, and would doubtless have had a great future in politics; but he was killed in the D-Day landings of June 1944. His successor was Sir William Beveridge, who had a very different background. He had never been a politician of any brand, but had had a brilliant career as an academic economist and a civil servant. In 1941, Beveridge was appointed Chairman of an inter-Departmental enquiry into the social services, the intention apparently being that it should not report until after the war. Beveridge perceived the potentials of this work and pressed ahead rapidly. The Committee's report, *Social Insurance and Allied Services*, was published in December 1942, and immediately attracted enormous public attention, while the government was visibly embarrassed by some of the proposals. Beveridge envisaged a free National Health Service, state policies to encourage full employment, and universal social insurance. He was soon drawn into the Liberal Party, and in October 1944 was returned as MP for Berwick-upon-Tweed. Thereafter he was used extensively in presentations of Liberal policy, and it was widely considered that he would attract a great deal of support to the Liberals.

As the war developed, the whole idea of the party truce came under severe criticism, and many Liberals saw a great chance of undermining the Conservative majority which still dominated the House of Commons. By the terms of the inter-party agreement of 1939, it was open to the Liberals to denounce the truce unilaterally. At the Liberal Assembly of 1942, a very serious, but unsuccessful, attempt was made to persuade the party to do so. Meanwhile, candidates with no official party support at all were polling strongly at by-elections, and soon began winning seats which had been held by Conservatives or Liberal Nationals. In March 1942, a thinly-disguised Labour candidate standing as an Independent captured the Conservative seat of Grantham, and in the folllowing month something very similar happened at Wallasey and at Rugby. In June this was repeated with a spectacular overturn of votes at Maldon. In April 1943, Acland's Common Wealth captured the Liberal National seat of Eddisbury.

Two by-election results in the second half of 1943 were particularly agonising for Liberals. In August Donald Johnson, a prominent figure in the party, resigned his membership to fight as an Independent Liberal in the Conservative seat of Chippenham. He missed election by 195 votes, and complained bitterly that this narrow defeat was due to the formal support which Sinclair gave to the Conservative out of loyalty to the electoral truce. In Samuel's old seat of Darwen another Independent Liberal, Honor Balfour, came even closer to victory, losing to the Conservative by only 70 votes.

In the mid-war period, another significant development seemed to be taking place, although eventually this, too, was frustrated. From 1931 onwards, Simon had been in every sense the leader of the Liberal Nationals. It is difficult to believe that the party would have come into existence without him, and he kept a close rein on its members thereafter. But when he became Lord Chancellor in 1940, it was impossible for him to continue as leader, and his office passed to Ernest Brown, a man conspicuously lacking in Simon's intellectual calibre and ruthlessness.

At that very moment, the position of the Liberal National Party became, from any point of view, anomalous. During the 1930s, there had been a sort of argument for the view that the interests of Liberalism were best served by continual and whole-hearted support for the National Government; but in 1940 the National Government came to an end. Once the war was over, it was most unlikely that political alignments would revert to what they had been in pre-war days, but the essential principles which had united Liberals before 1931 would remain. Just as Liberals had taken different views about the Coalition from 1918 to 1922, but soon came together again after that Coalition ended, was it not common sense that they should prepare to face problems which would follow the war as a united party?

Several MPs were already moving in that direction in the mid-war period. In 1942 Clement Davies rejoined the Liberals. In February of the same year three MPs, Hore-Belisha, Sir Henry Morris-Jones and Edgar Granville, withdrew from the Liberal National group in Parliament. In July 1943 Ernest Brown offered to inaugurate discussions on Liberal reunion – an offer which was eagerly taken up by the official Liberals. These talks continued until November 1944, when they collapsed. The fundamental point of difference was that Brown envisaged continued support for the Coalition into peace-time, while Sinclair recognised the need for complete independence.

Early in 1945, the Liberal Party lost its most famous twentieth-century personality. Towards the end of the previous year, Lloyd George was advised that there were considerable doubts whether he could retain his seat in Caernarvon Boroughs at the next General Election. It was considered important that a man with his enormous experience should retain some Parliamentary platform. He decided to accept a peerage, and was gazetted Earl Lloyd-George of Dwyfor. This necessitated a by-election under party truce conditions, which the Liberals duly won. Lloyd George, however, fell ill and died in March 1945.

As the European war approached its end, it was generally guessed that Churchill would attempt to capitalise on his immense wartime popularity, just as Lloyd George had done in 1918, by seeking to continue the Coalition into peacetime. Long before the war ended, both Liberal and Labour Parties had made it plain that they would have no part in such an arrangement. The House of Commons which had been elected in 1935 was still sitting, and its existence had been prolonged far beyond the normal lifetime by special con-stitutional provisions. On 18 May 1945, Churchill wrote to Attlee, Sinclair and Brown, proposing that the inevitable election should be delayed a little longer. There was some argument for this. The war in the Far East was still in progress, and in any event new electoral registers were due in October. It might be no bad thing to allow an interval between the main fighting and a political contest, in order to enable the voters to become familiar with the issues which would be important in peacetime. But both Attlee and Sinclair opposed the idea, so plans were made for an early General Election. The Coalition Government formally ended, while a new Ministry – the so-called 'Caretaker Government' – took office until the results could be declared. This new government was overwhelmingly Conservative, but included a number of Liberal Nationals. The Liberal and Labour Parties were not officially represented, but Gwilym Lloyd George, though still ranking as a Liberal, became Minister of Fuel and Power. Wheels were immediately set in motion for a General Election.

17

Nadir

> We carve out a niche for ourselves left of Centre ... in the sense that we stand for personal freedom against authority ... in the sense that we believe there is still too much poverty, too many slums, too much cruelty ... in the sense that we want and mean to have a wide dispersal of property and power.
>
> Jo Grimond, 29 March 1958[1]

Sir Percy Harris, who had been Liberal Chief Whip and the man primarily responsible for the adoption of Parliamentary candidates, recorded that

> Up to 1944 it was almost impossible to persuade Liberals to take any active interest in party politics or even to consider adopting candidates. It was not until early 1945 there was any real awakening of activity among the Liberals in the constituencies and the same applied to possible candidates ... With the hope of the war ending and victory assured, candidates came to us in a spate. If we had been able to put the organisation in order as rapidly as the candidates came forward we could have easily placed another hundred ... Most of the men and women who offered their services were ready to find money and were of an excellent quality.[2]

In the end, the Liberals were able to field 306 candidates for 640 seats, against 604 Labour and 624 Conservatives and other 'Nationals'. Among those Liberal candidates was a high proportion of young ex-service men: higher, in fact than in the other parties.[3] The Liberal tally of candidates was far in excess of the figures for the previous two General Elections, but was nothing like enough to convince voters that they had any prospect of forming a government. They received some support from the *News Chronicle* and the *Manchester Guardian,* but otherwise had little help from the national press. As for their own productions, one more or less objective account declares that 'the Liberal pamphlets in general were so high-toned as to be nearly academic'.[4] A good deal of emphasis was set on the Beveridge Report. 'Freedom through Security' was a popular slogan.

Polling was on 5 July 1945, but votes had to be collected from a great many Service men and women overseas, and counting was delayed until three weeks later. The upshot was a vast victory for the Labour Party, which won 393 seats, against 213 'Nationals' and only twelve Liberals, with various 'others'. This was far the lowest Liberal figure ever recorded, and the casualty list among the most eminent members of the party was fearful. The three most famous personalities, Sinclair, Beveridge and Harris, were all defeated. In Sinclair's case, this was one of the most agonising 'triple marginal' results ever recorded, for the three candidates in Caithness and Sutherland were within a bracket of 61 votes.

Examined in detail, the Liberal position was even worse than the crude figures suggested. Not a single seat was held in or near any large town. Six seats were held in remote parts of Wales, and a seventh in the University of Wales. Just five were held in England, and these were about as scattered as could be: North Cumberland, North Cornwall, North Dorset, the Eye division of Suffolk, the Buckrose division of Yorkshire. Nothing remained in once-Liberal Scotland. Only three of the elected MPs had survived both Conservative and Labour opposition. Four had had straight fights with Labour, four with the Conservatives and one with the Welsh Nationalists. Four Liberal MPs had majorities of less than a thousand. There was no Liberal seat anywhere which could be regarded as reasonably safe if both other parties chose to attack it. Two of the Liberal MPs, Clement Davies and Edgar Granville, had been elected in 1931 and 1935 as Liberal Nationals, but had returned to the Liberal Party in the early 1940s. All of the 53 Liberal National candidates had been spared Conservative opposition; yet they had fared as badly as the Liberals, for their representation had been reduced from 27 to thirteen.

Who was to lead the remnant of the Liberal Party? Sir Archibald Sinclair's victorious Conservative opponent had promised to submit to a by-election after the defeat of Japan. Sinclair's narrow defeat could reasonably be attributed partly to the fact that ministerial duties had caused him to neglect nursing his constituency, and partly to the disposition of Liberal organisers to regard it as safe, and therefore to use him extensively elsewhere. If the elected MP had kept his word, Sinclair might well have regained the seat later in 1945; but, to the high embarrassment of many members of his own party, the promise was forgotten. In any event, the Liberal MPs had to select somebody as Chairman for the time being.

Although there were already certain doubts about his loyalty, semi-official approaches were made to Gwylim Lloyd George, the only ex-Minister and Privy Counsellor. These approaches were rejected, as also were similar approaches from the Liberal Nationals.[5] There was no obvious choice among the remaining MPs, some of whom had never met each other. Eventually the job passed to Clement Davies, who had sat for Montgomeryshire since 1929, though for much of that period he had been a Liberal National. Initially the appointment was for one year only, but it was later renewed.[6] Tom Horabin, victor of the 1939 by-election in North Cornwall, became Chief Whip.

In spite of the general gloom, there were some circumstances in the Liberal Party's favour. A surprising number of Liberals who had been active in the party for many years were still active and well known, which gave weight to its activities. Sir Archibald Sinclair, Sir Percy Harris, Sir William Beveridge, Lord Samuel, Lady Violet Bonham-Carter, Lady Megan Lloyd George MP and Isaac Foot were examples. If, *per impossibile*, a Liberal had been invited to concoct a Cabinet from his own party in the late 1940s, he could have produced an impressive team. The second positive aspect of the Liberal Party in the aftermath of 1945 was that the General Election had brought forward a substantial number of able and relatively young people, most of whom had played little or no part in its activities before the war.

Liberals were convinced that the current weakness of their party had not come about because the British people had rejected Liberal policies, but because of a chapter of historical accidents which had damaged the party as an instrument for putting those policies over. When Lady Violet Bonham-Carter told the 1946 Liberal Assembly that the country was 'Liberal to the core', and that the recent Labour victory was due not to any desire for Socialism but to the pre-war record of the Conservatives, she expressed exactly what most Liberals believed. If a level playing field could be created, and the three political parties could be required to present their respective policies to the voters on their merits, the people would choose Liberalism. It was, therefore, incumbent on Liberals to create that level playing field. There must be a radical overhaul of organisation, so that all voters should be regularly confronted with Liberal candidates, backed by adequate propaganda, organisation and finance. Other great changes were required. In many constituencies no Liberal Association existed at all; in many others it was little more than nominal. Effective Liberal Associations must be set up everywhere.

Many of the younger and more active Liberals were coming to think and plan on such lines, but three names stand out. Frank Byers, the new MP for North Dorset, had risen to the rank of lieutenant-colonel in the wartime army. He was a go-getter, not willing to suffer fools gladly or to pull punches, whose personal vigour and determination had played a major part in his own rather unexpected victory. Philip Fothergill was a delightful little man who had come forward through the Young Liberal movement. His health was poor, but he had great determination, an excellent brain and a wonderful sense of humour, and was accessible to all. Edward Martell was

a wartime 'discovery' who was convinced that tactical efficiency was as necessary to produce results in politics as in the war. All were still in their
thirties in 1945.

As often happens when a party suffers a great electoral defeat, the Liberals set up a Reconstruction Committee in the aftermath. The Committee's
proposals were considered, and largely followed, at the Liberal Assembly in
May 1946. Plans were set out which would form the basis of party organisation until the next General Election. There was no doubt that a good many
Liberals were politically inexperienced, but were willing and eager to learn,
and to exert themselves to build up the party at local and national levels.

Much thought had been given to ways of utilising the available people
to best effect. The Liberal Party, all agreed, should seek to run candidates
in substantially every British constituency, ensuring that these candidates
were backed by efficient organisations. The aim, in theory at least, was to
produce a Liberal Government after the next General Election. Today that
goal seems wildly, ridiculously, optimistic; but it did inspire Liberals to
build up organisations in places where there had been little or no activity
for many years.

Where no Liberal Association existed in a constituency, plans were proposed for starting one. Simple instructions were provided, explaining step
by step what should be done to build a strong organisation, capable of field-
ing a candidate with reasonable prospects of victory. Grades of efficiency for
Liberal Associations were devised, and Associations were encouraged to
develop from one grade to the next. At the same time, Liberal finances must
be transformed beyond recognition. Constituencies were given advice on
money-raising. A 'Foundation Fund' was set up, designed to raise large sums
for the central machinery of the party. The original aim was to secure
£125,000 over a five-year period: a sum which was then worth many times
as much as it is now. At all major meetings, local or national, an appeal
would be launched, and this would be quite a protracted affair. An ingenious idea, bearing the recognisable stamp of the journalist Edward Martell,
was the institution of a weekly publication, initially called *Liberal Newscard*
but later *Liberal News*, which was to be priced at 3d, which at the time was
more than the retail price of most newspapers. Once a subscriber had signed
the appropriate form, the money would be collected automatically through
his newsagent, and no further effort by active Liberals would be required. If
a substantial proportion of Liberal sympathisers could be persuaded to take
Liberal News, the party's financial problems would be solved. Ideas like these
were applied with much enthusiasm and considerable effect at first. Reporting to the Liberal Assembly of 1947 on the first eight months of the new
operations, Philip Fothergill was able to tell delegates that the Foundation

Fund had received pledges of over £58,000, while already over 500 active Liberal Associations were in existence, compared with but 200 at the start.[7] Like most organisational and financial schemes, these plans ran into difficulties later, and by the time of the next General Election had fallen far short of early hopes; but they certainly put the Liberal Party in much better organisational and financial fettle than it had been for many years.

Questions of future relations with other Parties began to arise soon after 1945. Superficially, the Liberal Nationals seemed to be in a very similar position to the Liberals. They were clearly an Opposition Party, and most of them would have endorsed the bulk of established Liberal policy, at least as a *desideratum*. So why not reunite? Simon, prime author of the schism of 1931, had long ceased to be a Liberal in any meaningful sense.[8] But Simon no longer dominated the Liberal Nationals. In London, where neither party retained a single MP, the two formally reunited in June 1946. There were serious discussions between organisers of the two parties about fusion at a national level. Soon difficulties began to appear, and a flurry of correspondence in *The Times*, particularly from Frank Byers for the Liberals and Sir Geoffrey Shakespeare for the Liberal Nationals, brings out clearly what those difficulties were.[9] Would the reunited party seek to further positive and distinctive Liberal ideas, or would it be designed essentially to counter Socialism, which implied close and continuing cooperation with the Conservatives? The Liberals opted for complete independence, the Liberal Nationals for alliance with Conservatives. Late in October 1946, the English talks broke down. For a time it looked as if reunion might nevertheless take place in Scotland, but in December those negotiations also collapsed.[10]

The blow which the Conservatives sustained in 1945 was a very heavy and very unexpected one. But when Churchill decided to remain Conservative leader, the Conservative attitude to both Liberals and Liberal Nationals was swiftly defined. He soon brought in Lord Woolton, who had been the very popular Minister of Food in the wartime government as party chairman. Both men believed that the Conservative Party must greatly broaden its appeal, and in particular that they must win the support of Liberals. The character of the Conservative Party changed greatly. Instead of relying mainly on wealthy people and their deferential hangers-on, they made a massive effort to recruit middle-class and even working-class members.

After the Liberal rejection of Liberal National approaches in 1946, a definite alliance of Conservatives and Liberal Nationals was recorded in May of the following year – the 'Woolton-Teviot agreement'. This provided for the establishment of Conservative and Liberal National Associations with reciprocal membership, and for the adoption of candidates with either antecedents. But what deeply angered Liberals was the unscrupulous application of the name 'Liberal' to people who had no Liberal antecedents at all.[11] In several places meetings were called to form associations which included 'Liberal' in their title, from which actual Liberals were excluded. When the 1950 General Election came, no fewer than 53 candidates appeared with designations like 'Conservative and Liberal', 'Conservative and National Liberal', 'National Liberal', 'National Liberal and Conservative', or 'Liberal and Conservative'. These candidates, the so-called 'liquorice all-sorts', were all pledged to support a Conservative Government. Their existence caused great confusion among voters who often thought that a genuine alliance existed between the Liberal and Conservative Parties.

These misuses of the Liberal label were not the chief of the party's worries about Conservative intrusions into their territory. As time went on, large numbers of erstwhile Liberals decided that they ought to support Conservatives in order to 'beat the Socialists'. It was a demoralising experience for active Liberals to learn that people whom they had known as supporters, and sometimes as active members, of the party had hived off in that way.

There was some movement in a different political direction. Tom Horabin resigned as Chief Whip in March 1946. That was no great loss, for he was succeeded by the far more effective and charismatic Frank Byers. But a few months later Horabin left the Liberal Party. After sitting briefly as an Independent Liberal, he decamped to the Labour Party, but did not see fit to submit himself to the voters of North Cornwall in his new colours. Another significant loss to Labour was Sir Geoffrey Mander, who had sat as Liberal MP for Wolverhampton East from 1929 until his defeat in 1945.

The Liberal experience of by-elections and local elections began well. In the spring of 1946, two well-known Liberals, Sir Percy Harris and Edward Martell, were returned to the London County Council for Bethnal Green South-West – the first Liberal LCC victories for many years. In October, Arthur Comyns Carr polled 25 per cent of the votes in a Parliamentary by-election in the City of London. In the following month, Edward Martell won a similar proportion of the votes, and a respectable second place, in the London working-class constituency of Rotherhithe.

But from that moment forward, Liberal results turned very sour. Only one by-election of 1947 was even moderately encouraging. That was West Islington, where the Liberals polled 16 per cent. In other by-elections of the year, the Liberals either did not stand at all or forfeited their deposits. In January 1948 the Liberal finished sixth in a six-cornered contest in the Camlachie division of Glasgow, with a mere 1.2 per cent of the total vote. Even the North Croydon by-election in March was a disaster. The candidate was Air Vice Marshal Don Bennett, a war hero who had sat very briefly as MP for Middlesbrough West in 1945. He was supported by what was, for

Liberals of the time, a strong campaign; but Bennett, too, forfeited his deposit. Thereafter the Liberals dropped out of by-election contests entirely until after the 1950 General Election. In spite of these bad results, the vast majority of active Liberal workers were determined to promote candidates in their own areas at the next General Election. In this they received official encouragement. As late as the Liberal Assembly of March 1949, party workers were assured that their officials aimed to field 600 candidates. Whether a broad front was strategically desirable remains a matter of dispute; but it was really inescapable. At the constituency level, money had been raised and some sort of organisation established, and local Liberals were determined to fight.

The 1950 General Election differed in many ways from its predecessor. There had been a radical revision of constituency boundaries, and the total number of seats was increased slightly to 625. The university seats were abolished. Both Labour and Conservative Parties had a real hope of victory. Many ordinary voters had deep, and highly-coloured, fears of what damage 'Socialism' or 'Toryism' might do if the election went the wrong way. For the first time since 1929, the Liberals were putting forward candidates in the great majority of constituencies, though not as many as they had originally hoped. They would certainly win a lot of votes, though the idea that they might form a government after the election was not taken seriously anywhere. There were signs that some prominent Liberals were unhappy with the broad front which their Party was offering. As Churchill pointed out, neither Sir Archibald Sinclair nor Lady Violet Bonham-Carter delivered one of the party's election broadcasts, and Lady Violet was not even a candidate.

Results of the 1950 General Election demonstrated with great clarity some of the inadequacies of the British electoral system. Labour, with thirteen and a quarter million votes, returned 315 MPs, the Conservatives and their associates, with around twelve and a half million returned 298. The Liberals, with well over two and a half million votes, secured only nine seats. It required roughly 42,000 votes to return a Labour or a Conservative MP, but 291,000 votes to return a Liberal. The Liberals had received more votes than at any election since 1929, yet their representation was down to single figures.

Of the twelve MPs whom the Liberals had returned in 1945, two were no longer receiving the party whip at the Dissolution, for Horabin had defected to Labour and Gwilym Lloyd George was for practical purposes working with the Conservatives. One Liberal seat, the University of Wales, had disappeared under the redistribution. Of the remaining nine MPs, four had not had Labour opposition in 1945, but all were confronted with triangular contests in 1950. Three were defeated, all by Conservatives. The loss of Frank Byers, who failed by only 97 votes to hold North Dorset, was particularly serious. Another loss occurred in Yorkshire, where the former Buckrose division was remodelled as Bridlington, and the Liberal defender was defeated.

Against the various losses, the Liberals recorded but three gains. Jo Grimond, the son-in-law of Lady Violet Bonham-Carter, captured Orkney and Zetland, and Archibald Macdonald won Roxburgh and Selkirk, both in three-cornered contests. Shortly after the election Grimond was appointed Chief Whip in succession to the defeated Byers. The other gain caused some Liberal heartburning. In Huddersfield, the Liberals advanced Donald Wade as candidate for the West constituency, where the Conservatives did not stand, while the Liberals allowed the Conservatives a straight fight against Labour in the East. There was no formal pact, and either Liberals or Conservatives could have decided to fight both constituencies without incurring any complaints of ill-faith; but some Liberals viewed the nod-and-a-wink arrangement as a serious compromise of the party's independence. Fears that the new MP, Donald Wade, would temporise with the Conservatives were swiftly dispelled, and he behaved in an impeccably Liberal manner.

A profoundly disturbing feature of the 1950 General Election from the Liberal point of view was the loss of many deposits. In those days, the deposit stood at £150 – a good deal more in value than the £500 required today – and was forfeited by a candidate securing less than 12.5 per cent of the votes cast. This contrasts with the modern level of 5 per cent. Shortly before the election, Liberal headquarters negotiated an arrangement with Lloyd's to the effect that the first fifty deposits would be the party's responsibility, but that Lloyd's would cover the next two hundred for a premium of £5000. This arrangement was important in allowing the Liberals to field as many candidates as they did. It suggests that the underwriters did not anticipate more than 83 forfeitures. In fact no fewer than 319 deposits were lost. It is likely that there was a great squeezing of Liberal votes during the later stages of the election campaign.

Why did the Liberals fare so badly in 1950? In most places, the Liberal organisation was vastly inferior to that of their rivals. They had little media support. Television was of negligible importance in 1950, and the BBC, which still had a monopoly of sound broadcasting, was about as impartial as it could possibly be. The press was far more influential than it is today. The bulk of it was Conservative; the *Daily Herald* and the widely-read tabloid *Daily Mirror* supported Labour. Support for Liberals from the *News Chronicle* was minimal. The *Manchester Guardian* was better from a Liberal point of view, but its circulation in the south was very limited. The most telling argument advanced against the Liberals, most particularly by the Conservatives, was not that Liberal policies were wrong, but that a vote for a Liberal was 'wasted', because he had no realistic chance of being elected. As a variant on the 'wasted vote' argument, it was strenuously argued that the Conservative Party had become 'liberalised': that there were few issues of substance and immediate relevance on which the two parties differed.

The close result, with Labour's overall majority down to only five seats, made it likely that another election would be required at no distant date. Liberals had scraped together the money and the candidates they did in 1950 with extreme difficulty, and they could not hope to field anything like as many again. In the 1950 Parliament, new strains were put on the Liberals. No longer was there a comfortable working majority, and on top of that the Labour government was torn between traditional Socialists like Aneurin Bevan and modernisers like the new Chancellor of the Exchequer, Hugh Gaitskell. The way in which Liberals acted might easily determine whether the government survived or not. Differences in outlook between the MPs were considerable. As usual, what tore them apart was not attitudes to Liberal policies, but which of the other parties they preferred. Three of the nine – Lady Megan Lloyd George, Edgar Granville and Emrys Roberts, manifestly preferred Labour to the Conservatives. Some of the others were equally obviously dependent on Conservative votes for their seats in Parliament. Clement Davies and his new Chief Whip Jo Grimond were hard-put to prevent their little band breaking apart.

In the autumn of 1951, the government decided to go to the country again. This time, the Liberals were only able to field 109 candidates. The places where those candidates stood were mostly determined by the state of the local organisation and its finances – sometimes, perhaps, by the whim of particular individuals. Caernarvon, and Kinross and West Perthshire, where the Liberal had run second in 1950, and Rochdale, where he had polled over 10,000 votes, were left uncontested. Yet West Fulham and Bermondsey, in both of which places the Liberals had received fewer than 2000 votes – bad results even by Liberal standards – were contested again, and the Liberal was to fare even worse. Central finances were so straitened that there was no sanction which could be applied to produce a wiser disposition of resources.

Labour would give no quarter, not even in those constituencies like North Dorset where Labour had never polled well, and the presence or absence of a Labour candidate would be likely to make the difference between a Liberal and a Conservative victory. The Conservatives were more subtle. Where they had a realistic hope of winning a Liberal seat themselves – notably in the two Scottish Liberal constituencies and in the Eye division of Suffolk – they naturally put forward a candidate. Where they had no such hope, they considered the outlook of the particular MP. Lady Megan Lloyd George in Anglesey and Emrys Roberts in Merioneth were opposed by Conservatives, even though a Labour victory was the likely outcome. By contrast, four Liberal MPs were not opposed by Conservatives: Clement Davies in Montgomeryshire, Roderick Bowen in Cardiganshire, Hopkin Morris in Carmarthenshire, Donald Wade in Huddersfield West. There is no reason for thinking that the Conservatives sought, or obtained, any sort of Liberal reciprocity for abstention in the three Welsh constituencies.

Special problems arose in Bolton. As with Huddersfield, the town was divided into two constituencies, and all three parties had substantial support. In this case a more explicit arrangement was reached between Liberals and Conservatives, to the effect that the Liberal Arthur Holt would have a straight fight against Labour in Bolton West, and the Liberals would not stand in Bolton East. This deal caused more Liberal concern than the understanding in Huddersfield had done. Like Donald Wade, Arthur Holt showed no signs of temporising when he was eventually elected.

An even more difficult situation arose in Colne Valley, which borders Huddersfield, where Lady Violet Bonham-Carter was Liberal candidate. During the inter-war and wartime period, Lady Violet had acquired a massive reputation as a brilliant orator and an uncompromising Liberal. But by 1951 nobody had much doubt that she strongly preferred the Conservatives to Labour, and in particular that she had the highest regard for Churchill. These feeling were reciprocated, and the local Conservative Association decided, by a less than overwhelming majority, to support her. As the campaign developed, Churchill spoke on her platform. This caused much anger among Liberals, who regarded it as a serious qualification of her independence.

The overall result of the General Election was a small overall Conservative majority: 321 seats for Conservatives and their allies, 295 for Labour, just six for the Liberals, and three 'others'. The result was even more anomalous than that of the previous year, for the defeated Labour Party secured over a quarter of a million more votes than the Conservative victors. As for the Liberals, results followed roughly, though not exactly, the Conservative intentions. The Welsh Liberals who had received Conservative opposition were both defeated by Labour, while the three who had not been opposed were all returned. Of the three Liberal seats which the Conservatives hoped to win on their own account, they were successful in two, but Jo Grimond (who had already established himself as a very good and popular local MP) was able to increase his majority in the Northern Isles. Huddersfield West and Bolton West returned Liberal MPs. The result in Colne Valley was remarkable. In 1950, the combined Liberal and Conservative votes had been marginally greater than the vote of the Labour victor. In 1951, Labour was again victorious, this time in a straight fight against Lady Violet, and

actually picked up about 1500 votes. The explanation seems to be that a substantial number of Liberals and some Conservatives refused to support her,
and a number of Liberals actually voted for the Labour candidate in protest.

Liberal celebrities of pre-war days, like Sinclair and Harris, who had
been defeated in 1945 but had sought to regain their seats in 1950, dropped
out in 1951. Sinclair was created Viscount Thurso soon after the election, and
there were hopes that he would provide a valuable voice in the House of
Lords, and perhaps a successor to the octogenarian Viscount Samuel, who
still led the Liberal peers. But Thurso had a stroke soon afterwards, from
which he made only a partial recovery. Another stroke in 1959 left him a
bedridden invalid. He had the misfortune to endure a further eleven years
in that condition. By contrast, the much older Samuel remained both active
and effective, and played a considerable part in resisting any tendency for
Liberal peers to drift to the Conservatives.[12]

The much-reduced number of Liberal candidates inevitably meant a great
drop in the aggregate Liberal poll, which was down to 730,000. There was
again a heavy loss of deposits: 66 on this occasion. In most places the Liberal vote was substantially less than in 1950. The Liberal Party may have had
an important effect on results, but in a very negative sense. On the assumption that Liberals who had no candidate of their own divided about six to
four in favour of the Conservatives, this would explain eight of the 21 Conservative gains; if they divided seven to three, that would explain eighteen
of them.[13]

When Churchill formed his new government after the election, he hoped
to include at least one Liberal. Clement Davies was invited to become Minister of Education.[14] The Liberal leader, who was in his late sixties, and for
whom this was obviously the last chance of ministerial office, wished to
accept, but conversations with Liberal colleagues convinced him that this
would be unacceptable to the party, and, out of loyalty to colleagues, he
refused. Churchill told Lady Violet that she would have been offered a post
in the government if she had been elected. Unlike Clement Davies, Lady
Violet recorded in a private letter that 'had I been returned I should have
gone in without any hesitation'.[15] In the unhappy condition of the Liberal
Party after 1951, that could have proved the *coup de grâce*.

Despite the appalling election figures, there was no general collapse of
Liberal morale. In 1953 a General Director of the Party, H. F. P. Harris, was
appointed, a man hitherto unknown to Liberals. Yet there was no immediate improvement. Local election results were poor, and seemed to signal a
general decline in what Liberal support remained. There were 79 Liberal
Borough Councillors in 1951, 60 in 1953. In the following year numbers
bounced up to 74, but they were down to 56 in 1955.[16] Those by-elections

which the Liberals contested were, for the most part, rather discouraging but hardly disastrous. One result was good. At Inverness, in December 1954, John Bannerman polled 36 per cent of the votes cast. Realists recognised, however, that this was largely a personal acclaim for a former Rugby international and noted Gaelic singer. Much less encouragingly, two recent Liberal MPs, Lady Megan Lloyd George and Edgar Granville, were received into the Labour Party. Eventually Dingle Foot, the son of Isaac Foot, who had sat as a Liberal MP until 1945, trod the same road.

The second Churchill Government confounded the expectations of many supporters and opponents alike. Legislation which the Labour Government had carried in the previous period was largely untouched, the denationalisation of steel and road haulage (neither of which had been effectively taken over when Labour left office) being the main exceptions. 'Welfare State' legislation was left firmly in place, and the very low unemployment figures which had persisted since the mid-war period continued. There as no perceptible change in foreign policy. At the same time the Labour Opposition also did not appear eager to press Socialism much further. Thus there was a general cooling down of political passions, and voters became less fearful of terrible things happening should the 'wrong' party take office. This was good for the Liberals, because it meant that the intense squeeze on their support which had marked the late 1940s and early 1950s was relaxed.

Churchill celebrated his eightieth birthday in office, but shortly afterwards resolved to retire. His successor was Sir Anthony Eden, who settled into office, and then called another General Election in May 1955. This was one of the least exciting contests of modern times. Overall results showed a decline in votes of all three parties, though the number of government seats increased somewhat, to 344 – thus providing the Conservatives with a comfortable working majority. The Liberals remained exactly where they were, with the same six MPs. As in 1951, Grimond had a three-cornered contest, while the other five had no Conservative opposition. Overall, the Liberals showed a small, but just perceptible, improvement. 66 deposits had been forfeited in 1951; 60 were lost in 1955. The average vote for a Liberal candidate had been 14.7 per cent in 1951, in 1955 it was 15.1 per cent.

In the by-elections which followed the 1955 General Election, the Liberals showed a considerable upsurge, and were able to attract more protest votes from erstwhile government supporters who objected for various (and perhaps incompatible) reasons to what it was currently doing. At Torquay in December 1955, at Hereford and Gainsborough in February 1956, they improved substantially on recent performance. Clement Davies could reflect that his courageous leadership had kept the Liberal Party alive through a long and dark night, and the first grey streaks of dawn could be discerned in the sky. In September 1956, however, he decided that the time had come to retire from leadership, though he was to remain a Liberal MP for the rest of his life.

There was never much doubt about the succession. Jo Grimond was the only Liberal MP who could be confident of holding his seat in a triangular contest. He had been a successful Chief Whip almost since the moment of his election, and was still in his early forties. He had many admirers in the party, and no enemies. Grimond was intensely interested in ideas, and brought considerable freshness to the Liberal party. This attracted many people, particularly young people, who were becoming increasingly bored with the other parties, which seemed preoccupied with stale issues.

Then came the incredible Suez episode. In the summer of 1956, President Nasser of Egypt proclaimed the nationalisation of the Suez Canal, in which Britain and France had great financial interests. Towards the end of the year, British and French forces intervened in Egypt with the intention of toppling Nasser, using a dispute between Egypt and Israel as the pretext. This would not be the last occasion on which a British Prime Minister was to lose his reputation irretrievably by attempting to produce régime change in a Middle Eastern country. The upshot was a fiasco. The simultaneous collapse of Eden's policy and his health forced the Prime Minister to resign, and in January 1957 he was succeeded by Harold Macmillan. At first some Liberals seemed to be going along with the government, but soon the overwhelming majority swung against it. By the time of the last parliamentary vote on the crisis, Liberal MPs were unanimous.[17]

This adds poignancy to the Liberals' fate at Carmarthen in February 1957. Hopkin Morris, who had been knighted a couple of years earlier, died suddenly. He was a particularly lucid and inspiring exponent of Liberalism. As the Liberals were improving their position substantially, they might have had some hope of retaining Carmarthen at the supervening by-election, but the candidate selected was pro-Suez, and imparted little of the moral fervour of his predecessor. More agonising still, he was confronted by Lady Megan Lloyd George, fighting under her new Labour colours. Carmarthen was lost. This brought down the Liberal representation to five, the lowest figure ever.

Otherwise, the Liberals continued to do well in the by-elections. Some results were almost spectacular. At Dorset North in June 1957, and at Rochdale in February 1958, they secured substantially over one-third of the votes cast. Then, at Torrington in March 1958, came what looked like a breakthrough. Mark Bonham-Carter, the son of Lady Violet, was victorious, though by a desperately narrow margin, in a three-cornered contest. It was widely noted that the victory of Asquith's grandson seemed to atone for the defeat at the hands of Lloyd George's daughter in the previous year. Other good Liberal by-election results followed, though there were no actual victories. In constituencies as far apart as Weston-super-Mare, Argyll, East Aberdeenshire, Southend West and Galloway, they polled 24 per cent or more of the votes cast. Such returns would have been unthinkable a few years earlier.

The general lull in political fervour which had been interrupted by Suez was rapidly restored when Eden was succeeded by Harold Macmillan. The later 1950s witnessed unparalleled general prosperity – 'You've never had it so good,' in Macmillan's famous words. The Liberals were able to organise without either pretending that they were immediately ready to govern the country, or incurring furious obloquy for 'splitting the vote'. A long period of political peace enabled them gradually to improve their organisation and increase their funds.

When a General Election was called in October 1959, the Liberals fielded 216 candidates, almost double the number they had had on the two previous occasions. The Conservatives increased their overall majority to a very comfortable figure. Disappointingly, the Liberals still had only six MPs, but there were a few changes. The by-election gain of Torrington was lost, but the contiguous constituency of North Devon was captured by Jeremy Thorpe. This was a really spectacular personal victory for a very charismatic and hard-working candidate. Roderick Bowen was again returned with a comfortable majority in Cardiganshire, and Clement Davies held Montgomeryshire fairly securely, despite Conservative intervention. Jo Grimond's seat in Orkney and Zetland looked very safe indeed. In Huddersfield West and Bolton West, the special arrangements continued, and the Liberals were comfortably victorious.

As at earlier General Elections, enormous weaknesses in the Liberal political machine were revealed. Only 32 constituencies had full-time agents, just five more than in 1955, although there were many more part-time and honorary agents.[18] The linked problems of poverty and organisational weakness meant that they were unable to project a sharp image. A Gallup Poll of March 1959 showed that 59 per cent of people questioned did not claim to know what the Liberals stood for, and this number included almost half of the intending Liberal voters.[19] Grimond, by far the best-known Liberal personality, was largely tied up in his own remote constituency during the election, although he did contrive a quick and well-publicised helicopter tour of hopeful places. For all the defects in the party's organisation and finance, nobody was now disposed to foretell the Liberals' imminent demise. The worst seemed to have passed.

18

Uncertain Future

We do not know the secret of success ... but we fear that it may be hard work.

Anon.

Immediately the General Election results were announced, Jo Grimond made a press statement to the effect that he hoped that 'a new progressive movement' would arise.[1] Grimond was probably thinking in particular about the condition of the Labour Party. Hugh Gaitskell, who had succeeded Attlee as leader some time before, was seeking to make Labour less 'doctrinaire', but was encountering massive opposition within his own party. Grimond's statement may now be seen as a very early anticipation of the kind of thinking which would eventually link Liberals with 'Social Democrats'. For the time being, however, that initiative ran into the sands.

The next great change was essentially concerned with organisation, although it may have had policy overtones as well. During the General Election period, a Campaign Committee had been in existence, under the chairmanship of Frank Byers. Soon afterwards, a rather similar body, also with Byers as chairman, was established as a Standing Committee. The first important action of the Standing Committee was to cause the removal of H. F. P. Harris from the post of General Director, and to abolish his office, whose functions were to devolve on Heads of the Departments within the Party. This looks like a general loosening of organisation; in practice it meant transferring control to members of the Standing Committee. For a long time to come, Byers remained at the centre of Liberal organisation.

Liberal policy in relation to Europe underwent a fundamental change. From the end of the 1940s onwards there were important moves towards the removal of economic barriers between countries in western Europe. The disposition both of the 1945 Labour Government and (for several years) of its Conservative successor was to look sympathetically on these developments, but to take a more sceptical view of any active British participation. Non-European trade played a much greater part in the British economy than in that of most European countries.

At the turn of 1957–58, France, Western Germany, Italy and the three

Benelux countries set up the European Economic Community – the 'Common Market'. The EEC envisaged breaking down trade barriers between the member-states – a policy which naturally commended itself to all Liberals – but it also contemplated a common trading policy towards outsiders, which implied similar trade barriers against them, and also entailed a large measure of direction from an unelected Commission. This necessarily ran counter to traditional Liberal ideas of Free Trade and of democratic control. If Britain were to join the EEC, there would also be considerable problems for Commonwealth countries, some of which had built their economies largely on the assumption that entry to British markets would continue to be easy.

While the EEC was being formed, Britain took the initiative in forming a separate organisation, the European Free Trade Area – the so-called 'Outer Seven' – from more or less democratic European countries which for one reason or another were omitted from the original EEC. EFTA, like the EEC, planned to remove trade barriers between member states; but, unlike the EEC, left them free to take their own decisions about trade with outsiders. The initial reaction of the Liberal Party was to favour British membership of EFTA, but not of the EEC. Before either body had been fully established, an article in *Liberal News*, prepared 'after discussion among those chiefly responsible for guiding Party opinion, and ... with the endorsement of ... Mr Jo Grimond', explicitly supported membership of EFTA but not of the EEC, adding that 'the more countries are committed to lowering tariffs while still free to fix the level of their tariffs against countries outside the Common Market, the more likely it is that tariffs all round will be low, so that trade will be increased.'[2] This, one might say, was completely consistent with traditional Liberal attitudes towards Free Trade.

Soon, however, a great change of opinion took place. In July 1960, an all-Party group of MPs, which included Grimond, Thorpe and Davies, declared support for the idea that Britain should seek to enter the EEC. In September of the same year, the Liberal Assembly called the British Government 'to start consultations with other members of the Commonwealth and of the European Free Trade Area with a view to the entry of the United Kingdom and other countries into the Common Market.' This certainly did not commit the party to support membership if the terms proved oppressive either to Britain or to her Commonwealth and EFTA partners, but it was enough to produce a few resignations from the Liberal Party, though many anti-Market Liberals remained in place.

In August 1961 the Conservative government of Macmillan made a formal application for membership. It was made clear, however, that there was as yet no commitment. Everything would turn on whether the existing EEC members favoured the application, and – if so – what terms were offered. This approach came at a time when there was real public disquiet with the general progress of the economy, and membership of the EEC was seen by some people as a sort of panacea.

Meanwhile, the Liberal Party was becoming the accepted recipient of votes from disaffected former Conservatives, and Liberals were – on the whole – doing well. At the May local elections the Liberals registered an overall gain of 51 seats in the English and Welsh boroughs. Liberals were beginning to treat local elections much more seriously than in the past. In 1960, a Local Government Department was set up at party headquarters.

While this improvement in Liberal electoral performance was taking place, an event occurred in a different field which might have been catastrophic if it had happened a few years earlier. On 17 October 1960, the national daily *News Chronicle* and the London evening *Star* ceased publication. The *News Chronicle* had a circulation of well over a million, the *Star* was the second largest of the three London evening newspapers. Both were considered to be Liberal in their politics, though in practice neither had given much support to the Liberal Party for a number of years. Readers received no intimation whatever that suppression was contemplated. Senior Liberals had realised for some time that the newspapers were in difficulties, and sought without success to contact their directors, with view to a possible rescue operation; but they, like everybody else, had no advance warning. There was massive resentment: by readers; by the Liberal Party – Jeremy Thorpe described the manner of closure as a 'disgrace'; by the staff of the newspapers; by the National Union of Journalists; by people of all political persuasions who were apprehensive of the danger of monopolies developing.

Yet the demise of the two newspapers produced no discernible effect on political behaviour. In the course of the 1950s, most families had acquired television sets, and few still looked to newspapers as the source of political ideas. Grimond took easily to the new medium, and his appearances were frequent and popular. Electors, and particularly young electors, were attracted by his freshness, intelligence and transparent honesty. He was visibly receptive to new ideas, though he did not appear equally concerned to build up a distinctive all-embracing Liberal philosophy. A *Times* editorial reflected, not unjustly, on 'a fly-paper quality about Liberal policy exercises; ideas which happen to be buzzing around at the time tend to get stuck on',[3] and Grimond did not really resist that process.

The Liberal advance continued. In the 1960s, and for long afterwards, by-elections acquired considerable importance, both as indications of swings in public opinion and as influences on opinion. Active Liberals were naturally encouraged by good results; but Opinion Polls frequently showed a substantial Liberal upsurge in their aftermath. On 16 November 1960, six by-elections took place simultaneously, all in Conservative seats. In five of these cases, the result represented a substantial improvement on the party's recent performance. Less satisfactory was the result in Bolton East. The 1951 arrangement by which the Liberals had a straight fight against Labour in the West seat and the Conservatives had no Liberal opponent in the East was continued in the ensuing two General Elections. At the by-election, Frank Byers decided to contest the East seat. This was a high-risk strategy. The three 'serious' candidates in Bolton East each polled more than 10,000 votes, but the Conservative retained the seat, and Byers ran third. This sent a strong signal to the Conservatives, both in Bolton and in Huddersfield, that arrangements with the Liberals were not worth renewing, and made it virtually certain that both Holt and Wade would face Conservative opposition when the next General Election came.

With that interruption, the run of encouraging Liberal by-election results continued through 1961, and included a very good second place in Asquith's old seat of Paisley. Local elections in the spring were also good for the Liberals. In March 1962 Harry Hague, the Liberal candidate, came within a thousand votes of victory in Blackpool North. This was followed immediately by the real sensation of Orpington, an outer suburb of London, which was without argument the most remarkable by-election in the lifetime of that Parliament. The Liberal had run third in 1959. The prospective candidate was unable to stand for personal reasons, and Eric Lubbock, a local councillor, was chosen in his place. The Conservative, by contrast, was an incomer, who seems to have been at no particular pains to encourage his party's workers. Jeremy Thorpe was a major force in the campaign, while Pratap Chitnis, the agent, masterminded strategy and tactics. It soon became obvious that Lubbock would poll strongly. Very early on polling day, 14 March 1962, Chitnis surveyed the national press, and discovered that the *Daily Mail*, despite its Conservative proclivities, was predicting a Liberal victory. Chitnis bought up several thousand copies, and arranged for their free distribution at local railway stations. Most recipients probably thought that this was a promotional gimmick by the *Mail*. For whatever reason, the result was a massive Liberal victory, with a comfortable overall majority for Eric Lubbock.

For a brief moment, people suddenly took seriously the prospect of a Liberal government in the near future. At one point a public opinion poll even suggested that the number of intending Liberal voters exceeded that of the other two parties.[4] In the local elections a couple of months later, the Liberals were able to take full advantage of the situation. Not least significant were the excellent results in Liverpool, which had generally been a desolate spot for Liberals even in the great days of the early twentieth century. A new leaflet entitled *Focus* paid close attention to local issues, and not long afterwards the first breakthrough was made when Trevor Jones ('Jones the Vote') was returned at a local by-election. This presaged spectacular advances in Liverpool later on. One of Jones's most active helpers was David Alton, then a young Education student, who was a future Liberal MP. In July 1962, a big Liberal vote in the unpromising territory of Leicester North-East resulted in the Conservative being pushed into a bad third place. Next day, Macmillan sacked seven members of his Cabinet, including the Chancellor of the Exchequer. In the mordant and much-remembered words of Jeremy Thorpe, 'Greater love hath no man than this, that he lay down his friends for his life'.

For the remainder of 1962, the Liberals fought all but one of the by-elections, and in every case they improved their position by comparison with recent performance. There was a further victory, although this occurred in circumstances which were sad for the Party. Clement Davies lived just long enough to see the Orpington victory; but when he died the Liberals were required to defend Montgomeryshire. The seat had once looked like a personal holding of Clement Davies, and his majority in 1959 had been less than 3,000 which seemed precarious for a new candidate. But Emlyn Hooson secured an overall majority, leading his nearest rival by well over 7000 votes. There were also two more near-misses in 1962. At Derbyshire West in June, and at Chippenham in November, the Liberal was within 2000 votes of the elected MP. Local elections told the same story of general Liberal progress. There was an overall gain of more than 500 Council seats.

Most of these contests took place in the shadow of a growing public debate over membership of the EEC, for which a British application was lodged in the latter part of 1961. How far it affected by-election results in doubtful. All parties were conscious that many of the voters whom they sought to win, or to retain, were doubtful about, or even hostile to, their own party's official attitude. As time went on, there was a growing suspicion that the application would be rejected any rate, which would make the whole matter a sort of non-issue. Negotiations continued throughout 1962; but in January 1963 President de Gaulle of France interposed his country's *liberum veto*. With the EEC question in cold storage, British industry did not know what was going to happen, and it was inordinately difficult to plan ahead. This uncertainty produced predictable effects on the economy. As for the Liberals, they had invested a great deal of emotional capital into the Common Market question. Like the government, and – for that matter – the Labour Opposition, they had no real fall-back position: there was no other great topical question which any party was ready to bring forward for public attention.

At almost the same moment as the EEC fiasco occurred, Hugh Gaitskell, leader of the Labour Party, died suddenly and unexpectedly. His successor, elected in February 1963, was Harold Wilson. Labour, which had been making practically no progress at the various by-elections, began to press ahead. The Macmillan Government came under attack from pro-Marketeers, who blamed it for lack of enthusiasm, and from anti-Marketeers, who blamed it for ever making the EEC application. Soon it ran into difficulties of a more personal character. Eventually the Prime Minister had an experience not wildly different from that of his predecessor: his policies and his health both broke down, and Macmillan was succeeded by Sir Alec Douglas-Home.

Even before the end of 1962, there had been some signs that the great Liberal upsurge which had marked the first half of the year had run its course; but from the beginning ot 1963 until the General Election in October of the following year, it was a slow progress downhill. At local elections of May Liberals made overall gains. These results, however, were misleading, for the proper standard of comparison was with 1960, when most of the seats had last been contested, not with the previous year. At most of the 1963 by-elections, the Liberals continued to improve their performance, but as the year advanced the measure of improvement declined, and in the last two they actually slipped back a little. The 1964 by-elections were worse still for the Liberals. They fought three of the six constituencies which fell vacant, losing their deposits in two of them. Local election results were also far worse than in the earlier 1960s, with an overall loss of 63 seats in the English and Welsh boroughs.

The life of the 1959 Parliament ran almost to its legal limit, and polling took place in October 1964. The Liberals advanced 365 candidates for 630 seats: far more than in 1959. Labour, with 317 seats, won a very bare overall majority; the Conservative and their allies won 304. The Liberals returned nine MPs: more, indeed, than at any General Election since 1950, but a bitter disappointment after the heady days of Orpington. The distribution of gains and losses was remarkable. The Conservatives opposed the Liberals in the two North of England seats where arrangements had prevailed in earlier elections, and both seats were lost – Huddersfield West by fewer than 1300 votes. Four seats were gained: Bodmin in Cornwall, and three in the north of Scotland; Invernessshire, Ross and Cromarty and Sinclair's old constituency of Caithness and Sutherland. Against many expectations, Orpington held fast. North Devon, which Jeremy Thorpe had won with a tiny majority in 1959, gave him a comfortable margin of over 5000.

Yet despite their natural disappointment with the election results, the

Liberals had, after all, improved their parliamentary position; while in other respects they were building up quite rapidly and in a very solid manner. They had 60 full-time agents, nearly twice as many as in 1959. Over the same period, the party's membership had grown from 150,000 to 300,000, and its annual income had risen from £24,000 to £70,000.[5] They had been able to field far more candidates, they had secured well over three million votes, and had only forfeited 53 deposits. The Liberal share of the total poll had risen from 5.9 per cent to 11.2 per cent[6] and this increase was by no means exclusively attributable to the greater number of seats contested. In many 'commuter' seats they were in second place, though still far behind the Conservative holders.

The small Labour majority made it likely that a new General Election would be held in the fairly near future. It was predictable that every effort would be made to squeeze the Liberal vote, most particularly in places where the margin between Conservatives and Labour was small. By-elections soon gave clear indication that this was taking place. In 1964, the Liberals had run third in seven of the constituencies contested, all of them showing a drop in the Liberal share of the poll. By contrast, however, two results were remarkably good for the Liberals, and both of them occurred in places where the Liberals had been a comfortable second to the Conservatives in 1964. In those places it was the Labour vote which was squeezed. At East Grinstead in February 1965, the Liberal share of the poll rose by more than four points. More spectacularly, in the following month the young Liberal candidate, David Steel, was victorious in the three-county constituency of Roxburgh, Selkirk and Peebles – usually known locally as 'the Borders' – winning a seat from the Conservatives. But, meanwhile, local elections told a rather gloomy story for the Liberals. In May 1965 they sustained an overall loss of 169 seats in the urban elections.

For much of 1965, the tide seemed to be running against the Labour government, and it began to appear likely that the Liberals would soon face the unenviable choice which they had faced in 1929–31. Should they sustain in office a Labour government in which neither they nor the country seemed to have much confidence, or should they risk precipitating a General Election which threatened disaster? In June 1965, Grimond gave an interview to the *Guardian* (as the *Manchester Guardian* had been renamed).[7] That interview was reported under the alarming headline 'Coalition Offer to Labour by Mr Grimond'. The headline was misleading; but there could be little doubt that Grimond was contemplating the possibility that circumstances might soon arise when some kind of deal should be made. Liberal MPs were deeply divided on the idea of any kind of deal,[8] and Liberals in the country even more so. It was equally clear that any deal with the Liberals would have been anathema to a large section of the Labour Party. The matter was more or less fudged over, and – fortunately for both parties – the government retained a sufficient majority to ensure that the possibility of a deal never entered the realm of serious politics. Gradually the Labour Party began to appear more popular. A big swing to the government in the Hull North by-election of January 1966 – largely at the expense of the Liberals – may have played a significant part in persuading Wilson to call a General Election.

The Liberals were unable to fight on quite as broad a front as in 1964, only contesting 311 seats out of the 630. When the results emerged, Labour had pushed up its representation to 363 and the Conservatives had dropped to 253, while the Liberal tally rose from nine at the previous General Election – ten at the Dissolution – to twelve. This was by no means all progress for the Liberal Party. Three seats were taken from the Conservatives and one from Labour, against two losses, both to Labour. The popular vote, at 2.3 million, was down considerably. In 251 of the 278 seats which the Liberals fought in both 1964 and 1966, Liberal support fell.[9] There was a substantial national swing to Labour; but what particularly affected the Liberals was a third-party squeeze. That squeeze goes a long way towards explaining their four gains. In Aberdeenshire West, Cheadle and North Cornwall Labour had been in third place in 1964, and substantial numbers of Labour voters appear to have switched to the Liberals. Colne Valley is more anomalous, for it seemed to be bucking the trend of a general swing to Labour, but closer examination shows that this was not really the case. In 1964, Labour had been very narrowly ahead of the Liberal Richard Wainwright, with the Conservative in third place. In 1966 the Labour share of the poll rose slightly in Colne Valley, as in most places; but the Conservative vote slumped dramatically. No doubt a few 1964 Conservatives had switched to Labour; but many more had turned to Wainwright, as the candidate more likely to displace the Labour MP. A slump in Conservative morale led to Labour losing the only constituency which turned against it in the whole election.

There were some remarkable individual results. The Liberal gain of Cheadle, a Cheshire dormitory of Manchester, was impressive. Labour had been in third place in 1964, and there was a certain squeeze on the Labour vote, but this does not suffice to explain how Dr Michael Winstanley contrived to overturn a Conservative majority of well over 8000. He was a broadcaster and television personality, which may have helped. There was a striking Liberal upsurge in the far north of Scotland, where three of the four gains were recorded. Even in Caithness and Sutherland, which the Liberals lost, both the Liberal vote and the party's share of the poll actually increased in 1966. Another remarkable advance was in the Isle of Wight, where the Liberal poll rose by more than 4000, even though the 1964 candidate had run third. Eric Lubbock was able to retain Orpington. He was an excellent constituency MP, and the slogan 'Eric on Merit' appears to have been an effective one.

In 1957, Jo Grimond had challenged the Liberals to 'get on or get out'. In many ways, they certainly had 'got on' in the decade which followed, but they had not produced the effect which Grimond really desired: a great remodelling of politics, in which the Liberal Party, the non-Socialist element of the Labour Party, and many 'Liberal-at-heart' Conservatives would come together in a great new radical movement. For a moment after Orpington this had seemed a possibility, but the prospect soon vanished. By the time of the 1966 General Election it was out of the question, at least for a very long time to come. Like Gladstone before him, Grimond did not enjoy the pettiness which plays such a large part in day-to-day politics, and had no great interest in the mechanics of party organisation. He would probably have liked to lay down leadership of the Liberal Party long before the two General Elections of the 1960s, but loyalty to colleagues kept him at the helm until January 1967, when he intimated his intention to resign. As the rules then stood, the choice of a successor rested with the MPs. On first count, six voted for Jeremy Thorpe, and three each for Eric Lubbock and Emlyn Hooson. The others then stood down, and Thorpe was chosen unanimously. There was considerable protest among the rank-and-file against the manner, and the speed, in which the selection was made, and a strong demand for new procedures in the future.

For a long time to come, Liberal performance at the various by-elections did not follow a regular pattern. By far the most remarkable case was the Ladywood division of Birmingham on 26 June 1969, where Wallace Lawler captured what had looked like an impregnable Labour seat, albeit on a very low poll, but with a huge overturn of votes. This was the first Liberal parliamentary victory in the city since 1886.

What had happened in Ladywood? The answer seems to be 'community politics', which has curious echoes of tactics used by Chamberlain and Schnadhorst to build up Liberal support in the same city almost a century earlier, and – much more recently – had been applied in Liverpool. Ladywood was an extreme example of 'inner-city decay'. In 1950, it had had nearly 52,000 voters; nineteen years later it was down to just over 18,000, the lowest electorate in the country. It is not difficult to envisage the enormous social consequences which these bare figures reflect. In recent years, non-party local organisations had been set up, with Liberal guidance, to fight for improvements, and Lawler had become a Birmingham City Councillor. Liberals from outside the constituency canvassing in the by-election were astonished to discover how well known he was among the voters. The idea of 'community politics' was already being developed in many other constituencies long before the by-election, but the Liberal victory at Ladywood led to further emulation.

During the 1960s, considerable attention was directed to the question of the central finances and organisation of the party.[10] The great euphoria in the immediate aftermath of Orpington encouraged Liberals to spend lavishly, believing that a permanent breakthrough had been made. Expensive new premises were acquired, and staffing expanded. In the mid-1960s, long before he became leader of the Party, Jeremy Thorpe had been elected to the post of Party Treasurer, against the incumbent, Sir Andrew Murray, sometime Lord Provost of Edinburgh. The nub of Thorpe's argument was that finances were in an appalling condition, and that more attention should be given to the need to raise money from private industry. The Party's serious overdraft was reduced in time for the 1966 General Election, but the old problem soon recurred, and for most of the late 1960s the overdraft was never below £50,000, reaching £93,000 late in 1969 – when money values were far higher than they are today. In 1968 the Liberals moved to cheaper premises, but there was still a strong feeling among well-informed people that profligacy was continuing. Pratap Chitnis, the party's director, resigned in protest. Just before the ensuing General Election, however, Thorpe announced that the overdraft had been paid off. There has been speculation about what happened, and it has been suggested that most of the money came from a single source. The Party's new Treasurer, Sir Frank Medlicott, claimed that 85 per cent of the money given in the closing period of 1969 and the first half of 1970 derived from fewer than 25 people. Howbeit, the Liberal Party was solvent by the late spring of 1970, though it would be difficult to say that its finances were in a satisfactory condition.

Liberals have always opposed policies with any tinge of racism, and in the 1960s they campaigned vigorously against racist policies, most particularly against apartheid in South Africa and the white supremacy policy in what was then known as Rhodesia, now Zimbabwe. Some of the Young Liberals, however, went far beyond ordinary political campaigning, wilfully damaging sports pitches to 'Stop the Seventy Tour' of the South African 'Springboks'. This sort of behaviour was, of course, criminal, and was strongly condemned by the party authorities, but it may have done some damage to the Liberal cause in the minds of law-abiding citizens.

The Labour Government had a majority quite adequate for ordinary business, and there was no constitutional reason for going to the country before the autumn of 1971. It could point to few achievements which might be expected to gratify its own party rank-and-file, and it was beset more than most administrations by splits and intrigues, some concerned with policy questions, others with strong roots in personalities and personal ambitions. It was a period marked by many industrial disputes, and a serious attempt was made to legislate a sort of package deal between employers and workers. The attempt broke down primarily because of Trade Union opposition. Thereafter the government seemed to have little sense of direction, although a new British application was made for possible membership of the EEC soon after de Gaulle resigned in April 1969. Prime Minister Harold Wilson began to look for a moment when political signs were favourable for a General Election. By-elections gave little encouragement, but in the spring of 1970 there were indications of a more favourable nature elsewhere. The May local elections went well for Labour, and badly for both Conservatives and Liberals. About the same time, public opinion polls suggested that the Labour Party had moved ahead. Late in May, the government announced that a new General Election would be held in the following month. This time the Liberals were able to field 332 candidates, just a few more than in 1966. Although public opinion polls continued to point to a Labour victory, they were confounded by the results. Conservatives and their allies, with 330 seats, were well ahead of Labour with 287.

For the Liberals, the 1970 General Election was disaster. They were back with six seats – the same number as they had held in 1951, 1955 and 1959. Three of the four Liberal gains of 1966 were lost: Aberdeenshire West, Cheadle and Colne Valley. In the last of these, the remarkable circumstances in which Richard Wainwright had taken the seat in 1966 were reversed, and Labour recaptured it with a small majority. The Liberals lost Ross and Cromarty which they had captured in 1964, and Ladywood, which they had taken in the recent by-election. Orpington, which had been won in the *annus mirabilis* 1962, was at last retaken by the Conservatives. Another loss was Bodmin. Peter Bessell, the sitting MP, was in considerable financial difficulties and stood down; the new candidate, Paul Tyler, was defeated. There were no gains to compensate for seven losses. Of the six Liberals who did scramble home, Jeremy Thorpe had a majority of 369 in North Devon, John Pardoe a majority of 630 in North Cornwall and David Steel a majority of 550 in the Borders. As Thorpe noted, 'If 800 Liberals had voted Tory we three would have been out and the Parliamentary Party would have consisted of one Welsh MP and two Scottish MPs'.[11] Even those remaining three were hardly safe, for none had a majority as great as 3000. The Liberal overall vote was down by about 200,000, and the Liberal share of the aggregate vote fell from 8.5 per cent to 7.5 per cent. A substantial majority of all Liberal candidates forfeited their deposits. In Scotland the Liberal decline was particularly marked, and the Scottish Nationalists played an important part in eroding the Liberal vote. A quarter of a century of heroic effort appeared to have run into the sands.

And yet, amid the gloom, there were four constituencies where the Liberal vote had increased by more than 10 per cent by comparison with the previous General Election: Liverpool Wavertree, Rochdale, Southport and Ladywood. These four had vital features in common: a very active candidate, and a record of 'community politics'. At the Liberal Assembly later in the year, the message was taken, and a resolution calling for strategic emphasis on 'community politics' was carried. The leaflet *Focus*, which the Liverpool Liberals had produced eight years earlier and concentrated on local issues, was coming to be imitated in many places.

After the 1970 General Election, Edward Heath, who had succeeded Sir Alec Douglas-Home as Conservative leader, became Prime Minister. He was a keen supporter of the idea that Britain should join the EEC, and early in 1971 the public debate over membership began in earnest. The profound division in all Parties became apparent. In October, when it was more or less certain that the British application was acceptable to the other countries, the Government proposed a House of Commons resolution accepting the decision to join 'in principle'. In view of subsequent attitudes, it is noteworthy that at this date the Conservative Party was predominantly pro-EEC, the Labour Party predominantly 'Eurosceptic'. The Government allowed a free vote to Conservative MPs; the Labour Party imposed a three-line whip against the motion, but this was so extensively defied that it can have had little effect. The motion was carried by 356 to 244. The majority was comprised of 282 Conservatives, 69 Labour and five Liberals; the minority of 198 Labour, 39 Conservatives and one Liberal – Emlyn Hooson of Montgomeryshire. For all the enthusiasm of party spokesmen, public opinion polls taken rather later showed that most Liberal voters were opposed to membership.[12] At the end of 1972, Britain joined the EEC, though many people refused to accept the decision as final.

The other major measure contemplated by the government was a 'package deal' designed to improve industrial relations, very similar to what the outgoing Labour government had proposed. This also passed into law, but a large section of the Trade Union movement saw it as a 'dictated peace'. It is likely that it was counter-productive, and helped exacerbate rather than improve matters. Both measures had a considerable effect in unsettling political allegiances. At the by-elections of 1970 and the beginning of 1971 the Conservatives had been doing well, and the Labour and Liberal Parties had both been doing rather badly. The local elections of May 1971 and the by-elections later in the year, showed a great swing to Labour at the expense

9. Jeremy Thorpe, Liberal Leader 1967–76. (*Lib Dem News*)

10. Jeremy Thorpe and Cyril Smith. (*Lib Dem News*)

11. Roy Jenkins, Labour Minister who became a member of the 'Gang of Four'. (*Lib Dem News*)

12. Roy Jenkins, Shirley Williams, Dick Newby and David Owen at an SDP conference. (*Lib Dem News*)

13. David Owen, Leader of the Social Democrat Party, and David Steel. (*Lib Dem News*)

14. David Steel, Liberal Leader 1976–88. (*Lib Dem News*)

15. Simon Hughes, with his mother, Sylvia, celebrates winning the Bermondsey by-election, 1983. (*Lib Dem News*)

16. Paddy Ashdown, Liberal Democrat Leader 1988–99. (*Lib Dem News*)

17. Charles Kennedy, Liberal Democrat Leader since 1999. (*Lib Dem News*)

18. Charles Kennedy signing *The Future of Politics*. (*Lib Dem News*)

19. Charles Kennedy with Paddy Ashdown. (*Lib Dem News*)

partly of the Conservatives but to some extent of the Liberals as well. This pattern continued through the first half of 1972.

From the autumn of 1972 onwards, there was a run of by-elections which profoundly altered the position, not just in the eyes of political enthusiasts but in the eyes of the public as well. There were strong parallels with contests in the 'Orpington' period, a decade earlier. First was Rochdale. On the map, Rochdale looks like an outer fragment of the Greater Manchester sprawl. In truth, it was a civic entity with its own ideas, in which local personalities could exert great influence. In 1970 the Liberal candidate had been Cyril Smith, a popular and famously rotund figure who had been a local councillor – originally in the Labour interest but latterly as a Liberal – for a number of years, and was for a time mayor. Smith brought the Liberals from third place to second, which was no mean achievement in that miserable election; but he was still 5000 votes short of victory. At the by-election of October 1972, circumstances prevailed rather like those at Colne Valley in 1966. The Conservatives were losing popularity on a national scale, and the Rochdale Liberals were able to exert a powerful squeeze on their vote. A new Labour candidate, in place of an established MP, lost ground as well, and Cyril Smith was returned with a comfortable majority.

More remarkable still was the Sutton and Cheam victory of December 1972. The constituency was a dormitory outer suburb of London which had grown up largely in the inter-war period, with no more 'individualism' than any other similar place, and with what looked like an impregnable Conservative majority. The Liberal had never run better than a bad third, and Liberal support had fallen back in each of the previous two General Elections. At first sight, the only factor going for the Liberals in the constituency was that they had been building up strongly on the local council, and the young parliamentary candidate, Graham Tope, was an active campaigner. Tope received an early tip-off that a by-election was likely to occur, and plans were immediately set in play to organise the distribution of leaflets of the *Focus* type. Close attention was given to local issues. 'Death Stalks the Crossroads' was an early example, concentrating on traffic problems. Both Trevor Jones and David Alton played major parts in the campaign. Cyril Smith, victor of Rochdale, was also very active, persuading Liberal MPs and peers to telephone the chairmen and secretaries of every Liberal Association within a hundred miles of the constituency, urgently demanding help from their members. In the end 'the troops came pouring into town in unbelievable numbers'.[13] The upshot was a sensational victory for the Liberal.

It is instructive to contrast the gigantic Liberal victory in Sutton and Cheam with the wretched Liberal result recorded on the very same day in

Uxbridge, another London suburban Conservative seat. The Liberals targeted Sutton and Cheam, directing all available volunteers into the constituency, and they won the seat; they did not target Uxbridge and forfeited their deposit. Another difference between the two campaigns was that Uxbridge was fought on national issues, while in Sutton and Cheam local questions played a major part.

Liberal results in by-elections of 1973 fluctuated wildly. On 1 March, the Liberal candidate at Chester-le-Street in County Durham, which the Party had not fought at all for many years, recorded 38 per cent of the vote, yet on the very same day the Liberal in Dundee East, which had a strong, though interrupted, Liberal tradition, polled not much more than 8 per cent, while the Scottish Nationalist came close to capturing the seat. In the Exchange division of Manchester in June, results were very similar to those in Chester-le-Street. On 26 July, the Liberals were victorious in two erstwhile Conservative seats on the same day. In the Isle of Ely, which had been Liberal until 1945, the candidate was the well-known television personality Clement Freud. In Ripon the victor was David Austick, a local councillor. There was a large element of 'community politics' in the campaign.

On 8 November, another 'mini-General Election' underlined the enormous local variations in the support which Liberals were able to muster. Berwick-upon-Tweed, which had a strong Liberal tradition, but where the Liberal had been third in 1970, was captured by Alan Beith with a very narrow majority over the Conservative. In the traditionally Conservative seat of Hove, the Liberal took a good second place. Yet in two urban Scottish constituencies on the same day – Edinburgh North and the Govan division of Glasgow – the Liberal finished fourth, behind the two main parties and the Scottish Nationalist as well. It looks as if the 'protest vote' which in England had been going largely to the Liberals was passing in Scotland to the Nationalists, who even recorded a victory in Govan.

Local elections of 1973 were favourable to the Liberals. At the Greater London Council elections in April, where the electoral areas were the same as parliamentary constituencies, the Liberals were victorious in Sutton and Cheam, and also in Richmond. A few weeks later, the Metropolitan District Council elections showed a substantial rise in Liberal support. Most remarkable of these results was in Liverpool, which had sometimes been poor territory for Liberals even in the days of Liberal Governments. This time the Liberals won 48 seats, against 42 for Labour and nine for the Conservatives. This result was clearly linked with 'community politics' and the great skill of local organisers such as Trevor Jones.

Taking 1973 as a whole, the Liberals had performed sensationally well. Not only had they captured three parliamentary seats, but the aggregate

Liberal vote at by-elections of the year was actually ahead of that of each of the other two parties. They had won substantial victories in local elections. The media were disposed to give them massive coverage. Public opinion polls showed a big rise in intending Liberal voters, which in August passed 20 per cent.[14] Yet less than two years earlier it seemed possible that the Party was heading for early extinction. The by-elections had played a major part in the Liberal advance, and opinion polls regularly showed a sudden upsurge in the immediate aftermath of a good result.

Until almost the end of 1973, it had been generally believed that the Conservatives, with their fairly comfortable overall majority, would not call another General Election before the autumn of 1974. But in the concluding weeks of the year, troubles of various kinds beset the government – some long-standing, some recent; some of the government's own making, some not. A great pre-war problem, which many believed had been removed for ever, returned. With occasional relatively brief lapses, usually attributable to some special cause, the number of unemployed had been kept well below a million ever since he war. Figures had already risen far above that number long before the crisis came; but the January 1974 figures of two and a quarter millions came as a considerable shock. Then, early in February, the National Union of Mineworkers called a strike throughout the industry. On 7 February, the Prime Minister responded by declaring a General Election, to be held just three weeks later.

The Liberal Party, with five recent by-election victories to its credit, appeared a serious factor in its own right, and not just for its 'nuisance value', even though the first few public opinion polls suggested that it had slipped back a great deal since its high point a few months earlier.[15] But great enthusiasm had already been generated among Liberal workers, and it was able to field 517 candidates for 635 seats – nearly 200 more than in 1970, and more than at any General Election since 1906. As the campaign proceeded, the number of intending Liberal voters revealed by the public opinion polls rose rapidly. After his narrow victory in 1970, Jeremy Thorpe more or less confined himself to North Devon, though arrangements were made for him to engage in press conferences connected from Barnstaple to London.

The results were as perplexing as the circumstances of the election, and can hardly have given unalloyed pleasure to either major party. The Conservatives secured 296 seats, the Labour Party 301, the Liberals fourteen. Small parties did remarkably well. The Ulster Unionists, who by this time had broken their traditional links with the Conservatives, took eleven seats, the Scottish Nationalists seven, the Plaid Cymru two and 'others' four. Numbers of seats bore little relation to votes cast. Labour had marginally more seats than the Conservatives, though the Conservative polled 200,000 votes in excess of Labour. The fourteen Liberal MPs represented over six million voters. With rather more than half as many votes as each of the larger parties, the Liberals had obtained fewer than one-twentieth the number of seats.

Constituency results are not entirely comparable with those of 1970, for there had been a number of changes in boundaries. All six seats which the Liberals had held in 1970 were kept. Jeremy Thorpe increased his bare majority to one of 11,000. The other two narrow majorities, in the Borders and in North Cornwall, were also replaced by very comfortable margins. Three of the by-election gains were kept – at Rochdale, the Isle of Ely and Berwick-upon-Tweed – but Sutton and Cheam and Ripon were lost to the Conservatives. There were five Liberal gains. Colne Valley and Cardiganshire were captured from Labour, Hazel Grove near Manchester, the Isle of Wight and Bodmin from the Conservatives – the last of these by a margin of only nine votes. Stephen Ross's victory in the Isle of Wight was the most impressive of all. In 1964, the Liberal vote had been a little under 15 per cent. Ross raised it to over 22 per cent in 1966 and 1970, but was still in third place. In February 1974 he won the seat, with more than 50 per cent of the votes cast, and the Labour candidate sustained a lost deposit. But there were some heavy disappointments.[16] Old Liberal territories like St Ives and Dorset North were missed by a considerable margin. The new hopeful, Liverpool, which had performed so well in the recent local elections, fell far short of expectations. Only in one of the eight constituencies in the city did the Liberal secure as good as second place.

Edward Heath still hoped to remain in office. He offered Jeremy Thorpe a seat in the Cabinet – it was never stated what the post would be – and also offered to set up a Speaker's Conference to consider the possible introduction of Proportional Representation. As soon as it became known that Thorpe was about to see the Prime Minister (surely, one reflects, he could hardly refuse an invitation to do so?), there was a furious reaction by Liberals who feared that he was about to accept office, and some recent candidates threatened public resignation from the party.[17] The Liberal MPs agreed that the offer should be rejected. In the end, Heath resigned and Harold Wilson formed another Labour Government, though he was far short of an overall majority – defying the miscellaneous group of Liberals, Celtic Nationalists and Ulstermen who nominally controlled the balance of power between them to put him out. The new Ministry, however, was most unlikely to last for long without a further General Election. There was little to show how the political wind was blowing in the lifetime of that short Parliament. Only one by-election took place – at Newham South, on the eastern fringe of London, in May, and that did not suggest any strong swing of opinion, although the Liberal lost a little ground. In compensation, a few weeks later Christopher Mayhew, Labour MP and former Cabinet Minister, transferred to the Liberal Party.

In June, the Chief Whip David Steel made a broadcast appealing for a 'Government of National Unity', and immediately Jeremy Thorpe endorsed the suggestion. But what did they mean? It was really unthinkable that the three parties would come together in a general coalition – and, even if they had done so, the precedent of 1931 was not an encouraging one. Or did it mean that the Liberals were prepared to consider some kind of alliance with one other party to the exclusion of the other? If so, there was no more certain recipe for disrupting the Liberal Party altogether. Wisely, the party's National Executive carried a resolution rejecting the idea. But perhaps both views were wrong, and the Liberal spokesmen wished to demonstrate to the electorate that they set national interests before factionalism. Who knows? But there can be little doubt that considerable numbers of active Liberals were dismayed at the possibility of Liberal MPs making some kind of arrangement or alliance with either of the other parties. This point was made emphatically and authoritatively at the Liberal Assembly in September 1974.

Meanwhile, the Liberal Party went ahead with plans to expand its electoral front further when a new General Election came. That moment arrived on 18 September, when the Prime Minister announced that Parliament was about to be dissolved, and polling would take place on 10 October. This time the Liberal Party put forward 619 candidates, contesting every seat in England and Wales except Lincoln (where the sitting 'Independent Labour' MP was treated as a Liberal for many purposes), and all but three in Scotland. Another remarkable feature of the election was that the Scottish Nationalists and Plaid Cymru contested every seat in their respective countries.

Labour made a few overall gains, bringing its representation to 319, against 276 for the Conservatives. The Liberals were down to thirteen, while the Scottish Nationalists and Plaid Cymru both improved their position, to eleven and three seats respectively. There was a substantial reduction in the overall turnout, and all three parties polled fewer votes than in February. Despite the increased number of candidates, the Liberal percentage poll dropped a little. An academic study of the October 1974 election suggests that the February Liberal voters were far more fickle than the crude figures suggest. It argued that the Party actually lost two and a half million votes.[18] If so, it largely compensated for these by winning two million new ones.

Two of the seats captured in February were lost – Bodmin and Hazel Grove. The one Liberal gain was Truro, where David Penhaligon was narrowly victorious. This was a remarkable personal triumph. In 1970 the Liberal had been third, far behind the other two contenders. Penhaligon brought this to a good second place in February 1974, from which he was able to capture the seat in October. The new convert Christopher Mayhew transferred from his former seat to the more hopeful territory of Bath, but was unsuccessful. Although the three Scottish seats were held, the Liberals fared abominably in much of the country, particularly the industrial belt. Liberals fought twelve of the thirteen Glasgow seats, losing their deposits in every one and scoring fewer than a thousand votes in five. In the seven Edinburgh seats they did not perform much better, forfeiting five deposits. In most of Scotland the 'protest vote' was moving ever more strongly to the Nationalists, and the Liberals were being swept aside.

The new government had little difficulty in enacting new Industrial Relations legislation which was more satisfactory to trade union critics. At the General Election it had also promised to renegotiate Britain's accession to the EEC, and submit proposals on the matter to the electorate. The new terms seemed very similar to those negotiated by the Heath government, but a referendum was held in 1975, which resulted in a a substantial majority of the electorate endorsing membership.

Soon a new and unexpected matter arose, which attracted enormous public attention. In January 1976, a man named Norman Scott, who was completely unknown to the general public, gave evidence in a case heard in Barnstaple to the effect that he had had homosexual relations with the Liberal leader: which, at the time of the alleged incident, would have been a criminal offence. The case in which Scott gave this testimony was unconnected with Thorpe, who strenuously denied the allegation. It was impossible for him to give full attention to party leadership with a matter like that hanging over his head. David Steel, who is not given to overstatement, reflected that 'the endless speculation had a devastating effect on party morale. No one could go canvassing because no satisfactory explanation could be given of anything which kept appearing in the newspapers'.[19] And so, in May 1976, Jeremy Thorpe resigned the Liberal leadership. It is disturbing, one reflects, that an unsubstantiated allegation by an unknown man should be able to shatter the career of an important politician, and wreak much damage on his Party as well.

Choice of a successor presented special difficulties. In the previous year, long before this trouble arose, the Liberal Assembly had decided that new procedures should be adopted for future leadership elections, but had not decided what those procedures should be. When Thorpe resigned, the MPs wanted Jo Grimond to return to the leadership, and if that had happened there would have been little dissent among the rank and file. Grimond was unwilling to accept, but agreed to return as acting leader, until new procedures could be determined and an election held.

New election procedure was quickly agreed. The Liberals were the first national party to arrange for a leader to be selected by ordinary members. Two candidates appeared: David Steel and John Pardoe. The issue was more than a simple choice between two MPs, both anxious for the job. Pardoe proposed an aggressive assault on the existing political system, while Steel emphasised his willingness to cooperate with one of the major parties in the hope of desirable reforms. Pardoe, noted for his 'knockabout style', contrasted with Steel's 'serious and cautious tone'.[20] Steel was eventually elected, by 12,546 votes to 7032. One suspects – though this can never be proved – that the Party activists tended to support Pardoe while the rank-and-file backed Steel, who had had long experience of the post of Chief Whip. He had also been responsible, very early in his parliamentary career, for a Private Member's Bill, which was eventually carried on a free vote, greatly extending the grounds on which abortion could be lawfully performed.[21]

Soon a new difficulty arose. In the 1976, the same year as the Thorpe issue broke, Harold Wilson resigned the premiership, and was succeeded by James Callaghan. The Labour Government was under great pressure. Economic problems were mounting, and inflation seemed almost out of control. Early in the year, two Labour MPs joined a splinter body known as the Scottish Labour Party. At by-elections in November, two Labour seats were lost to the Conservatives, both with a large overturn of votes. Labour's overall majority had been tiny after October 1974; now it had disappeared altogether. Margaret Thatcher, who had recently succeeded Edward Heath as Conservative leader, was eager to force a new General Election. An Opposition motion of No Confidence was tabled for 23 March 1977.

The last thing either the Liberals or the government wanted was a General Election. On the day of the debate, Callaghan and Steel announced an agreement, usually known as the 'Lib-Lab Pact'. The Liberal MPs would support the government on the No Confidence motion. This action could be justified on 'national interest' grounds, since the alternative would be a third General Election in just over three years, and one whose upshot was by no means a foregone conclusion. The two parties agreed to consult together, but it was explicitly stated that the agreement 'will not commit the Government to accepting the views of the Liberal Party or the Liberal Party to supporting the Government on any issue'. A Joint Consultative Committee would examine Government policy and Liberal policy proposals. There would be regular meetings between Denis Healey, Chancellor of the Exchequer, and the Liberal economics spokesman, John Pardoe. Callaghan and Steel would meet 'as necessary'. The government agreed that when legislation for direct elections to the European Assembly, and for the proposed devolved Assemblies in the United Kingdom, was submitted to Parliament, there should be a free vote as to whether they should be conducted with Proportional Representation. Provision would also be made to allow parliamentary time for the Housing (Homeless Persons) Bill proposed by Liberal MP Stephen Ross. The whole arrangement would be made public, and would continue to the end of the current parliamentary session, when both parties would consider whether to renew it. On the basis of this agreement, the Government was able to survive the Conservative motion of No Confidence by 322 to 298.

Peacetime arrangements with other parties have usually been decried by large sections of the Liberal Party. Two prominent MPs, Jo Grimond and David Penhaligon, were unhappy about the 'Pact' from the start.[22] The great majority of officers of constituency Liberal Associations were prepared to accept it, not least because there was no sort of commitment to support the Government in the lobbies after the crucial March vote. When the matter was considered by the Liberal Assembly at Brighton in September, it was endorsed by a substantial majority, and it was soon renewed for a further year. But, as time went on, the 'Lib-Lab Pact' proved increasingly disappointing. There was little, if any, legislation which had a distinctively Liberal stamp, although Liberals could claim to have had some effect on such matters as petrol prices and post office organisation.[23] Steel and Callaghan cooperated easily, but relations were bad between Pardoe and Healey. The Party rank-and-file, and – among the MPs – Cyril Smith in particular, became increasingly restive. A straw vote of MPs in December 1977 only agreed to continue it by six votes to four; and it was understood that Steel intended to resign if they did not approve.[24] The Special Assembly of the Party at Blackpool in January 1978 rejected a motion openly condemning the arrangements; but it was obvious that many Liberals were distinctly dubious. By-election results while the Lib-Lab Pact endured were even worse than they had been before. At last, in March 1978, Steel promised that it would not be renewed beyond the end of the current Parliamentary session, and in August it was formally terminated.

During 1978, and in the early weeks of 1979, the government ran into more and more trouble. Inflation was reaching unprecedented heights. There was much industrial strife. Then it fell foul of the Scottish and Welsh Nationalists. Acts had been passed accepting, in principle, the establishment of devolutionary bodies for those countries, but referenda were called for 1 March Unconvincing results were recorded and the proposals lapsed. Thus neither Scottish nor Welsh Nationalists had any further interest in keeping the government in existence. The *coup de grâce* was delivered on 28 March, when a motion of No Confidence, moved from Conservative benches, received support form Liberals and most MPs from the smaller parties, and was carried by 311 votes to 310. A new General Election was immediately called.

Then, suddenly, the Liberals received good news. On the day after the government's defeat, there was a by-election in the Liverpool constituency of Edge Hill, where the Liberals had been working furiously. A seemingly impregnable Labour seat fell to the Liberal candidate, David Alton, who polled more than 64 per cent of the votes cast. Edge Hill had been the only Liverpool constituency where the Liberal had run second in October 1974, and the by-election candidate was the man who had stood on that occasion. The swing of 32 per cent was enormous: the greatest swing in any post-war by-election. At last Liverpool 'community politics' had paid off in parliamentary as well as local government terms. The news could not have come at a better time for the Liberals, and it had a great effect on party morale. Opinion polls showed an immediate surge in the intending Liberal vote from around 5 per cent to around 10 per cent – a figure which was itself greatly exceeded on polling day.

At that moment, the Liberals needed every encouragement they could get. The Thorpe affair was becoming steadily more disturbing. In August 1978, Thorpe and three others were charged with conspiracy to murder Norman Scott. In December there was a hearing before a magistrates' court, as a result of which Thorpe was committed to trial. Much sensational evidence was given, and many casual observers probably failed to realise that the hearing was not a trial, and that committal did not imply guilt.

At the General Election of 1979, 579 Liberal candidates were nominated, considerably fewer than in October 1974. The result, as most people had expected, was a Conservative victory. The victors took 339 seats, against 269 for Labour and eleven for the Liberals. Both groups of Celtic Nationalists dropped back to two seats. The remaining twelve MPs were from Northern Ireland.

The Liberals were able to keep their very recent trophy at Edge Hill, but they suffered three casualties. There can be little doubt that Jeremy Thorpe's loss of North Devon took place because voters refused to give him the benefit of the doubt in the current court case. John Pardoe's failure in North Cornwall may perhaps be related to the same matter, for the Liberal vote fell away particularly badly in the south-western peninsula. Emlyn Hooson's loss of Montgomeryshire – Clement Davies's old constituency – may be attributed, in part, to local opposition to the 'Lib-Lab pact'. There were no Liberal gains to compensate for the three losses. The Liberal poll declined by about a million votes, to 4.3 million, while the percentage poll dropped from 18.3 per cent to 13.8 per cent. These figures are partly, but by no means entirely, attributable to the diminished number of candidates.

In the aftermath of the General Election, the Thorpe affair would have two more twists. When the trial was held some weeks later, It became clear that the two most significant prosecution witnesses, Peter Bessell, Liberal MP for Bodmin from 1964 to 1970, and Norman Scott, were both suffering from serious mental illness, and Thorpe was triumphantly acquitted on all charges;[25] but this did not save the immediate position. The second twist was a personal tragedy. About the same time, Jeremy Thorpe was diagnosed with Parkinson's disease, which meant that there could be no question of him returning to an active political career, although he continued, and still continues, to support the Liberal cause both in his former constituency and nationally.

Reflecting on the 1979 election, many Liberals must have heaved sighs of relief that the results were not worse. For all the violent fluctuations in their fortunes during the previous twenty years, the Liberal Party did seem firmly established as a permanent feature of British politics, which had not been the case for much of the 1950s. The Liberal Party's future was still uncertain, but there was little doubt that it would have a future, and that it would continue to influence the course of events for a long time to come.

19

Alliance and Fusion

> By the end I was forced to admit to myself that I did not much want to
> be governed by either [David Steel or David Owen] and the thought of
> being governed by both was too appalling for words.
>
> John Pardoe on his experience as Chairman
> of the Alliance Planning Group in the 1987 General Election[1]

On 4 May 1979, the day after her party's electoral victory, Margaret Thatcher
was appointed Prime Minister. Few would have anticipated it at the time,
but that was the commencement of eighteen years of Conservative Government, during which profound changes would take place which would
affect all parties. At first the Cabinet had included a wide spectrum of
Conservatives, though the omission of Edward Heath was immediately
noticed. As time went on, however, various other Ministers – the so-called
'wets' – found themselves unable to work with Thatcherite policies and
dropped off.

The feature of the new administration which first attracted adverse attention was the rise in unemployment. For thirty years after 1945, successive
governments had followed the Beveridge vision of 'full employment', which
meant in practice that the level of unemployment should normally be held
at around 2.5 per cent or less of the working population. In the Wilson-
Callaghan period, unemployment had moved far above that level, and stood
at rather over 5 per cent when the Labour Government fell. One of the most
effective Conservative posters at the General Election had been a picture of
a dole queue, with the words 'Labour isn't working'. But from early 1980
onwards, unemployment began to climb rapidly. By the end of 1981 it stood
at more than double the level two years earlier, corresponding with well over
two and a half million jobless, and it was still rising. Nor could such figures
be extenuated as unfortunate but temporary side-effects of a resolute war
against inflation. Far from it; inflation continued apace. The money supply
at the end of 1979 was below £60 thousand millions; two years later it was
over £86 thousand million.

Not surprisingly, the government was rapidly losing popularity. Public
opinion polls showed that Labour had caught up with the Conservatives in

the third quarter of 1979, and thereafter was well ahead. At the by-elections, the Conservatives lost support heavily, with Labour and the Liberals both making headway. In the District Council elections of May 1980, Labour made an overall gain of 476, the Liberals of 75. But changes within the Labour Opposition set matters on a different course. The Wilson-Callaghan Government, like the Labour Government of the 1960s, had been a considerable disappointment for many Labour activists. In 1979, the Labour Conference asserted the right of constituency Labour parties to reselect MPs. This meant that parliamentarians could no longer assume that tenure of a safe Labour seat meant a job for life, and great pressures could be set on MPs to conform to the views of local supporters. In October 1980, Callaghan announced that he was resigning the Labour leadership. Michael Foot was chosen as his successor, while in the following year Denis Healey was chosen as deputy leader, with the barest of majorities over Tony Benn. It looked to many Labour supporters as if their party was lurching sharply towards what was vaguely called the 'left'. Thus at the same moment as many Conservatives were becoming alarmed with the Thatcher government, many Labour people were becoming similarly alarmed with their own party. By early 1981 there were indications that Liberals were winning support at the expense of both.

There were soon signs that the unquiet in the Labour Party would lead to open revolt. At first, the main initiative rested with the so-called 'Gang of Three', Shirley Williams, Bill Rodgers and Dr David Owen. All had been members of Callaghan's Cabinet, although Shirley Williams had been narrowly defeated in the 1979 General Election. All were eager supporters of the EEC, and were generally regarded as 'moderates' (whatever that means) in the Labour Party. The term 'Social Democrat' was often used to describe them, although, oddly enough, it had been originally employed in the late nineteenth century to label H. M. Hyndman's movement, which was strongly Marxist in outlook. For much of 1980, it was by no means clear what the Gang of Three proposed to do – indeed, they were far from clear themselves. Would they set up a powerful pressure group in the Labour Party, or would they break away from it entirely; and, in that event, where would they go?

Roy Jenkins now entered the scene. He had been an even more important figure then the Gang of Three in the Wilson and early Callaghan periods, having occupied successively the positions of Home Secretary and Chancellor of the Exchequer. Then, in 1976, he departed to Brussels, becoming the first British President of the European Commission, which necessarily excluded him from political activity in the United Kingdom. He signalled his return to Britain by giving the BBC Dimbleby Lecture of

November 1979, in which he urged the formation of a party of what he called the 'radical centre'.

Jenkins and the Gang of Three were by no means in an identical position. Jenkins was much closer to the Liberals than they were. He was already a sympathetic biographer of Asquith, and author of a famous book on the Liberals-versus-Lords period. He was close to Steel both politically and personally, and his relationship with the younger man has been called avuncular. Jenkins was almost certainly prepared to join the Liberal Party if asked, though the story that Jenkins told Steel that he would like to join, and Steel discouraged him, has been denied by both men.[2] Steel must have realised that if such an important political figure did join the Liberal Party, his claim on the leadership would have been unanswerable. Steel and Jenkins agreed that a mass exodus from the Labour Party into a new organisation should be encouraged. Eventually contact was made between Jenkins and the Gang of Three, and soon people were speaking of the 'Gang of Four'.

In March 1981, the 'Gang of Four', plus a dozen MPs who had been elected as Labour, and one Conservative, formally launched the Social Democratic Party (SDP). It is a fair guess that an important factor in some, at least, of these cases had been the reselection process accepted by the Party Conference of 1979. People like Jenkins and Williams were likely to find it difficult to get a seat at all, and a substantial number of the existing MPs would probably be displaced. Soon a number of other Labour MPs joined the original defectors. All this attracted a great deal of media attention, much of it very sympathetic with the SDP. The SDP was a good deal more than a breakaway from the Labour Party. It drew in large numbers of people who had played no part in politics before, and in the first year or so of its existence it had a welcome element of freshness,[3] though hardly of political maturity.

Would the Liberals and the SDP cooperate? From the SDP's point of view, there was every reason to do so. If they had been faced with out-and-out opposition from Liberals as well as the other two parties, they would have found it difficult to get a foothold. From the Liberal point of view, it was a very different matter. Not long before the formal launch of the SDP, Cyril Smith expressed the opinion that the new party should have been 'strangled at birth'. Perhaps the Liberal Party could, and should, have shown an active concern to attract SDP supporters into its own ranks, rather than permit a potential rival to come into existence. Furthermore, as the authors of the standard work on the SDP have observed, urban radicals like Michael Meadowcroft and Tony Greaves who set the tone of the Association of Liberal Councillors 'saw themselves as being just as distinct from social democracy as from Conservatism. They believed in the dispersal of power, a weak state and the primacy of the individual. Ex-Labour Social Democrats were not their obvious allies'.[4] Another writer has noted that the SDP 'was an elitist, centralised and patrician party in which the strategic and the more important tactical decisions were usually taken at the centre',[5] contrasting with the far more democratically-organised Liberals. Thus there were widespread doubts as to whether the SDP was either basically Liberal in its outlook, or politically useful.

Steel and his immediate associates did not share those doubts. Representatives of the two parties met in May 1981, and in the following month a statement by Shirley Williams and David Steel made it clear that they considered a large range of agreement to exist between them, and that 'our two parties wish to avoid fighting each other in elections'. In confirmation of that view, the publication *A Fresh Start for Britain* was issued under joint authority. The principle of an alliance with the SDP was approved at the Liberal conference in Llandudno in September by a large majority. The SDP had not yet adopted a formal constitution, but at conferences held early in October the idea seemed also to receive general approbation in that quarter. Representatives of the two parties had already begun to discuss arrangements under which the British constituencies would be divided between them, so that neither would oppose the other.

The first attempt by the SDP to win a new parliamentary seat was in the Warrington by-election of July 1981. This looked like a very safe Labour seat indeed, but Jenkins, as SDP candidate, ran within 2000 votes of the Labour victor, and the Conservative forfeited his deposit. Very significantly, there was no Liberal candidate. Jenkins insisted on describing himself on the ballot paper as 'SDP with Liberal support', and he received much Liberal assistance during the campaign.

There soon followed a by-election in the traditionally Conservative territory of North West Croydon. At the 1979 General Election the Liberal candidate, Bill Pitt, fighting his third contest in the constituency, had fared badly. Steel was anxious for Shirley Williams to be the candidate, despite his special duty to the Liberals and a tacit agreement that Liberals and SDP should alternate in by-election contests. Pitt was invited to lunch with Steel, and thereafter was bombarded with telephone calls from leading Liberals;[6] but neither he nor his constituency organisation budged. Why in the world should a Liberal Association, which had regularly fought Parliamentary elections over a great many years,[7] withdraw its candidate to support a recent apostate from the Labour Party, who even then did not rank as a Liberal? And why should a man who had slogged on for a cause in which he believed for so long, withdraw now that victory seemed to be in the air? The Liberal Party Council took the same view. So Pitt went forward as 'Liberal SDP

Alliance' candidate. There was a great barrage of *Focus*-type leaflets, while the active presence of Jenkins, Steel and Shirley Williams ensured that the media gave much attention to the campaign. To the amazement of many people, Bill Pitt was elected with a comfortable majority.

In the following month, November 1981, the second 'Alliance' by-election was fought, this time in Crosby. In 1979, the constituency had had a Conservative majority of over 19,000 and a Liberal candidate, Anthony Hill, was already in the field. The Party leaders were eager to push forward Shirley Williams (although there was evidence that her past association with comprehensive schools might damage her campaign), and Hill was persuaded to withdraw in her favour. Huge numbers of supporters, both Liberal and SDP, were poured in, and some of the public meetings attracted audiences of over a thousand, requiring overspills in adjacent buildings and open spaces. The *Liverpool Echo* and local television gave the matter immense attention. In the end, Shirley Williams was elected as 'SDP/Liberal Alliance' candidate.

The next critical election arose in the Hillhead division of Glasgow, which included many members of the city's university among its electorate. Jenkins was exceedingly anxious to get back into Parliament, and his decision to stand was a high-risk strategy. If he had failed, this would almost certainly have ended his political career. As in Crosby, a huge effort was put into the campaign, and Jenkins was elected.

By this time, the Alliance Parties formed a significant force in the House of Commons. The SDP had 29 seats – two by-election victories, one defection from the Conservatives, and 26 defections from Labour. The Liberals had twelve – eleven returned at the General Election and one by-election victory. MORI Public Opinion Polls from the last quarter of 1981 and the first quarter of 1982 showed intending Alliance voters running ahead of intending voters for either of the other two parties. Many people thought that there was a real prospect that they would be equal, or even senior, partners in the next government. In the early part of 1982 there was some indication from public opinion polls which suggested that the original impetus of the Alliance was beginning to flag slightly, but not very much.

Then came one of those wholly unexpected events which sometimes change the political scene completely. At the beginning of April 1982, just over a week after the Hillhead by-election, Argentinian forces invaded the British colony of the Falkland Islands, to which the Argentine had long claimed *de jure* right. Margaret Thatcher, who had something of Boadicea in her make-up, was completely in her element. A great task-force was amassed, and proceeded slowly towards the South Atlantic. The other parties supported the Prime Minister's action, though some individuals were noticeably more enthusiastic than others; but she dominated them all in her eagerness for battle. The media gave the affair huge coverage. In March, most people in Britain would probably have been hard-put to say where the islands were or to whom they belonged; a few weeks later they seemed to be the most important place in the world. By mid-June, they had been recaptured.

In the thrill of battle far away, many people forgot the political controversies of 1981. The media lost interest in the Alliance as quickly as they had developed that interest in the first place. Public opinion polls showed a huge swing to the government, particularly at the expense of the Alliance. The Gallup public opinion poll had given the Alliance top, or equal top, position among the three political groupings from October 1981 to April 1982, peaking at 50 per cent of intending voters in December. By July 1982 the Conservatives stood at 46 per cent and Labour at 27 per cent, while the Alliance had fallen back to 24 per cent.[8]

In June, the SDP failed to take Mitcham and Morden, which on earlier form they would have expected to win. There was only one more Alliance by-election victory for the remaining life of the Parliament, which was the remarkable Liberal capture of Bermondsey in February 1983. Superficially, Bermondsey looked impregnable, with a Labour vote of over 63 per cent in 1979 and the Liberal polling less than 7 per cent. But it was one of several working-class constituencies where control of the local Labour Party had passed into the hands of a wholly unrepresentative group of extremists – some would call them revolutionaries. The Labour leader Michael Foot and the National Executive of the Party made no secret of their dislike of the candidate Peter Tatchell, yet in the end they had little choice but to accept the nomination. The Liberal candidate, Simon Hughes, secured a great victory, with over 57 per cent of the votes cast. The Alliance was back in business.

In the following month, there was a contest in Darlington. In 1979, and in several earlier elections, Darlington had returned Labour, with a small majority over the Conservative, and the Liberal a poor third. This time the SDP was the Alliance standard-bearer, and the candidate was Tony Cook, a television presenter.[9] Media interest was great, and at the beginning of the campaign the SDP appeared to be in front. Technically, the campaign was excellent, with plenty of literature and outside help. Much criticism has been heaped on the candidate, who does not seem to have been well informed, and who contrasted unfavourably with his two serious rivals. This is unfair on him. If anyone is to blame, it is surely his party for adopting a candidate without testing such matters beforehand. The upshot was another narrow Labour majority over the Conservative, though the SDP vote was more than double the Liberal vote of 1979. A much-needed fillip to Alliance support was lost.

Meanwhile, negotiations between the Liberal Party and the SDP continued. Somebody claimed that the Alliance was working because Jenkins was
a Liberal and Steel a Social Democrat. The negotiations were complex, and
neither party's leadership was a free agent; but the eventual result was agreement on the allocation of seats between them. The Liberals got most of the
seats where they had come reasonably close to victory in 1979, while the SDP
was so placed that if the Alliance had won a couple of hundred seats, they
would have had rough parity with the Liberals. Many Liberal Associations
were less than pleased when they discovered that arrangements between the
party leaders had resulted in their constituency being allocated to the SDP.
In three places – Liverpool Broad Green, and the London constituencies of
Hackney South and Hammersmith – no local agreement at all was reached,
and an 'official' SDP candidate was opposed by a nominee of the local Liberals. In retrospect, it is remarkable that the national arrangements for
constituency allocation worked as well as they did. Perhaps fortunately, SDP
policy was not very clearly worked out, while Liberal enthusiasts for the
Alliance did not care to lay stress on distinctive Liberal policies.

During the spring of 1983, it became increasingly clear that a new General
Election would be called very soon. In conditions of considerable haste, and
some difficulty, the Alliance leaders concocted a Manifesto entitled *Working
Together for Britain*.[10] The sharpest commitment was to reduce unemployment by one million within the next two years; but there was a wide range
of policies, most of which looked like short-term expedients rather than a
long-term vision of a new kind of society. There was a general understanding that if some particular individual was required to speak officially for the
Alliance – in the event, for example, of the Alliance being invited to form a
government, or needing to decide which other party (if either) should be
supported in event of a hung Parliament – that person would be Roy
Jenkins. On 9 May, a new General Election was officially announced, with
polling day on 9 June.

In the course of the campaign, there was considerable dissatisfaction with
Roy Jenkins's leadership, and the stormy character of a meeting at David
Steel's house was – fortunately for the Alliance – not appreciated by the
media. Until a week or so before polling, the Alliance seemed, nevertheless,
to be running ahead of Labour.

The result, in terms of seats won, was a huge triumph for the Conservatives, with 397 MPs, against 209 for Labour, 23 for the Alliance, two each for
the Scottish and Welsh Nationalists, and the remainder for the various
Northern Ireland parties. These crude results, however, give a wildly misleading picture of what the electors wanted. For the first time, every seat in
Britain (though not in Northern Ireland) was contested by all of the three

political groupings. The turnout was 73 per cent – a drop of 3 per cent from four years earlier. Although the Conservative majority had increased considerably, the Conservative percentage poll had dropped from 43.9 to 42.4. More dramatic was the change in support for the other parties. Labour fell from 36.9 per cent to 27.6 per cent. The Alliance won 25.4 per cent of the vote, compared with 13.8 per cent given to the Liberals in 1979. Here, surely, was the most astonishing reflection of all on the workings of the British electoral system. The Labour Party, with rather fewer than eight and a half million votes, won 209 seats; the Alliance, with over seven and three quarter million votes, won 23. Even within the Alliance there was a disparity. The 322 Liberal candidates polled 4.22 million votes and won seventeen seats; the 311 SDP candidates polled 3.57 million votes and won six seats.

The Liberals did well by comparison with 1979, though they fell far behind earlier hopes and expectations. All of their 1979 seats were retained. So was their recent by-election gain of Bermondsey – now remodelled as Southwark and Bermondsey – but they lost their other by-election gain of N. W. Croydon. They won six new seats – two in England, one in Wales and three in Scotland. Two of these victories would prove particularly significant for the party's future: 'Paddy' Ashdown's capture of Yeovil, and Michael Meadowcroft's capture of Leeds West. The SDP, by contrast, fared badly by any test. There was one victory: Ross, Cromarty and Skye, where the very young Charles Kennedy, future leader of the Liberal Democrats, was elected: the only SDP candidate ever to take a seat at a General Election. Only five of their existing seats were held. Of the original 'Gang of Four', Owen and Jenkins were returned, while Williams and Rodgers were defeated. Just three of the rank-and-file defectors from the Labour Party survived. Even with Liberal support, the SDP appeared to have lost nearly all of the force it possessed a couple of years earlier.

In the immediate aftermath of the 1983 General Election, two parties changed their leaders, and both changes would have a significant effect on the Liberals. Michael Foot resigned leadership of the Labour Party and was succeeded by Neil Kinnock: who appeared more credible as an alternative Prime Minister than did his predecessor. Roy Jenkins resigned from the SDP leadership. As the new leader had to be an MP, there was no other serious possibility but David Owen.

There were important questions about the purpose and future of the Alliance which seemed to call for urgent attention. Whether or not the Liberals had been wise in allowing the SDP to become established in the first place, matters had now moved on. If the two parties were indeed similar in outlook and essential policies – as the 1983 arrangements seemed to imply – then why not amalgamate them completely? To do otherwise was necessarily to waste money and effort at all levels, from Parliament through constituency organisations down to campaigning for seats in local government. Alternatively, if there were irreconcilable differences, then the best course was to break the Alliance as quickly as possible, and for the Liberals to prepare to fight every constituency at the next General Election. Either course would have made sense; dithering between them would make no sense at all.

But for Owen, the two parties would probably have moved towards amalgamation at all decent speed. Before the 1983 change in SDP leadership, contacts between Steel and Jenkins had been on a friendly basis; but dealing with Owen was like dealing with a truculent foreign power. Many of the SDP found him difficult to work with, and he showed little intention of cooperating with the Liberals. Owen's whole idea of the nature of the Alliance was fundamentally different from that of either Steel or Jenkins, and he never dissembled that fact. The Alliance, to Owen, was never more than an electoral expedient. Consistently with that view, he resisted ideas like choosing a single leader, or joint spokesmen in the House of Commons, or joint procedures for policy making, or close organisational links. All this, of course, was necessarily an impediment on the efficiency of the Alliance.

And would people, Liberal or SDP, work with enthusiasm in the future for a candidate in whose selection they had been denied any part? All agreed that it was necessary to reach some arrangement to determine which candidate stood in any particular constituency. There were at least three possible ways of handling the matter, and there was no uniformity of practice. There might be a repetition of the 1983 arrangement, under which the leaders divided the country between the two parties. Or there might be 'joint closed selection', by which a particular place was allocated to one party or the other, but members of both parties would have a say in choosing the candidate. Or there might be 'joint open selection', by which all members of either party in a constituency would be entitled to vote on their candidate, who also might belong to either Party. Generally the Liberals, who were the more numerous, favoured joint open selection.

There were other considerations. Owen claimed – probably rightly – that there were some voters whom the SDP could attract, who were inaccessible to the Liberals. The converse, however, was also true. There were important differences in political outlook as well, which had been brought out in the mid-1980s. Thus, the Liberals had a strong anti-nuclear streak, and in 1986 the Party Assembly voted down a proposal (with which Steel had concurred) for European nuclear weapons. Again, at the time of the 1984–85 miners' strike, the Liberals favoured compromise rather than confrontation. To Owen, whose attitude on such matters was a good deal more Conservative than Liberal, this was anathema. The overall result was that when the next

General Election approached in 1987 the two Alliance Parties were still separate bodies.

In spite of such difficulties, both the Liberals and the SDP performed remarkably well at by-elections which followed the 1983 General Election. There were sixteen contests, all of which were fought by the Alliance. Usually, the Alliance Party which had fought the seat in 1983 also contested the by-election, but in two places where the Liberal had fought in 1983 the Alliance candidate at the by-election was a member of the SDP, and in one it was the other way round. The aggregate Alliance vote over the period exceeded that of each of the other two parties. In all but one of the by-elections, the Alliance share of the total poll was better than in 1983. The only contest in which the Alliance candidate ran worse than second was at Fulham in April 1986, which was also the only Labour gain.

There were two SDP gains: at Portsmouth South in June 1984 and at Greenwich in February 1987. There were also two Liberal gains. Richard Livsey captured Brecon and Radnor in July 1985, and Elizabeth Shields took Ryedale in Yorkshire in May 1986. After the tragic death of David Penhaligon, Liberal MP for Truro, his former research assistant, the 24-year old Matthew Taylor, held the constituency at the by-election of March 1987, with a three-point increase in percentage poll. In local elections, the Alliance's performance was more variable, but by the end of the four-year period it had made a net gain of 200 seats.[11] It is striking to note that in most of these by-election contests, either the Liberals or the SDP ran the campaign, with little help from the other. The one exception was Greenwich, late in the Parliament, where the two parties were probably more closely integrated than at any other election of the 'Alliance' period. The machinery was largely provided by the SDP, while the Liberals gave special flavour to the election literature, and supporters from both Parties gave unstinting help.

A new General Election was held on 11 June 1987, just over four years after the previous one. As in 1983, there was a delicate balance between the numbers of candidates of the two Alliance parties, but the preference for joint open selection in some places led to a small tilt in favour of the Liberals, who received 327 candidatures against 306 for the SDP. Organisation was much better than in 1983, but the political handling was worse. John Pardoe was put in charge of the Alliance campaign, apparently because he was the only person whom both Steel and Owen would countenance. Pardoe was left with an extremely baleful view of the whole operation. The manifesto he considered 'a disgrace to any kind of political party', adding that 'you have a damned hard job finding anything positive in it'. Owen and Steel were brought together at major events during the election because the organisers 'were stark staring terrified of what they would say if we allowed them to speak separately'.[12] They had reason for this apprehension. At one point in the campaign Owen made a statement about Labour defence policy which could be taken as a very broad hint that he would personally prefer a Conservative government,[13] while Steel indicated at another point that working with Thatcher would be unimaginable. Mobile phones, which had only recently come into widespread use, made it easy for a journalist who had just interviewed one of the leaders to contact a colleague who was about to interview the other, and prime him with questions which would reveal the gulf between them. Whatever else was clear at the end of the campaign, it was obvious that joint leadership by two ambitious men with very different outlooks was a disaster and must on no account be repeated.

The overall result looked remarkably similar to 1983. The Conservative representation fell by 21, from 395 to 374, but the majority was still very comfortable; while Labour increased its representation by twenty, from 207 to 227. The Liberals held seventeen seats, as in 1983, while the SDP fell from six to five. There were more changes than these crude figures suggest. Two established Liberal MPs, Richard Wainwright in Colne Valley and Stephen Ross in the Isle of Wight, retired, and both seats were lost by their successors. In addition, Clement Freud lost North-East Cambridgeshire. Of the two by-election gains, Brecon and Radnor was retained by a tiny majority, but Ryedale was lost. Against these losses, the Liberals made three gains, all from Conservatives. Mrs Ray Mitchie won Argyll and Bute, Menzies Campbell captured North-East Fife, and Ronnie Fearn was returned for Southport. Of the SDP members who had been elected in 1983, Roy Jenkins lost Hillhead and Ian Wrigglesworth lost Stockton South. The SDP by-election gain of Greenwich was held, but Portsmouth South was narrowly lost.

From the point of view of the Alliance parties, the period between the General Election of 1987 and the next contest, in 1992, may conveniently be divided in three. First was the confused phase of merger, which ended with the final establishment of a united party in March 1988. This was followed by a period in which the new party took its bearings, selecting a new leader and a new designation. This period ended with the collapse of the Owenite rump which persisted in calling itself the SDP in June 1990. In the third phase the new party established itself as a credible body, able to face a new General Election with a measure of confidence.

The merger phase began immediately after the General Election of 1987. With the defeat of Jenkins, Owen was the only member of the original SDP 'Gang of Four' who remained in the House of Commons. Any case for maintaining the SDP as a separate party seemed to have disappeared. For many years the Liberals had been struggling to keep a third national party in existence; the prospect of keeping a fourth alive was small, particularly when that party had but five MPs, and little prospect of getting more. Although the SDP had much stronger reason than the Liberals for desiring a merger of the Alliance parties, Owen was implacably opposed to the idea, and made that point clear at a press conference in Plymouth on the day after polling. Almost immediately Jenkins and Williams on the SDP side, and Ashdown on the Liberal, called publicly for a merger. David Steel soon followed, announcing three days after the election that he proposed soon to present a memorandum supporting the 'democratic fusion' of the two parties. To this view the Liberal MPs gave unanimous assent.

The other Alliance party moved in the opposite direction. A few days later, the SDP's National Committee voted by eighteen to thirteen against a merger. The split was remarkable. Owen, and three of the other SDP MPs, were opposed, while Williams, Jenkins and Rodgers, along with one of the MPs, Charles Kennedy, were in favour. In August a ballot of SDP members resulted in 57.4 per cent supporting the merger. At that point, to the immense relief of many members of both parties, Owen resigned the SDP leadership. After some hesitation, Robert Maclennan was chosen in his place. Maclennan was one of only three MPs who broke with the Labour Party in 1981 who were still in the House. Accepting the popular vote of his party, Maclennan henceforth worked to assist the merger.

In September 1987, both the SDP and the Liberal Party held their annual conferences, and both decided, by large majorities, to work for fusion. Meanwhile, a group of SDP supporters opposed to fusion, headed by Owen, campaigned in the opposite direction. There were considerable doubts within, and between, the Alliance Parties as to the precise form the union should take.[14] Almost every aspect of the arrangement was open to some argument: the name of the amalgamated party, its underlying principles, the membership, the organisational structure.

Nevertheless, the leadership of both parties judged that an agreement could be reached which would be acceptable to the great majority of their members. Plans were accordingly laid for an Assembly of the Liberal Party and a Conference of the SDP in late January, which would be expected to give authority to proceed with the establishment of a new party in which the two would be united. At the beginning of 1988, an article in support of speedy union was published, with support of 650 Liberals, of whom a hundred were recent candidates and 250 were local councillors.

Meanwhile, Steel and Maclennan began to prepare a joint declaration of aims, though this was hampered by the fact that the SDP leader was in the United States. The document appeared on 13 January 1988. Its official title was *Voices and Choices for All*, but it was widely known as 'the dead parrot document', after the famous Monty Python sketch. Much of it was innocuous and unlikely to cause serious controversy within either party. Incredibly, however, its proposals included the extension of VAT to food, children's clothes, fuel and newspapers, the phasing out of tax relief on mortgages, an end to universal child benefit and a pledge of support for Trident nuclear missiles, all of which were likely to be intensely unpopular with the members of both parties, and disastrous with the electorate. Just possibly the authors had hoped to placate Owen and his immediate adherents. They did not win over Owen, but they angered nearly everybody else, Liberals and SDP alike.

The Liberal MPs exploded in fury. Des Wilson, former director of Shelter, and more recently President of the Liberal Party, described the document as 'barely literate' as well as 'politically inept'. It was very rapidly disowned. Steel and Maclennan were both shattered at the response. A team consisting of three members of each party was set up to devise a new statement. Owen gloated visibly, and urged the errant SDP MPs to return to him.

Enormous pressure was imposed by the Liberal leadership to force the merger through. On 23 January the Liberal Assembly at Blackpool accepted the principle of merger by 2099 votes to 385. Eight days later the Council for Social Democracy meeting at Sheffield accepted it by 273 to 28. Merger proposals were then referred to party members. On a 52.3 per cent poll, the Liberals voted 46,376 in favour, 6365 against. The SDP, on a 55.5 per cent poll, voted 18,722 in favour, 9929 against. The low poll in both parties may signal apathy; equally well, it may signal genuine uncertainty. On 3 March 1988, the new body was launched, with the working title Social and Liberal Democratic Party. Everybody agreed that the name was a mouthful, and nobody felt much enthusiasm for it, but that designation, or the short title 'Democrats', was allowed to remain for the time being. Steel and Maclennan acted as joint interim leaders.

In the second phase, the new party needed to choose a regular leader. In the summer of 1988, two candidates appeared, both of them Liberals: Paddy Ashdown, a former Marine officer, whose victory at Yeovil had been one of the sensations of the 1983 General Election, and Alan Beith, sometime university lecturer who had held Berwick-upon-Tweed since the by-election of 1973. Ashdown was victorious, with about 72 per cent of the votes cast.

Ever since 1981, an enormous amount of Liberal attention had been devoted to relations with the Social Democrats. We may ask ourselves Little Peterkin's famous question: 'What good came of it at last?' From one point of view – as in Southey's poignant poem about the battle of Blenheim – the conclusion seems to be: not much; and the good which did follow the operation was outweighed by the bad. That judgement suggests that the Liberal leadership of 1981 made two grave errors. First, it assumed that the leading Social Democrats were ideologically close to the Liberals. This was probably true of Jenkins; it was certainly not true of Owen, and one may suspend judgement about most of the MPs who broke with the Labour Party. They were not Socialists, and they were not Conservatives, at least in Thatcher's sense; but those two negatives did not make them Liberals.

The second misjudgement was that the SDP would play a major part in (to use the jargon of the time) 'breaking the mould' of contemporary politics. Evidence soon appeared, and it was proved down to the hilt in 1983 that things were not going to work in that way. It was a great error of judgement to take the Social Democrats at their own valuation, assume that they would be able to bring over great numbers of voters who would not only back the Alliance in a few exciting by-elections, but would remain with it thereafter. The results of the 1983 General Election showed beyond reasonable doubt that the SDP had struck no deep roots. From that point of view, the judgement of Michael Meadowcroft accurately summed up the whole episode:

> For six years of the Alliance loyalty required many Liberals to defend the indefensible and to explain the inexplicable, all to produce the remarkable result of June 1987. Remarkable, that is, in that it got us back, *pro rata*, to precisely where the Liberals were on their own in February 1974.[15]

Others would disagree sharply with that view, and would argue that the comparison with 1974 was not a valid one, for the high Liberal support on that occasion was the product of exceptional circumstances. If the Liberals had been required to fight the SDP as well as the other two parties after 1981, they might have suffered greatly. Other people might draw different lessons from the experience. There was everything to be said for trying to attract anybody with essentially Liberal opinions into the Liberal Party. There might well have been a case for promising any Labour MP who broke from his Party that he would have no Liberal opposition, or even that he could expect active Liberal support, at the next General Election. Whether the initial decision to form an Alliance with the SDP was wise or unwise, there can be little doubt that the Liberals made a serious error by failing to force the issue after 1983, and requiring the SDP either to fuse with the Liberals quickly, or face all-out Liberal opposition.

The first great task which Paddy Ashdown had to perform on becoming leader of the new party was to deal with the appalling condition into which finances had been allowed to lapse. A few weeks after assuming office, he attended a crisis meeting, and recorded, 'We are in a desperate situation. A potential deficit of a quarter of a million and an immediate cash flow problem which means we cannot pay any bills except for salaries and even those are precarious.'[16] It would soon be shown that the potential deficit was much greater than this gloomy note records. Ashdown was compelled to report to the party's dismayed and angry staff that many of them would have to be sacked, while immediately afterwards he faced a meeting of chairs of the regional parties who considered that the leadership's view of the financial position was actually too sanguine. Happily, it was possible to reduce the deficit greatly before the next General Election. There remains, however, a serious question as to how and why the deficit was allowed to develop in the antecedent period without effective action being taken. The terrible lesson burned into Ashdown's mind. Much later, the party officers proposed that the deficit should be increased by £70,000 for the next Election. Ashdown refused to countenance this, insisting that they should 'not be forced, once again, to sack our excellent employees just to pay off election debts'.[17]

In the early part of Ashdown's leadership, the legacy of the events in the previous few years was received in full measure. In the European elections of June 1989 the 'Democrat' vote of 6 per cent was not only much less than that of the two major parties, but also far below the 15 per cent accorded to the Greens, whom most people had regarded more as a pressure group than as a political party. In an unusual phase of deep depression, the new leader confided in his diary, 'I am plagued with the nightmare that the party which started with Gladstone will end with Ashdown'.[18] At one moment, the party's intending voters, as recorded in the opinion polls, were down to 4 per cent.[19] There were some fearful by-election results, culminating in the Glasgow Central disaster of June 1989, when the candidate languished in fifth place, behind Labour, Scottish Nationalists, Conservatives and Greens, with a mere 411 votes.

During mid-1989, there was deep argument over the name which the united party should adopt. The long-winded official name, and the short title 'Democrats' were generally felt to be unsatisfactory. People tended to lose their sense of proportion, and MPs were even threatening to resign the Whip if the matter was not resolved in a manner acceptable to themselves.[20] 'Liberal Democrat' eventually proved tolerable to the parliamentarians. It was then submitted to the rank-and-file members through a postal ballot, and the decision to adopt it was recorded in October 1989. They were not allowed the option of choosing 'Liberal', which would have been so much simpler. The name still took a long time to register with the public. Almost a year later, the Gallup Poll recorded that a large majority of the respondents either did not profess to know the name, or got it wrong.[21]

The position of the Owenites, and their claim to be the authentic SDP, took some time to resolve. At the Richmond (Yorkshire) by-election of February 1989, the SDP fared remarkably well, running within 3000 votes of the

Conservative victor, and leading the 'Democrat' candidate by more than 5000 votes. Is it possible that one of the factors which led to this result was confusion, both among voters and among pollsters, as to the distinction between a Social and Liberal Democrat on one side, and a Social Democrat on the other? To many observers, the difference between them must have appeared to carry all the subtlety of a Byzantine dispute on theology.

Richmond represented a false dawn for the Owenites, who thereafter fell back rapidly, and never again polled better than the Liberal Democrats. Their ultimate disaster was at the first Bootle by-election, in May 1990, when the SDP candidate not only ran far behind Labour, Conservatives, Liberal Democrats and 'continuing Liberals', but was beaten into seventh place, below the Monster Raving Loony Party's candidate, the eccentric 'Scream- ing Lord Sutch'. In the aftermath, Sutch generously offered to unite his party with that of Owen. The SDP was finally wound up in the following month, and the three MPs thenceforth sat as Independents, although for some pur- poses the name 'Social Democrat' was still used, down to the General Election of 1992. Owen tried, without success, to persuade the Conservatives not to oppose his two colleagues, while he prepared to retire from the House of Commons. He must stand with Joseph Chamberlain as one of the great wreckers of British politics.

A body of 'continuing Liberals' who resented the merger, and were headed by Michael Meadowcroft – once a member of the merger negotiat- ing team – also appeared. Their rise and fall was not as meteoric as that of the SDP. The party still exists; it has returned a number of local councillors, but has never come close to securing an MP. On a few occasions it has produced an effect which its organisers never intended, taking enough votes from a Liberal Democrat candidate to enable another party to win by a tiny margin. The clearest example here was the Devon East seat in the Euro-elections of 1994; but there have been several other occasions when the same thing seems to have happened.

In the third phase, from mid-1990 onwards, the party's position improved very rapidly. When Ian Gow, MP for the apparently impregnable Conservative constituency of Eastbourne was murdered by a terrorist attack of the IRA, Ashdown's first reaction was that the Liberal Democrats should stand down as a mark of indignation at the crime, and he was preparing to make an almost immediate announcement to that effect. Chris Rennard, the chief organiser, got wind of this at the last moment, and there were furious altercations between them. Eventually Ashdown was persuaded to recant,[22] and in October 1990 the Liberal Democrat candidate David Bel- lotti recorded a massive victory. Generously conceding the error of his earlier stand, Paddy Ashdown described this as his best day as leader of the Lib Dems. Intending Lib Dem supporters as indicated by the opinion polls surged by around ten points in the immediate aftermath. Perhaps this result was of decisive importance in persuading the Conservatives to displace Margaret Thatcher as Prime Minister in the following month. In Eastbourne, as in a considerable number of places over many years, the by-election victory was only possible because of the patient build-up at local elections over a long period, which was followed by close attention to local issues during the by-election campaign itself. Eastbourne was followed by two more Liberal Democrat victories. In March 1991 Michael Carr captured Ribble Valley. This result may also have had a big effect at a high level of government, for it is quite likely that it decided the Conservative government to kill off the notorious 'poll tax'. In November of the same year Nicol Stephen won Kincardine and Deeside – both seats being taken with convincing majorities, and large overturns of votes.

In this period, three factors operated particularly in favour of the Liberal Democrats: the personality, and perhaps the sheer obstinacy, of Paddy Ashdown; the sound base they had built in local government, where they currently held around 3,000 seats, and the run of successful by-elections. Meanwhile, they began to make serious plans for the long-term future. In June 1990, Ashdown confided in his diary a personal view of the matter. The next General Election, he recorded, should be 'a development election for us, which [we] should not put the party in hock. I wanted to use the two or three years after it to build the party.'[23] This sort of far-sightedness is unusual; more commonly, politicians are unable to look beyond the next General Election.

In March 1992 John Major, who had succeeded Margaret Thatcher as Prime Minister, announced that the next General Election would take place in the following month. Like their predecessors in several earlier elections, the Liberal Democrats contested almost all the British constituencies. There were just two exceptions: the contiguous London Thames-side constituencies of Greenwich and Woolwich, both of which had been held by Social Democrats who refused to enter the new united party.

The Lib Dem campaign was run by Des Wilson. It got off to an unfortunate start. A theft from the office of Paddy Ashdown's solicitor led to the disclosure that, some years previously, he had had an affair with a former secretary. This produced the scurrilous (but inspired) *Sun* headline, 'Paddy Pantsdown'. Ashdown admitted the incident in a dignified manner, and his wife gave her full support. The matter seems to have done no damage either to Ashdown or to his party. A remarkable feature of the campaign was the LIb Dem proposal to increase income tax by 1p. in the pound to pay for education. Contrary to the widespread view that proposals for extra taxation are always unpopular, this appears to have done no harm at all. As in 1987, the question of a possible alliance with other parties in the aftermath was raised late in the campaign and may have done some damage. In the end, the Conservatives, with 336 seats, lost a considerable amount of ground, but retained their overall majority, against 271 seats for Labour, twenty for the Liberal Democrats, four for the Plaid Cymru, three for the Scottish Nationalists and seventeen for the various Northern Ireland parties.

Liberal Democrat results followed a curious pattern. At the dissolution, they held 22 seats: 17 of which had been won by Liberals, and two by Social Democrats who decided to join the Liberal Democrats, The remaining three seats represented by-election victories. The three by-election gains were all wiped out at the General Election. Otherwise, there were three losses and four gains. Ceredigion (once Cardiganshire) and Pembroke North fell to the Plaid Cymru; Brecon and Radnor and Southport to the Conservatives. Against these were four gains, all of them in the west country: Bath, captured by Don Foster, Cheltenham by Nigel Jones, North Cornwall, taken by Paul Tyler, and North Devon by Nick Harvey. All but two of the Liberal Democrat seats were held by people whose antecedents were Liberal. Those two were in the north of Scotland, an area where the personality of the candidate is often more important than party. The three seats which had been held by Social Democrats who were not prepared to join the new party were all taken by Labour. The candidate described as a Social Democrat who succeeded Owen in Devonport fared very badly; but the other two who were defending their seats, and had no Liberal Democrat opposition, only lost to Labour by a narrow margin.

20

Into a New Millennium

Our last five minutes were spent in enthusiastic discussion of Gladstone
and the similarity between the present fluidity of politics and the thirteen years after the repeal of the Corn Laws.

Paddy Ashdown, on meeting with Roy Jenkins, 2 May 1996 [1]

The General Election of 1992 produced yet another Conservative majority,
albeit smaller than the previous three had been. Some people began to wonder whether the traditional 'swing of the pendulum' mechanism had broken
completely. The Conservatives had already been in office for fourteen years,
and – barring unpredictable accidents – were set for another four or five to
come. During the lifetime of the 1992 Parliament, however, three important
developments took place, which greatly altered the political pattern. Each
was a gradual process, and each had considerable influence on the other
two.

The first was the growing unpopularity of the Conservative government.
During the Thatcher years, that government had followed profoundly divisive economic and social policies. When John Major took over the
premiership in 1990, these policies were softened considerably, but by that
time the Conservatives were showing a dearth of new ideas. As the 1990s
advanced, a series of personal scandals began to erupt – 'sleaze', as they were
popularly called – which led many people to think that corruption was
widespread in the government. The declining popularity of the government
was signalled in the various by-elections of the period. Not a single Conservative seat which came up for challenge was retained, and by the end of the
Parliament the government's overall majority had disappeared.

The second process was a radical shift in policy and outlook within the
Labour Party. Almost immediately after the General Election, Neil Kinnock
resigned the leadership, and after an interval was succeeded by John Smith.
Smith occupied a more or less central position in the various issues which
were debated in the Labour Party. In May 1994, however, he died suddenly
and unexpectedly, and a couple of months later Tony Blair was chosen as
his successor. It was evident from the start that Blair had no sort of commitment to socialist policies, and it was also plain that the people who voted

for him were prepared to make many sacrifices of the traditional principles of their party in order to win the next election. Perhaps they hardly needed to make concessions, for growing numbers of ordinary voters were determined to throw out the government, whatever policies Labour might have on offer. Blair was soon able to persuade Labour to modify the celebrated Clause 4 of its constitution, which had committed the party to a policy of general nationalisation. In wider terms, he sought to give the Labour Party a much more popular image, and to damp down policies like high state expenditure and taxation which in the past had upset many voters. Even before Blair became Labour leader, Ashdown committed to his diary the view that his appointment would be something of a mixed blessing for the Liberal Democrats. On the negative side, 'he'll steal our clothes and appeal to our voters'. On the positive side, he would make Labour 'less frightening to potential Lib Dem voters who flood to the Tories for fear of Labour in the last few days before every election', and 'he's very interested in cooperation' with the Liberal Democrats.[2]

The third process which developed during the lifetime of the 1992 Parliament was the gradual abandonment, both in the Labour Party and among the Liberal Democrats, of 'equidistance' – the idea that they were as distinct from each other as each was from the Conservatives. Both parties had a strong tradition of complete separateness. The 'Lib-Lab Pact' of 1977–78 had represented a small and tentative move away from that tradition, but it was far from universally popular in either of the parties from the start, and it ended with almost audible sighs of relief all round. 'Equidistance' had long seemed particularly important to Liberals, who were well aware that some of their voters preferred Labour to Conservative while others preferred Conservative to Labour. Any significant shift in either direction was likely to drive a lot of people into the opposing party. The necessity of a very delicate balancing act was brought out again at the 1987 General Election when Owen appeared to favour the Conservatives and Steel the Labour Party.

Just after the 1992 election, Ashdown circulated a strategy paper to his parliamentary colleagues, arguing for the abandonment of 'equidistance', and envisaging eventual participation with Labour in a coalition. Most of the MPs reacted very strongly against 'the Project' – as the idea soon became known in inner circles of the party – and when Ashdown broached it in a more muted form at a meeting at Chard, in his own constituency, shortly afterwards, responses among the MPs were equally adverse.[3] A resolution seeking to move away from 'equidistance' was drafted for the Liberal Democrat Conference at Harrogate in September 1992, but was withdrawn in favour of a more innocuous one when it became clear that the original would probably be rejected. Nor did Ashdown have much more early success with the Labour Party. In October he had a meeting with Smith which was friendly in tone, but the Labour leader left him in no doubt that pacts and alliances were out of the question.[4] So there, for the time being at least, matters rested. Yet throughout the lifetime of the 1992 Parliament there was considerable tension among Lib Dems (the abbreviation was now widely used), though no open breach.

When Tony Blair became Labour leader in 1994, Ashdown's ideas obtained a much more welcome reception. There were many meetings between Blair and Ashdown, sometimes involving colleagues as well. At times Roy Jenkins performed towards both of them something of the 'avuncular' role he had once adopted towards Steel. Evidence soon emerged that Blair would contemplate a government containing some Liberal Democrats if Labour emerged as the largest party but without an overall majority; indeed, that he would prefer to have a government including Lib Dems even if he did secure a majority.[5] There is every reason for thinking that this represented his real wishes, not a reluctant concession to political necessity. He did not disagree with Ashdown on many questions of policy, although he had considerable reservations about Proportional Representation – but he disagreed profoundly with many of his own putative followers on numerous matters.

Yet Liberal Democrat opposition to any abandonment of 'equidistance' did not appear to have weakened. Ashdown described a meeting with the MPs' researchers in March 1995 as 'very tough' and 'very hostile to the abandonment of equidistance, reflecting, they said, the views of their MPs'. In a moment of despair, he even asked himself, 'Is this the time to pack it in?'[6] The argument continued to rage. It became evident that some MPs, including Alex Carlile and Menzies Campbell were eager to accept close cooperation with Labour, while others, including Chris Davies – victor in a recent by-election[7] – and Liz Lynne, who had succeeded Sir Cyril Smith in Rochdale, were implacably opposed. But Ashdown set up various unofficial *ad hoc* groups of sympathisers, MPs and others, to engage in discussions with members of the Labour Party. It gradually emerged, however, that while both Ashdown and Blair personally desired a coalition including two or three Liberal Democrats, neither man could lead his own party into such an arrangement without enormous ructions.

These conversations were, of course, largely secret at the time, though many must have guessed that they were taking place. Meanwhile, the electorate was moving more and more sharply away from the Conservatives, and seemed to care little which party should be favoured as the alternative. When a by-election occurred, all three parties regularly put forward candidates, but the voters plumped heavily for the one who seemed better placed to beat the Conservative, with the result that there was often a very substantial slump in votes of the other.

A by-election at Newbury in May 1993 resulted in a massive Lib Dem victory in traditionally Conservative territory, with a huge overturn of votes. As in all the Lib Dem campaigns of the 1992 Parliament, Chris Rennard, now Lord Rennard, was in charge of operations. Newbury was followed in July by an even more remarkable victory at Christchurch, with a record swing of 35 per cent. Soon the Lib Dems pushed the Conservatives into third place in opinion polls. The pattern of Lib Dem victories in hitherto Conservative seats was followed in the next two years: a by-election gain at Eastleigh in June 1994, and another at Littleborough and Saddleworth in July 1995. In this last case it was not a simple question of Liberal Democrats winning Conservative votes and squeezing Labour votes in a constituency where Labour had no chance, for Labour also had some reasonable hopes of winning the seat and was fighting much more vigorously against the Liberal Democrats. This result showed that the Lib Dems were still able to capture Conservative seats, despite the apparent appeal of 'New Labour'. Then, at the end of 1995, Emma Nicholson, one of the Devon Conservative MPs, transferred to the Lib Dems.

Labour was also doing well in by-elections where it was seen as the principal challenger, winning three in the course of the Parliament. Like the Lib Dems, Labour made a convert from among the Conservative MPs. In Scotland, the Nationalists were the main beneficiaries of Conservative unpopularity, and were able to capture Perth and Kinross in May 1995. Local elections told the same general story of Conservative collapse, to the benefit of whatever party appeared to be the main local challenger. By the end of the 1992 Parliament, only one County Council remained in Conservative hands, while the Conservatives held only 4700 local council seats, against 5100 for the Lib Dems and 10,800 for Labour. In the European elections of June 1994, the Lib Dems carried two west country seats, and came close in several others. What a contrast with the fearful results of 1989! One of the oddities of the situation, however, was that these very marked Liberal Democrat advances in elections were not paralleled by the public opinion polls. In 1993 voters proposing to support them stood at 25 per cent, but three years later they were down to 12 per cent.[8]

In March 1997, almost at the end of the 1992 Parliament, tentative cooperation between Labour and Lib Dems resulted in an agreed statement on a number of issues. A joint consultative committee with members from each of the two parties, chaired jointly by Robin Cook for Labour and Robert Maclennan for the Lib Dems produced a report indicating agreement on constitutional issues.[9] Matters considered included ending the right of hereditary peers to sit and vote in the House of Lords; adoption of a fairer system for elections to the European Parliament; directly elected legislatures for Scotland and Wales; and the establishment of a commission to consider voting reform in elections to the House of Commons. Other agreed measures included incorporation of provisions of the European Convention on Human Rights into UK law, and a Freedom of Information Act. Technically, these proposals were not binding on either party; but they would probably have considerable effect on future legislation in the not unlikely event of the next General Election producing a Labour majority.

The 1992 Parliament ran almost to the legal limit, and the next General Election was held in May 1997. By that time, most people were coming to think that a Labour victory was likely, but the magnitude of that victory – 418 Labour seats against 165 Conservative – was astonishing. One of the remarkable features of the election was the big rise in Lib Dem representation to 46 seats: substantially more than any 'third party' had won at a General Election since 1929.

How had the Lib Dems contrived to make this massive advance? Far from improving, the party's vote had declined: from practically six million in 1992 to a shade under five and a quarter million in 1997. So had the percentage poll dropped – from 17.8 per cent to 16.8 per cent. The explanation of the paradox is twofold. The 'tactical voting' which had been so marked in the by-elections continued, though to a lesser extent, in the General Election, and where the Lib Dems had been in a good second place to the Conservatives in 1992, they had a fair chance of capturing enough former Labour votes to win. Conversely, the Lib Dem vote was likely to collapse where Labour was seen as the challenger. The other explanation is the better use of resources. The Lib Dems targeted the seats they were defending, plus fifty more – half of which they won. Ed Davey was even victorious in a seat, Kingston and Surbiton, which had not originally been targeted.[10] This general advance owed much to the far greater sense of strategy promoted by the chief organiser Chris Rennard, and supported by Paddy Ashdown, though targeting winnable seats was no new idea. The practice began in local elections perhaps forty years earlier, and was gradually extended to parliamentary contests. What was new, however, was the much more extensive and intelligent way in which it was carried out. Winnable seats were selected long beforehand. Regional Lib Dem organisations were encouraged to part-fund these constituencies, and the places chosen were encouraged to produce development plans extending over at least two years, whose progress was carefully monitored. The Lib Dems recognised that it was worth allowing some falling away of support to take place in impossible constituencies if this produced victories elsewhere. They were also able to raise election funds more effectively than in previous contests. Something like £2,750,000 was spent by the central organs of the Party, compared with about £2,200,000 in 1992.

There was also a shift in policy emphasis, which resulted from a careful study of voters' reactions through opinion polling. It was decided, for example, that particular emphasis should be given to matters of wide public interest, like education, health and the environment; while questions like constitutional reform and Europe, which did not excite much positive enthusiasm, should be soft-pedalled. A cynic might suggest that there was another reason for soft-pedalling Europe. Among actual and potential supporters of the Lib Dems – as of both other parties – were many people who were far from convinced supporters of the official Party line on the subject. On the positive side, considerable media attention – much of it very sympathetic – was given to the Lib Dem proposal to add 1p. to the current rate of income tax, to be earmarked for education.[11] At one point Ashdown had considered the possibility of holding joint pre-election rallies with Blair; the idea, however, was later dropped.

Seen in more detail, the 1997 General Election displayed a number of remarkable features. The number of constituencies had been increased from 651 to 659, but the smallness of this numerical change obscures the massive measure of redistribution which had taken place. Most constituencies had been altered to some extent, many of them radically. As in several previous General Elections, Conservatives, Labour and Lib Dems stood almost everywhere in Great Britain, but almost ignored Northern Ireland. The main parties did not stand in the Speaker's seat; while in Tatton, Labour and the Lib Dems both decided to support an Independent, Martin Bell, who stood as an 'Anti-Corruption' candidate. Both parties had some difficulty with their Tatton constituency organisations, which were eager to fight.

The much-increased Lib Dem representation was secured by 26 gains, all from Conservatives. Two Lib Dems who had been defeated in 1992 returned to the House: Ronnie Fearn in Southport, Richard Livsey in Brecon and Radnor. The by-election captures of Newbury and Eastleigh were retained, but Christchurch reverted to the Conservatives. The other constituency which had been taken by the Lib Dems in a by-election, Littleborough and Saddleworth, disappeared as a result of redistribution. The Liberal seat of Mossley Hill, in Liverpool, was also abolished, and there were two losses to Labour, both of which took place in rather special circumstances. In the Highland constituency which was redrawn as Inverness East, Nairn and Lochaber, Sir Russell Johnston, who had sat there since 1964, retired. As often happens in North of Scotland constituencies, voters who had been loyal to one MP did not transfer their affections to his successor. In

Rochdale and in the new constituency of Oldham East, which included much of the former Littleborough and Saddleworth, there had been boundary changes, and there appears to have been tactical voting by Conservatives, which may explain the disappearance of the Lib Dem majorities.

Once the overall result of the General Election was clear, John Major resigned the premiership and Tony Blair took over. It was not necessary to incorporate Lib Dems in the new Ministry in order to give the government a comfortable majority, and no doubt Blair would have found opposition within his own party insuperable if he had tried. Astonishingly, he told Roy Jenkins almost immediately afterwards that he intended to have Lib Dems in the Ministry 'within a matter of months'.[12] Whether or not this arrangement would be acceptable to both parties – indeed, to either – there certainly appeared to be a serious prospect of cooperation on the matters which had been considered before the election by the joint consultative committee.

One constituency had presented a special problem at the General Election – more common when electorates were much smaller than today, but rare in recent times. In Winchester, the majority of Mark Oaten the Lib Dem over the Conservative was only two votes. In the aftermath of the election, this desperately narrow majority was challenged by the defeated Conservative. Recounts had naturally taken place, but these could hardly remove all doubts about the electors' wishes, and (as usual) there were some ballot papers on which the voter's intention was unclear. The matter was referred to the courts, which ordered a new election. Polling took place in November, and Oaten secured the sensational majority of 21,556. Plainly, supporters of the Labour Party, perceiving that it was a 'two-horse race', decamped *en masse* to the Lib Dems.

The close contacts between Blair and Ashdown which had existed in the old Parliament continued in the new. The two men discussed political problems with considerable frankness. They agreed that they should seek 'to mend the schism that split apart the progressive forces in British politics in the early years of the [twentieth] century, giving the Tories more chance to govern than they deserved'.[13] The views of the two men, though similar, were not identical. Blair appears to have been eager that this 'mending' should lead to the eventual merger of the two parties; Ashdown was significantly more cautious. While Ashdown was anxious to secure a system of electoral reform which would represent the voters' wishes more accurately, Blair was (at least in public) unconvinced. Like most Prime Ministers, he was conscious that the parliamentary representation of his party was far in excess of its electoral support, and in the current House of Commons this excess was something like 100 seats.

Some of the two-party consultative committee's proposals went forward in the new Parliament, though occasionally in a somewhat modified form. In May 1997, a Referendum Bill for Scottish and Welsh devolution was published. The government indicated that, in both cases, simple majorities of those actually voting would be sufficient to inaugurate the legislative process. The Lib Dem MPs, however, were deeply divided in their reactions to the Bill. The Welsh MPs favoured it; the Scottish MPs reacted strongly against it. With considerable difficulty, Ashdown at last persuaded his Scottish followers to abstain from voting.[14] In the end, Parliament accepted the Bill, and the referenda took place in September 1997. The people of Scotland voted for their own Parliament by a very convincing majority. Wales supported the establishment of an Assembly which would not have taxing powers, but by the narrowest of majorities. The required legislation was duly passed. In mid-July, Blair indicated that the government would support legislation for a modified electoral system (though one which did not correspond closely with the traditional Liberal policy of Proportional Representation (PR)) in the European elections which were due in 1999. This was a less controversial question than electoral reform in UK elections, for other EU countries had long adopted similar systems. There was some danger that it would be blocked in the House of Lords; but Ashdown was able to put enough pressure on Blair to enable the measure to pass.

Blair and Ashdown continued to seek much closer cooperation between their two parties. In the late spring and early summer, secret discussions took place about the establishment of a more 'official' Joint Consultative Committee (sometimes wrongly called a Cabinet Committee) to examine constitutional questions and other matters of mutual concern, on which members of both parties would sit. The news leaked, and Ashdown had a furious meeting with one of the Scottish Lib Dem MPs, Jim Wallace, in the course of which Wallace accused his leader of 'betrayal', and 'we shouted at each other for about two minutes'.[15] Most of the MPs appear to have known nothing either of the incident or of the subject, and they were not told of the proposals until 22 July, the very day on which the Joint Consultative Committee was to be announced officially. Not surprisingly, 'there was much talk of being bounced'. In the end, Ashdown reflected, 'I got it through, but at considerable cost'.[16] It is not difficult to sympathise with the feelings of the aggrieved MPs. The announcement was duly made, and the committee was set up.

The importance of electoral reform for the Liberal Democrats was never in doubt, and there were protracted discussions on the subject. In December 1997, a commission was set up under Roy Jenkins, who by this time had become Lord Jenkins of Hillhead and leader of the Lib Dem peers. Towards the end of October 1998, the Commission at last made its proposals.

These were very different from Proportional Representation, as Liberals had always understood the term, although they would probably have produced somewhat fairer elections than in the past. In the end they did not even satisfy that modest objective, for they went much too far for many in Blair's Cabinet and were eventually dropped.

A difficult situation arose both in Scotland and in Wales when the first elections for the Scottish parliament and Welsh assembly were held in May 1999. In both countries, some seats were awarded on the 'first past the post' principle, while others were chosen on a 'top-up' system designed to ensure fairer representation for the parties. This was rather like the Jenkins proposals for the UK. The results followed a similar general pattern in both countries. Labour led, but with no overall majority, with the respective Nationalist parties second and the Conservatives third, followed closely by the Lib Dems. In Scotland, Labour and the Liberal Democrats formed a coalition. In Wales, Labour initially formed a minority government, but eventually reached a partnership agreement with the Lib Dems.

The European parliament elections in June 1999 were marked by a very low turn-out, with only 23.1 per cent of the electors bothering to vote at all. Euro-elections were generally regarded as – at best – a sort of opinion poll for 'the real thing' at Westminster. Very few even of those who did bother to vote appear to have been influenced by issues which were within the competence of the European Parliament. A sharp contrast exists between British apathy and the far greater interest which these elections attracted in nearly all continental countries. 36 of the UK seats were taken by the Conservatives, 29 by Labour, ten by the Lib Dems, three by the anti-EU United Kingdom Independence Party, and two by the Greens. The big increase in Lib Dem representation seems due overwhelmingly to the changed electoral system.

Long before this, it was clear that Ashdown had pushed the party to the very limit. In November 1997, the view that 'a Lib-Lab pact would be a disaster' was expressed publicly by an active and influential Lib Dem peer and was widely endorsed.[17] Even after that, some talks about possible Lib Dem places in a Labour Cabinet continued,[18] but nothing came of them. Ashdown still did not abandon the idea of the 'Project', and at one point late in 1998 he and Blair had issued a joint statement to the effect that they hoped later to extend the committee's remit. This provoked a very strong hostile reaction among the MPs and party activists, and probably persuaded him that further progress in that direction was impossible.

Ashdown had really come to the end of the line. Whatever he or Blair might have wished, there was no real prospect of Lib Dems being brought into the government in the foreseeable future, and there was the certainty of gigantic explosions in both the Labour and Lib Dem Parties if any further moves were made in that direction. Ashdown's diaries are peppered with entries to the effect that he did not propose to remain either leader of the Lib Dems or MP for Yeovil beyond the lifetime of the current Parliament, and he informed the Prime Minister to that effect as early as July 1997.[19] Yet there were occasional indications thereafter of a very different kind. A year later, he announced that it was his intention 'to lead this party through this parliament, through the next election and into the next government'.[20] Very likely he vacillated from time to time. But he had many interests outside party politics, and recognised that by the next General Election he would be sixty. This age worried him, as it had also worried Harold Wilson. On 20 January 1999 Ashdown announced his intention to resign the leadership as soon as a successor could be chosen.

Selection of a new Lib Dem leader was a protracted process. Each candidate had to be nominated by some of the MPs, and all party members were entitled to vote. Five candidates appeared, and on the first count none secured an overall majority. After the usual eliminations, it came to a contest between Charles Kennedy and Simon Hughes. When the result was announced on 9 August, Kennedy led by 28,425 votes, against 21,833 for his rival, on a turn-out of a little under 62 per cent of those entitled to vote.

The change in leadership was not marked by any immediately obvious changes in the party's electoral performance. Apart from Winchester, the most encouraging parliamentary contest for the Lib Dems in the lifetime of the 1997 Parliament was in the contiguous constituency of Romsey in May 2000, when Sandra Gidley overturned a Conservative majority of over 9000. Collapse of the Labour vote – from 9,623 in 1997 to 1,451 in 2000 – seems to be the main explanation of the change. Elsewhere results were less encouraging, and two of the central Scotland results were atrocious. At Hamilton South in September 1999, the Lib Dem had run sixth with a mere 3.3 per cent of the vote, while at Falkirk West in December 2000 the proportion was marginally smaller than that. In general, the turn-out at by-elections was exceedingly poor. The worst was at Leeds Central in June 1999, when fewer than 20 per cent of the electorate bothered to vote at all. The local Lib Dems had modest satisfaction in moving up to second place in the contest.

Local elections also showed an erratic pattern, and – like the by-elections – do not appear to have been much influenced by the change in Lib Dem leadership. In the May elections of 1998, 1999 and 2000, the overall picture was of some Conservative recovery and of losses by both Lib Dems and Labour, but there were substantial variations. On the whole, the Lib Dems did rather badly in the south, losing control of – for example – Eastbourne, and finishing fourth in the London mayoral contest. Yet in parts of the north the picture was very different. They ousted Labour from control in Sheffield and also captured Liverpool and Oldham, places which had not always been good for the party in its great days. Public opinion polls continued, almost without interruption, to give Labour the lead, with the Lib Dems continuing in third place, though without signs of a general collapse.

The next General Election was held on 7 June 2001. The contest was a quiet one. The intense hopes and fears which had marked some of the recent elections were both absent. No intending Conservative voter had reason to fear that a majority for Blair would lead to 'Socialism'; no intending Labour voter had reason to fear that a Conservative majority would result in a return to 'Thatcherism'. From the Lib Dem point of view, that was good; for their potential supporters were not likely to be frightened into voting for some other party out of fear of the alternative.

In the run-up to the 2001 General Election, the Lib Dems had remained solvent, and were able to staff their central office more fully than in the past. 'Targeting' of hopeful seats continued. In the view of the authors of the Nuffield monograph on the election, Charles Kennedy 'seemed to grow from "a lightweight couch potato" to a formidable leader'.[21] Seven Lib Dem MPs did not seek re-election. Chief of these were Paddy Ashdown himself and Robert Maclennan, while two other Scottish Lib Dem MPs, Jim Wallace and Donald Gorrie, decided that their duties in the Edinburgh Parliament were more pressing than those at Westminster.

The turn-out, at under 60 per cent, was the lowest by a substantial margin of any General Election since the wholly exceptional circumstances of 1918. Overall results were remarkably similar to those of 1997. Labour held 413 seats, compared with 419, the Conservatives 164 instead of 165. Contrary to widespread predictions, the Lib Dems improved their position: 52 seats, compared with 46 in 1997 and 47 at the dissolution. They also increased their share of the vote in British constituencies by 1.8 per cent. Two Lib Dem seats were lost – the Isle of Wight and Taunton, both to the Conservatives. Against this were six gains from the Conservatives, while the by-election capture of Romsey was retained. There was also a gain from Labour, at Chesterfield, which was taken by Paul Holmes. Many years before, the seat had been held by Barnet Kenyon, last of the miners' MPs to take the Liberal whip. More recently Chesterfield had been Tony Benn's seat, but he stood down in 2001. Benn had often been treated as something of a bogey man by his political opponents, but he was also a hard-working and popular constituency MP, and attracted a strong personal vote. The seat had been changing radically in character, and by the beginning of the twenty-first century it had become largely a middle-class dormitory. The Lib Dem gains from Conservatives were also striking. Cheadle, captured by Patsy Calton, had been marginal between the two parties for a long time. The other gains were in new territory, which had no recent record as Liberal seats. Guildford, taken by Sue Doughty; Ludlow, captured by Matthew Green; Mid-Dorset and North Poole, won by Annette Brooke; North Norfolk, gained by Norman Lamb; and Teignbridge, taken by Richard Younger-Ross. North Norfolk had last returned a Liberal MP in 1910, Guildford in 1906 and Ludlow in 1885.

The considerable progress made by Lib Dems both in 1997 and in 2001 was essentially the result of persuading supporters in hopeful constituencies to work effectively, not the result of funnelling activists in from outside. That had been an important factor in some of the by-elections, and had occurred to some extent in earlier General Elections, but it only took place to a limited degree on those two occasions. Tactical voting and successful 'targeting' both appear to have been important. In all seats which the Lib Dems gained from Conservatives, the Labour vote declined, in some cases dramatically so. In the four rural Dorset seats, 'tactical voting' was developed in a sophisticated manner. In 1997, all four had been Conservative, but without an overall majority in any of them. The Lib Dems had run a close second in three and Labour a close second in the other. A Labour-sympathising pop celebrity, Billy Bragg, opened a web site proposing vote exchanges between Labour and Lib Dem supporters, seeking to unseat as many Conservatives as possible. Whether as a consequence of this initiative or for other reasons, Labour was able to capture South Dorset with a considerable slump in the Lib Dem vote, while the Lib Dems were able to capture Mid Dorset and Poole North, with a corresponding slump in the Labour vote.

The local elections of 2001 were held on the same day as the General Election and this may have distorted the result in various ways. On the whole, the Conservatives improved their standing, while Liberal Democrats and Labour both lost ground. But the spring local elections in 2002 and 2003 showed a pattern markedly different from most of the previous decade, when the fortunes of Lib Dems and Labour had tended more or less to march together. On the two most recent occasions, the Conservatives made substantial, though not enormous, overall gains: around 238 seats in 2002, around 565 in the following year. Most of those gains were at the expense of Labour, while the Lib Dems also contrived to make overall gains, though on a more modest scale: 42 seats in 2002, nearly 200 in 2003.

Since the 2001 General Election, the close association between the Lib Dems and the Labour leadership which was crumbling long before, has broken down completely. Interviewed in September 2003, Charles Kennedy declared that 'the distancing is complete'.[22] The very limited nature of the results from the Joint Consultative Committee set up in 1997 has already been noted; but the committee continued in existence until September 2001, when the Lib Dems withdrew. A year later, Kennedy became the first non-Labour leader to address the TUC's annual conference, thus encroaching on territory long regarded as exclusive to the Labour Party, and he appears to have been well received. John Monks, the General Secretary, indicated that the TUC sought to foster alliances beyond its traditional links with Labour. This development may lead to nothing; but it may represent the first step in a major political change.

Soon there were other signs of a widening gap between Lib Dems and the Blair government. After the famous 11 September 2001 attacks in the United States, the Bush administration took this as the occasion to declare a 'war on terrorism' whose first phase was a military assault on the real or believed headquarters of Al Qaida terrorists in Afghanistan. This action received support form the British Government, but began to shake the loyalty of Paul Marsden, Labour MP for Shrewsbury and Atcham, who disagreed profoundly. Later in the year, Marsden defected to the Lib Dems, criticising in particular the 'continual freakery and spin' of the government. Liberal Democrat reactions were by no mean unanimous. Marsden had been in close contact with Lembit Öpik and Matthew Green, Lib Dem MPs for constituencies contiguous with his own, and his defection was at once welcomed by Charles Kennedy; but Simon Hughes expressed public concern, contending that it would have been more appropriate for him to sit as an independent for the duration of the current Parliament.[23]

This individual decision was followed some months later by disagreement between the Lib Dems and the government on a much wider issue. In the second half of 2002, signs began to appear that the United States government contemplated military action in Iraq, with the primary object of inducing 'régime change' – that is, toppling the dictator Saddam Hussein. There were also signs that the Blair government proposed to cooperate with the Americans in this action, while the Lib Dems, like many Labour MPs and a number of Conservatives, viewed the prospect of war in Iraq with great concern.

Resolutions at the Lib Dem annual conference at Brighton in September 2002, and the 'keynote' speech by Kennedy, left no doubt of the party's attitude on the matter. Lib Dems deplored the Saddam Hussein government as much as anybody, but they held that military action by outsiders would create a most dangerous precedent unless it was performed with the full authority of the United Nations, and could well lead to long-term consequences of a most appalling kind. In the Lib Dem view, the UN is far from perfect, but it is the only world organisation which exists and anything which tends to undermine its authority presents incalculable risks for the future. These views continued to be maintained as Britain slid into war as America's vassal. In February 2003, Kennedy was one of the speakers at a great rally which formed the culmination of a march of a million people protesting against the imminent war. In the following month, an amendment declaring that the case for war was 'not yet proven' was debated in the House of Commons. 52 Lib Dem MPs were present, and voted for the amendment, in which they were supported by 139 Labour and fifteen Conservative MPs, plus a further eleven from minor parties.

In the summer of 2003, the death of a Labour MP precipitated a by-election in the apparently safe outer London constituency of Brent East. The Lib Dem position seemed very weak. At the General Election two years earlier, they had run a poor third, with just over 3000 votes. When the new campaign began, there were no Lib Dem councillors in the constituency (though a Conservative councillor soon defected), and the local organisation was poor. The Lib Dems decided to make a massive effort. As a result the Lib Dem candidate Sarah Teather was victorious with a 28 per cent swing. However interpreted, it was an astonishing victory, and seemed to justify Charles Kennedy's claim that 'there is no such thing as a no-go area for the Lib Dems'. In the previous few years, they had proved that they were capable of capturing what looked like impregnable seats from both Labour and Conservatives.

A little later, by-elections followed in two other Labour constituencies where the Lib Dem had run third in 2001: Leicester South, and the Hodge Hill division of Birmingham. In Leicester South the Liberal Democrat was victorious, in Hodge Hill he came a close second, within 500 votes of the elected Labour candidate. A further by-election occurred at the end of September 2004 in Hartlepool, another seemingly impregnable Labour seat, where also the Lib Dem had run third, substantially behind the Conservative, in 2001. This time Labour retained the seat, but with the Lib Dem a couple of thousand votes behind. As for the Conservatives, they were reduced to fourth place, behind the United Kingdom Independence Party.

Yet the Lib Dems have fared less well in some other recent contests. On 10 June 2004, elections were held simultaneously for the Euro-Parliament, for the Mayor and Assembly of Greater London, and for some of the English and Welsh local councils. Considering only the votes polled, the Lib Dems ran fourth in the Euro-elections, third in the London elections and second in the English and Welsh local elections. A great deal is still wide open.

Whatever else has happened since the General Election of 2001, the Lib Dems have begun to take a new view of themselves and their own future. For the first time in the lifetime of most people, the prospect of Liberals becoming the alternative government within the foreseeable future does not appear ridiculous to outside observers. The fixed points of politics from which everybody used to navigate are beginning to vanish, and the situation is far more fluid than it has been since the Second World War. In the last decade, great changes have taken place in the Labour Party, and it appears likely that equally great changes will soon take place in the Conservative Party. At the same time, ordinary voters are far less firmly attached to their traditional allegiances than for many years. Lib Dems have enormous opportunities; but it remains to be seen whether those opportunities will be realised.

21

Reflections

In short, wee may gather out of History a policy no lesse wise than eternall; by the comparison and application of other men's fore-passed miseries, with our owne like errours and ill deseruings.

Sir Walter Raleigh

The reasons for the varied fortunes of the Liberal Party and its successor have been the subject of much historical study and continuing controversy. What has caused people either to join, or to desert, the Liberals? Both parts of the question require attention.

The strongest bond between the disparate politicians who came together to form the Liberal Party in the 1850s and 1860s was a common belief in Free Trade, underpinned by Gladstonian ideas about the management of public finance, and a disposition to favour 'reform' in various areas. In the late 1860s and the 1870s, Liberals developed a strong concern to remedy the most obvious grievances of the Irish people, and a firm conviction that foreign policy should be based on moral principles and not just perceived British interests. By this time, the nonconformist element in the Liberal Party was becoming increasingly influential, and concern for causes which were particularly popular in nonconformist circles, like temperance and curtailment of privileges of the Anglican Church, was growing. In the 1880s, the Liberals became committed to Irish Home Rule, and showed a deepening interest in social reform. In the early twentieth century, interest in ameliorating the condition of the poor and deprived by state action had become much stronger and the idea of radical land reform, which had been growing in Liberal circles right back to the 1880s, became general in the party.

By the time of the Campbell-Bannerman – Asquith government, Liberals with a philosophical bent were coming to develop a sort of political *Weltanschauung*. The principle underlying their thinking was the general idea of liberty. 'I was brought up to distrust and dislike liberty. I learnt to believe in it. That is the key to all my changes', declared Gladstone in a private conversation in the last decade of his life.[1] That idea persisted. 'There is no man alive who is sufficiently good to rule the life of the man next door to him', observed Hopkin Morris, the most impeccable of Liberal MPs, around 1950. In the twenty-first century, the idea remained. 'We want less government and less interference in people's lives. We favour more choice and a better chance', asserted Charles Kennedy in 2003.[2] Liberals were disposed to derive many of their policies from this principle. Free Trade, in the sense in which the term was traditionally used (very different from the meaning which is often given to the same words today) was a natural corollary. So was the idea of land value taxation, and a general preference for direct to indirect taxation. Liberals freely endorsed the need for a great deal of 'welfare' legislation designed to achieve a rough-and-ready rectification of past injustices; but they never lost sight of the need to create a system which would be prove largely self-regulating. In areas outside the field of economics, Liberals were also anxious to promote the cause of liberty. Without proper influence over the formation of laws which they were required to obey, people could hardly be called free. On that principle most Liberals had come by 1914 to accept the principle of universal franchise. They were also moving towards the view that colonial people had a right to self-government, long before that view was universally acknowledged. The decision to grant what would later be called 'dominion status' to South Africa was in some ways ill-starred, but the principle behind it was sound. Montagu's Indian policy during the Coalition period showed great vision.

After 1922, when Liberals would have wished to take up the 'unfinished business' of the pre-war Asquith government, it was necessary to counter actual retrogression which had occurred in the interval: qualifications to Free Trade through the McKenna Duties and the 'Safeguarding' legislation; repeal of the land valuation. It was also urgently necessary to counter the chronic unemployment of the inter-war period. A person who is willing to work, but cannot get a job, is not free in any meaningful sense of the word. The Liberal Party therefore addressed itself to the problem. 'We can conquer unemployment' was the slogan in 1929, and the Beveridge programme of 'full employment in a free society' profoundly influenced thinking in all parties in the 1940s.

In the aftermath of the 1914 war, there was widespread agreement that international relations should henceforth be governed by universal law, and each state should no longer act as judge in its own cause. Liberals could fairly claim that they had been acting on those lines for a very long time. It was natural that Liberals should give strong support to the League of Nations. After 1945 they gave similar support to the United Nations, which appeared to be built on a sounder basis.

We come to the second part of the original question. People have departed from the Liberal Party at various times and for various reasons.

The one nineteenth century mass-departure over a specific issue of policy arose over the Home Rule split of 1886, though even that schism was not really as clear as might at first appear. Some who remained with Gladstone, like Sir William Harcourt, can hardly be called enthusiastic Home Rulers, while Joseph Chamberlain on the other side appeared to stand at least half way in the Home Rule direction shortly before the split occurred. In the early 1880s many people had anticipated a division in Liberal ranks, but nobody would have guessed that Hartington and Chamberlain would be on one side of the great divide, with Gladstone, Granville and Dilke on the other.

After the Home Rule split of 1886 which occasioned the departure of the Liberal Unionists, various issues have arisen where Liberals have disagreed with each other. A few of these disagreements have produced large numbers of departures and consequential damage to the party; most have not. The Boer War of 1899–1902 resulted in great divisions of opinion within the Liberal Party, but no definite split. Just as the war was coming to an end, the Liberal League was set up. It had the makings of a schismatic body which would attract many people from the regular ranks of the party, but matters did not work out that way, and most of the principal members of the League were glad enough to cooperate fully with the rest of the party as soon as the Tariff Reform banner was raised. When the League was wound up in 1910, the event was scarcely noticed.

There were many differences between Liberals during the 1914 war, but it was not those differences which produced a major split in the party. Even the celebrated Maurice debate of May 1918 would have been almost forgotten today if it had not been for events immediately after the Armistice. It was when the Lloyd George Coalition continued into peacetime that the Liberal Party did indeed seem to be breaking apart. In a short time, the division between Coalition Liberals and 'Independent' or 'Asquithian' Liberals appeared unbridgeable. Yet the issue was whether some Liberal objectives should be sacrificed in order to secure success for others, not what the objectives of Liberalism ought to be. It was a dispute over strategy, not over principle, and it was quickly resolved, first by the collapse of the Coalition and then, a year later, by an issue which united all Liberals. The Liberal National secession of 1931 appeared at first to be another issue between compromisers and purists, both seeking to preserve as much Liberalism as possible in a difficult situation, but it eventually turned into a permanent rupture. The fact that some of most famous compromisers of the 1930s had been ultra-purists a dozen years earlier added poignancy to the situation. As with the Liberal Unionist split, but unlike the split of the Coalition period, the division proved permanent and final.

The most significant Liberal division on a policy question which arose after 1945 was the disagreement over British membership of the European Common Market in the 1960s and 1970s. A glance at the voting figures, whether at Liberal Assemblies or in the House of Commons, suggests that anti-Market Liberals were an insignificant minority; in truth the division within the Liberal Party, like the division within both other parties, was a good deal more equal than such numbers suggest. A few Liberal anti-Marketeers dropped out of politics altogether; nobody of note joined another party. As Oliver Smedley, a Vice-President of the party and best known of the Liberal anti-Marketeers, put it, 'Where else can we go?'

The Liberal Unionist secession of the 1880s and the Liberal National secession of the 1930s may therefore be regarded as the two great occasions on which a major disagreement on policy led to large-scale departures from the Liberal Party in a different political direction. The first of these splits goes a long way towards explaining the Liberal weakness in the twenty years after 1886; the second goes some way towards explaining why the Liberal Party, which was already in a parlous state in 1931, declined even more rapidly thereafter.

Yet no disagreement over long-term policy suffices to explain the Liberals' decline from being the party of government in 1914 to their wretched condition a decade later, which must be explained in other ways. That decline is clearly related to the rise in the Labour Party. There are two main theories which seek to explain the change, both of which have been strenuously argued by historians. First of these is what might be called the 'strange death' theory, deriving from George Dangerfield's book *The Strange Death of Liberal England*, which appeared in 1936. This argues that the Liberal Party was already showing signs of inevitable decline before 1914. The Great War accelerated, but did not cause, that decline. The theory has Marxist overtones: the *bourgeois* Liberal Party was bound to cede place to the proletarian Labour Party. The second theory, which might be called the 'bus' theory, was argued in Trevor Wilson's 1966 book, *The Downfall of the Liberal Party, 1914–1935*. Certainly the Liberal patient had some health problems before 1914 – what patient doesn't? – but whether those problems would prove mortal was never determined, because he was run over by a bus – the 1914 war. Perhaps significantly, the dust-cover of the book shows a picture of Lloyd George.

The present author does not wholly accept either view. In his judgement, Lloyd George – in some ways the best, in other ways the worst, of the twentieth century Liberals – deserves to be shown on Trevor Wilson's dust-cover, but a number of other Liberals, including some of his most vehement opponents, deserve to be there as well. Before 1914 several afflictions, including self-inflicted wounds, had troubled the patient, and these afflictions made it more difficult for him to recover from the impact of the bus. He also sustained a number of blows subsequent to the impact which severely delayed his recovery from the initial accident. Nor did the bus kill him: at the beginning of the twenty-first century, by this time almost a sesquicentenarian, he appears in better health than he has been for a long time;

Liberal afflictions sustained before 1903 may safely be excluded from the diagnosis, because by the General Election of 1906 the patient appeared in general good health, and there was only one serious adverse symptom: the election of 29 LRC MPs who, along with one Lib-Lab, constituted themselves the Labour Party. The large majority of those MPs evidently owed their election to the Herbert Gladstone – Ramsay MacDonald pact of 1903, and Liberal forbearance in their constituencies. Inspection of figures suggests that a small LRC contingent, perhaps half a dozen, would have been returned whatever the Liberals had done about it, but certainly not enough to constitute a serious political party, or to attract the Mineworkers' Federation from its Liberal moorings a couple of years later. The damage done was still not irreparable, and there is plenty of evidence that in the period 1910 to 1914 it was the Labour Party, not the Liberal Party, which was grievously sick.[3] The Liberals could probably have removed the threat altogether by a judicious mixture of carrot for those Labour supporters who were prepared to join them in a common cause, and stick for the recalcitrants.

The great disaster for millions of human beings, and for the Liberal Party as well, was the British decision to engage in the 1914 war. In the view of the present author, that decision was neither necessary nor right.[4] This is not the place to discuss whether that judgement was correct or not. But whether the decision to declare war was right or wrong, it was disaster all the way for the Liberals thereafter. Concessions to Unionist sensitivities at the beginning destroyed the best chance of applying Home Rule, and saving Ireland from complete alienation. Other concessions took the heart out of the land reformers who had been the most active and positive element in pre-1914 Liberalism. Further concessions followed formation of the first Coalition in 1915. The thin end of the Protectionist wedge was soon inserted, and military conscription followed a few months later. More concessions of Liberal principles followed formation of the second Coalition in 1916, and by the end of the war the Liberal Party seemed to have lost its sense of purpose and vision for the future.

In the four years which followed the war, the Lloyd Georgeites were impossibly entangled with the Conservatives, while the some of the Asquithians – not Asquith himself – were too busy conducting an internecine party feud to look to the great outside. There were notable achievements of a truly Liberal kind during the Coalition period, but events of those four years nearly completed the Liberal ruin. When the 1922 General Election gave Labour more MPs than the two Liberal groups combined, that development owed little to the inherent attractiveness of the Labour Party, but much to the Liberal feuding. Who could expect a young person who came on the register in 1918 to feel enthusiasm for a party whose leading figures were constantly at loggerheads?

Baldwin's conversion to Protectionism in 1923 gave the Liberals an opportunity which – properly handled – might well have saved them many of the consequences of earlier mistakes. At first the Liberals acted wisely, and achieved general reconciliation within their own ranks. After the supervening election, however, they took the disastrous decision to allow Labour to take office, instead of striking out for power themselves. Whether they would have succeeded in such an attempt, nobody can tell; but it was well worth the try. The period of the first Labour government witnessed more internecine Liberal feuding, this time over party finances. The *dénouement* came at the 1924 General Election. Credit for the quite considerable achievements of that government in a Liberal direction went to the Labour Party; blame for its failures was visited largely on the Liberals. The field of Liberal candidates was so small that everybody could see there was no prospect of a Liberal government in the aftermath. Liberal representation was almost quartered. The fundamental error had been for Liberals to allow themselves to be pushed into a position where they had to choose between Conservative and Labour policies, rather than to advance their own policies. Inevitably, some Liberals preferred one of the opposing parties, and other Liberals preferred the other.

The revival of the later 1920s was possible because, at last, the Liberals addressed themselves to the need to provide Liberal solutions to current problems. But the accident of a new balance-of-power situation in 1929, followed by the further accident of the Great Depression a few months later, wrecked most of the good that had been done. By mid-1931, the Liberals were facing the fearful choice between a Labour Government which was manifestly incompetent in dealing with economic disaster and a Conservative Opposition which was becoming daily more avid for Protection. Even before the National Government was formed, the Liberals had begun to split.

When the National Government was established in August, the stricken Lloyd George missed a real opportunity to limit damage and isolate Simon and his two confederates by recommending a broad range of the other Liberals for inclusion in the government. Instead, he made a lopsided selection. This inevitably meant that able and ambitious men with some claim on preferment who had been excluded despaired of any advancement through the ranks of the official party, and many were willing to join Simon when he raised the Liberal National banner.

The 1931 General Election was fought in conditions of more than usual confusion. Lloyd George rightly perceived that the real issue was Free Trade versus Protection. Otherwise, why call a General Election at all, when the government had an adequate majority to take whatever emergency measures it deemed necessary to deal with the crisis which had brought it into existence? If the Liberals had followed Lloyd George's lead and gone into opposition immediately the decision to call and election was taken, they would probably have suffered much electoral damage; but the bulk of the party would have been united, and the survivors would have been ready to form the nucleus of a real Free Trade opposition.

Having lost that opportunity for taking a clear stand in 1931, the Liberals were soon presented with another one, when the decision was taken early in the following year to go for tariffs. Free Traders could have broken with the government on a clear issue of principle, and crossed into opposition. They might even have been able to force another General Election, with the Free Trade issue set squarely before the public. The 'agreement to differ' on the tariff question involved no concession of substance by the Protectionists, for the result was a foregone conclusion. The Liberal rank-and-file, working through the NLF, showed a good deal more wisdom than their leaders and evinced visible disquiet at the decision to remain in the government. Even the Ottawa agreements later in the year, though they drove the Samuelites out of the government, did not suffice to make them cross the floor into opposition.

For most of the 1930s, there was no major issue on which Liberals could make a distinctive appeal. The darkening international situation was not such an issue, for the great division of opinion ran within, not between, the parties. Sinclair, Churchill and Attlee leaned one way; Samuel, Chamberlain and Lansbury leaned the other. Unlike its predecessor, the 1939 war did not produce any great Liberal splits; but the 1945 General Election was a further disaster for the party. The main consolation from the Liberal point of view was the substantial influx of young and able supporters, and a brief revival followed. No doubt part of the reason for this revival was negative. There were many people who disliked the class basis of both other parties. They were appalled at the Conservative record in the 1930s, yet opposed the prospect of wholesale nationalisation to which the Labour Party was then committed. There was a great freshness among Liberals in that period. Older people were impressed by the calibre of the newcomers, and all concerned felt themselves engaged in the challenging and exciting task of re-establishing Liberalism as a major force in politics.

The euphoria did not last. The Conservatives contrived to develop a new and more attractive image; the Labour Government, like others before it, worked itself out of a job. Many Liberals became convinced that the Conservatives were liberalised, while others admired the social welfare legislation of the Labour Government, whatever reservations they may have felt about other items of its programme. The Liberal MPs were few in number, and most of the famous names in the Party were not included among them. By 1947 the post-war Liberal revival was faltering. The dreadful electoral results of the 1950s convinced most people, including many Liberals, that the party had no future at all. If the Conservatives had chosen to oppose all the existing Liberal MPs in 1951 and 1955, that gloomy assessment might well have proved correct.

Since the mid-1950s. there has been a substantial revival which is as remarkable as the decline which preceded it. Part of the explanation of this revival seems to be the diminishing difference between the two great parties. If Conservatives and Labour had become so similar, why should Liberals compromise their principles by voting for one to keep out the other? From time to time, this was reinforced by particular incidents which threw great doubt on the argument that other parties been 'liberalised'. The Suez expedition of 1956 was a spectacular example. Many Conservatives were shocked, and this goes some way towards explaining Mark Bonham-Carter's capture of Torrington in 1958. That victory was soon reversed; but Jeremy Thorpe's victory in the contiguous constituency of North Devon at the 1959 General Election proved that it was possible for the right candidate with a good organisation and a vigorous campaign in the right constituency to win in the teeth of opposition from both other parties. From then on it was a slow and interrupted climb back to a position of influence.

The sensational Liberal victory at Orpington in 1962 and later successes at Roxburgh and Ladywood were possible because there was already a good Liberal organisation when the vacancy occurred, and it was possible to pour outside assistance into the constituency. Such events encouraged Liberals to believe that their cause was not lost; but in 1970 they were back again to six seats. In the early 1970s they benefited from the growing unpopularity of the Heath government and were able to score four impressive by-election victories. From the first 1974 General Election onwards they were always in double figures, and their MPs had always faced opposition from both other parties.

The end of the 1970s and the 1980s brought a great change in the political scene. Margaret Thatcher became Prime Minister and Michael Foot became Leader of the Labour Party. Here was real political polarisation; and yet, from the Liberal point of view, the effect was exactly the reverse of the polarisation of the late 1940s and early 1950s. This time both major parties began to lose support, and the Liberals profited.

Liberals had long believed that there were many people in other parties whose natural place was in their own ranks. The beginnings of the SDP secession from the Labour Party in 1980 and 1981, and the formation of the Alliance, seemed to confirm that view. At first the Alliance made dramatic progress at the expense of both Conservative and Labour Parties, but then it fell back considerably. The two Alliance Parties were nevertheless able to make great headway in votes at the 1983 General Election. Results in terms of seats won were far less encouraging. The Liberals made some progress, though nothing like as much as would have been expected a couple of years earlier. The SDP fared much worse, and a large majority of the Labour MPs who had defected were unseated. Roy Jenkins's departure from the SDP leadership in the immediate aftermath was really an admission of failure, and the appointment of Owen as his inevitable successor was a disaster from the point of view of all who wished the two parties to work closely together.

In the period between the General Elections of 1983 and 1987 the Alliance was able to make considerable headway at by-elections, and yet no progress at all was made in the direction of establishing a permanent relationship between the two parties. If they were sufficiently close to support each other's candidates, why were they not sufficiently close to join together? At best, there was a duplication of organisation. It is easy to say that the fault lay with David Owen; that any other possible SDP leader would have handled matters very differently. That, however, is only part of the answer, for it is also likely that a firm stand by the Liberals early in that Parliament could have resolved the matter. As Harcourt and Rosebery had demonstrated in the 1890s, and as Asquith and Lloyd George had demonstrated in the mid-1920s, dual leadership of a political movement by two strong-willed men with very different long-term aspirations is unlikely to work.

The 1987 General Election campaign proved beyond dispute that current arrangements could not last, and both Alliance parties were fortunate that the differences between their respective leaders were not recognised more clearly by the electorate at large. Those close to the centre of the campaign could see how unsatisfactory the existing state of affairs was, and prominent Liberals immediately set to work to force the pace. Either there must be fusion of the two parties or they must go their separate ways. It was touch and go which course would be followed, and at one point separation seemed the likelier result. The eventual upshot was amalgamation, but a substantial number of able people in both parties found the arrangement unpalatable, and were soon driven out of serious politics altogether. In spite of this, the amalgamation succeeded in the long term, and at the dawn of the twenty-first century it had become impossible to discern from current political attitudes which members derived from one source and which from the other. There is also a substantial generation of active Lib Dem workers who were much too young to have had any serious interest in politics when the fusion took place, and for whom events of the 1980s are remote history.

It has been said that the chief value of history is that it tells us so much about the future. Certainly the history of the Liberal Party and its successor provides many hints for the future: ways of making progress, pitfalls to be avoided.

In the period after 1945, when the party was at its lowest ebb, some Liberals had been disposed to take a kind of gloomy consolation in the view that their historic mission had been fulfilled, because both other parties had become 'liberalised'. Everybody supported the United Nations; everybody accepted Beveridge ideas about full employment. The idea that education should be much more widely accessible to all who were capable of benefiting from it was enshrined in the Act of 1944 promoted by the wartime Coalition Government. The idea that ownership of property should be much more generally distributed had been pressed by Liberals in the 1930s; in the aftermath of war it was widely supported. The idea that the peoples of colonies and other dependent territories should be entitled to self-government if they so desired seemed very radical before 1939; by the early 1960s hardly anybody in British politics seriously disputed it.

Even in that period there were other directions in which liberalisation was far from universal, and Liberals of the post-1945 period felt that they had a unique message to proclaim. The Liberal Party, its members decided, must be preserved because there was so much of its essential policy which no other party could be trusted to put into effect.

Events would show that even the degree of 'liberalisation' which appeared to have pervaded both other parties was in some important respects only skin-deep. The support for United Nations principles which everybody seemed to have endorsed in 1945 was violated by a Conservative Government in 1956 and by a Labour Government in 2003. Full employment – 'more jobs than there are people looking for jobs' – appeared to be an inflexible policy of Conservative and Labour Governments alike for thirty years. Then unemployment began to soar, first under the Labour Government of Callaghan, then – even more so – under the Conservative Government of Thatcher. The Blair administration at the turn of the millennium, to its credit, reduced the jobless figures very substantially; yet by the early twenty-first century they remain far above the level of 'frictional unemployment' contemplated by Beveridge so long ago.

Liberals therefore feel entitled to claim that they have a vital part to play in contemporary politics for two reasons: because some traditional Liberal policies are not even theoretically endorsed by other parties, and policies which once seemed to have been adopted universally are liable to be abandoned. The Liberal view on these points has been widely endorsed by the public in recent years, and the present Lib Dem representation in the House of Commons would have appeared to be far beyond all realistic hopes not many years ago. A Liberal government remains the long-term objective of many members of the Party, but cannot be expected in the near future. Liberals have often, therefore, considered whether some of their immediate policy objectives can be secured in some other way. May corners be cut?

At various times, some kind of coalition or understanding between Liberals and supporters of one of the larger parties has been recommended, or actually applied, but, without exception, the experience of peacetime arrangements of that kind has been profoundly discouraging. In addition to the cases where coalitions actually came into existence, there have been others where they were seriously bruited. Churchill had wished to include Lady Violet Bonham-Carter in his 1951 government, and actually offered a place to Clement Davies. If Lady Violet had been elected in Colne Valley, or if Clement Davies had been less loyal to his Liberal colleagues, the fatal step would have been taken. Those who remember Liberal feeling at the time, and particularly feeling among the Party's younger and more active members, will appreciate that the continued existence of the Liberal Party would have been in doubt if Liberals had joined a predominantly Conservative government.

The possibility of some sort of understanding with the Labour Party was raised twice in the late twentieth century, and in both cases the upshot was discouraging. The so-called 'Lib-Lab Pact' of the 1970s was ended with sighs of relief from both quarters. In the second half of the 1990s, close cooperation appeared to be developing between Paddy Ashdown and Tony Blair. But for Ashdown's very candid published diaries, not much might be known for certain about the reactions of parliamentarians, but it is now evident that what was called 'the Project', which pointed towards the inclusion of Lib Dems in a Blair Cabinet, would have been fatal to the Lib Dems, at the very moment when they were poised to achieve very substantial advances in their parliamentary representation.

Although inclusion of Liberals in governments composed mainly of people with different political affiliations has usually proved disastrous, it has sometimes been suggested that Liberals might benefit from such an arrangement if it were conducted on a *quid pro quo* basis. Liberals, for example, have a strong interest in electoral reform, partly because they consider it is desirable on its merits and partly because it would be likely to improve their own parliamentary position. In all General Elections from 1935 onwards, Liberals have returned far fewer MPs than their support among the electorate warranted. But it would be exceedingly difficult for a government of another party to deliver on such a bargain, even if it honestly desired to do so. It would be vulnerable to revolts by its own backbenchers, and to delaying tactics by the House of Lords. Furthermore, even the most qualified support for a government of a different political colour is likely to generate tensions among Liberals – as Asquith, Lloyd George, Samuel, Steel and Ashdown all discovered. Experience also suggests that Liberals who enter some kind of coalition government – even Liberals with an impeccable record of devotion to Liberal principles – will be under a strong temptation to remain in office. In politics, no course of action is without disadvantages; but the safest and best course is complete independence.

If the Lib Dems find themselves in a position of power, what will they do with that power? For fifty years, that question was purely academic; now it is not. During a large part of those fifty years, the Liberals and their successors have dealt with political problems largely on a short-term basis. Many of the proposals which they have made have been concerned with some current issue, rather than expressions of long-term aspirations. Perhaps they had little alternative. Most people were not interested in the long-term policies of the Liberal Party, because they did not consider that Liberals would ever have the chance of implementing those policies. On the other hand they could sometimes be persuaded to vote Liberal for essentially short-term reasons.

Now matters are changing. The larger the Lib Dem representation becomes, the more insistently voters will demand to know what sort of long-term policies they will pursue. Comparisons might be drawn with the early history of the Labour Party. Down to 1918, when they seemed to have no prospect of becoming the government of the country in the near future, if ever, Labour gave little thought to long-term policies. In the last year of the Great War they suddenly realised that a Labour Government was a serious possibility, and addressed the task of devising a programme for such a government. The Lib Dems are now in a rather similar position to Labour at that time, and the sooner they get down to the job of proposing action which a Lib Dem government would seek to pursue in a full term of office, the less the risk that they will fall at that last hurdle.

It is worth considering how much of traditional Liberal policy is still 'unfinished business' today. Of course many of the things for which Liberals fought best part of a century ago have long been swept aside by events; but a surprising lot have not, and are likely to interest a modern electorate.

Gladstonian financial principles are every bit as relevant today as they were in the past. People of all political persuasions are conscious that an enormous amount of public money, even money which is earmarked for thoroughly worthy and necessary causes, is in fact wasted, and goes to feed a self-sustaining bureaucracy. The principle that public money is a trust which should always be spent with great care is still valid, even though few modern Chancellors of the Exchequer, Labour or Conservative, have shown much sign of acting on that principle. The idea that taxation should be col-lected in a way which causes the minimum disruption of useful economic activities, not on the principle of extracting the maximum number of feath-ers from the goose for the minimum number of squawks, is as valid as it has ever been. Clearly stated, and linked to practical taxation measures, it is likely to be popular. Many Lib Dems believe, for example, that the taxation of land values, towards which Asquith's government was moving in 1914, is both feasible and desirable. It would allow existing taxes which damage the economy to abate, and would produce a great many sometimes unexpected beneficial side-effects.

Modern Lib Dems will find it useful to examine other old Liberal poli-cies. 'Trade with all, friendship with all, alliance with none' is a good basis for both foreign policy and international trading policy. The fact that the time-honoured words 'Free Trade' are sometimes used today in a pejorative sense which nobody on either side of past controversies would have recog-nised should not preclude people of our own time from re-examining Free Trade in its original meaning. The cry, 'We can Conquer Unemployment' is highly relevant still. Electoral reform for central and local government is as necessary as ever, and Lib Dems could usefully study the form of Pro-portional Representation which Liberals traditionally favoured, which has many advantages over the expedients which have recently been applied in regional and Euro-elections.

Lib Dems may also learn from the past on matters of party organisation. The idea of 'community politics', as we have seen, is simply a restatement in contemporary terms of practices which were applied by Liberals in Birm-ingham in the 1870s. Where this strategy has been applied with vigour, it has proved exceedingly beneficial both in local and in national contests.

It is useful, however, to consider some implications which are not always clearly drawn. Today, there are numerous cases where one constituency returns a Lib Dem MP, while in the constituency next door, where the social distribution is very similar, and considerations which interest the electors are also very similar, the Lib Dem fares badly. The constituency which is now Southwark North and Bermondsey returns a Lib Dem MP with a large majority, and has done so for two decades; in other nearby constituencies with similar largely working class electorates the Lib Dem candidate performs poorly. Carshalton and Wallington is a Lib Dem constituency; in adjacent Croydon South, which is a similar outer London suburban area, the Lib Dem runs third. In the very bleakest days, Cardiganshire looked like the safest Liberal constituency in the UK, while contiguous Brecon and Radnor, after an abominable result in 1950, was not fought at all for many years. Today what is now called Ceredigion has been lost, while Brecon and Radnor returns a Lib Dem MP. Equally sharp comparisons between neighbouring areas may be drawn from local government. Such facts reinforce Charles Kennedy's judgement that there are no 'no-go areas' for Lib Dems; but they also warn against complacency. It might be worth Lib Dems reflecting on one of the positive achievements in the generally unhappy 1940s: how eager but inexperienced Liberals were encouraged and taught to build up local organisations where little or nothing existed.

Insofar as guidance may be drawn from past experience, the prospect for Lib Dems in the foreseeable future is completely open. They could slip back into insignificance; or they may become the government of the country. One conclusion, however, emerges strongly from a close study of the Liberal Party and its successor. Where there has been success, this has been due to the appropriateness of Liberal policies. Where there has been failure, that failure has been due not to the inadequacy of Liberalism but to the inadequacy of Liberals.

Appendix

The date of formation of the Liberal Party is arbitrary; but this is here taken to be 1859, the date of the Willis's Rooms meeting. Throughout the nineteenth century, and until well into the twentieth, there was no regular method of appointment of a leader; but it was assumed that anyone invited to constitute a government composed of Liberals was the Party Leader, and remained so until death or resignation, or until somebody else headed a Liberal government. Thus a substantial period could elapse without a Leader, and at that time the Chairmen, or Leaders, of the party in the House of Commons and the House of Lords divided the functions between them. When Lloyd George became Prime Minister in 1916, Asquith continued to be acknowledged as Party Leader, and remained so until his retirement in 1926. Then there was no formal appointment of a new leader, but for all practical purposes the functions of leadership were exercised by Lloyd George, though his official rank remained no more than chairman of the MPs.

Thereafter the chairman of the MPs, who was chosen by the MPs alone, continued to be treated as leader of the Liberal Party for many years to come. It was not until 1976 that a new method of election of a definitive party leader was devised. MPs could nominate candidates for the post of leader, but the choice between those candidates lay with the rank-and-file of the party membership. When the Social and Liberal Democrats, later known as the Liberal Democrats, were formed in 1988, a similar method of selection for new leaders was adopted.

Liberal Party

1859	3rd Viscount Palmerston (second Ministry)
1865	1st Earl Russell (second Ministry)
1868	William Ewart Gladstone
1875	Chairman of the MPs: Marquis of Hartington;

Chairman of the Peers, 2nd Earl Granville.

1880	William Ewart Gladstone
1894	5th Earl of Rosebery
1896	Chairman of the MPs: Sir William Harcourt (succeeded by Sir Henry Campbell-Bannerman 1899); Chairman of the Peers 1st Earl of Kimberley (succeeded by 5th Earl Spencer 1902)
1905	Sir Henry Campbell-Bannerman
1908	Herbert Henry Asquith (Earl of Oxford and Asquith 1925)
1926	David Lloyd George (1st Earl Lloyd-George 1945)
1931	Sir Herbert Samuel (1st Viscount Samuel 1937)
1935	Sir Archibald Sinclair (1st Viscount Thurso 1952)
1945	(Edward) Clement Davies
1956	Joseph Grimond (Baron Grimond 1983)
1967	(John) Jeremy Thorpe
1976	Joseph Grimond (interim)
1976	David Martin Scott Steel (Baron Steel 1997)

Social and Liberal Democrats/ Liberal Democrats

1988	John Jeremy Durham ('Paddy') Ashdown (Baron Ashdown)
1999	Charles Peter Kennedy.

CHIEF WHIPS IN THE HOUSE OF COMMONS

Until well into the twentieth century, the duties of a Chief Whip included not only parliamentary responsibilities but also general control of the organisation of the party in the country through the office of Chairman of the Liberal Central Association. When the Liberal Party was in office, the Chief Whip became Patronage, later Parliamentary, Secretary to the Treasury.

Normally, the Chief Whip is appointed by the Leader, but there have been two exceptions. In 1919, Asquith appointed G. R. Thorne, but the Liberal MPs insisted on J. M. Hogge serving as joint Chief Whip with him. In 1935, the Chief Whip was elected by the MPs.

1852–58	Sir William Goodenough Hayter
1859	(Sir) Henry Bouverie William Brand (later Speaker of the House of Commons. 1st Viscount Hampden 1881; 23rd Baron Dacre 1890.)
1868	George Grenfell Glyn (1st. Baron Wolverton 1873)
1871–73	Arthur Peel (1st Viscount Peel, 1895)
1874	William Patrick Adam
1880	Lord Richard Grosvenor (1st Baron Stalbridge 1886)
1886	Arnold Morley
1892	Edward Marjoribanks (2nd Baron Tweedmouth 1894)
1894	Thomas Edward Ellis
1899	Herbert Gladstone (1st Viscount Gladstone 1910)
1905	George Whiteley (1st Baron Marchamley 1908)
1908	Joseph Albert Pease (1st Baron Gainford 1917)
1910	Alexander William Charles Oliphant Murray, Master of Elibank (1st Baron Murray, 1912)
1912	Percy Holden Illingworth
1915	John William Gulland
1919	George Rennie Thorne and James Myles Hogge
1923	Vivian Phillipps
1924	Sir Godfrey Collins
1926	Sir Robert Hutchison (1st Baron Hutchison 1932)
1930	Sir Archibald Sinclair (1st Viscount Thurso 1952)
1931	(Sir) Goronwy Owen

1931	(Sir) Walter Rea (1st Baron Rea 1937)
1935	Sir Percy Harris
1945	Thomas Lewis Horabin
1946	(Charles) Frank Byers (Baron Byers, life peer, 1964)
1950	Joseph Grimond (Baron Grimond, life peer, 1983)
1956	Donald Wade (Baron Wade, life peer, 1965)
1963	Eric Reginald Lubbock (4th Baron Avebury 1971)
1970	David Martin Scott Steel (Baron Steel, life peer, 1997)
1975	(Sir) Cyril Smith
1976	Alan Beith
1985	David Alton (Baron Alton, life peer, 1997)
1987	James Robert Wallace
1992	Archibald Johnstone Kirkwood
1997	Paul Tyler
2001	Andrew Stunell

BY-ELECTIONS AFFECTING LIBERAL REPRESENTATION
FROM 1901

Liberal Gains

Date	Constituency	Loser	Liberal MP
10 May 1902	Bury	Conservative	G. Toulmin
29 July 1902	Leeds North	Conservative	R. H. Barran
2 January 1903	Newmarket	Conservative	C. D. Rose
17 March 1903	Rye	Conservative	C. F. Hutchinson
26 August 1903	Argyll	Conservative	J. S. Ainsworth
17 September 1903	St Andrews Burghs	Liberal Unionist	E. C. Ellice
15 January 1904	Norwich	Conservative	L. J. Tillett
30 January 1904	Ayr Burghs	Conservative	J. Dobbie
12 February 1904	St Albans	Conservative	J. B. Slack
16 March 1904	Dorset East	Conservative	C. H. Lyell
20 June 1904	Devonport	Conservative	J. W. Benn
26 July 1904	Oswestry	Conservative	A. H. Bright
10 August 1904	Lanarkshire North-East	Liberal Unionist	A. Findlay
7 January 1905	Stalybridge	Conservative	J. F. Cheetham
26 January 1905	Dorset North	Conservative	A. W. Wills
3 March 1905	Bute	Conservative	N. Lamont
5 April 1905	Brighton	Conservative	E. A. Villiers
1 June 1905	Whitby	Conservative	N. E. Buxton
29 June 1905	Finsbury East	Conservative	J. A. Baker
3 August 1905	Barkston Ash	Conservative	J. O Andrews
24 May 1912	Hackney South	Independent Liberal	H. Morison
13 July 1912	Hanley	Labour	R. L. Outhwaite
23 December 1916	Sheffield Hallam	Conservative (collusive)	H. A. L. Fisher
1 March 1919	Leyton West	Coalition Unionist	A. E. Newbould
29 March 1919	Kingston upon Hull Central	Coalition Unionist	J. M. Kenworthy

Date	Constituency	Loser	Liberal MP
16 April 1919	Aberdeen and Kincardine Central	Coalition Unionist	M. M. Wood
3 June 1920	Louth (Lincolnshire)	Coalition Unionist	T. Wintringham
24 February 1922	Bodmin	Coalition Unionist	I. Foot
3 March 1923	Willesden East	Conservative	Harcourt Johnstone
7 June 1923	Anglesey	Independent Labour	Sir R. J. Thomas
21 June 1923	Tiverton	Conservative	F. D. Acland
28 March 1927	Southwark North	Labour	E. A. Strauss
3 May 1927	Bosworth	Conservative	Sir W. Edge
9 February 1928	Lancaster	Conservative	R. P. Tomlinson
6 March 1928	St Ives	Conservative	Hilda Runciman
28 June 1928	Carmarthen	Conservative	W. N. Jones
20 March 1929	Eddisbury	Conservative	R. J. Russell
21 March 1929	Holland with Boston	Conservative	J. Blindell
27 March 1957	Torrington	N.L. & Conservative	Mark Bonham-Carter
14 March 1962	Orpington	Conservative	Eric Lubbock
24 March 1965	Roxburgh, Selkirk and Peebles	Conservative	David Steel
26 June 1969	Birmingham Ladywood	Labour	Wallace Lawler
26 October 1972	Rochdale	Labour	Cyril Smith
7 December 1972	Sutton and Cheam	Conservative	Graham Tope
26 July 1973	Isle of Ely	Conservative	Clement Freud
26 July 1973	Ripon	Conservative	D. Rustick
29 March 1979	Liverpool Edge Hill	Labour	David Alton
22 October 1981	Croydon North-West	Conservative	William Pitt
24 February 1983	Southwark Bermondsey	Labour	Simon Hughes
4 July 1985	Brecon and Radnor	Conservative	Richard Livsey
8 May 1986	Ryedale	Conservative	Elizabeth Shields

Liberal Losses

Date	Constituency	Victor
26 September 1901	Lanarkshire North-East	Liberal Unionist
22 October 1902	Devonport	Conservative
24 July 1903	Barnard Castle	Labour Representation Committee
3 August 1906	Cockermouth	Conservative
26 February 1907	Brigg	Conservative
4 July 1907	Jarrow	Labour
18 July 1907	Colne Valley	Socialist
17 January 1908	Ashburton	Conservative
31 January 1908	Ross	Liberal Unionist
24 March 1908	Peckham	Conservative
24 April 1908	Manchester North-West	Conservative
20 June 1908	Pudsey	Conservative
1 August 1908	Haggerston	Conservative
25 September 1908	Newcastle upon Tyne	Conservative
2 March 1909	Glasgow Central	Conservative
4 May 1909	Sheffield Attercliffe	Labour
4 May 1909	Stratford-on-Avon	Conservative
15 July 1909	Mid-Derbyshire	Labour
28 October 1909	Bermondsey	Conservative
28 April 1911	Cheltenham	Conservative
13 November 1911	Oldham	Conservative
20 December 1911	Ayrshire North	Conservative
5 March 1912	Manchester South	Conservative
26 July 1912	Crewe	Conservative
8 August 1912	Manchester North-West	Conservative
10 September 1912	Edinburghshire	Conservative
16 May 1913	Newmarket	Conservative
8 November 1913	Reading	Conservative
12 December 1913	Lanarkshire South	Conservative

Date	Constituency	Victor
19 February 1914	Bethnal Green South-West	Conservative
26 February 1914	Leith Burghs	Conservative
23 May 1914	Ipswich	Conservative
2 November 1917	Salford North	Independent Labour
20 December 1919	Widnes	Labour (from Coalition Liberal)
7 February 1920	Wrekin	Independent (from Coalition Liberal)
27 March 1920	Dartford	Labour (from Coalition Liberal)
27 July 1920	Norfolk South	Labour (from Coalition Liberal)
4 March 1921	Kirkcaldy Burghs	Labour (from Coalition Liberal)
5 March 1921	Penistone	Labour
8 June 1921	Heywood and Radcliffe	Labour (from Coalition Liberal)
14 December 1921	Southwark South-East	Labour (from Coalition Liberal)
30 March 1922	Leicester East	Labour (from Coalition Liberal)
25 July 1922	Pontypridd	Labour (from Coalition Liberal)
18 October 1922	Newport	Conservative (from Coalition Liberal)
31 May 1923	Berwick-upon-Tweed	Conservative (from National Liberal)
5 June 1924	Oxford	Conservative
8–12 March 1926	English Universities	Conservative
29 November 1926	Kingston-upon-Hull Central	Labour
13 July 1928	Halifax	Labour
31 July 1929	Preston	Labour
7–12 March 1934	Scottish Universities	Liberal National
23 October 1934	Lambeth North	Labour
28 February 1957	Carmarthen	Labour

Social Democratic Party Gains
(No By-Election Losses)

Date	Constituency	Loser	SDP MP
26 November 1981	Crosby	Conservative	Shirley Williams
25 March 1982	Glasgow Hillhead	Conservative	Roy Jenkins
14 June 1984	Portsmouth South	Conservative	M. T. Hancock
26 February 1987	Greenwich	Labour	Rosie Barnes

Liberal Democrat Gains
(No By-Election Losses)

Date	Constituency	Loser	LD MP
18 October 1990	Eastbourne	Conservative	David Bellotti
7 March 1991	Ribble Valley	Conservative	M. Carr
7 November 1991	Kincardine and Deeside	Conservative	N. R. Stephen
6 May 1993	Newbury	Conservative	David Rendel
29 July 1993	Christchurch	Conservative	Diana Maddock
9 January 1994	Eastleigh	Conservative	David Chidgey
27 July 1995	Littleborough and Saddleworth	Conservative	C. Davies
4 May 2000	Romsey	Conservative	Sandra Gidley
18 September 2003	Brent East	Labour	Sarah Teather
15 July 2004	Leicester South	Labour	Parmit Singh Gill

GENERAL ELECTION RESULTS

In many cases, particularly in the early period, exact numbers are debatable.

Year	Liberal [a]	Conserva- tive [b]	Irish Nation alist [e]	Labour [c]	Others [d]	Total
1859	356	298	–	–	–	654
1865	369	289	–	–	–	658
1868	387	271	–	–	–	658
1874	242	350	60	–	–	652
1880	352	237	63	–	–	652
1885	335	249	86	–	4	670
1886	192 + 77	316	85	–	–	670
1892	273	268 + 45	81	–	3	670
1895	177	340 + 71	82	–	–	670
1900	184	334 + 68	82	2	–	670
1906	400	133 + 25	83	29	–	670
1910 Jan	275	241 + 32	82	40	–	670
1910 Dec	272	236 + 36	84	42	–	670
1918	30 + 132	332 + 48	7	4 + 60	12 + 82	707
1922	64 + 53	347	–	142	9	615
1923	158	258	–	191	8	615
1924	42	415	–	152	6	615
1929	59	260	–	288	8	615
1931	33 + 4 + 35	471	–	52 + 13	7	615
1935	21	387 + 33 + 8	–	154	12	615
1945	12	213	–	393	22	640
1950	9	298	–	315	3	625
1951	6	321	–	295	3	625
1955	6	344	–	277	3	630
1959	6	365	–	258	1	630
1964	9	304	–	317	–	630
1966	12	253	–	364	1	630
1970	6	330	–	287	7	630
1974 Feb	14	297	–	301	23	635
1974 Oct	13	277	–	319	26	635
1979	11	339	–	269	16	635
1983	17 + 6	397	–	209	21	650
1987	17 + 5	376	–	229	23	650

Year	Liberal [a]	Conservative [b]	Irish Nationalist [e]	Labour [c]	Others [d]	Total
1992	20	336	–	271	24	651
1997	46	165	–	419	29	659
2001	52	166	–	412	29	659

Notes

[a] In 1886, the first figure is of 'Gladstonians', the second of Liberal Unionists, who are added to the Liberal total because they proposed to continue taking the Liberal whip. In subsequent elections, Liberal Unionists are added to the Conservative total. In 1918, first figure is of Liberals elected without the 'Coupon', the second figure is of Liberals elected with the 'Coupon'. (whether or not they actually used it). In 1922 the first figure is 'official' Liberals, the second is National Liberals (Lloyd George). In 1931 the first figure is 'official' (Samuelite) Liberals, the second is 'independent' (Lloyd George) Liberals, the third is Liberal Nationals (Simonite). Liberal Nationals are added to the Liberal total for that election because it was believed, or hoped, that they would take the Liberal whip. In 1983 and 1987 the first figure is Liberals, the second SDP. From 1992 onwards the column is for Liberal Democrats.

[b] For elections from 1892 to December 1910, the first figure is of Conservatives, the second of Liberal Unionists. After the two parties formally united in 1912, the name 'Unionist' was commonly employed to describe them. but gradually dropped out of use in favour of 'Conservative'. In the 1918 General Election, the first figure is for Conservatives/Unionists elected with the 'Coupon', the second for those elected without it. Ulster Unionists are included in the Conservative total from 1918 until 1974, by which date the parties had formally separated. In the 1935 General Election the first figure is for Conservatives, the second for Liberal Nationals, the third for National Labour. In subsequent General Elections, no distinction is made between Conservatives and other MPs ('Liberal National', 'Liberal and Conservative', 'Conservative and National Liberal', etc.), who acted as Conservatives.

[c] In 1900, the two MPs in this column were elected under the aegis of the Labour Representation Committee. So were the 29 MPs elected in 1906, but after election they almost immediately constituted themselves the Labour Party. In the 1918 election, the first number (4) is of members elected with support of the Coalition, the second is of members without Coalition support. In the 1931 election, the first number is of MPs formally supported by the Labour Party, the second of erstwhile Labour MPs who were declared supporters of the National Government.

[d] In 1885, the four MPs in this column are sometimes counted as Liberals, sometimes as members of a 'Crofters' Party'. In 1892, the three MPs in this column may be described as 'Independent Labour'. In the 1918 election, the distinction is drawn between twelve MPs (ten of them members of the National Democratic Party) who had received the 'Coupon', and the remainder who had not. 73 seats at that election

were won by Sinn Féin, but in some cases a Sinn Féin candidate was elected for more than one constituency.

[e] The MPs elected as Irish Nationalists of various brands after 1918 are listed under 'Others'.

Notes

Notes to Chapter 1: Origins

1. See George L. Bernstein, 'The Origin of Liberal Politics, 1830–1874' *Journal of British Studies*, 28 (1989) pp. 75–89; T. A. Jenkins, *The Liberal Ascendancy, 1830–1886* (Basingstoke 1994).

2. See Elie Halévy, *The Liberal Awakening, 1815–1830* (London, 1961), pp. 81–82.

3. J. R. Vincent: *The Formation of the British Liberal Party, 1857–1865* (Hassocks 1970), p. 3.

4. For examples see H. J. Hanham, *Elections and Party Management: Politics in the Time of Disraeli and Gladstone* (Hassocks, 1978).

5. R. G. Thorne, *The House of Commons, 1790–1820* (London, 1986), ii, p. 436.

6. M. R. D. Foot, 'The Hawarden Kite', *Journal of Liberal Democrat History*, 20 (1998), p. 26.

7. See C. H. Stuart, 'The Formation of the Coalition Cabinet of 1852', *Transactions of the Royal Historical Society*, fifth series, 4 (1954), pp. 45–68.

8. A. J. P. Taylor, *Essays in English History* (1950), p. 110.

9. Anthony Taylor, 'Palmerston and Radicalism, 1847–1865', *Journal of British Studies*, 33 (1993), pp. 157–79.

10. Paul Smith, 'Ginger Beer or Champagne …', *Modern History Review*, 4 (1993), pp. 2–4.

11. 1 Samuel 22:2.

12. Henry Brand to W. E. Gladstone, 28 September 1868, BL, Add. MS 44194, fol. 107.

13. See M. Ostrogorski, *Democracy and the Organization of Political Parties* (London, 1902).

14. T. A. Jenkins, *The Liberal Ascendancy, 1830–1886* (Basingstoke, 1994), p. 39.

15. Henry Brand to W. E. Gladstone, 3 March 1860, BL, Add. MS 44193, fol. 10f.

16. G. W. T. Ormond, *The Lord Advocates of Scotland, 1834–1880* (1914), p. 245; cited in J. R. Vincent, *The Formation of the British Liberal Party*, p. 49.

Notes to Chapter 2: Exhausting the Volcanoes

1. R. V. Comerford, in *A New History of Ireland*, v (Oxford, 1989), p. 442.
2. See W. E. Vaughan, in *A New History of Ireland*, v, pp. 726–34.
3. Robert Blake, *Disraeli* (London, 1967), p. 523.
4. See F. W. S. Craig, *Chronology of British Parliamentary By-Elections, 1833–1987* (Chichester, 1987).
5. See David Thornley, *Isaac Butt and Home Rule* (London, 1964), esp. pp. 82f.
6. Thornley, *Isaac Butt and Home Rule*, pp. 148–53.
7. For the circumstances, see Anthony Denholm, *Lord Ripon, 1827–1909: A Political Biography* (London, 1982), pp. 106–13.
8. H. C. G. Matthews, ed., *The Gladstone Diaries, 1871–1874* (Oxford, 1982), pp. 442f.
9. Gladstone to Spencer, 6 February 1874, in Matthews, ed., *The Gladstone Diaries, 1871–1874*.
10. T. A. Jenkins, *Gladstone, Whiggery and the Liberal Party, 1874–1886* (Oxford, 1988), pp. 5–7.
11. Aaron Watson, *A Great Labour Leader: Being the Life of the Rt Hon. Thomas Burt MP* (London, 1908), p. 4.
12. Coleraine, Dungannon, County Down (one seat gained); County Londonderry (two seats gained.)
13. R. V. Comerford, in *A New History of Ireland*, vi, p. 13.

Notes to Chapter 3: In the Wilderness

1. See Allen Warren, 'The Return of Ulysses: Gladstone, Liberalism and Late Victorian Politics', *Parliamentary History*, 9 (1990) pp. 184–96; Matthew R. Temmel, 'Gladstone's Resignation of the Liberal Leadership, 1874–1875', *Journal of British Studies*, 16 (1976) pp. 153–75.
2. Patrick Jackson, *Education Act Forster* (London, 1997), p. 223.
3. Temmel, 'Gladstone's Resignation of the Liberal Leadership, 1874–1875', p. 170.
4. M. Ostrogorski, *Democracy and the Organization of Political Parties* (London, 1902), i, pp. 161f.
5. H. J. Hanham, *Elections and Party Management* (Hassocks 1978), pp. 125, 133.
6. Ostrogorski, *Democracy and the Organization of Political Parties*. pp. 173f.
7. F. H. Herrick, 'The Origins of the National Liberal Federation', *Journal of Modern History*, 17 (1945), pp. 116–29.
8. R. Spence Watson, *The National Liberal Federation* (London, 1907), p. 10.
9. Ostrogorski, *Democracy and the Organization of Political Parties*, pp. 184–85.
10. Hanham, *Elections and Party Management*, p. 133.
11. Watson, *The National Liberal Federation*, p. 19.

12. George L. Bernstein, 'Sir Henry Campbell-Bannerman and the Liberal Imperialists', *Journal of British Studies*, 23 (1983), p. 108.

13. John Morley, *Life of Gladstone* (London, 1908), ii, pp. 152–53.

14. *Annual Register* (1879), pp. 1–2.

15. B. R. Mitchell, *British Historical Statistics* (Cambridge 1988), p. 195.

16. Ibid., p. 198.

17. Jackson, *Education Act Forster*, p. 220.

18. T. A. Jenkins, 'Gladstone, the Whigs and the Leadership of the Liberal Party, 1879–1880', *Historical Journal*, 27 (1984), pp. 331–60.

19. *Annual Register* (1880), p. 51.

20. *Times*, 13 April 1880.

21. See Jenkins, 'Gladstone, the Whigs and the Leadership of the Liberal Party, 1879–1880'.

Notes to Chapter 4: Events Take Charge

1. R. V. Comerford, in *A New History of Ireland* (Oxford, 1996), vi, p. 40.

2. Ibid., p. 45.

3. *Annual Register* (1881), p. 29.

4. John Morley, *Life of Gladstone* (London, 1908), ii, p. 220.

5. *Nineteenth Century*, October 1881, p. 473.

6. Gladstone to Granville, 4 January 1882, in Agatha Ramm, ed., *Political Correspondence of Mr Gladstone and Lord Grenville* (Oxford, 1962), i, p. 326.

7. 1 June 1882, *Parliamentary Debates*, vol. 269, col. 1781.

8. Peter Mansfield, *The British in Egypt* (London, 1971), p. 39.

9. Gladstone to Bright, 12 July 1882, BL, Add MS 43385, fol. 303.

10. 12 July 1882, Parliamentary Debates, vol. 272, col. 169.

11. R. A. J. Walling, ed., *Diaries of John Bright*, entry for 8 July 1882 (London, 1930), p. 485.

12. Ibid., entry for 17 July 1882, p. 723.

13. Morley, *Life of Gladstone*, ii, pp. 288–90.

14. Gladstone to Granville 16 January 1884, in Ramm (ed.), *Political Correspondence of Mr Gladstone and Lord Grenville*, ii, p. 150.

15. Morley, *Life of Gladstone*, ii, p. 325.

16. Figures in this section are based on those quoted in B. R. Mitchell, *British Historical Statistics* (Cambridge, 1988).

17. Elwood P. Lawrence, *Henry George in the British Isles* (East Lansing, Michigan, 1957), p. 34.

Notes to Chapter 5: Schism

1. H. J. Hanham, *Elections and Party Management* (Hassocks 1978), pp. 369f.
2. Down to the 1960s, there was a story current in rural Lincolnshire that enthusiastic Liberals knocked up a friend late at night, with the message 'We've got you three acres and a cow'. The weary response was 'Tether the cow in front, and put the three acres at the back'.
3. A. R. D. Elliot, *Life of George Joachim Goschen, First Viscount Goschen* (London, 1911), ii, pp. 35–36.
4. Quoted in J. Loughlin, *Gladstone, Home Rule and the Ulster Question, 1882–93* (Dublin 1986), p. 36.
5. H. C. G. Matthews, ed., *Gladstone Diaries* (Oxford, 1990), xi, p. 403.
6. J. L. Hammond, *Gladstone and the Irish Nation* (2nd edn, London, 1964), p. 401.
7. Richard Shannon, *Gladstone: Heroic Minister, 1865–1898* (London, 1999), p. 394.
8. Sir Charles Mallet, *Herbert Gladstone: A Memoir* (London, 1932), p. 119.
9. *Times*, 18 December 1885.
10. Elliot, *Life of Goschen*, p. 10.
11. John Morley, *Life of Gladstone* (London, 1908), ii, p. 398.
12. At Holloway, 17 June 1885.
13. Notably at Warrington, 8 September 1885.
14. Lewis Harcourt journal, cited in Patrick Jackson, *The Last of the Whigs* (London, 1994), p. 215.
15. See J. L. Garvin, *Life of Joseph Chamberlain* (London, 1933), ii, p. 185f.
16. Graham Goodlad: 'The Liberal Party and Gladstone's Land Purchase Bill of 1886', *Historical Journal*, 32 (1989), pp. 627–41.
17. Lewis Harcourt journal, 26. March 1886, cited in W. C. Lubenow, *Parliamentary Politics and the Home Rule Crisis* (Oxford, 1986), p. 12.
18. See M. Ostrogorski, *Democracy and the Organization of Political Parties* (London, 1902), ii, pp. 289–99; R. Spence Watson, *The National Liberal Federation* (London, 1907), pp. 54–59; B. McGill, 'Francis Schnadhorst and Liberal Party Organisation', *Journal of Modern History*, 34 (1962), pp. 19–39; P. C. Griffiths: 'The Caucus and the Liberal Party in 1886', *History*, 61 (1976), pp. 183–97.
19. Griffiths, 'The Caucus and the Liberal Party in 1886', p. 192.
20. *Times*, 1 May 1886.
21. Elliot, *Life of Goschen*, pp. 62–63.
22. *Birmingham Daily Post*, 9 June 1886.
23. 3rd Viscount Chilston, *Chief Whip* (London, 1961), p. 77.
24. See *Life of Goschen*, pp. 242–45.
25. Hansard, third series, vol. 306, col. 1240.
26. As usual, there was a small awkward squad who were difficult to classify, so

exact numbers are debatable. See W. C. Lubenow, 'Irish Home Rule', *Historical Journal*, 28 (1985) pp. 125–42.

27. Garvin, *Life of Joseph Chamberlain*, ii, p. 250.

28. Arnold Morley to Gladstone, 19 June 1886, BL, Add. MS 44253, fos 13–14.

29. *Times*, 22 April 1886.

30. William O'Brien, *An Olive Branch in Ireland* (London, 1910), p. 169n.

31. Roy Douglas, *Land, People and Politics* (London, 1976), pp. 60–72, 86–92.

32. *Annual Register* (1886), p. 252.

33. Arnold Morley to Gladstone, 25 June 1886, misdated 25 July 1886, BL, Add. MS 44253, fos 27–30.

34. *Times*, 21 June 1886.

35. Viscount Wolmer (Petersfield) defeated the Conservative challenger. The 3rd Viscount Chilston describes in detail the problems in Petersfield, *Chief Whip*, pp. 80–81. L. McIver (Torquay), and J. Westlake (Romford) lost their seats to Conservatives, the latter in a three-cornered contest.

36. Jackson, *Last of the Whigs*, p. 242.

Notes to Chapter 6: Reconstruction

1. M. Ostrogorski, *Democracy and the Organization of Political Parties* (London, 1902), ii, pp. 300f.

2. Arnold Morley to Gladstone, 2 September 1887, BL, Add. MS 44253.

3. Thomas W. Heyck, 'Home Rule, Radicalism and the Liberal Party, 1886–1895', *Journal of British Studies*, 13 (1974), at pp. 78–79.

4. B. McGill, 'Francis Schnadhorst and Liberal Party Organisation', *Journal of Modern History*, 34 (1962), pp. 19–39. Campbell-Bannerman Papers, BL, Add. MS 41216, fos 135–45.

5. Heyck, 'Home Rule, Radicalism and the Liberal Party, 1886–1895', pp. 69–70.

6. D. A. Hamer, *Liberal Politics in the Age of Gladstone and Rosebery* (Oxford, 1972), pp. 124–26.

7. Ibid., p. 127.

8. Arnold Morley to Gladstone, 31 December 1886, 14 January, 13 and 19 April 1887, BL, Add. MS 44253, fos 52–53, 57, 86–87, 88–89.

9. Chamberlain to Hartington, 9 September 1886, JC5/22/124, University of Birmingham and Devonshire Papers, 340.2043; cited in Michael Hurst, *Joseph Chamberlain and Liberal Reunion: The Round Table Conference of 1887* (London, 1967), p. 54, and in Peter Davis. 'The Liberal Unionist Party and Irish Policy, 1886–1892', *Historical Journal*, 18 (1975), pp. 85–104.

10. J. L. Garvin, *Life of Joseph Chamberlain* (London, 1933), ii, pp. 277f.

11. Arnold Morley to Gladstone, 31 December 1886, BL, Add. MS 44253.

12. Peter Davis, 'The Liberal Unionist Party and Irish Policy, 1886–1892'. The MPs

were A. B. Winterbotham (Cirencester), C. R. M. Talbot (Mid-Glamorgan), Sir Hussey Vivian (Swansea) and Sir T. F. Grove (Wilton).

13. Garvin, *Life of Joseph Chamberlain*, pp. 354f.
14. John Morley, *Life of Gladstone* (London, 1908), ii, p. 505.
15. Ibid., p. 506.
16. William O'Brien, *An Olive Branch in Ireland* (London, 1910), p. xxii.
17. See Garvin, *Life of Joseph Chamberlain* p. 508f.
18. *Times*, March 1891.
19. *Annual Register* (1891), p. 213.
20. T. A. Jenkins, 'The Funding of the Liberal Unionist Party and the Honours System', *English Historical Review*, 414 (1990), pp. 920–38.
21. Arnold Morley to Gladstone, 6 July 1892, BL, Add. MS 44254.

Notes to Chapter 7: End of an Era

1. Burt to Gladstone, 6 March 1894, BL, Add. MS 44518, fos 82–84.
2. John Morley, *Life of Gladstone* (London, 1908), ii, p. 547.
3. Arnold Morley to Gladstone, 21 April, 1 August 1892, BL, Add. MS 44254.
4. Gladstone to Queen Victoria, 25–26 August 1893, *Letters of Queen Victoria*, third series (London, 1931), ii, p. 307.
5. *Times*, 11 September 1893.
6. Morley, *Life of Gladstone*, ii, p. 558.
7. Dudley W. R. Bahlman, ed., *Diary of Sir Edward Walter Hamilton, 1885–1906* (Hull, 1993), 28 December 1893, p. 215.
8. Ibid., 10 January 1894, p. 215.
9. Ibid., 25 January 1894, p. 227.
10. Ibid., 25 January 1894, p. 226.
11. Marjoribanks to Gladstone, 2 February 1894, BL, Add. MS 44332, fos 251–54.
12. Bahlman, ed., *Diary of Sir Edward Walter Hamilton, 1885–1906*, 8 February 1894, p. 233.
13. Morley, *Life of Gladstone*, ii, p. 558.
14. H. C. G. Matthews, ed., *Gladstone Diaries* (Oxford, 1978), xiii, p. 385.
15. At Liberal Unionist Club, 7 March 1894, J. L. Garvin, *Life of Joseph Chamberlain* (London, 1933), ii, p. 593.
16. See A. G. Gardiner, *Life of Sir William Harcourt* (London, 1923), ii, pp. 268–70.
17. Lewis Harcourt's journal, 28 February 1894, unpublished, cited in R. R. James, *Rosebery* (London, 1963), p. 329n.
18. Ibid., p. 334.
19. Ibid., pp. 334–35
20. Wyn Griffiths, *Thomas Edward Ellis, 1859–1899* (Llandybie, 1959), p. 30.
21. *Parliamentary Debates*, 4, 12 March 1894.

22. See F. S. L. Lyons, in *A New History of Ireland* (Oxford, 1989), vi, pp. 85–86.

23. *Letters of Queen Victoria*, third series, ii, p. 437.

24. Ibid., p. 446.

25. See Wynn Jones, *Thomas Edward Ellis* (1986), pp. 65–69.

26. James, *Rosebery*, p. 370.

27. See Tweedmouth to Gladstone, 20, 23 June 1895, BL, Add. MS 44332, fos 322–28.

28. Lord Askwith, *Lord James of Hereford* (London, 1930), p. 238.

29. Tweedmouth to Gladstone, 20, 23 June 1895, BL, Add. MS 44332, fos 322–28.

30. Rosebery, *Sir Robert Peel*, cited in James, *Rosebery*, p. 384.

31. See, e.g., his Scarborough speeches of 18 October 1896.

32. Tweedmouth to Gladstone, 12 July 1895, BL, Add. MS 44332, fos 330–33.

33. J. A. Spender, *Sir Robert Hudson* (London, 1930), p. 23.

34. Old issues remain to this day a valuable, though often neglected, source of information about events in the late nineteenthth century and the first half of the twentieth.

Notes to Chapter 8: Collapse and Recovery

1. Rosebery to Ripon, 12 August 1895, BL, Add. MS 43516, fos 220–21.

2. Harcourt to Rosebery, 14 August 1895, quoted in A. G. Gardiner, *Life of Harcourt* (London, 1923), ii, p. 375.

3. Rosebery to Gladstone, 26 August 1895, BL, Add. MS 44290, fos 264–65.

4. R. R. James, *Rosebery* (London, 1963), pp. 385–88.

5. The present author has discussed the situation in 'Britain and the Armenian Question, 1894–97', *Historical Journal*, 19 (1976), pp. 113–33.

6. Lady Gwendolen Cecil, *Life of Salisbury* (London, 1921), v, p. 87.

7. Salisbury to Victoria, 19 February 1896 (copy) Salisbury Papers, A/84, fos 15–16.

8. Herbert Gladstone to Campbell-Bannerman, 12 April 1899, BL, Add. MS 41215, fos 66–67; Campbell-Bannerman to Herbert Gladstone, 13 April 1899, BL, Add. MS 45987, fol. 11.

9. See, e.g., Sir Charles Mallet, *Herbert Gladstone: A Memoir* (London, 1932); H. W. McCready: 'Chief Whip and Party Funds: The Work of Herbert Gladstone, 1899–1906', *Canadian Journal of History*, 6 (1971) pp. 285–303.

10. See particularly McCready, 'Chief Whip and Party Funds'.

11. At Manchester, 15 September 1899, *Liberal Magazine* (1899), p. 489.

12. Memo. of conference of 4 October 1899, BL, Add. MS 41215, fos 105–6.

13. Herbert Gladstone to Campbell-Bannerman, 5 October 1899, BL, Add. MS 41215, fos 108–9.

14. *Times*, 12 October 1899.

15. Hansard, *Parliamentary Debates*, fourth series, 18 October 1899, vol. 77, col. 210.

16. See Peter Jacobson, 'Rosebery and Liberal Imperialism, 1899–1903', *Journal of British Studies*, 13 (1973), pp. 83–107.

17. Herbert Gladstone to Campbell-Bannerman, 3 April 1900, BL, Add. MS 41215, fos 278–79.

18. *Liberal Magazine* (1900), p. 492.

19. Ibid., pp. 520–25.

20. Herbert Gladstone to Campbell-Bannerman, 22 October 1900, BL, Add. MS 41216, fos 23–24

21. 4 October 1900, cited in James, *Rosebery*, p. 418.

22. *Times*, 19 October 1900; *Annual Register* (1900), p. 165; T. Boyle, 'The Liberal Imperialists, 1892–1906', *Bulletin of the Institute of Historical Research*, 52 (1979), pp. 48–82.

23. And see Campbell-Bannerman to Herbert Gladstone, 18 December 1900 (copy), BL, Add. MS 45987, fos 211–12.

24. Herbert Gladstone to Campbell-Bannerman, 17 December 1901, BL, Add. MS 41216, fos 171–72.

25. Campbell-Bannerman to Herbert Gladstone, 18 December 1901, BL, Add. MS 45987, fos 211–12.

26. *Times*, 21 February 1902.

27. Marquis of Crewe, *Lord Rosebery* (London, 1931), ii, p. 574.

28. Herbert Gladstone to Campbell-Bannerman, 12 November 1901, BL, Add. MS 41216, fol. 154.

29. Mark Rathbone: 'The Rainbow Circle and the New Liberalism', *Historian*, 71 (2001), pp. 16–21; David Powell, 'The New Liberalism and the Rise of Labour, 1886–1906', *Historical Journal*, 29 (1983), pp. 369–93.

30. Richard A. Rempel, *Unionists Divided* (Newton Abbot, 1972), pp. 49–63.

31. Ibid., p. 95, and appendixes.

32. Ibid., especially pp. 76–93.

33. The present author has discussed Liberal–Labour relations of the period more fully in *The History of the Liberal Party, 1895–1970* (London, 1971), pp. 64–79.

34. See Powell, 'The New Liberalism and the Rise of Labour, 1886–1906', pp. 369–93.

35. Herbert Gladstone notes, esp. 19 June and 10 July 1902, BL, Add. MS 46484.

36. Jesse Herbert to Herbert Gladstone, 6 March 1903, BL, Add. MS 46425, fos 126–36.

37. *Daily News*, 7 July 1903.

Notes to Chapter 9: Triumph and After

1. *Pall Mall Gazette*, 5 February 1906.
2. Herbert Gladstone to Campbell-Bannerman 24, 25 November 1905, BL, Add. MS 41217.
3. Balfour, Cabinet letters, 24 November, 8 December 1905, PRO, CAB 41/30/33, 34.
4. See, for example, Morley to Campbell-Bannerman, 28 November 1905, BL, Add. MS 52518; Hudson to Herbert Gladstone, 28 November 1905, BL, Add. MS 46021.
5. See Stephen Koss, *Asquith* (2nd edn, London, 1985), pp. 65–73; John Wilson, *CB: A Life of Sir Henry Campbell-Bannerman* (London, 1973), pp. 423–58.
6. Campbell-Bannerman, Cabinet letter, 20 December 1905, PRO, CAB 41/30/36.
7. *Liberal Magazine* (1905), p. 708; (1906), pp. 14–15.
8. H. W. McCready, 'Chief Whip and Party Funds: The Work of Herbert Gladstone', *Canadian Journal of History*, 6 (1971), pp. 285–303.
9. Herbert Gladstone to Campbell-Bannerman, 21 January 1906, BL, Add. MS 41217.
10. R. A. Rempell, *Unionists Divided* (Newton Abbot, 1972), pp. 228–29; Peter Rowland, *The Last Liberal Governments: The Promised Land, 1905–1910* (London, 1968), p. 44 and n.
11. See *Times*, 3, 5, 7 March 1906.
12. Campbell-Bannerman, Cabinet letter, 8 February 1906, PRO, CAB 41/30/39.
13. Rowland, *The Last Liberal Governments*, pp. 89–97
14. Campbell-Bannerman, Cabinet letters, 7 November 1906, 18 December 1906, PRO, CAB 41/30/74, 82.
15. Campbell-Bannerman, Cabinet letter, 30 March 1906, PRO, CAB 41/30/52.
16. George Whiteley to Ponsonby, 20 December 1906, BL, Add. MS 41231, fol. 220.
17. Whiteley to Campbell-Bannerman, 1 March 1907, BL, Add. MS 41231, fol. 230; and see Cabinet letter, 13 March 1907, PRO, CAB 41/31/9.
18. Asquith, Cabinet letter, 1 May 1908, PRO, CAB 41/31/54.
19. Hansard, *Parliamentary Debates*, fourth series, 20 July 1908, vol. 192, cols 1379–89.
20. See Koss, *Asquith*, p. 105.
21. Anthony Denholm, *Lord Ripon, 1827–1909* (London, 1982), pp. 258–59.
22. The titles in the family are a little confusing. Frederick Robinson (1782–1859) was the second son of Lord Grantham. He was created Viscount Goderich, and later Earl of Ripon. In 1859 his son George (1827–1909) first succeeded his father as Earl of Ripon, then his uncle as Earl de Grey. His Ripon peerage was later advanced to a marquisate.
23. Denholm, *Lord Ripon*, pp. 139–65.

24. B. R. Mitchell, *British Historical Statistics*, p. 123.

25. Whiteley to Campbell-Bannerman, 19 January 1908 (misdated 1907), BL, Add. MS 41231, fol. 213.

26. See Roy Gregory, *The Miners and British Politics, 1906–14*.

Notes to Chapter 10: Climax

1. Asquith, Cabinet letter, 5 April 1911, PRO, CAB 41/33/9.

2. Asquith, Cabinet letter, 20 October 1908, PRO, CAB 41/31/68.

3. Asquith, Cabinet letter, 19 December 1908, PRO, CAB 41/31/74.

4. Asquith, Cabinet letter, 21 July 1909, PRO, CAB 41/32/26.

5. Winston Churchill, *The World Crisis, 1911–1918* (abridged edn, London, 1942), p. 39.

6. Asquith, Cabinet letter, 24 March 1909, PRO, CAB 41/32/8.

7. Asquith, Cabinet letter, 24 April 1909, PRO, CAB 41/32/11.

8. *Land Values*, March 1906; *Liberal Magazine* (1906), pp. 64–65.

9. See Paul Mulvey, 'The Single Taxers and the Future of Liberalism', *Journal of Liberal Democrat History*, 34/35 (2002), pp. 11–15.

10. Lloyd George memo, 13 March 1909, PRO, CAB 37/98/44.

11. Asquith, Cabinet letters, 19, 24 March 1909, PRO, CAB 41/32/7, 8.

12. To Walter Runciman, Runciman Papers.

13. Asquith, Cabinet letter, HHA CL 30. vii, 21 October 1909, PRO, CAB 41/32/28, 38.

14. Peter Rowland, *The Last Liberal Governments: The Promised Land, 1905–1910* (London, 1968), pp. 224–25.

15. Asquith, Cabinet letter, 3 November 1909, PRO, CAB 41/32/40.

16. Asquith, Cabinet letters, 3, 17, 24 November 1909, PRO, CAB 41/32/40, 41, 42.

17. *Liberal Magazine* (1909), pp. 491–97.

18. Asquith, Cabinet letter, 10 February 1910, PRO, CAB 41/32/45.

19. Asquith, Cabinet letter, 22 February 1910, PRO, CAB 41/32/50.

20. Some would suggest a smaller number. See note, 'The O'Brien Movement', in Elibank Papers, National Library of Scotland, MS 8802, fos 39–45.

21. Much of the information about Elibank is derived from Arthur C. Murray, *Master and Brother* (London, 1945). On the assessment of Elibank's calibre, see R. H. Davies to Elibank, 2 January 1911 (misdated 1910), Elibank Papers, National Library of Scotland, 8802, fos 3–4.

22. Elibank memorandum, Murray, *Master and Brother*, p. 40.

23. *Liberal Magazine* (1909), p. 747.

24. *Parliamentary Debates*, fifth series, 1, 55.

25. Murray, *Master and Brother*, p. 39.

26. Asquith, Cabinet letter, 25, 28 February 1910, PRO, CAB 41/32/51, 52.

27. *Parliamentary Debates*, fifth series, 16, 1548.

28. Murray, *Master and Brother*, p. 45.

29. Asquith, Cabinet letter, 10 May 1910, PRO, CAB 41/32/57.

30. Asquith, Cabinet letter, 7 June 1910, PRO, CAB 41/32/60.

31. Lloyd George Papers, C/16/3/1, 3. It does not appear clear who were the intended recipients.

32. C. F. G. Masterman, quoted in Murray, *Master and Brother*, p. 59.

33. Crewe, 8 August 1911, *House of Lords Debates*, fifth series, 9, 837.

34. 7 August 1911, *Parliamentary Debates*, fifth series, 29, 811.

35. Summarised in J. A. Spender and Cyril Asquith, *Life of Asquith* (London, 1932), i, pp. 307–8.

36. Asquith, Cabinet letter, 10 May 1911, PRO, CAB 41/33/14.

37. Spender and Asquith, *Life of Asquith*, ii, p. 308.

38. Asquith, Cabinet letter, 30 March 1911, PRO, CAB 41/33/8.

39. Asquith, Cabinet letter, 14 July 1911, PRO, CAB 41/33/66.

40. Elibank Papers, fos 252–265; Spender and Asquith, *Life of Asquith*, pp. 329–31.

41. Asquith, Cabinet letter, 5 April 1911, PRO, CAB 41/33/9.

Notes to Chapter 11: When Troubles Come

1. This matter is discussed more fully by the present author in his essay, 'Labour in Decline, 1910–14', in Kenneth D. Brown, ed., *Essays in Anti-Labour History* (London, 1974), at pp. 111–12.

2. *Times*, 23 November 1910.

3. Asquith, Cabinet letter, 10 May 1911, CAB 41/33/13, 14.

4. See Douglas, 'Labour in Decline, 1910–14', pp. 113–25.

5. J. C. Wedgwood, *Memoirs of a Fighting Life* (London, 1941), 83–84.

6. P. F. Clarke: 'The Electoral Position of the Liberal and Labour Parties, 1910–1914', *English Historical Review*, 90 (1975), p. 831.

7. John Hancock (Mid-Derbyshire), John Wadsworth (Hallamshire), Fred Hall (Normanton).

8. *Liberal Magazine* (1914), p. 323.

9. See, e.g., Martin Gilbert, *Churchill: A Life* (London, 1991), pp. 219–21.

10. Crewe, Cabinet letter, 4 June 1912, PRO, CAB 41/33/51.

11. Asquith, Cabinet letter, 7 February 1912, PRO, CAB 41/33/35.

12. Asquith, Cabinet letter, 14, 26 November 1913, PRO, CAB 41/34/34, 36.

13. Asquith, Cabinet letter, 14 November 1913, PRO, CAB 41/34/34.

14. Ibid.

15. Ibid.

16. Asquith, Cabinet letter, 5 March 1914, PRO, CAB 41/35/6.

17. Asquith, Cabinet letter, 28 March 1914, PRO, CAB 41/35/10.

18. Cabinet paper, 4 July 1914.

19. George V to Asquith, 18 July 1914, Asquith Papers, 3, fol. 237.

20. *Parliamentary Debates*, fifth series, 38, cols 1326–27.

21. For further examples, see *Liberal Year Book* (1914), p. 205.

22. A report submitted by J. Renwick Seager, of the Liberal Registration Depart-
    ment, to Elibank, 8 November 1911, gives considerable detail of Liberal agents'
    comments on the matter. See Peter Rowland, *The Last Liberal Governments:
    Unfinished Business, 1911–14* (London, 1971), pp. 90–91.

23. See Lloyd George to Fawcett, 30 November 1911, cited in Rowland, *Unfinished
    Business*, p. 92.

24. Asquith, Cabinet letter, 22 January 1913, PRO, CAB 41/34/3.

25. Asquith, Cabinet letter, 25 January 1913, PRO, CAB 41/34/4.

26. See analysis in *Liberal Magazine* (1913), pp. 301–2, and division list 6 May 1913,
    in *Parliamentary Debates*, fifth series, 52, cols 2001–6.

27. *Land Values*, June 1911, pp. 17–18.

28. Sir Edgar Harper, *The Lloyd George Finance (1909–10) Act 1910: Its Errors and
    How to Correct Them*, International Union for Land Value Taxation and Free
    Trade (1929).

29. Ian Packer: 'The Land Issue and the Future of Scottish Liberalism in 1914', *Scot-
    tish Historical Review*, 75 (1996), pp. 52–71.

30. Lloyd George to Asquith, 5 December 1913, Asquith Papers, 25, fol. 63.

31. Lloyd George to Percy Illingworth, 24 October 1913, Lloyd George Papers,
    C/5/4/7.

32. Illingworth to Lloyd George, 28 December 1913, Lloyd George Papers, C5/4/8.

33. Ian Packer: 'The Liberal Cave and the 1914 Budget', *English Historical Review*
    (1996), pp. 620–35; *Liberal Magazine* (1914), pp. 398–99.

34. Earl of Oxford and Asquith, *Memories and Reflections, 1852–1927* (London,
    1928), i, pp. 207–12.

Notes to Chapter 12: Catastrophe

1. John Burns, note to a friend, 3 August 1914, BL, Add. MS 46282, fol. 158.

2. See G. P. Gooch and Harold Temperley, *British Documents on the Origin of the
   War, 1898–1914*, ii, esp. p. 392.

3. Viscount Grey, *Twenty-Five Years, 1892–1916* (London, 1925), i, p. 70f; Gooch
   and Temperley, *British Documents*, iii, p. 170.

4. A. J. A. Morris, *Radicalism against War, 1906–14* (London, 1972), pp. 54–70.

5. Asquith, Cabinet letter, 20 July 1910, PRO, CAB 41/32/67.

6. Asquith, Cabinet letter, 9 March 1911, PRO, CAB 41/33/5.

7. G. M. Trevelyan, *Grey of Fallodon* (London, 1937), p. 225.

8. Asquith, Cabinet letter, 4 July 1911, PRO, CAB 41/33/20.

9. Asquith, Cabinet letter, 19 July 1911, PRO, CAB 41/33/22.

10. Asquith, Cabinet letter, 2 November 1911, PRO, CAB 41/33/28.

11. Asquith, Cabinet letter, 3 February 1912, PRO, CAB 41/33/34.

12. Grey, *Twenty-Five Years*, pp. 243–44.

13. Asquith, Cabinet letter, 29 January, 11 February 1914, PRO, CAB 41/35, 1, 3.

14. Asquith, Cabinet letter, 25 July 1914, PRO, CAB 41/35/20.

15. Grey, *Twenty-Five Years*, pp. 302–3.

16. Asquith, Cabinet letter, 30 July 1914, PRO, CAB 41/35/22.

17. Nicolson to Grey, 1 August 1914. PRO, FO 800/94, fol. 529.

18. Crowe memo, 31 July 1914, PRO, FO 800/94, fol. 522.

19. Trevelyan, *Grey of Fallodon*, i, pp. 255–57.

20. Crewe, Cabinet letter, 2 August 1914, PRO, CAB 41/35/23.

21. Beauchamp, Lloyd George, Harcourt, Morley, Pease, Samuel, Simon, McKinnon, Wood.

22. Viscount Morley, *Memorandum on Resignation, August 1914* (London, 1928), p. 15.

23. Asquith, Cabinet letter, 3 August 1914, PRO, CAB 41/35/24.

24. Asquith, Cabinet letter, 3 August 1914 (no. 2), PRO, CAB 41/35/25.

25. Burns to Asquith, Kitchener and McKenna, BL, Add. MS 46282, fos 175–77.

26. Morley to Rosebery, 7 August 1914, Rosebery Papers, 37.

27. *Manchester Guardian*, 5 August 1914; discussed in A. J. A. Morris, *C. P. Trevelyan, 1870–1958: Portrait of a Radical* (Belfast, 1977).

28. The subject is discussed more fully by the present author in *The History of the Liberal Party, 1895–1970* (London, 1971), pp. 97–98, 107.

29. R. J. Q. Adams, *Bonar Law* (London, 1999), pp. 176–77.

30. Peter Fraser, 'British War Policy and the Crisis of Liberalism in May 1915', *Journal of Modern History*, 54 (1982), pp. 1–26.

31. Viscount Simon, *Retrospect* (London, 1952), p. 103.

32. Asquith, Cabinet letter, 12 October 1915, PRO, CAB 41/36/48.

33. Asquith, Cabinet letter, 28 December 1915, PRO, CAB 41/36/56.

34. 4, 16 May 1916, *Parliamentary Debates* (Commons), vol. 82, cols 263, 1487.

35. Asquith, Cabinet letter, 6 May 1916, PRO, CAB 41/37/18.

36. Asquith, Cabinet letter, 27 June 1916, PRO, CAB 41/37/24.

37. See Stephen Koss, *Asquith* (London, 1985), pp. 211–12.

38. H. H. Asquith, *Memories and Reflections* (London, 1927), ii, pp. 138–47; Lord Newton, *Lord Lansdowne: A Biography* (London, 1929), pp. 449–52.

39. James Pope-Hennessy, *Lord Crewe, 1858–1945* (London, 1955), pp. 188–89.

40. J. M. McEwen, 'Lloyd George's Liberal Supporters in December 1916: A Note', *Bulletin of the Institute of Historical Research*, 53 (1980) pp. 265–72.

41. *Liberal Magazine* (1916), pp. 620–26.

Notes to Chapter 13: The Era of Lloyd George

1. G. M. Trevelyan, *Grey of Fallodon* (London, 1937), p. 329.
2. Asquith to Montagu, 19 June 1917, Asquith Papers, 18, fos 11–14.
3. Edward David, 'The Liberal Party Divided, 1916–1918', *Historical Journal*, 13 (1970), pp. 509–33; *Liberal Magazine* (1917), pp. 142–46, 152.
4. War Cabinet 144, 23 May 1917, PRO, CAB 23/2.
5. Philip Kerr to Lloyd George, 4 December 1917, Lloyd George Papers, F/89/1/9.
6. McKenna to Runciman, 27 August 1917, Runciman Papers.
7. L. Harcourt to Runciman, 21 May 1918, Runciman Papers.
8. Guest to Lloyd George, 3 August 1918, Lloyd George Papers, F/21/2/30.
9. Discussed in Roy Douglas, 'The Background to the "Coupon" Election Arrangements', *English Historical Review*, 86 (1971), pp. 318–36, at pp. 321–22. See also David, 'The Liberal Party Divided'.
10. F. E. Guest to Lloyd George, 20 July 1918, Lloyd George Papers, F/21/2/28; and see discussion in Douglas, 'The Background to the "Coupon" Election Arrangements'.
11. Memorandum of 2 October 1918, Elibank 8804, fos 193–96; A. C. Murray, *Master and Brother* (London, 1945), pp. 175–56.
12. Guest to Lloyd George, 21 October 1918, Lloyd George Papers, F/21/2/43.
13. *Liberal Magazine* (1918), p. 669.
14. Douglas, 'The Background to the "Coupon" Election Arrangements'.
15. Correct allocation of MPs presents considerable difficulty. It is discussed by the author in 'A Classification of the Members of Parliament Elected in 1918', *Bulletin of the Institute of Historical Research*, 47 (1974), pp. 74–94.
16. Sir Percy Harris, *Forty Years In and Out of Parliament* (London, 1949), p. 76.
17. Gulland to Runciman, 4 January 1919, Runciman Papers.
18. *Manchester Guardian*, 4 February 1919.
19. S. Galbraith, E. Hayward, P. W. Raffan and J. C. Wedgwood. See list in *Liberal Magazine* (1919), p. 89.
20. *Annual Register* (1919), p. 5; contrast *Liberal Magazine* (1919). pp. 90, 284.
21. J. C. Wedgwood, *Memoirs of a Fighting Life* (London, 1941), p. 144.
22. Maclean to Runciman, 8 January 1920, Runciman Papers. A good study of Hogge is provided by R. Ian Elder in *Journal of Liberal Democrat History*, 30 (Spring 2001), pp. 20–22, 32.
23. See Viscount Gladstone to Maclean, 13 January 1922 (copy), BL, Add. MS 46474, fol. 2.
24. *Times*, 4, 6, 7 February 1919. The Coalitionists were Sir Archibald Williamson, Sir Ivor Philipps, Albion Richardson and Sir Thomas Whittaker; the 'Wee Frees' were Wedgwood Benn, Penry Williams, Frank Briant and J. M. Hogge.
25. *Times*, 7 February 1919.

26. *Times*, 28 February 1919.

27. John Ramsden, ed., *Real Old Tory Politics* (London, 1984), p. 131.

28. *Liberal Magazine* (1920), p. 70; J. A. Spender and Cyril Asquith, *Life of Asquith* (London, 1932), ii, p. 331.

29. *Times*, 17 March 1920.

30. *Times*, 18, 19 March 1920.

31. Guest to Lloyd George, 1 November 1920, Lloyd George Papers, F/22/2/18.

32. Mond to Lloyd George, 15 March 1919, Lloyd George Papers F/36/6/46; Guest to Lloyd George 18 June 1920, Lloyd George Papers, F/22/1/45.

33. *Liberal Magazine* (1920), pp. 394, 437–39; and see *Lloyd George Liberal Magazine*, 1 (1920), p. 6.

34. McCurdy to Lloyd George, May 1921, Lloyd George Papers, F/34/4/8.

35. Cabinet, 12 (21), 8 March 1921, PRO, CAB 23/24.

36. The *Liberal Year Book* lists 126, but perhaps one or more of C. L'E Malone, A. S. Moreing and J. H. Wilson should be added.

37. Sir F. D. Blake, G. Collins, J. Gardiner, S. G. Howard, G. Lambert, J. T. Rees, Sir W. H. Seager and E. Hilton Young.

38. J. C. Wedgwood (who received, but did not use, the Coupon) joined the Labour Party in 1919. H. Barnes, D. Davies, S. Galbraith, E. Hayward, B. Kenyon, P. W. Raffan and A. Rendall took the Asquithian Whip.

39. See F. S. L. Lyons, in *New History of Ireland*, vi (London, 1996), pp 240f.

40. Memorandum, 3 November 1920, PRO, CAB 23/23.

41. Notes of meeting, 25 August 1920, PRO, CAB 23/22.

42. See *Lloyd George Liberal Magazine*, 1 (1920), pp. 95–96.

43. *Liberal Magazine* (1922), pp. 676–80.

44. Vivian Phillipps, *My Days and Ways*, p. 110.

45. M. Bentley, 'Liberal Politics and the Grey Conspiracy of 1921', *Historical Journal*, 20 (1977), pp. 461–75.

Notes to Chapter 14: Politics in Chaos

1. Michael Hart, 'The Liberals, the War and the Franchise', *English Historical Review*, 97 (1982), pp. 820–32.

2. G. Collins, G. Lambert, C. C. Barnes, A Lyle-Samuel, A. C. Murray and J. H. Whitley.

3. 1910: eight County seats, plus Darlington, Durham City, Gateshead and South Shields; 1918 and 1922: eleven County seats, plus Darlington, Gateshead and South Shields.

4. *Lloyd George Liberal Magazine*, December 1922, p. 168.

5. *Liberal Magazine* (1923), p. 215.

6. *Lloyd George Liberal Magazine*, July 1923, p. 787.

7. *Manchester Guardian*, 31 May 1923.

8. Asquith Papers, 141, fol. 2; Malcolm Thompson, *David Lloyd George* (London, 1948), p. 369.

9. Maclean to Viscount Gladstone, 29 December 1923, BL, Add. MS 46474, fol. 52.

10. Chris Cook, *A Short History of the Liberal Party, 1900–1997* (Basingstoke, 1998), pp. 93–94; Jaime Reynolds, 'Spectacular Victories', *Journal of Liberal History*, 44 (Autumn 2004), pp. 4–9.

11. Vivian Phillipps, *My Days and Ways* (Edinburgh 1932), p. 98.

12. Trevor Wilson, ed., *The Political Diaries of C. P. Scott, 1911–28* (London, 1970), pp. 459f.

13. Letter to *The Times*, 18 January 1924.

14. With the government: J. Duckworth, J. H. Edwards, Colonel A. England, Sir Ellis Griffith, H. C. Hogbin, W. A. Jenkins, Sir W. Beddoe Rees, Sir Thomas Robinson, W. E. Robinson and J. Leng Sturrock. Absent unpaired: Sir Clifford Cory, Sir R. Newbald Kay, Sir Murdoch Macdonald, Brigadier-General E. L. Spears, Colonel John Ward, Sir Robert Thomas and Sir William Sutherland.

15. *Liberal Magazine* (1924), p. 315.

16. Ibid., p. 375.

17. Viscount Gladstone to Asquith, 28 April 1924, Asquith Papers, 34, fol. 132.

18. Phillipps suggests otherwise in *My Days and Ways*, p. 111; but the present author has been unable to find evidence of this.

19. See, for example, Lloyd George to Asquith, 20 August 1924, Asquith Papers, 34, fos 136–43.

20. Viscount Gladstone to Runciman, enclosed memo, 31 August 1924, Runciman Papers.

21. Viscount Gladstone to Maclean, 30 December 1923, fol. 54; Maclean to Viscount Gladstone, 10 January 1924, fol. 60, BL, Add. MS 46474.

22. Interview, Maclean and Lloyd George, 5 March 1924, BL, Add. MS 46474, fol. 83.

23. Hudson memo, 1 July 1924, BL, Add. MS 46475, fol. 110.

24. Phillipps, *My Days and Ways*, p. 104.

25. Martin Gilbert, *Winston S. Churchill*, v, *1922–1939* (London, 1976), p. 29.

26. R. Alstead, Captain Berkeley, Percy Harris, A. E. Hilary, Colonel Hodge, J. M. Hogge, W. A. Jowitt, Commander Kenworthy, J. J. O'Neill, A. Rendall, Dr Spero and Mrs Wintringham. So also did two Nationalists, and even two Conservatives.

27. Asquith Papers, 141, fol, 202.

28. J. A. Spender and Cyril Asquith, *Life of Asquith* (London, 1932), pp. 350–51.

29. Frank Briant (Lambeth North), Percy Harris (Bethnal Green South West). Leslie Hore-Belisha (Devonport), H. H. Jones (Merioneth), A. M. Livingstone

(Inverness), Walter Runciman (Swansea West) and G. R. Thorne (Wolverhampton East).

Notes to Chapter 15: Recovery and Collapse

1. See analysis in Vivian Phillipps, *My Days and Ways* (Edinburgh, 1932), p. 119.
2. Anti-Lloyd George voters: W. W. Benn, Frank Briant, J. M. Kenworthy, Mackenzie Livingstone, R. Hopkin Morris, W. T. Thompson and G. R. Thorne. Other Radical Group members: H. E. Crawfurd, Percy Harris and Walter Runciman.
3. The other members were Mrs Wintringham, C. A. McCurdy, Sir Godfrey Collins and Major-General Sir Robert Hutchison.
4. Hudson to Viscount Gladstone, 23 February 1925, BL, Add. MS 46475, fol. 152.
5. J. A. Spender, *Sir Robert Hudson: A Memoir* (London, 1930), pp. 172–73.
6. Edge to Stevenson, 9 March 1925, Lloyd George Papers, G/6/10/8.
7. The present author has discussed the fund at greater length in *The History of the Liberal Party, 1895–1970* (London, 1971), pp. 199–201.
8. Phillipps, *My Days and Ways*, p. 110.
9. Lord St Davids to Samuel, 9 July 1929, Samuel Papers, A/71, fol. 26.
10. *Times*, 3 December 1927.
11. Collins to Lloyd George, 10 May 1926, Lloyd George Papers, G/5/1/10.
12. Lords Beauchamp, Buckmaster and Buxton; Collins, Hudson, Maclean, Phillipps, Pringle, Runciman, Simon.
13. Maclean to H. G., 20 May 1926, BL, Add. MS 46474, fol. 189.
14. Winifred Coombe-Tennant to Lloyd George, 30 September 1926, Lloyd George Papers, G/31/1/39.
15. Beauchamp to Lloyd George, 3 May 1926, Lloyd George Papers, G/3/5/18.
16. Guest to Lloyd George, 1 June 1926, Lloyd George Papers, G/8/13/4. The MPs indicated as supporters were J. Duckworth, J. H. Edwards, Colonel England, W. Forrest, Captain F. E. Guest, Sir M. MacDonald, Sir Beddoe Rees, Sir Tom Robinson, W. M. Wiggins and C. P. Williams. 'Likely supporters' were Ellis Davies, Ernest Evans, E. A. Harney, L. Hore-Belisha, Major-General Sir R. Hutchison, H. H. Jones, B. Kenyon, J. I. Macpherson, Goronwy Owen and Sir Archibald Sinclair.
17. See *Manchester Guardian*, 20 January 1927; *Daily News*, 20 January 1927; Trevor Wilson, *The Downfall of the Liberal Party, 1914–1935* (London, 1966), pp. 337–39.
18. *Times*, 12 February 1927.
19. *Times*, 5 February 1927.
20. Samuel Papers, A/71, fos 16–18.
21. Jamie Reynolds, 'Spectacular Victories', *Journal of Liberal History* (Autumn 2004), pp. 4–9.

22. Wilson, *The Downfall of the Liberal Party*, p. 351.

23. Ibid., pp 352–55.

24. J. Graham Jones, 'Lloyd George, Welsh Liberalism ... 1931', *Welsh Historical Review*, 19 (1998), pp. 68–102.

25. Cabinet, 5 (32), 21 January 1932, PRO, CAB 23/70.

26. Viscount Snowden, *Autobiography*, ii, pp. 883–86.

27. Viscount Simon, *Retrospect* (London, 1952), p. 163.

28. The Liberal votes are listed in *Liberal Magazine* (1931), p. 194.

29. *Liberal Magazine* (1931), pp. 154–59.

30. Snowden, *Autobiography*, ii, pp. 905–16.

31. 3 July 1931, *Parliamentary Debates*, House of Commons, fifth series, vol. 254, col. 1667.

32. Hore-Belisha diary, 29 June 1931, cited in Graham D. Goodlad, 'The Liberal Nationals, 1931–1940', *Historical Journal*, 38 (1995), pp. 133–43.

33. Frank Owen, *Tempestuous Journey* (London, 1954), p. 717.

34. Viscount Samuel, *Memoirs* (London, 1945), p. 205.

35. Technically, Lloyd George was not Leader but only Chairman of the MPs.

36. Sir Geoffrey Shakespeare, *Let Candles be Brought in* (London, 1949), p. 136.

37. Samuel, *Memoirs*, p. 219.

38. Shakespeare, *Let Candles be Brought in*, p. 138.

39. Cabinet, 70 (31), 5 October 1931, PRO, CAB 23/68.

40. See *Manchester Guardian*, 6 October 1931.

41. Owen, *Tempestuous Journey*, p. 720.

42. *Times*, 9, 10 October 1931.

43. *Manchester Guardian*, 6 October 1931.

44. Discussed in more detail in Roy Douglas, *The History of the Liberal Party, 1895–1970* (London, 1971) pp. 219–23.

45. These figures are slightly different from those given by the present author in *The History of the Liberal Party, 1895–1970*.

46. David Dutton, '1932: A Neglected Date in the History of the Decline of the British Liberal Party', *Twentieth-Century British History*, 14 (2003), p. 48.

47. Figures based on *Times* analysis, 29 October 1931.

Notes to Chapter 16: Salvage

1. Cabinet, 85 (31), 7 December 1931, PRO, CAB 23/69.

2. Cabinet Papers, 25 (32); and see Cabinet 5 (32), 21 January 1932, PRO, CAB. 23/70.

3. Cabinet 7 (32), 22 January 1932, PRO, CAB 23/70.

4. Snowden to Samuel, 23 August 1932, Samuel Papers A/89, fol. 1.

5. See list in *Liberal Magazine* (1932), p. 148. Like the *Liberal Year Books*, *Liberal Magazine* did not yet recognise the Liberal Nationals as a separate party.

6. An amusing dialogue, summarising the debate among Liberals at the time, but reaching a 'Samuelite' conclusion, is provided in *Liberal Magazine* (1932), pp. 157–60.

7. See David Dutton, '1932: A Neglected Date', *Twentieth-Century British History*, 14 (2003), pp. 43–60.

8. Shakespeare to Simon, 23 September 1932. See Dutton, '1932: A Neglected Date', pp. 51–52.

9. Grey to Samuel, 12 September 1932, Samuel Papers, A/89, fol. 84.

10. Geoffrey Shakespeare, *Let Candles be Brought in* (London, 1949), pp. 140–41.

11. Robert Bernays (Bristol North), William McKeag (Durham) and J. P. Maclay (Paisley). The present author originally considered William Mabane (Huddersfield) to be one of their number, in *The History of the Liberal Party 1895–1970* (London, 1971), p. 229, but now recognises that he was a Liberal National. In the 1935 General Election, Bernays and Maclay both stood as Liberals, McKeag as a Liberal National.

12. *Liberal Magazine* (1933), pp. 551–52.

13. *Liberal Magazine* (1933), p. 566.

14. The two parties also collided at the two-member constituency of Oldham. In 1931 both seats had been won by Conservatives; no Liberal of any kind stood. In 1935, evidently as the result of some collusive arrangements, a Conservative and a Liberal National defended the two seats together.

15. David Marquand, '1924–1932', in David Butler, ed., *Coalitions in British Politics* (London and Basingstoke, 1978), p. 73.

16. Sir Percy Harris, *Forty Years In and Out of Parliament* (London, 1949), p. 126.

17. For a critique of the arrangements, see *Liberal Magazine* (1936), pp. 129–32.

18. Neville Chamberlain to Hilda Chamberlain, 22 May 1935, NC 18.1/918, cited in Graham D. Goodlad, 'The Liberal Nationals, 1931–1940', *Historical Journal*, 38 (1995), pp. 133–43, where the statements from Shakespeare and Hore-Belisha are also cited.

19. *Liberal Magazine* (1938), p. 188.

20. Bernard Wasserstein, *Herbert Samuel: A Political Life* (Oxford, 1992), p. 392.

21. For example, the French Foreign Minister had warned the British Ambassador not to rely on France; the Prime Minister had received military advice that Britain would have a better chance of success if war was delayed six or twelve months; there were big doubts about Russia; and some Dominion attitudes were uncertain.

22. Sinclair to Countess of Aberdeen, 12 December 1938, copy, Thurso Papers, 2/38/1.

23. *Liberal Magazine* (1936), p. 348.

24. *Liberal Magazine* (1939), pp. 205, 246.

25. *Liberal Magazine* (1939), p. 297.

26. Ian Hunter, 'Sir Archibald Sinclair: The Liberal Anti-Appeaser', *Journal of Liberal History*, 42 (2004), p. 35.

27. John Vincent, 'Chamberlain, the Liberals and the Outbreak of War, 1939', *English Historical Review*, 113 (1998), pp. 367–83.

28. 8 May 1940, *Parliamentary Debates*, Commons, fifth series, vol. 360, col. 1283.

29. H. W. Butcher, Leslie Hore-Belisha, Captain Medlicott and J. Henderson Stewart.

30. See Harris, *Forty Years In an Out of Parliament*, p. 151.

31. Ibid., p. 142.

Notes to Chapter 17: Nadir

1. *News Chronicle*, 29 March 1958, cited in Michael McManus, *Jo Grimond: Towards the Sound of Gunfire* (London, 2001), p. 129.

2. Sir Percy Harris, *Forty Years In and Out of Parliament* (London, 1949), p. 184.

3. R. B. McCallum and Alison Readman, *The British General Election of 1945* (Oxford, 1947), p. 86.

4. Ibid., p. 68.

5. Information from the late Lord Tenby; and see *Guardian* 15 February 1967.

6. *Manchester* Guardian, 3 August 1945.

7. J. S. Rasmussen: *Retrenchment and Revival* (Tucson, Arizona, 1964), p. 15.

8. See David Dutton: 'John Simon and the Post-War National Liberal Party: An Historical Postscript', *Historical Journal*, 32 (1989), pp. 357–67.

9. *Times*, 3, 4, 11, 15, 18 June 1946.

10. *Times*, 28 October, 8 December 1946.

11. See Clement Davies's public letter to Churchill, *Times*, 24 January 1950.

12. Michael McManus, *Jo Grimond: Towards the Sound of Gunfire*, p. 88.

13. David Butler, *The British General Election of 1951* (London, 1952), p. 242.

14. Martin Gilbert, *Winston S. Churchill*, viii (London, 1988), p. 655.

15. Violet Bonham-Carter to Gilbert Murray, 20 December 1951, cited in Mark Pottle, ed., *Daring to Hope: The Diaries and Letters of Violet Bonham Carter, 1946–1969* (London, 2000), p. 105.

16. Chris Cook, *A Short History of the Liberal Party, 1900–2001* (London, 2002), p. 134.

17. Michael McManus, 'Liberals and the Suez Crisis', *Journal of Liberal History*, 42 (2004), pp. 38–41.

18. D. E. Butler and Richard Rose, *The British General Election of 1959* (London, 1960), p. 121.

19. Ibid., p. 33.

Notes to Chapter 18: Uncertain Future

1. *Guardian*, 10 October 1959; *Observer*, 11 October 1959.
2. *Liberal News*, 1 February 1957.
3. *Times*, 10 September 1963.
4. D. E. Butler and Anthony King, *The British General Election of 1964* (London, 1965), pp. 204–5.
5. Ibid., p. 101.
6. Chris Cook, *A Short History of the Liberal Party, 1900–2001* (Basingstoke, 2002), p. 143.
7. *Guardian*, 24 June 1965.
8. D. E. Butler and Anthony King: *The British General Election of 1966* (London, 1966), p. 78.
9. Ibid., p. 261.
10. See discussion in David Butler and Michael Pinto-Duschinsky, *The British General Election of 1970* (London, 1970), pp. 144–45.
11. Jeremy Thorpe, *In My Own Time* (London, 1999), p. 96.
12. David Butler and Dennis Kavanagh, *The British General Election of October 1974* (London, 1975), p. 48.
13. Cyril Smith, *Big Cyril* (London, 1977), p. 146.
14. David Butler and Dennis Kavanagh, *The British General Election of February 1974* (London, 1974), p. 26.
15. Ibid., p. 80.
16. Cook, *A Short History of the Liberal Party, 1900–2001*, pp. 155–57.
17. Smith, *Big Cyril*, p. 161.
18. David Butler and Dennis Kavanagh, *The British General Election of 1979* (London, 1980), p. 87, citing J. Alt, J. Crewe and B. Sarlvik, 'Angels in Plastic: Liberal Support in 1974', *Political Studies*, September 1977.
19. David Steel, *Against Goliath* (London, 1989), p. 97.
20. Butler and Kavanagh, *The British General Election of 1979*, p. 92.
21. It is sometimes wrongly said that the measure legalised abortion. A celebrated case of the 1930s established that, in very limited circumstances, abortion was lawful even then.
22. Michael McManus, *Jo Grimond: Towards the Sound of Gunfire* (London, 2001), p. 331; Philip Norton, in Vernon Bogdanor, ed., *Liberal Party Politics* (London, 1986), at pp. 168–69.
23. Arthur Cyr, *Liberal Politics in Britain* (Oxford, 1988) pp. 124–25.
24. Butler and Kavanagh, *The British General Election of 1979*, p. 94.
25. Jeremy Thorpe's own account of this tragic affair is remarkably sympathetic to his deluded accusers. See Thorpe, *In My Own Time*, pp. 197–206. The part played by Bessell.

Notes to Chapter 19: Alliance and Fusion

1. In Ivor Crewe and Martin Harrop, eds, *Political Communications: The General Election Campaign of 1987* (Cambridge, 1989), p. 58.

2. John Pardoe, in Crewe and Harrop, eds, *Political Communications: The General Election Campaign of 1987*, p. 55. Roy Jenkins, *A Life at the Centre* (London and Basingstoke, 1991), p. 526; David Steel, *Against Goliath* (London, 1989), p. 216.

3. *Journal of Liberal History*, 39 (Summer, 2003).

4. Ivor Crewe and Anthony King, *SDP: The Birth, Life and Death of the Social Democratic Party* (Oxford, 1995), p. 171.

5. Don MacIver, ed., *The Liberal Democrats* (Hemel Hempstead, 1986), p. 7.

6. Crewe and King, *SDP*, p. 139.

7. North-West Croydon was approximately, though not exactly, the same as the pre-1950 North Croydon.

8. MacIver, ed., *The Liberal Democrats*, pp. 27, 28.

9. See Bill Rodgers, with commentary by Chris Rennard, 'What Went Wrong at Darlington?', *Journal of Liberal History*, 39 (2003), pp. 12–17.

10. Butler and Kavanagh, *The British General Election of 1983* (London, 1984), pp. 79–80.

11. See David Butler and Dennis Kavanagh: *The British General Election of 1987* (Basingstoke, 1988), passim.

12. Pardoe in Crewe and Harrop, *Political Communications*, pp. 56–58.

13. Steel, *Against Goliath*, p. 279.

14. Chris Cook, *A Short History of the Liberal Party, 1900–2001* (Basingstoke, 2002), pp. 188–201.

15. *Times*, 14 January 1988.

16. Paddy Ashdown, *The Ashdown Diaries*, i, *1988–1997* (London, 2000), p. 8, entry for 6 September 1988.

17. Ibid., p. 90, entry for 26 June 1990.

18. Ibid., p. 50, entry for 15 June 1989.

19. Butler and Kavanagh *The British General Election of 1992* (Basingstoke, 1992), p. 69.

20. Ashdown, *The Ashdown Diaries*, i, p. 52, entry for 19 June 1989.

21. MacIver, ed., *The Liberal Democrats*, p. 34.

22. Ashdown, *The Ashdown Diaries*, i, p. 90, entry for 1 August 1990.

23. Ibid., p. 90, entry for 26 June 1990.

Notes to Chapter 20: Into the Millennium

1. Paddy Ashdown, *The Ashdown Diaries*, i, *1988–1997* (London, 2000), entry for 2 May 1996.

2. Ibid., p. 262, entry for 15 May 1994.

3. Ibid., pp. 576, 590, 161–62, 167, 169.

4. Ibid., p. 196, entry for 19 October 1992.

5. Ibid., p. 346, entry for 24 October 1995.

6. Ibid., p. 307, entry for 2 March 1995.

7. Ibid., p. 446, entry for 12 July 1996.

8. David Butler and Dennis Kavanagh, *The British General Election of 1997* (Basingstoke, 1997), p. 69.

9. Peter Riddell, *Times*, 7 March 1997.

10. Butler and Kavanagh *The British General Election of 1997*, pp. 210–11.

11. See discussion by Richard Holme and Alison Holmes, at pp. 16–27, in Ivor Crewe et al., eds, *Political Communications: Why Labour Won the General Election of 1997* (London, 1998).

12. Paddy Ashdown, *The Ashdown Diaries*, ii, *1997–1999* (London, 2001), p. 3, entry for 4 May 1997. For a rather different angle on these events, see Alan Leaman's review in *Journal of Liberal History*, 41 (Winter, 2003), pp. 37–39.

13. Ashdown, *The Ashdown Diaries*, ii, p. 15, entry for 15 May 1997.

14. Ashdown, *The Ashdown Diaries*, ii, p. 21, entry for 21 May 1997.

15. Ashdown, *The Ashdown Diaries*, ii, p. 64, entry for 16 July 1997.

16. Ashdown, *The Ashdown Diaries*, ii, pp. 68–70, entry of 22 July 1997. Among the MPs supporting Ashdown were Cable, Campbell, Foster, Livsey, Oaten and Öpik; among his critics were Baker, Ballard, Bruce, Davey, Hughes, Rendel, Smith, Stunell, Taylor, Tonge and Willis.

17. Conrad (Earl) Russell, *Times*, 22 September 1997.

18. See discussion in Chris Cook, *A Short History of the Liberal Party, 1900–2001* (Basingstoke, 2002), p. 242; and see Ashdown, *The Ashdown Diaries*, ii, pp, 102–9.

19. See Ashdown, *The Ashdown Diaries*, ii, p. xiv.

20. Cook, *A Short History of the Liberal Party, 1900–2001*, p. 246n.

21. Butler and Kavanagh, *The British General Election of 2001*, p. 103.

22. *Times*, 6 September 2003.

23. *Times*, 10, 11 December 2001.

Notes to Chapter 21: Reflections

1. 27 December 1891, John Morley, *Life of Gladstone* (London, 1908), ii, p. 535.

2. 25 September 2003.

3. Roy Douglas, 'Labour in Decline, 1910–14', at pp. 105–25, in Kenneth D. Brown, ed., *Essays in Anti-Labour History* (London, 1974).

4. Morley to Haldane, 16 August 1920, Haldane Papers, 5914, fol. 224. Morley may have pitched it a bit high when he wrote that 'I count "the guilt of Wilhelm Hohenzollern" as far less than the guilt of three English Ministers'.

Bibliography

PRIMARY SOURCES

Unprinted Papers

Asquith papers, Bodleian Library, Oxford

John Burns Papers, British Library

'Cabinet Letters' (Prime Minister to Sovereign), Public Record Office, CAB 41

Cabinet Minutes, National Archives, Public Record Office, CAB 23

Sir Henry Campbell-Bannerman Papers, British Library

John Burns Papers, British Library

Elibank (Lord Murray, formerly Master of Elibank) Papers, National Library of Scotland

David (Earl) Lloyd George Papers, Beaverbrook Library, now at House of Lords Record Office

Herbert (Viscount) Gladstone Papers, British Library

W. E. Gladstone Papers, British Library

Viscount Grey Papers, National Archives, Public Record Office, FO 800/94, 800/100

'Hansard', *Parliamentary Debates (Lords and Commons)*

Marquis of Ripon Papers, British Library

Viscount Runciman Papers, University of Newcastle-upon-Tyne

Josiah Wedgwood Papers

Periodicals

Daily Chronicle

Daily News

Land Values

Liberal Magazine

Liberal News/ Liberal Democrat News

Liberal Year Books

Manchester Guardian/ Guardian

News Chronicle
Observer
Times

SECONDARY SOURCES

Books

Annual Register.

Ashdown, Paddy, *The Ashdown Diaries*, i, *1988–1997*; ii, *1997–1999* (London, 2000, 2001).

Asquith, H. H., *Memories and Reflections, 1852–1927* (London, 1928).

Asquith, H. H., *The Genesis of the War* (London, 1923).

Asquith, H. H., *The Paisley Policy* (London, 1920).

Bartram, Peter, *David Steel: His Life and Politics* (London, 1981).

Bassett, R., *Nineteen Thirty-One* (London, 1958).

Bealey, F., and Pelling, H., *Labour and Politics, 1900–1906* (London, 1958).

Bentley, Michael, *The Liberal Mind, 1914–1929* (Cambridge, 1977).

Biagini, Eugenio F., *Liberalism, Retrenchment and Reform: Popular Liberalism in the Age of Gladstone, 1860–1880* (Cambridge, 1992).

Biographical Dictionary of Modern British Radicals.

Blake, Robert, *The Conservative Party from Peel to Churchill* (London, 1970).

Bogdanor, Vernon, ed., *Liberal Party Politics* (Oxford, 1983).

Brown, Kenneth D., ed., *Essays in Anti-Labour History* (London, 1974).

Brown, Kenneth D., ed., *The First Labour Party, 1906–1914* (London, 1985).

Butler, David, *The British General Election of 1951* (London, 1952).

Butler, David, *The British General Election of 1955* (London, 1955).

Butler, David, *The British General Election of 1966* (London, 1966).

Butler, David, ed., *Coalitions in British Politics* (London and Basingstoke 1978).

Butler, David, and King, Anthony, *The British General Election of 1964* (London, 1965).

Butler, David, and Kavanagh, Dennis, *The British General Election of February 1974* (London, 1974).

Butler, David, and Kavanagh, Dennis, *The British General Election of October 1974* (London, 1975).

Butler, David, and Kavanagh, Dennis, *The British General Election of 1979* (London, 1980).

Butler, David, and Kavanagh, Dennis, *The British General Election of 1983* (London, 1984).

Butler, David, and Kavanagh, Dennis, *The British General Election of 1987* (Basingstoke, 1988).

Butler, David, and Kavanagh, Dennis, *The British General Election of 1992* (Basingstoke, 1992).

Butler, David, and Kavanagh, Dennis, *The British General Election of 1997* (Basingstoke, 1997).

Butler, David, and Kavanagh, Dennis, *The British General Election of 2001* (Basingstoke, 2002).

Butler, David, and Pinto-Duschinsky, Michael, *The British General Election of 1970* (London, 1970).

Butler, David, and Rose, Richard, *The British General Election of 1959* (London, 1960).

Campbell, John, *Lloyd George: The Goat in the Wilderness, 1922–1931* (London, 1977).

Campbell, John, *Roy Jenkins: A Biography* (London, 1980).

Chamberlain, Joseph, preface to *The Radical Programme* (London, 1885).

Chilston, 3rd Viscount, *Chief Whip: The Political Life and Times of Aretas Akers-Douglas, 1st Viscount Chilston* (London, 1961).

Churchill, Winston S., *The World Crisis, 1911–1918* (abridged edn, London, 1942).

Clarke, P. F., *Lancashire and the New Liberalism* (London, 1971).

Cook, Chris., *A Short History of the Liberal Party, 1900–2001* (6th edn, Basingstoke, 2002).

Cooke, A. B. and Vincent, John, *The Governing Passion: Cabinet Government and Parliamentary Politics in Britain, 1885–86* (Brighton, 1974).

Craig, F. W. S., *British Parliamentary Election Results, 1832–1885* (2nd edn, Aldershot, 1989).

Craig, F. W. S., *Chronology of British Parliamentary By-Elections, 1833–1987* (Chichester 1987).

Crewe, Ivor, and Harrop, Martin, eds, *Political Communications: The General Election Campaign of 1987* (Cambridge, 1989).

Crewe, Ivor Gosschalk, Brian and Bartle, John, eds, *Political Communications: Why Labour Won the General Election of 1997* (London, 1998).

Crewe, Ivor, and King, Anthony, *SDP: The Birth, Life and Death of the Social Democratic Party* (Oxford, 1995).

Cross, Colin, *The Liberals in Power, 1905–1914* (London, 1963).

Cyr, Arthur, *Liberal Politics in Britain* (Oxford, 1988).

Dangerfield, George, *The Strange Death of Liberal England, 1910–1914* (London, 1936).

David, Edward, ed., *Inside Asquith's Cabinet: From the Diaries of Charles Hobhouse* (London, 1977).

de Groot, Gerard J., *Liberal Crusader: The Life of Sir Archibald Sinclair* (London, 1993).

Dictionary of Liberal Biography (London, 1998).

Dictionary of National Biography.

Douglas, Roy, *Land, People and Politics: A History of the Land Question in the United Kingdom, 1878–1952* (London, 1976).

Douglas, Roy, *The History of the Liberal Party, 1895–1970* (London, 1971).

Dutton, David, *A History of the Liberal Party in the Twentieth Century* (Basingstoke, 2004).

Dutton, David, *Simon: A Political Biography of Sir John Simon* (London, 1992).

Dyer, Michael, *Men of Property and Intelligence: The Scottish Electoral System Prior to 1884* (Aberdeen, 1996).

Elliot, A. R. D., *Life of George Joachim Goschen, 1st Viscount Goschen* (London, 1911).

Encyclopaedia Britannica.

Ensor, R. C. K., *England, 1870–1914* (Oxford, 1966).

Fyfe, Hamilton, *The British Liberal Party* (London, 1928).

Gardiner, A. G., *The Life of Sir William Harcourt* (London, 1923).

George, David Lloyd, *War Memoirs* (2 vols, London, 1938).

George, Henry, *Progress and Poverty* (many editions, 1879 onwards).

Gilbert, Martin, *Churchill: A Life* (London, 1991).

Gilbert, Martin, *Winston S. Churchill* (8 vols, London, 1967–88).

Gregory, Roy, *The Miners and British Politics, 1906–1914* (London, 1968).

Grey, Viscount, *25 Years, 1892–1916* (London, 1925).

Halévy, Elie, *History of the English People in the Nineteenth Century* (6 vols, London, 1961).

Hamer, D. A., *Liberal Politics in the Age of Gladstone and Rosebery* (Oxford, 1972).

Hamilton, Sir Edward Walter, *Diary, 1885–1906* (Hull, 1993).

Hanham, H. J., *Elections and Party Management: Politics in the Time of Disraeli and Gladstone* (London, 1959; Hassocks, 1978).

Harris, Sir Percy, *Forty Years In and Out of Parliament* (London, 1949).

Hazlehurst, Cameron, and Woodland, Christine: *A Liberal Chronicle: Journals and Papers of J. A. Pease, 1st Lord Gainsford, 1908–1910* (London, 1994).

Historical Abstracts.

Hurst, Michael, *Joseph Chamberlain and Liberal Reunion: The Round Table Conference of 1887* (London, 1967).

Iremonger, Lucille, *Lord Aberdeen* (London, 1978).

Jackson, Patrick, *Education Act Forster: A Political Biography of W. E. Forster (1818–1886)* (London, 1997).

Jackson, Patrick, *The Last of the Whigs* (London, 1994).

James, Robert Rhodes, *Rosebery: A Biography of Archibald Philip, 5th Earl of Rosebery* (London, 1963).

Jenkins, Roy, *A Life at the Centre* (London and Basingstoke, 1991).

Jenkins, Roy, *Asquith* (London, 1964).

Jenkins. Roy, *Gladstone* (London and Basingstoke, 1995).

Jenkins, T. A., *The Liberal Ascendancy, 1830–1886* (Basingstoke, 1994).

Jones, Wyn, *Thomas Edward Ellis, 1859–1899* (Cardiff, 1986).

Keesing's Contemporary Archives.

Keesing's Record of World Events.

Loughlin, J., *Gladstone, Home Rule and the Ulster Question* (Dublin, 1986).

Lubenow, W. C., *Parliamentary Politics and the Home Rule Crisis: The British House of Commons in 1886* (Oxford, 1988).

Lyons, F. S. L., *Ireland since the Famine* (London, 1985).

McCallum, R. B. and Readman, Alison, *The British General Election of 1945* (Oxford, 1947).

McCalmont's Parliamentary Poll Book, 1832–1918 (3rd edn, Hassocks, 1971).

Maccoby, S., *English Radicalism, 1786–1832* (London, 1955).

MacIver, Don, ed., *The Liberal Democrats* (Hemel Hempstead, 1986).

McManus, Michael, *Jo Grimond: Towards the Sound of Gunfire* (London, 2001).

Magnus, Philip, *Gladstone: A Biography* (London, 1954).

Mallet, Sir Charles, *Herbert Gladstone: A Memoir* (London, 1932).

Mansfield, Peter, *The British in Egypt* (London, 1971).

Matthew, H. C. G., *Gladstone, 1809–1898* (Oxford, 1997).

Matthew, H. C. G., ed., *W. E. Gladstone Diaries* (Oxford, 1978).

Mitchell, B. R., *British Historical Statistics* (Cambridge, 1988).

Moody, T. W., *Davitt and Irish Revolution, 1846–82* (Oxford, 1981).

Morley, John, *The Life of William Ewart Gladstone* (2 vols, London, 1908).

Morris, A. J. A., *Radicalism Against War, 1906–14* (London, 1972).

Murray, Arthur C., *Master and Brother* (London, 1945).

New History of Ireland (NHI), vol. v, *Ireland Under the Union, 1801–1870* (Oxford, 1988); vol. vi, *Ireland Under the Union, 1870–1921* (Oxford, 1996).

Nicholas, H. G., *The British General Election of 1950* (London, 1951).

Ostrogorski, M., *Democracy and the Organization of Political Parties* (2 vols, London, 1902).

Owen, Frank, *Tempestuous Journey: Lloyd George, his Life and Times* (London, 1954).

Oxford and Asquith, 1st Earl of, *see* Asquith, H. H.

Packer, Ian, *Lloyd George, Liberalism and the Land: The Land Issue and Party Politics in England, 1906–1914* (Woodbridge, 2001).

Parry, J. P., *Democracy and Religion: Gladstone and the Liberal Party, 1867–1875* (Cambridge 1986).

Pelling, Henry, *A Short History of the Labour Party* (London, 1961).

Phillipps, Vivian, *My Days and Ways* (Edinburgh, 1932).

Poirier, Philip, *The Advent of the Labour Party* (London, 1958).

Pottle, Mark, ed., *Daring to Hope: The Diaries and Letters of Violet Bonham Carter, 1946–1969* (London, 2000).

Rallings, Colin, and Thrasher, Michael, *British Electoral Facts, 1832–1999* (Aldershot, 2000).

Rasmussen, J. S., *Retrenchment and Revival: A Study of the Contemporary Liberal Party* (Tucson, Arizona, 1964).

Rempell, Richard A., *Unionists Divided: Arthur Balfour, Joseph Chamberlain and the Unionist Free Traders* (Newton Abbot, 1972).

Rowland, Peter, *The Last Liberal Governments: The Promised Land, 1905–1910* (London, 1968).

Rowland, Peter, *The Last Liberal Governments: Unfinished Business, 1911–1914* (London, 1971).

Samuel, Viscount, *Memoirs* (London, 1945).

Searle, G. R., *Corruption in British Politics, 1895–1930* (Oxford, 1987).

Searle, G. R., *The Liberal Party: Triumph and Disintegration, 1886–1929* (Basingstoke, 1992, 2001).

Shakespeare, Sir Geoffrey, *Let Candles be Brought In* (London, 1949).

Shannon, Richard, *Gladstone and the Bulgarian Agitation 1876* (Hassocks, 1975).

Shannon, Richard, *Gladstone: Heroic Minister, 1865–1898* (London, 1999).

Simon, Viscount, *Retrospect* (London, 1952).

Smith, Cyril, *Big Cyril* (London, 1977).

Skidelsky, Robert, *Politicians and the Slump: The Labour Government of 1929–1931* (London, 1967).

Spender, J. A., and Asquith, Cyril, *Life of Asquith* (2 vols, 1932).

Stansky, Peter, *Ambitions and Strategies: The Struggle for the Leadership of the Liberal Party in the 1890s* (London, 1964).

Steel, David, *Against Goliath: David Steel's Story* (London, 1989).

Taylor, A. J. P., *English History, 1914–1945* (Oxford, 1965).

Taylor, A. J. P., *Lloyd George: Twelve Essays* (1971).

Thomson, Malcolm, *David Lloyd George: The Official Biography* (London, 1948).

Thorne, R. G., *The House of Commons, 1790–1820* (London, 1986).

Thornley, David, *Isaac Butt and Home Rule* (London, 1964).

Thorpe, Jeremy, *In My Own Time* (London, 1999).

Trevelyan, G. M., *Grey of Fallodon* (London, 1937).

Vincent, J. R., *The Formation of the British Liberal Party, 1857–1868* (Hassocks, 1976).

Walter, David, *The Strange Rebirth of Liberal England* (London, 2003).

Wasserstein, Bernard, *Herbert Samuel: A Political Life* (Oxford, 1992).

Watson, Aaron, *A Great Labour Leader: Being the Life of the Rt Hon. Thomas Burt MP* (London, 1908).

Watson, R. Spence, *The National Liberal Federation 1877 to 1906* (London, 1907).

Wedgwood, Josiah C., *Memoirs of a Fighting Life* (London, 1941).

Wilson, R. J. M., *CB: A Life of Sir Henry Campbell-Bannerman* (London, 1973).

Wilson, Trevor, *The Downfall of the Liberal Party, 1914–1935* (London, 1966).

Wilson, Trevor, ed., *The Political Diaries of C. P. Scott, 1911–1928* (London, 1970).

Woodward, Sir Llewellyn, *The Age of Reform, 1815–1870* (Oxford, 1962).

Wrigley, Chris: *Lloyd George* (Oxford, 1992.

Articles

Bentley, M., 'Liberal Politics and the Grey Conspiracy of 1921', *Historical Journal*, 20 (1977), pp. 461–78.

Bernstein, George L., 'The Origin of Liberal Politics, 1830–1874', *Journal of British Studies*, 28 (1989), pp. 75–89.

Bernstein, George L., 'Sir Henry Campbell-Bannerman and the Liberal Imperialists', *Journal of British Studies*, 23 (1983), pp. 105–24.

Boyle, T., 'The Liberal Imperialists, 1892–1906', *Bulletin of the Institute of Historical Research*, 52 (1979), pp. 48–82.

Brown, Kenneth D., 'Explaining the Liberal Working Man', *Labour History Review*, 58 (1993), pp. 56–58.

Clarke, P. F., 'The Electoral Position of the Liberal and Labour Parties, 1910–1914', *English Historical Review*, 90 (1975), pp. 828–36.

Clarke, P. F., 'Liberals, Labour and the Franchise', *English Historical Review*, 92 (1977), pp. 582–90.

Comerford, R. V., 'Isaac Butt and the Home Rule Party, 1870–77', *New History of Ireland*, vi (1996), pp. 1–25.

Comerford, R. V., 'The Land War: The Politics of Distress, 1877–82', *New History of Ireland*, vi (1996), pp. 26–52.

Comerford, R. V., 'The Parnell Era, 1883–91', *New History of Ireland*, vi (1996), pp. 63–65.

David, Edward, 'The Liberal Party Divided, 1916–1918', *Historical Journal*, 13 (1970) pp. 509–33.

Davis, Peter, 'The Liberal Unionist Party and Irish Policy, 1886–1892', *Historical Journal*, 18 (1975), pp. 85–104.

Douglas, Roy, 'A Classification of the Members of Parliament Elected in 1918', *Bulletin of the Institute of Historical Research*, 47 (1974), pp. 74–89.

Douglas, Roy, 'Britain and the Armenian Question, 1894–97', *Historical Journal*, 19 (1976), pp. 113–33.

Douglas, Roy, 'God Gave the Land to the People!', in A. J. A. Morris, ed., *Edwardian Radicalism, 1900–1914* (London, 1974), pp. 148–61.

Douglas, Roy, 'Labour in Decline, 1910–14', in Kenneth D. Brown, ed., *Essays in Anti-Labour History* (London, 1974), pp. 105–25.

Douglas, Roy, 'The Background to the "Coupon" Election Arrangements', *English Historical Review*, 86 (1971), pp. 318–36.

Dutton, David, '1932: A Neglected Date in the History of the Decline of the British Liberal Party', *Twentieth-Century British History*, 14 (2003), pp. 43–60.

Dutton, David, 'John Simon and the Post-War National Liberal Party: An Historical Postscript', *Historical Journal*, 32 (1989), pp. 357–67.

Fair, John D., 'Labour's Rise and the Liberal Demise, 1906–18', *Albion*, 34 (2002), pp. 58–73.

Fraser, Peter, 'British War Policy and the Crisis of Liberalism in May 1915', *Journal of Modern History*, 54 (1982), pp. 1–26.

Goodlad, Graham D., 'The Liberal Nationals, 1931–1940: The Problems of a Party in "Partnership Government"', *Historical Journal*, 38 (1995), pp. 133–43.

Goodlad, Graham D., 'The Liberal Party and Gladstone's Land Purchase Bill of 1886', *Historical Journal*, 32 (1989), pp. 627–41.

Griffiths, P. C., 'The Caucus and the Liberal Party in 1886', *History*, 61 (1976), pp. 183–197.

Gutzke, D. W., 'Rosebery and Campbell-Bannerman: The Conflict over Leadership Reconsidered', *Bulletin of the Institute of Historical Research*, 54 (1981), pp. 241–50.

Hart, Michael, 'The Liberals, the War and the Franchise', *English Historical Review*, 97 (1982), pp. 820–32.

Herrick, F. H., 'The Origins of the National Liberal Federation', *Journal of Modern History*, 17 (1945), pp. 116–29.

Heyck, Thomas W., 'Home Rule, Radicalism and the Liberal Party, 1886–1895', *Journal of British Studies*, 13 (1974), pp. 66–91.

Hunter, Ian, 'Sir Archibald Sinclair: The Liberal Anti-Appeaser', *Journal of Liberal History*, 42 (2004), pp. 32–48.

Jacobson, Peter D., 'Rosebery and Liberal Imperialism, 1899–1903' *Journal of British Studies*, 13 (1973), pp. 83–107.

Jenkins, T. A., 'Gladstone, the Whigs and the Leadership of the Liberal Party, 1879–1880', *Historical Journal*, 27 (1984), pp. 337–60.

Jenkins, T. A., 'The Funding of the Liberal Unionist Party and the Honours System', *English Historical Review*, 414 (1990), pp. 920–38.

Jones, J. Graham, 'Lloyd George, Welsh Liberalism and the Political Crisis of 1931', *Welsh Historical Review*, 19 (1995), pp. 68–102.

Laybourn, Kevin, 'The Rise of Labour and the Decline of Liberalism: The State of the Debate', *History*, 80 (1995), pp. 207–26.

Lowe, Michael, 'Are the Liverpool Liberals Really Different?', *British Journal of Political Science* (1984), pp. 243–49.

Lubenow, W. C., 'Irish Home Rule and the Social Basis of the Great Separation in the Liberal Party in 1886', *Historical Journal*, 28 (1985), pp. 125–42.

Lyons, F. S. L., 'The War of Independence 1919–21', in W . E. Vaughan, ed., *New History of Ireland*, vi (Oxford, 1996), pp. 240–58.

McCready, H. W., 'Chief Whip and Party Funds: The Work of Herbert Gladstone, 1899–1906', *Canadian Journal of History*, 6 (1971), pp. 285–303.

McEwan, J. M., 'Lloyd George's Liberal Supporters in December 1916: A Note', *Bulletin of the Institute of Historical Research*, 53 (1980), pp. 265–72.

McGill, B., 'Francis Schnadhorst and Liberal Party Organisation', *Journal of Modern History*, 34 (1962), pp. 19–39.

Mann, Kevin, 'Whig/Liberal Dominance: An Age of Personality?' *Modern History Review*, 12 (2000), pp. 21–24.

Matthew, H. G. C., McKibben, R. I., and Kay, J. A., 'The Franchise Factor and the Rise of the Labour Party', *English Historical Review* (1976), pp. 723–52.

Packer, Ian, 'The Land Issue and the Future of Scottish Liberalism in 1914', *Scottish Historical Review*, 75 (1996), pp. 52–71.

Packer, Ian, 'The Liberal Cave and the 1914 Budget', *English Historical Review*, 111 (1996), pp. 620–35.

Parsons, F. D. 'Ignis Fatuus v. Pons Asinorum: William Gladstone and Proportional Representation, 1867–1885', *Parliamentary History*, 21 (2002), pp. 374–85.

Powell, David, 'The Liberal Ministries and Labour, 1892–1895', *History*, 68 (1983), pp. 408–26.

Powell, David, 'The New Liberalism and the Rise of Labour, 1886–1906', *Historical Journal*, 29 (1986), pp. 369–93.

Rathbone, Mark, 'The Rainbow Circle and the New Liberalism', *Historian*, 71 (2001), pp. 14–21.

Rodgers, Bill (with commentary by Chris Rennard), 'What Went Wrong at Darlington?' *Journal of Liberal History*, 39 (2003), pp. 12–17.

Searle, Geoffrey, 'Did the Liberals Have a Future in 1914? *Historian*, 35 (1992), pp. 10–12.

Smith, Paul, 'Ginger Beer or Champagne? Palmerston as Prime Minister', *Modern History Review*, 4 (April 1993), pp. 2–4.

Stuart, C. H., 'The Formation of the Coalition Cabinet of 1852', *Transactions of the Royal Historical Society*, fifth series, 4 (1954), pp. 45–68.

Tanner, Duncan, 'Election Statistics and the Rise of the Labour Party, 1906–1931', *Historical Journal*, 34 (1991), pp. 893–908.

Taylor, A. J. P., 'Lord Palmerston', *History Today* (January 1991), pp. 15–20.

Taylor, Anthony, 'Palmerston and Radicalism, 1847–1865', *Journal of British Studies*, 33 (1993), pp. 157–79.

Temmel, Matthew R., 'Gladstone's Resignation of the Liberal Leadership 1874–75', *Journal of British Studies*, 16 (1976), pp. 153–75.

Vaughan, W. E., 'Ireland, *c.* 1870', *New History of Ireland*, v (1988), pp. 726–800.

Vincent, John, 'Chamberlain, the Liberals and the Outbreak of War, 1939', *English Historical Review*, 113 (1998), pp. 367–83.

Warren, Allen, ' "The Return of Ulysses": Gladstone, Liberalism and Late Victorian Politics', *Parliamentary History*, 9 (1990), pp. 184–96.

Watts, Duncan, ' "Juggler Joe": Radical and Unionist', *Modern History Review*, 5 (1993), pp. 20–23.

Woodward, David R., 'David Lloyd George: A Negotiated Peace with Germany and the Kuhlmann Peace Kite of September 1917', *Canadian Journal of History*, 6 (1971), pp. 75–93.

Wrigley, Chris, 'Labour and the Trade Unions', in K. D. Brown, ed., *The First Labour Party, 1906–14* (London, 1985), pp. 129–57.

Index